Intuition On Tap

*Mastering Your Inner Wisdom
to Transform Your Life*

Heidi Jane

BALBOA.
PRESS
A DIVISION OF HAY HOUSE

Balboa Press books may be ordered through booksellers or by contacting:

Balboa Press
A Division of Hay House
1663 Liberty Drive
Bloomington, IN 47403
www.balboapress.com
1-(877) 407-4847

ISBN: 978-1-4525-7431-8 (sc)
ISBN: 978-1-4525-7432-5 (hc)
ISBN: 978-1-4525-7436-3 (e)

Library of Congress Control Number: 2013908581

Printed in the United States of America

Balboa Press rev. date: 06/07/2013

Contents

Acknowledgments vii

Introduction ix

The Heart Center VIP (Very Intuitive Person) Community
and Forum xiii

Getting Started xv

Part 1   Understanding Yourself 1

Chapter 1   The Journey Begins 3

Chapter 2   I Am 13

Chapter 3   As Within So Without 18

Chapter 4   Shadow Self 24

Chapter 5   The Witch's Wound 32

Chapter 6   As Above So Below 38

Chapter 7   Defining Intuition 44

Chapter 8   The Three Levels of a Human Being 52

Part 2   Understanding Your Universe 59

Chapter 9   The Universal Structure 61

Chapter 10   Interdimensional Interference 69

Chapter 11   Spiritual Boundaries 76

Chapter 12   Energy Vampires 83

Chapter 13 Torus Field 88

Chapter 14 Meditation...93

Chapter 15 Discovering Your Ray.............................104

Chapter 16 Working with Your Medicine and
            Animal Totems......................................110

Chapter 17 Empaths and Highly Sensitive People 119

Part 3   Turning on the Tap...129

Chapter 18 Intuition and Clairsentience 131

Chapter 19 Intuition and Clairvoyance....................................139

Chapter 20 Intuition and Clairaudience 147

Chapter 21 Your Ego Mind, Ego Voice, and Emotional
            Addictions 153

Chapter 22 Embodying Your Spirit 158

Chapter 23 Past Lives or Concurrent Lives? 166

Chapter 24 Reincarnation 172

Chapter 25 Soul Family 179

Chapter 26 Intuition on Tap 183

Acknowledgments

I would firstly like to acknowledge the people in my life who have been an integral part of my journey and in the creation of this book. Some have been my greatest teachers, some my greatest challenges, and some my greatest gifts. This includes my two children, without whom my life would be incomplete and unfulfilled. My daughter, Taelor-Jane, has always been able to shine a light on my life and into my heart, especially in the moments when I was stumbling, blind in the dark. In those dark moments, it felt easier to give up than to keep moving forward. Without unconditional love and encouraging words of truth from Taelor-Jane, I don't think I would have been able to continue to put one foot in front of the other, journeying back into my heart. Taelor-Jane inspires me to be a better woman, a better mother, and a better human being.

From the moment my son, Lachlan, was born, the words "Thank God you've come back to me" drifted through my mind. We have such a special understanding, a connection that surpasses time and words, a deep bond that allows us to communicate with one another simply through our hearts. I admire Lachie's courage and his sensitivities. He is a true leader in every sense of the word, and when I look at him I am reminded of the fabled King Arthur—strong, compassionate, open hearted, honorable. Thank you for choosing me, again.

To my beautiful partner, Wayne: You are my rock and my shelter. You are my soft place to land. I am so thankful you found me.

To my soul sister, Min, how could I possibly have done this without you? Thank you for being a shoulder to cry on, an ear to listen, and a bottomless well of inspiration. I love you.

To my birth family, who have difficulty understanding me at times and even more difficulty relating to my perspective of the world, you have given me a firm foundation in logic, analysis, and intellect with a drive to do better, to reach my personal best, and for this I thank you.

To my soul family, words cannot express my heartfelt gratitude for the courage you have shown me, for the love you have given me and for the support you continue to provide. We're almost there.

Introduction

There are only two mistakes one can make along the road to truth: not going all the way and not starting.—Buddha

This book takes you through an unfolding process, a journey. It has been created to turn on the tap of your intuition, teaching you how to use it in your everyday life. You don't have to be aware of your intuition to gain value from this book, and conversely, this book has much to offer the more advanced intuitive. It will work to guide you, no matter where you are in your life, intuitively and personally.

This book is experiential in nature and contains many exercises, self-care tips, and homework exercises that have been tried and tested. If completed, there is no doubt that these tools will help you to connect to and deepen your intuition. By following simple instructions you will have access to your intuition on tap, being able to turn it on whenever you choose. I have created a companion workbook for you to use alongside of this text. This workbook offers exercises and gives you space to record your experiences, your findings, and your discoveries along the way.

After teaching meditation and spiritual development for many years, I developed a training and therapeutic modality called Intuitive Dynamix™ that is professionally accredited internationally.

I understand the keys, tools and methods that enable a healthy, balanced approach toward developing your intuitive abilities. I have also seen the negative effects of some methods that only focus on psychic development or developing clairvoyance before the student is ready. Such methods can cause mental, spiritual, and emotional problems and potentially create illness and imbalance.

This book will guide you through a balanced, step-by-step process that will allow you to take the journey at your own pace, moving forward or backing off in alignment with what your intuition is telling you. *Intuition on Tap* is unique in its approach to intuition and spirituality, containing a strong link between personal and spiritual growth throughout. I believe you cannot open your intuitive gifts without honoring your own personal process and evolution. Addressing both aspects of yourself while reading this book will give you the ability to open, deepen, and express your intuition like never before.

Even though this book has the same exercises for all readers, it is a doorway to gaining deep understanding into your own unique way of experiencing the world. I know one size does not necessarily fit all, and as you journey through the book, continue to ask yourself:

- "What are my strengths?"
- "How do I enjoy working with my intuition?"
- "Are there particular exercises that I find easy and feel attuned to?"
- "Are there exercises or topics that I don't resonate with?"
- "What is my unique way of accessing and using my intuition?"

There are no wrong answers; trust what you feel is right for you.

It is not my intention to try and squeeze you into a box or to tell you who you are. That is, and always will be, your work and your journey. I am here to pave the road and to give you a map so that you may make your own discovery. When you understand this, the rest will follow.

You may have been told that you are not enough, that you are less-than, or that you can't be spiritual or intuitive because you aren't gifted, or aren't special, or don't come from a long line of gypsies, or aren't the seventh daughter of a seventh daughter. In my experience, these are all limiting beliefs and concepts created, in part, to keep you small and separate from who you are as an amazingly talented being. This is one of the reasons I don't use the word "gifts" or "gifted" when referring to developing your intuition. This creates a belief that some people have the "gift" and that others don't. I believe you have the ability to develop and utilize your intuition to whatever level you desire. It is always your choice, always. Don't allow other people's opinions and egotistic projections to limit your ability to shine.

I, as a fellow traveler, acknowledge your courage, strength, and spirit for taking this journey. Travel deep and well.

If you are interested in pursuing more of your intuitive gifts and have a desire to work in the spiritual industry professionally, then this book will give you a taste of the Internationally Accredited Intuitive Dynamix™ Training with me. You can find more details on my website, www.heidisvision.com.

The Heart Center VIP (Very Intuitive Person) Community and Forum

Be who you are and say what you feel,
because those who mind don't matter,
and those who matter don't mind.

—Dr. Seuss

Sometimes when your intuitive abilities awaken, it can be quite scary to find the people around you don't quite understand what you're going through. This is one of the main intentions for creating the online community The Heart Center and Forum, where you can become a VIP (Very Intuitive Person) member and connect and share with like-spirited people who will understand you and the processes you are learning. If you become a member of the VIP forum, you will be able to discuss the exercises and topics of this book and your experiences within each chapter. There will be other students to share with, and you will have access to me and my expertise. Visit http://www.heidisvision.com for more information.

Getting Started

Congratulations! The fact that you are holding this book in your hands and reading these words is a great example of you following your intuition! It is no mistake that this book has found its way into your life. I invite you to open your heart and open your mind as you read on, allowing the words that are written and the energy behind them to weave their magic into the fabric of your life.

You are probably already aware of the desire you feel to expand and explore your intuition and create the life of your dreams. You feel that cloying internal thirst that can't be quenched by anything else, the yearning to experience more, have more, and be more in your life. This desire stems not from an egotistical need to attain more things but rather from a beautiful quality that dwells within your own heart and spirit, the desire to simply become more of your true self. This imperative you feel may be the result of a loss, a crossroads moment, a divorce, or dissatisfaction in your job, or it may simply be from an intention to become more heart-centered, intuitive, and connected to your own spirit. Whatever the reason that has led you to this moment, it is perfect and will undoubtedly add to the richness of your experience.

Each of us has our own unique way of viewing and interacting with the world. We all contain our own distinctive spiritual and energetic blueprint or DNA. This means that your experience of this book will be unique to you, which is perfect.

The outcome that you are seeking will affect your experience of this book. In fact, you may read multiple times, each time with a different intent. The first time may be read as a personal growth exercise and the second time as a professional guide to deepen your intuitive abilities. However you feel drawn to utilize the content is perfect for you right now. Take a few moments, still your mind, and feel into what your heart is telling you. Do you feel ready to simply read the book through first, feeling your way into the lessons? Or is your mood brave and enthusiastic, wanting to get stuck into the exercises and challenge yourself?

Ask yourself, "Do I want to extend my spiritual and intuitive gifts to the next level and possibly create a new life for myself, one of working with spirit day to day?", or "Would I prefer to simply learn more about myself, who I am, and what makes me tick?"

Again, there are no right or wrong answers to these questions.

This book should be transformative. It may be used at a professional level, but even more than that, if you follow the processes in this book you will learn who you are as an inimitable spiritual being having a human experience. This journey will lead you to knowing who you truly are, warts and all. You will be encouraged to learn to love your limitations, your shadow, your beliefs, your beauty, and your natural gifts. You will learn how you naturally interact with the world, what your natural abilities are, what your ray is, what your medicine is, and how you can best fulfill your soul's yearning and desire to work with spirit and turn on your intuition, like turning on a tap. Within that, it is important that you have trust in the process, in the content, and most of all in yourself. You may find it challenging at times to stay in a state of trust, but this is what will help you to return the greatest rewards for your time and energy investment.

I work very differently compared to other professionals in the new age and psychic industry, and in fact I don't relate to many of these people at all. After researching, experiencing, and putting into practice a great number of belief systems, teachings, and techniques, I believe the processes in this book are the most responsible way to teach you to access your intuition.

I will never ask you to call in anything outside of yourself, including guides, masters, or angels, or to give your power away to another person. I will explain this more in later chapters, so for now rest assured that after many years of my own triumphs and failures, I offer you a way to channel more of your power back into your life, creating a deeper connection to your own heart and an acknowledgement that you are a sovereign being, capable of creating miracles.

The book will continue to affect you and your life, even after you have completed the exercises and read the chapters. It will continue to weave itself within your subconscious mind, your body, your spirit and your heart, often bringing to light old ways of being, judgments, fears, criticisms, and doubts. It will also open up new ways of seeing the world and opportunities that, to this point, may have been unimaginable.

If, when reading, your ego mind becomes quite noisy and active, I implore you to stick with it. Even if your mind, body, and emotions are screaming at you to stop, stick with it. Even if your mind, body, and emotions are telling you, "you can't succeed" or "you can't do this work" or "you're not gifted" or "who do you think you are?" please stick with it. It is absolutely normal and an expected part of the process of development. You see, we want the ego mind to become more active initially! Then you can get to the heart of your shadow self and learn to love it, honor it, heal it, and bring it into the light of awareness. Without this light of awareness, your shadow self will invariably filter through into your intuition, into your relationships with loved ones, and into your relationship with yourself. This may leave you feeling resentful, empty, overwhelmed, and fearful. There must always be balance when undertaking any new spiritual lessons, and this book is no different. If you are to develop yourself spiritually and intuitively, then it is vital that you develop yourself personally. Otherwise you may find yourself with no desire to develop your intuition anymore.

This book can empower you and transform your life, if you open your heart and allow it to. Having said that, it is not a stand-alone therapeutic process. If you are at any time feeling overwhelmed by your emotions or thoughts, please seek professional support, either with me or another professional with whom you feel comfortable and who has an understanding of spiritual work, processes, and concepts.

Taking responsibility, by taking care of you and also being gentle and compassionate with yourself, is a nonnegotiable requirement of this book. Can you make that commitment to yourself?

Throughout the book are self-care requests that are intended to assist and support you with this. Like most things in life, you will get out what you put in! Where do you place your value? That is where you will get results.

I invite you to purchase your own workbook to complete the written exercises in or the *Intuition on Tap Companion*, which has been specifically designed to help you record your experiences and observations and includes room for you to journal.

Part One

Understanding Yourself

At back of Mirrors of Time Journal
there's a list of Crystals that might be
of use here.

CHAPTER ONE

The Journey Begins

My favorite thing to do is to go where I've never been.—Diane Arbus

To begin to develop your intuition and reach a place of self-awareness and understanding, let's start with some simple reflective exercises.

Setting Your Intention

It is paramount that you set a clear and strong intention when starting anything important, and this book is no different. As with most things, the way you begin is often the way you will finish. If you get really clear with yourself about your expectations, your desires, your dreams, and your goals and express these within an intention, it gives your higher self and spirit the opportunity to get you what you want. Again, it will give *your* higher self the opportunity to get *you* what *you* want. Please sit with this statement for a few moments and explore its importance. You decide what you want to experience, and you decide what you want to create. You as an amazing manifestation machine are able to cocreate your life with spirit. You have a choice.

You have always had a choice, and anyone who tells you differently is attempting to place his or her own limitations upon you. You are not simply waiting for your life to happen or unfold, and if that is how you have been living up to this point, I invite you to reflect upon your results. Do you have what you desire? Have you reached your goals? Are you happy and fulfilled? Stating your aim at the beginning of any journey and checking in with it as you move forward will help you to steer the course as a cocreator. Otherwise, the road can become unclear and confusing, and you may feel lost. Reading the intention that you create often throughout the process is necessary if you are using it as a map to your destination. Keep checking in to see if you are on track to your objective.

What Is an Intention?

An intention, in the context of this book, is an aim or plan expressed through words, both verbally and written. This is for those people who are auditory, visual, and kinesthetic. You can hear, see, and feel your intention when you read it and say it aloud. Again, this will help to keep you on track. Your initial intention may change throughout the reading of this book, or it may not. If you feel that your initial intention no longer resonates with you after a while, then please go through the process again, creating a new intention that is more in alignment with where you are.

Creating an Intention Exercise

To create an intention, write down a list of all the things you choose to create and receive through this process. When you have your list, cut it down into the main points and start to create a short, succinct sentence that is easy to remember. Please don't create an intention that seems unrealistic to you now, as every time you read this or state it, your mind will say "that's not true" or "no you can't" or "you're lying to yourself." Your intention must be believable to you. You may like to start the statement with, "My clear and strong intention is ..."

Here are some examples to get you started.

"My clear and strong intention is to live abundantly and joyously. I am thankful for the healing I bring to this world as I walk upon my spiritual path."

"My clear and strong intention is to experience love, abundance, and joy."

Please play around with words until you find an intention that makes your heart feel full and your body tingle! If it does, then you know you are on the right track.

When you have created your intention, write it down clearly and place it somewhere at work or home where you can see it and read it often. State your intention at least once every morning and every night. Feel your body, mind, and heart respond or react to this statement. Does it need adjusting? If so, then adjust and restate it. Now, does that feel more resonant with you? If you answered yes, then stick with your intention. Do this process until you feel your body zing with excitement and your heart open.

Stages of Intention

Your intention statement may also be created in stages. For example, you may want to be a professional intuitive but feel you are not ready for this quite yet. Instead of setting your intention as already having what you desire, set it as a goal you are working toward. This helps to make it believable to your mind, body, and emotions, and you won't get "push-back" when you state or read a statement you don't believe. An example of this is,

"My clear and strong intention is to work toward becoming a professional intuitive."

As you can see, your intention is to "work toward." This is resonant with your mind, body, and emotions because it is your truth.

Intention Ceremony

The term "ceremony" has many connotations. In the context of this process, it means creating a sacred manifestation of intent, a personal expression that is set aside from the mundane world. Within this exercise, you will design a way to express your intention to your spirit and out to the universe, also bringing your thoughts and words of intent into the third dimension, or the physical world.

Utilize the intention statement you have already created with words to guide you in your ceremony. In an expression of intent or an intention ceremony, you use focus to define your intent. The objects you choose can symbolize your intent and can help to manage your focus. For example, you may light a candle to symbolize light coming into your life. You might make an elixir of rose quartz crystal and water and drink it, to show that you are ready to receive love. You may write a declaration that best represents what you want to state and then burn it, denoting that you are letting the spirit winds of life bring you what you desire.

In your ceremony, choose objects that are meaningful to you and represent your intent. These may be candles, feathers, crystals, leaves, pictures, photographs, or incense, for example. You can use whatever you feel drawn to; you are only limited by your own imagination. Using the colors that you feel best represent your intention can be a powerful addition. For example, to express passion and power you may use the color red, and to express love and compassion you may use pink and green. Use the color that you feel best symbolizes your intention. You may also like to use suitable music to set the mood if you are doing your ceremony indoors.

As you are creating your ceremony, make sure it is truly meaningful to you. If you're looking to enhance certain qualities within your spiritual abilities, create metaphors to symbolize these. For example you may like to use a clear quartz crystal to symbolize your clarity in receiving messages from spirit.

Take time to make sure your expression is meaningful and authentic and that it contains all of the elements that are important to you. This expression is sending a very strong ripple out to the universe. It is like saying in a loud voice: "I am ready. Here is what I want to create and experience."

Within the ceremony, it is important to have a beginning, middle, and end. This does not need to be a long process, only what you feel is appropriate to you and what you are trying to achieve. You may like to write down the steps, including what you would like to say, in your workbook and read from the pages. Alternatively, you may like to allow your intuition to guide you during the ceremony to add depth and spontaneity.

The Beginning

- Collect your tools and objects that represent your intention, and have them within easy reach.

- Ensure you will not be disturbed or interrupted during the ceremony. Take your phone off the hook and turn off your mobile.

- Choose a time and place that is appropriate and private. This can be inside or outside.

- Burn white sage[1] to clear the area.

- Sit or stand quietly and close your eyes, thinking about what you want to achieve.

- Create a Torus Field, which is simply a bioelectric barrier or field of your own energy or life force that surrounds your physical body and auric field, creating a barrier to any external energy. Picture it coming out from your heart center and encircling you. In your mind's eye, envision a circular force field or bubble that surrounds you. State that only your spirit and your soul family with specific soul contracts may enter this sacred space. This will ensure you do not attract

---

[1] White Sage or Grandfather Sage is a plant that has been used for centuries to remove negative energy in the atmosphere. It comes in a dried form, as either loose leaves or wrapped in a stick. The best way to use White Sage is to place loose leaves in a bowl or hold the sage stick and then light the loose leaves or the top of the stick with a lighter. After the leaves are well alight, blow them out. The smoke that is generated will clear away any discordant energy in your auric field or in the environment. White sage can also be used to clear crystals. You may like to use a feather or handheld fan to wave the smoke into the room, making sure the smoke reaches under furniture and into the corners. It is more effective to leave the windows and doors closed whilst you are burning the sage. When you intuitively feel the space has been cleared, then make sure the leaves or stick are properly extinguished to avoid any fire hazards. Then open the space up, including doors and windows, letting the smoke leave the space and take the negative energy with it. White sage will only neutralize energy; it does not create positive energy, nor will it remove entities. You may like to burn some essential oils or pure incense afterwards to attract more positive energies into your space. You can use white sage as often as you feel you need to, being respectful of the plant and only using a small amount each time.

any external interference and ensure this process is only about you.

- Ask only your spirit or higher self to connect with you to protect you, guide you, and inspire you during the process.

- State something like, "I intend to create a personal expression of my intention regarding intuitive and spiritual work and development. I ask that this be created in alignment with my spirit, my higher self, and my divine will and that it happen with ease and grace."

The Middle

- Enjoy your ceremony, taking as much time as you need to experience with your mind, emotions, physical body, and spirit all that you desire. Feel the emotions that are present, as these are very powerful tools of manifestation.

- Know that what you state with your intention will send out ripples of information to the universe. Like a pebble dropped in the center of a pond, these ripples of intent will then flow back to you.

- To open the door to joyful and positive experiences, include a statement similar to, "Let my ceremony be for the highest good of all and according to my soul's original free will and choice. Let my intent manifest in the ways I imagine or in even better ways. Let this occur with ease and grace."

This statement means if you have to learn something before your intent will manifest, it will happen very easily, that you won't manipulate anyone's free will in the process, and that the result could be even better than you imagine.

- It is also important that you only use your own spirit and higher self to state this intention and its expression, as otherwise you may not like who turns up to help! (We will be discussing this in later chapters.)
- Using your chosen object, express your intention. For instance, light your candle, drink your elixir, or burn your words.

The End

- On completion of your ceremony, take time to thank your spirit, your higher self, and your physical body for their help and support. Thank, also, any members of your soul family who may have assisted you during the ceremony.
- Clear the space again with white sage.
- Pack up your tools or objects in a respectful manner. You may also like to thank the energies of the objects you have worked with, such as the deva or life force within the crystals.
- Write in your journal or workbook what you experienced during the ceremony. Did a vision, a feeling, an epiphany, or any other form of clarity come through to your awareness?
- Be quiet and gentle with yourself for a while after the ceremony, as it can be quite a powerful experience.

As the universe responds to your ceremony, it is up to you to interpret the ripples coming back. Please keep a journal each day for the rest of the month, after you exact your ceremony of intent, to observe what responses you are receiving. One aspect of what you're looking for is this. During each day, does anything happen which pushes your buttons? Do you respond emotionally, negatively or positively, to any situation you are presented with? If so, this is a sign from the universe that you have more to learn about an aspect of yourself before your personal magnets will draw to you what you want. These signs from the universe are saying you still have something to work on regarding your intention. Look at the encounters closely. What feelings did they raise within you? Where do these feelings come from? All people you encounter and all situations you experience are messages from your higher self, helping you to live with more love and clarity, so see these situations as messages from your spirit and from the universe.

The other aspect to observe is any positive ripples that flow back to you. Watch to see if new people, new opportunities, or new ways of thinking, feeling, and being arrive in your life. Do you feel a more concrete connection to your intention? Do you feel that the strong foundation of your spiritual journey has been built? Are you receiving signs of confirmation through other people, places, and events? Are you experiencing a number of synchronicities?

Observation of the smallest occurrence can add to the greater picture of your ceremony. It is also a good idea not to talk to anyone about your ceremony or your practice, keeping the details, the energy, and the magic private and potent. Other people's uneducated opinions and comments can diminish the strength of what you have created and seek to achieve. Sharing the ceremony can also indicate that you are looking for validation from outside of yourself. If this is the case, please be aware of this need and what this may mean to you. No-one else's opinion is more important or valid than yours.

It is always key to be very mindful of what you ask for in your ceremony ... you just might get it! Do not ask for anything that you feel you cannot handle with ease and grace. You will only ever say to the universe "bring it on" once, as the universe will respond in kind, and you may find yourself regretting your momentary enthusiasm.

Vision Board Exercise (Optional)

As an added tool to stating your intention, you may like to create a vision board. This is a board, canvas, or piece of paper where you place images from magazines, papers, or the Internet that relate to your intention and create a pictorial representation. When you look at these images, you should feel them lift you up and feel a connection to them. I request that if you choose to complete a vision board, you also include your sentence in words. Vision boards have become very popular of late, but it is important to understand that this process is more effective for people who are predominately visual.

If you would like to interact on the secure *Intuition on Tap* forum through the Heart Center to discuss the topics and exercises in this chapter and interact with me and with other readers, please go to http://www.heidisvision.com/community and become a member of the VIP forum. After you have joined, you may follow the topic heading to this or any other chapter, for example: "Setting Your Intention."

CHAPTER TWO

———•—•———

I Am

Because one believes in oneself, one doesn't try to convince others. Because one is content with oneself, one doesn't need others' approval. Because one accepts oneself, the whole world accepts one.—Lao Tzu

I -am statements connect you to your higher self, or to your spirit, and resonate with you on a higher level. They reflect your state of being rather than being goal oriented like your intention statement. These very powerful statements connect you to the essence of who you are as a spiritual being in the present tense, living as a human being. Understanding the concept of having an eternal spirit can help you to define your I-am statement. Your statement is not constrained to mental constructs or limiting belief structures. It expresses who you are on the deepest level of self. Your I-am statement will open the doorway to your understanding of just how beautiful, amazing, gifted, and special you are.

The reason I encourage you to discover your true essence through creating your I-am statement is so that you begin to build the foundation from which you will develop your intuition. This is another piece of the puzzle of self-discovery, allowing you to connect to the limitless part of yourself. If you struggle at any time during your progress through this book, you can come back to your I-am statement and read it to yourself out loud as you look at yourself in the mirror. Allow yourself to reconnect with your amazing core, remembering your own divinity. This will help you to not get too caught up in your personal beliefs or limitations, reinstilling the reason that you are developing your intuition in the first place.

I-Am Exercise

When creating your I-am statement, always state it in the here and now, in terms of who you already are, not who you wish to become. Don't use the words *hope*, *wish*, *want*, or *create* within your I-am statement, as these words all imply that the state of being you desire does not already exist! Likewise, do not set your I-am statement in a future date or time. Most importantly, the statement must ring true to you.

Here are some examples to get you started.
I am abundantly wealthy in body, mind and spirit.
I am a powerful intuitive.
I am love in physical form.
Write these in your workbook until you find a statement that resonates with you. Think about what makes you truly special and unique, what differentiates you from other people. We all have at least one thing that is different from others, and that adds to our own distinctive spiritual signature. Let this be your guide.

When you are happy with what you have created, speak out loud your I-am statement, along with your intention statement, a minimum of twice a day. Observe the difference in your life. Write what you observe in your journal.

Continually stating to the universe who you are solidifies this truth within your own heart, spirit, and mind.

"Who Am I?" Exercise

Spend time contemplating who you are as a human being. Start by thinking about yourself as a spirit, then a soul, and then a human. Then think about all of the amazing qualities you have.

- Sit in a room where you won't be disturbed, in front of a mirror. A handheld mirror will work fine.
- Look directly at yourself in the mirror and ask the question, "Who am I?"
- Ask this question again and again, leaving a few moments between each question to hear, feel, or experience a response.
- Write the answers in your workbook.
- Do this practice for at least thirty minutes, and then read what you have written. You may be surprised at what you find.

This can be a deeply altering experience if you truly allow yourself to witness *you*.

Inspiration

I also encourage you to collect statements, quotes, and affirmations from other people and use these to inspire you and keep you on track throughout your journey. I have included these throughout the book and one of my very favorites below. No matter how many times I read this quote, I still feel inspired! It has helped me through many tough times in my own journey.

> Our deepest fear is not that we are inadequate. Our deepest fear is that we are powerful beyond measure. It is our light, not our darkness, that most frightens us. We ask ourselves, who am I to be brilliant, gorgeous, talented, fabulous? Actually, who are you not to be? You are a child of God. Your playing small does not serve the world. There is nothing enlightened about shrinking so that other people won't feel insecure around you. We are all meant to shine, as children do. We were born to make manifest the glory of God that is within us. It's not just in some of us; it's in everyone. And as we let our own light shine, we unconsciously give other people permission to do the same. As we are liberated from our own fear, our presence automatically liberates others.
>
> —Marianne Williamson

Journaling

As a part of the process of self-discovery, I highly encourage you to write in a journal. Buy yourself a beautiful journal that is used only for this purpose, or use the *Intuition on Tap Companion,* to record your deepest thoughts and understandings. Treat yourself to something sacred and special; this will increase the level of your enjoyment. You don't have to spend a lot of money; you may want to decorate the outside of an inexpensive, plain exercise book to personalize and beautify it, putting your energy into and onto it.

Above and beyond the set work, it is important that you journal any thoughts, dreams, epiphanies, realizations, struggles, challenges, joys, triumphs, and breakthroughs. There will be many coming through as you progress, and more than anything else, your journal is a testament to your journey and your continuation upon it. It can become your very best friend.

You may, over time, forget the profound experiences you have as you work through this book. Even though they seemed so amazing when they occurred, your mind will slowly lose the recollection. If you journal these experiences, then you will always have a record of your journey. It's also fun to look back at what you've written to see just how far you've come.

Self-Care

I ask that you journal daily, and if that is not possible due to time constraints, then a minimum of three times a week. Please also be clear that what you put into developing your intuition, you will get out. This simply means that if you do not do the exercises, the journaling, the meditations, the reading, the self-care, and any other tasks suggested to you, you won't get as much from the book.

If you feel you are having trouble in this regard, spend a few moments reflecting on where your value is placed in your life. Reflect upon how important it is to set aside some time for yourself and your evolution and development. If you have no time, then it is often a case of self-sabotage in play! The bottom line is, where you place your value is where you will put your focus.

CHAPTER THREE

———✦———

As Within So Without

We are what we think. All that we are arises with our thoughts. With our thoughts, we make the world.— Buddha

A s mentioned, as you travel on this journey of self-discovery, you will uncover limitations, judgments, and fears in regard to intuitive work and to yourself as an intuitive. The clear and strong intention of this work is to hold you in your divine light until you are able to achieve this for yourself. I am able to hold you, see you, and relate to you as a divine being of love until such time as you come home to yourself. In other words, I am very clear that you are not your shadow, nor your ego mind, nor your personality—and yet, paradoxically, you are all of these. These somewhat uncomfortable parts of yourself have made you who you are today, for better or worse. They have helped you to survive, and so you must thank them for that service. However, what you are reaching for is not simply survival but living, thriving, loving unreservedly and unconditionally. To attain this state you must begin to look at, acknowledge, and own the parts of you that are limiting, constricting, uncomfortable, challenged, challenging, and fearful.

This is what I call the shadow self. The processes below are tools to liberate you from the energetic and emotional burden that the shadow self can create.

If you are unaware of a limiting belief or pattern, then it is impossible to change it. At the very moment you become aware of these limitations or attitudes, you have access to freedom from them. When you are conscious of what you are doing, thinking, feeling, or saying, you have a choice. You have a choice to be, do, think, feel, or speak differently, thus creating the change within and without. I look at this moment as receiving the "key to the golden door." When you have this key of self-realization, you can use it to unlock any layer, constraint, challenge, or limitation you may have. The golden door will then open to reveal the next level of your development and evolution as a balanced human and spiritual being. This will then begin to be reflected back to you through positive outcomes, people, and experiences in your life.

Have you ever had a day where everything seemed to be going wrong? From the moment you woke, you felt unsettled and grumpy. Your family certainly didn't help your state of mind with their thoughtlessness; they drank all the milk and left a sink full of dishes from last night's dinner. As a result, you found yourself running late for work. You asked your ten-year-old approximately seven times to brush his teeth, and then he could find only one shoe. By the time you were in the car, you felt stressed. As you pulled into traffic, you found that it was at a standstill. A rude person cut in front of you and then flipped his middle finger. You could feel the anger, the injustice, and the frustration building in your belly and running through your body, climbing toward your throat and boiling over as you opened your mouth to express your own feelings of anger ... and all this before you were even at work.

If you have often had similar experiences, then you know how hard it is at these times to take control of your feelings, your words, and your thoughts. Perhaps you experience this type of day regularly. It is now your opportunity and your responsibility to address these situations and feelings when they occur. This will be part of your work as you embrace your intuitive abilities, and it is imperative to attain a level of self-mastery if you want to maintain your heart-centered connection.

Going back to the scenario given, what do you think your body, mind, and soul are communicating to you through your thoughts, feelings, and experiences? What are the thoughtless, inconsiderate, or rude people showing you? If you believe it has nothing to do with you and that they are the problem, then I strongly encourage you to take another look! The outer world is always trying to reflect what lies unresolved within us. Perhaps you have some unexpressed anger toward your boss or partner. Perhaps there are some old behaviors regarding victimization that have not been fully integrated and healed. Maybe you experienced abuse as a child. Regardless of the underlying reason, it is always your responsibility, as a heart-centered intuitive, to not only change the outcome of your downward-spiraling day but also to take responsibility for your feelings, words, and reactions as a human being. This in no way condones rude or abusive behavior from others, nor does it land taking responsibility for them upon your lap. What it does, however, is pave the way for you to live consciously and responsibly.

Each time you find yourself in conflict, confusion, or turmoil, look within and see what is lurking beneath the surface. When you find what is there, try out some of these processes to get the energy of your emotions, thoughts, and limiting beliefs moving. Often when people are experiencing anxiety or panic attacks, it can be attributed to an excess of unresolved emotional energy. It's important to remember that emotions and thoughts are simply a form of energy. If you view them as such, then you can simply access this energy and begin to release it from your body, mind, and soul. Once released, they no longer have the power to cocreate your reality by attracting a person or experience to you that reflects your own unresolved issues, feelings, or negative thoughts.

Dumping: Writing your thoughts down onto a piece of paper is a great way of dumping your negative state of being, releasing thoughts out of your body and mind and onto the pages. It can have quite an emptying effect. It isn't necessary to read over your work once written; in fact, you can simply dump any negative thoughts onto the paper and throw away or burn the pages afterward.

Some people's minds are like a mouse on a wheel, expending a great deal of energy but never moving forward. This is very common, with the mind going over and over the same topics, worrying and creating stress. This can also create more negative flow-on thoughts, with the mind making up stories as it goes along. It can then move into the next mode of collecting evidence to support a certain belief structure. For example, if the mind believes, "I can't trust myself," it is likely that it will create situations where you will make poor choices. The mind will then use that as evidence to prove its perspective. If you can dump these thoughts out of your head and onto the pages, then you have more room to create the thoughts and beliefs that will actually support you, rather than debilitate you.

Pillow Therapy: Go into your bedroom or a place where you won't be disturbed, ask your higher self to surround you with protective energy (ensuring no-one bears the energetic brunt of your anger or emotions), and let it rip! Beat the fluff out of your pillows and your mattress, really unleashing your innermost feelings of frustration, grief, or anger through your physical movement of punching or throwing. When you are finished, burn white sage to neutralize any discordant energies in the room and the emotions that you have released. It is always important to clear any space after a releasing process, especially if it is in your home or work environment. When you have cleared all you feel you need to, then ask your higher self to release the protective energy. If you feel that you want to take a shower or lie in the sun to reenergize or to refill the space within you, please do. This can be a very helpful process when needed.

Embracing the Banshee: Again, be in a place where you won't be disturbed or heard and allow yourself to feel the negative feelings. Open your throat and mouth, and let your voice and sound move through you. Often, you won't form words but rather sounds that connect you to the place in your body where your shadow feelings are stored. Before you know it you will be screaming like a banshee. Choose a private place where you won't be heard, such as the car with the radio turned up, the top of a headland on a windy day, or your bedroom with loud music playing. You don't want the neighbors to mistakenly call the police!

Physical Exercise: Kickboxing, running, martial arts, and free-form dancing are all great ways of managing the feelings stored in your cellular body. The endorphins, or feel-good hormones, released in your brain after physical exercise can also lighten your mood and feelings and give you a clearer perspective of a situation. Why not vocalize as well as exercising to really dig into any stuck energy?

It is extremely important that through the process of self-realization you do not begin to abuse yourself mentally or emotionally. As an intuitive, your depth of compassion, acceptance for what is, and understanding of others will aid you in achieving ever-greater states of evolvement. It all starts at home, though, and so the most important work is with yourself. Please be gentle with yourself as you uncover these shadow aspects, and show yourself the same depth of compassion you would a loved one or friend.

It is also important to note that your shadow emotions are not "bad." Be very careful about placing judgment on yourself and others in this regard. The shadow emotions are simply energy that needs to be acknowledged, owned, and released. If you notice yourself criticizing and judging your feelings, then stop. Take a moment and acknowledge your courage for moving toward self-mastery. This is challenging, and most people never extend themselves out of their comfort zone of dysfunction and unhappiness. Be proud of yourself for daring to be different.

Self-Care

Take some time to recognize your bravery, and write a small letter of acknowledgement to yourself. Write this on beautiful paper. Make it really heartfelt and special so that you can acknowledge and accept your journey and your courage.

CHAPTER FOUR

Shadow Self

It is not the road ahead that wears you out—it is the grain of sand in your shoe.—Arabian proverb

For all actions in the universe, there is an equal and opposite reaction. This concept is important when dealing with the shadow aspects of yourself. We all have a shadow self, no matter how much therapy, praying, volunteering, meditating, or donating we do or have done in the past. Where there is light, there is shadow.

Picture in your mind a sunny, clear day. You are standing outside in the middle of a clearing, surrounded by trees. You can easily see everything the light touches, but what about the shadows the trees' shapes cast? Can you see what is behind them? Do you prefer just to enjoy the light of the sun on your face and ignore the shadow behind the trees?

This is a picture of what lives within each of us. It is possible to have both light and shadow coexisting. Discovering your shadow self can also be a doorway to revealing more of your light. There is nothing wrong with your shadow. But allowing this aspect of yourself to take control can be limiting and debilitating.

"Shadow self" is a term used throughout this book to describe the limiting beliefs, thoughts, feelings, and experiences that are created by fear. If there are only two emotions in the universe, love and fear, then your shadow is the expression of your fear. This can be given as an imprint to you by others, including your friends and family, or can be self-created.

Shadow Recording Exercise

Over a week, write down in your workbook every time you experience your shadow. Record where you are, what you're doing, and whom you are with. Begin to gain clarity of when these feelings or situations arise. Likewise, note down any incidents with other people that are conflicting or unsettling. Please don't judge or analyze; simply record your experience.

Begin to create a list of people with whom you have unfinished business. They can be passed over or alive—it doesn't matter. Look back through your life to the present and see if there are people who stand out to you as being difficult or whom you are carrying a wound with. A good indication of this state is that when you think of a person, your belly knots or you feel anxiety. There are probably people who really stand out to you and others who are not so clear. Be honest with yourself, and write these in your workbook. When you have your list, take some time to think of the person and the conflict. Observe what your body does, what emotions come up, and what your thoughts are, and then note these down too. Simply observe yourself rather than plugging into the stories, the drama, or the states of being you are experiencing. As if watching a scene play out on a screen in front of you, you are viewing, not engaging.

When you are finished with the list, read it through and see if there are any patterns or feelings that seem to reoccur. Once again, observe what you find. These findings will give you a clue of where you may have stuck or residual beliefs, resentment, anger, shame, or guilt connected to a person or to people in your life. Through the reflection that these people offer, you can begin to see what issues you may be holding on to. Remember, others are simply reflections of an aspect of you.

If you are wondering what relevance this has to being and developing your intuition, it can be explained like this. If you have unresolved and unowned shadow aspects, you will attract people with very similar baggage or issues to yours. You will also attract events that will magnify your shadow self. If you are in an emotionally abusive relationship, you will have friends attracted to you who seem to be going through exactly the same thing as you. This is the way your higher self works, and I understand this to be true for a few different reasons.

- to get you very clear on your own unresolved issues
- to enable you to have a depth of compassion, empathy, and understanding so that people around you will feel heard, acknowledged, and held (This makes you a great intuitive. People who resonate with you will surround you, in accordance with your level of self-mastery!)
- to ensure that you have a clear and strong boundary within your relationships and that you do *not* energetically plug in to other people's pain, negating the temptation to carry it on their behalf

Once you come to have a deeper understanding of any limitation or patterns that you have discovered with the people in your life, utilize some of the processing techniques above or simply journal regarding what you have discovered about yourself.

Optional Exercise

If you feel you would like to achieve completion with the people on your list, you are welcome to write them a letter detailing all you need to express to them. You do not have to send it to them, but I would recommend you dispose of it by burning it or burying it.

Completion Exercise

Sometimes there are people in your life around whom you have a deep sense of incompletion and who cause you to experience a great deal of energy and power loss. These can be people currently in your life or people with whom you have had a past relationship. This could include former partners, parents, siblings, friends, and colleagues. Sometime this loss of power related to people in your life can be so profound and marked that there is a need to complete matters with this person or people once and for all. On a soul level you have an unrealized or unfinished contract or agreement with this person. This leaves a very real response and reaction to this person and can create a continued difficulty in moving forward, with you cycling into similar relationships in the future.

I suggest you try this completion ceremony for the people in your life with whom you just can't seem to find a sense of resolution. Perhaps they are abusive, unwilling, difficult, or unavailable on the body level, i.e., emotionally, mentally, and physically. This completion exercise will allow you to complete with them on the soul level, bypassing the ego mind that may not be willing to yield its perceived control over you or the situation. I think it is important to note that you may actually still do this exercise with people who are actively in your life and with whom you want a continued relationship. This exercise will not banish them from your life; it will simply complete the agreement or contract that is still active. This can in fact pave the way for a deeper and healthier connection to them. Imagine how this relationship would look and feel without any drama.

You will need:

A photo of the person you desire completion with.

A ribbon or string of any color.

A candle and lighter or matches.

A pair of scissors.

Your journal and a pen.

- Prepare a quiet and private place where you will not be disturbed.
- Bring with you all of your items, placing the photo of the person across from you but facing you.
- Sit on a comfortable cushion on the floor.
- Extend the ribbon or string from you and out toward the photo across from you.
- Place the candle in between you and the photo. This may be resting on the ribbon if you like.
- Set your Torus Field around you, stating your clear and strong intention. "I set my clear and strong intention that nothing may enter my field and my space that wishes to harm me or cause me pain or that has any other negative intentions."

- Using the photo as a tool, close your eyes and picture that person sitting across from you in the same room. (If there is a history of violence with this person, know that you are safe, as you have set your Torus Field for a clear boundary.)

- Ask the person's soul to come forward and communicate with you. You may feel the soul's presence intuitively in your body, you may see it in your mind's eye, or you may simply have a knowing that it is with you.

- Ask the person's soul whether you have permission to communicate with it and to work with it through a completion exercise. Open your intuition to receive the response.

- If you feel it is a "no" response, then do not proceed. You cannot go against another person's free will and choice without causing more karma and incomplete contracts with them. Please be respectful of this and honor their choice. Thank them and release them back to their lives. Complete the optional exercise above that includes writing a letter to the person to communicate your unexpressed feelings, thoughts, and issues, and then burn this letter outside and allow the wind to carry it away from your life.

- If you feel a "yes" response from them, then continue with the following.

- Imagine the person's soul sitting across from you. Take the opportunity to express to them, out loud or within your mind, all of the unexpressed communications that you have. Say everything that you have always wanted to say and how you feel, including any injustices you think they have perpetrated against you. I also invite you to express any regrets, shame, or guilt that you may be carrying regarding your own actions and behaviors. This is your opportunity to get it all out. Please don't edit yourself or hold back in your communication.

- When you have completed your expression, allow the soul aspect of the person to communicate to you any unexpressed communications or feelings they may be holding on to. Open your heart and mind to receive what is being offered to you. This may feel strange at first, but trust your intuition. What you are doing is listening to their soul, not their ego, and you will receive this best on the intuitive level of yourself. You may get quite a different response to the one you are expecting, including possibly an apology from them.

- When you feel their soul has completed their communication, you then thank them for their sharing.

- You then state out loud, "I, (say your name), now complete and finish any and all vows, oaths, commitments, promises, contracts, agreements, marriages, pledges, initiations, deals, bets with (say their name), throughout all distance, dimensions, time, and space, including all lifetimes past, present, and future. I clearly and strongly intend that this cause no harm to either of us and that it is enacted in alignment with our divine will. I also ask that this take place with ease and grace and that no negativity or ongoing karma is created through this act of completion."

- Now cut the ribbon or string with the scissors, symbolizing the act of cutting ties and the current karmic connections.

- You may then blow out the candle, again symbolizing the end of the flame that may contain any negativity between you.

- Again say to the person's soul, "I thank you for agreeing to complete with me, and I wish you goodness and joy in your journey of life, if that is what you choose. You may now return to your place of creation. Travel safely and well."

- You may like to take some time to sit quietly with yourself, taking a moment to write in your journal all that you have experienced and felt, including what you received from the other person's communication. Observe any realizations, epiphanies, or deeper understandings that may have surfaced during the exercise. This may include understanding how this difficult relationship began and why it was difficult to complete.

- Clear the space with white sage and have a drink of water to help ground you.

- Note in your journal anything you observe in relation to this experience throughout the next month, including what you find reflected back to you through other people.

Self-Care

Create a special celebratory dinner with lovely flowers and nourishing home-cooked food. You may invite the people whom you love and feel supported by to share this joyous meal.

CHAPTER FIVE

———◆———

The Witch's Wound

And the day came when the risk to remain tight
in a bud was more painful than the risk it took to
blossom.—Anais Nin

O ver the years I have been aware, through teaching and
facilitating thousands of intuitive sessions, of a wounding
that many people hold within their souls. This is called
the "Witch's Wound." It simply means that throughout the many
incarnations or lives that we have lived upon the earth, many of
us, particularly those who feel drawn to this type of work, have
been persecuted, tortured, shamed, humiliated, or murdered for our
difference and our abilities.

There was a time in history that was deeply steeped in fear
of the unknown, prejudice, lack of education, and an attempt to
control people with "gifts" by those in power. This is documented
throughout history as the "witch hunts," and it is a good example of
what happened to people who stood out from the crowd as different.
During these terrible times in Europe and North America between
AD 1480 and 1750, anyone who stood out as gifted, spiritual,
healing, magical, different, unusual, or simply bad-tempered found

themselves at risk of persecution, torture, and murder. Depending on the historical source, the number of people murdered during this period ranges anywhere from one hundred thousand to eleven million, with 85 percent of those killed being women. When you reflect upon those numbers, you begin to have an understanding of what an effect this has had not only on a personal level but also on a collective level. It can be easy to fathom how this has affected and continues to affect those choosing to step into their spiritual power and the abilities that are their birthright.

Often, this imprint is carried so deeply that it is contained within the cellular memory of the body-mind-soul. This fear of persecution can then begin to seep into your awareness when you decide to embark upon your spiritual journey, the decision itself triggering the sleeping memory of this trauma. This fear can fill the cellular matrix of your body-mind-soul, limiting and inhibiting your intuitive abilities and landing you in work and relationships that keep you safe, but unfulfilled and unhappy. It is unlikely that in Australia or the United States of America in 2013 you will be tortured or murdered for being intuitive, although it is important to note that it was only in 2005 that witchcraft and psychic readings using tarot cards were legalized in some parts of Australia.

I want to be very clear that this book is not about witchcraft. It is also important, however, to address the perceived fears that some people still hold within their consciousness and souls. The Gendercide, as some historians call it, which occurred during "the burning times" is a fact that cannot be ignored. Again, it is better to address what lurks beneath the surface than to have it control and limit your life without your awareness.

It is important to recognize, also, that some people in your life may not accept your choice to become intuitive and embrace your abilities. These can be family, friends, or members of the public. This is often due to their own ignorance and fear, based both on the collective consciousness, their conditioning, and the culture in which they live. Perhaps it is also their cellular memory of the burning times coming into play. Often with a little bit of education and explanation, these fears can be alleviated. It is a natural human condition, it seems, to be afraid of what you don't know. Communicating calm, considerate information about what you do and how you do it can go a long way toward bridging that gap, if it is shared compassionately and not defensively.

When I first started spiritual work professionally, I held a fear of abandonment and persecution in my soul that was directly related to being different and intuitive. As a direct result, I had people mirror this fear back to me through misunderstanding and ignorance. I have had a number of Bibles sent to me throughout my professional career by some well-meaning and some not-so-well-meaning members of the public. At first I would allow this to upset me, as I would take it as a personal attack. Now I don't react, as I no longer hold any issues regarding religious persecution in my soul. I have dealt with the past trauma that I held in my cellular memory and soul, of being persecuted and murdered, by following the processes in this book. I can now see the well-meaning people as being compassionate and caring enough about me to offer me their perspective. It's up to me what I choose to do and how I choose to react to this offering. I think it's important to also say that I haven't received any Bibles for a number of years!

It is important that you first recognize what fears you hold yourself. Then, as we have already discussed, you can minimize any criticisms, opinions, or negative judgments coming your way.

Shadow and Light Exercise

In your workbook, write two lists. One can be titled "Light" and the other "Shadow." In each list, write down all of your perceived positives or negatives regarding your intuition and your uniqueness. Be very honest with yourself. These may include two aspects of the same thing in both lists. For example,

Light	Shadow
Gaining new, like-minded friends	Losing friends who don't understand
Being connected to my inner knowing and guidance	Having to take responsibility for my actions and thoughts
Developing my intuitive gifts	Becoming oversensitive to people and situations
Feeling part of a community of like-spirited people	Feeling misunderstood and isolated

When you have completed your list, write down the title "Fears" and continue in the same vein. What are you truly afraid of? These fears may, as mentioned, live on the soul-body-mind level and do not need to be "rational." Perhaps you fear losing your children, or being physically harmed, raped, or persecuted. Whatever the fear, please write it down. For example,

Fears

Mind   My husband won't understand me if I embrace my spiritual abilities.

Body   He may leave, and I won't be able to support my children.

Soul   I was abandoned by a man in a past life because I was accused
        of being a witch.

As you are writing your lists, be gentle with yourself and give yourself enough time and space to process what comes through. You may have difficulty realizing these fears on all three levels, and that's okay. Simply write down what you are aware of, for example, "I don't know what to say to people about what I am studying because I'm afraid they will judge me." Perhaps after a while there will be more clarity coming through around this fear. If so, write down what you discover.

After you go through this process of realizing your fears, they are less likely to hold you back and creep up when you least expect it. Fears can contribute to self-sabotaging behaviors, and this is very important to recognize. Remember, you are bringing your shadow into the light. The moment when you realize you are holding limiting beliefs is the exact moment when you have the opportunity to choose differently, creating a different outcome and therefore a different result in your life. This may be hard at first, as we are often addicted to old patterns and fears, but little by little with self-awareness you will be able to reclaim your power and your birthright to be free to choose the outcome and experience of your life.

Continue with this exercise, and every time a fear or a limiting belief regarding your intuition arises, write it down. Feel what bubbles to the surface, and become conscious and aware around this. We will address this more deeply in a later chapter, so for now, be gentle and compassionate with yourself as you become aware of your shadow.

Self-Care

Treat yourself to an outing at the beach, the mountains, or somewhere in nature. Spend time soaking in the beauty of the natural world, remembering that you are a part of and are connected to this beauty, that you are not separate from this but one with it. You may also like to treat yourself to a massage or a facial—something that will pamper you and make you feel special.

CHAPTER SIX

As Above So Below

Personal transformation can and does have global effects. As we go, so goes the world, for the world is us.—Marianne Williamson

The next step is to gain understanding of your intuitive strengths. In later chapters you will be connecting to and deepening your relationship with your higher self. For now, though, let's focus on the way your intuitive self is set up.

There are many forms of intuitive abilities, and everyone on this planet is capable of developing theirs. It's important to note that the intuitive ability that stands out to you now may change over time. My own abilities were predominantly clairsentient to begin with, but I now work on many levels at once. I am also aware that the more intuitive work I do, the more advanced my skills become. This journey is limited only by you and the focus you bring.

So what are the intuitive abilities? Here are the main ones to focus on for now.

Clairsentience: the ability to receive information from people, animals, environments, or other forms of consciousness through your body.

Clairvoyance: the ability to receive information from people, animals, environments, or other forms of consciousness through visions or visual pictures.

Clairaudience: the ability to receive information from people, animals, environments or other forms of consciousness through auditory experience. This can include hearing words, sounds, and sentences from both outside and within you.

Empathy: the ability to merge your own consciousness with another, especially through your body and emotions, and experience life as they do.

Interaction Exercise

Observe over a week how you interact with the world and with people.

Are you visual? Feeling? Auditory? Do you love watching movies, listening to music, receiving hugs, and getting massages? This will give you clues as to where your natural intuitive strengths lie.

Take note of the language you use while in conversation with different people. Do you use description words like "I can see what you mean," "I know how you feel," or "I hear what you're saying?" This will also give you clues to your own personal language and how this can be an indication of your natural intuitive abilities.

Is there an intuitive ability that you would like to develop more strongly? Why? What advantages do you feel you may gain with this new intuitive ability? Write this in your workbook.

What Is a Psychic?

Exercise

Write down what you think the term "psychic" means.

Write down what you think the term "medium" means.

Write down what you think the term "intuitive" means.

What do you think is the difference between the three? Include any stereotypes related to these terms that you may have come across.

Can a person be all three—psychic, a medium, and intuitive? If yes, how? If not, why not?

In later chapters we will discuss the benefits and the challenges related to the different ways of working with spirit and intuition, so for now take the opportunity to observe professional psychics, mediums, and intuitives working and see if you can determine the difference.

Grounding

Grounding is the concept of having your consciousness fully engaged in your physical body. The importance of being in the physical whilst connecting to your intuition cannot be understated. If you are ungrounded or flighty, you will be less effective as an intuitive and in your life, generally speaking. There is a misconception of the new age that you need to be out of your body to be connected. Nothing could be farther from the truth! If you are ungrounded, you will be more affected by the energy around you and other people's shadows. This can eventually lead to health issues, including mental illness and energetic illness.

A great number of highly skilled intuitives have at some point taken medication to numb themselves, including antidepressants and painkillers, legal and illegal, and food, alcohol, and cigarettes. Once you have trained your soul and mastered your own energy, you won't need to dumb down the experience of your life. Likewise, I have seen many new agers blissed out on spirit. This is a great indication that they are not fully engaged in their lives and that they are numbing themselves with the "bliss" drug. You may have met people like this, who perceive themselves as enlightened but can't pay the rent. Developing your intuition is a holistic experience, and if you can't pay your bills because you prefer to meditate, then I would seriously suggest addressing what is going on under the surface.

Here are a few examples of being ungrounded:

- being accident prone
- bumping into furniture
- dropping things
- feeling light headed
- being forgetful
- losing the thread of a conversation
- losing your train of thought
- driving and not remembering the journey
- being emotionally reactive
- being emotionally oversensitive
- being physically oversensitive

If you experience these symptoms at all, please make it your aim to work strongly with grounding every day, especially while developing your intuitive abilities. This state can be such a habit for some people they are not even aware what it feels like to be fully embodied!

Grounding Exercise

1) Sit quietly, cross-legged on the earth and preferably in the sun, for a minimum of five minutes, morning and night. Imagine that your heart center energy flows down and connects to the earth. Ensure that your heart center energy travels down to the very center of the earth and into her crystalline heart. If you only tap into the surface or just below, you will actually be tapping into the astral realm, or fourth dimension, that is held within the earth. This layer is about three hundred kilometers in depth and contains the residue of human emotions, entities, and other unpleasant energies that you do not want to connect with or draw into your body, mind, or heart. Your clear and strong intention is to connect with the earth, heart to heart. When you have connected right into the heart, allow the earth's healing love to flow up to you, filling your heart and connecting you to your own body. Visualize the earth's heart at the center of her body and then see your heart at the center of your body.

2) Meditate every day for the next week, concentrating on your consciousness anchoring into the very heart of the earth mother. Visualize your consciousness traveling down through the layers of rock and stone, down through the underground rivers and streams, down though the rivers of fire and lava, and then merging into the earth's crystalline heart. Perhaps imagine that, just like a ship's anchor, your consciousness is now held in the heart of the earth mother. Stay there in this

connection for as long as you choose. This is a great way to begin any meditation or to prepare yourself for your day.

This is a very healing process and can be used as much as you wish. Please journal after each meditation, noticing any realizations and experiences you've had.

During the week, notice if anything changes in terms of you being more present in your life and if there are differences you perceive.

I have developed an amazing guided visualization called "Heart of the Earth Mother," which can be purchased and downloaded at http://www.heidisvision.com/audios. This will help you to ground and can be listened to three times a week initially while you are learning to be in a natural state of being grounded and present.

Self–Care

Take a number of baths, showers, or swims during the week, and do one thing each day that feels great and is just for you. This will help to clear your auric field of any discordant energy, thought forms, or judgments. It will also help to clear and stabilize your physical body. You may also like to imagine a shower of father sun's golden light washing down over you while you are standing in the shower or any other time you need it. State in your mind that the father sun's golden light is washing away any negativity or stuck energy.

CHAPTER SEVEN

Defining Intuition

Just as in the body, eye and ear develop as organs of perception, as senses for bodily processes, so does a man develop in himself soul and spiritual organs of perception through which the soul and spiritual worlds are opened to him. For those who do not have such higher senses, these worlds are dark and silent, just as the bodily world is dark and silent for a being without eyes and ears.—Rudolf Steiner

Heart-Centered Intuition

You were asked earlier to write down your understanding of the terms "psychic," "medium," and "intuitive" and the differences between them. Here I will explain my perspective of these three abilities, and you can compare it with what you have written yourself. Before I begin, I would like to say that I am aware that my point of view may push some buttons. I can only speak from my experience.

What Is a Psychic?

A psychic is a person who receives information from people, places, items, animals, plants, crystals, and other forms of consciousness, in various ways. A psychic receives information and can gain insight, guidance, and information on behalf of another regarding the past, present, or future. This information comes from outside of the psychic, is filtered through her belief systems and experiences, and is then communicated in whatever way she finds comfortable. Psychics may also use tools such as tarot cards, oracle cards, jewelry, or crystals to assist with the information gathering. Once the psychic is disconnected from the person, place, or thing, she can usually disconnect from the flow of information or energy for that situation or person.

What Is a Medium?

A medium communicates to other forms of consciousness that are not necessarily within the physical world. Similar to a translator, mediums often receive images or specific words to pass on messages to the living. This includes human souls who are in other dimensional planes as well as other nonhuman life forms in other dimensions. The most popular understanding of this is a person who can communicate and relay messages from passed-over people in spirit to the living. The medium translates the communication from the soul, which may come in the form of words, visions, or feelings, to the recipient.

Mediums can also communicate to animals, angels, guides, and masters, depending on their level of ability and their interest. Again, the interaction comes from a form of consciousness outside or separate from the medium.

What Is an Intuitive?

An intuitive accesses a higher aspect of himself or herself, called the spirit or higher self, to bring through understanding and information and to facilitate healing and transformation on behalf of themselves and others. Intuitives usually work better with animate objects and people.

This can be experienced through clairsentience, through clairvoyance, and through clairaudience, the same as a psychic, the main difference being that the guidance originates from within, rather than being received from the external.

Where Is Your Intuition?

There is a common misconception around intuition these days. A lot of people believe, or think, that their intuition stems from something outside of themselves and that this intuition can only be accessed through practices such as meditation, trance, or prayer. Of course, we have all heard of the stories that make reference to angels or guides or beautiful beings assisting people in their moment of need, giving direction, guiding, and bringing clarity to the big questions—and sometimes even saving lives. We hear of people using the guidance of angels for many things, from finding their keys to finding the love of their life. We pray, we ask for help, and we listen to the guidance that comes from outside of ourselves, believing that what we are receiving from the external has authority, wisdom, and power.

When professional psychics use their ability, they receive impressions from other people, divine beings, and forms of consciousness to gather information on behalf of their clients. Amazing and profound insights can be received which bring healing and insight to the client. This information may be received through a vision, a smell, a feeling, words, or sound. Psychics receive information from outside of themselves, and they then translate and share this in whatever way is relevant.

My question is this, though. Why, necessarily, does another person, being, soul, or consciousness know more about you than you do? Why do they possess authority over your life and the choices you make?

After reading for thousands of clients, I have become very aware of the temptation to externalize our own power and responsibilities. Imagine you have a very difficult decision to make about a relationship that you are in. Rather than looking within, you ask others about what you should do. Imagine phoning your mum and asking her what she thinks you should do about this relationship. Should you stay or go? More than likely, your mother's response will be one of love and support, and she will offer her advice and direction from this level. Your mother will also likely have an underlying agenda, however, within the advice she offers you. Perhaps she's always wanted grandchildren and thinks her time is running out, so she encourages you to stay. Maybe she doesn't like your partner or the work he does, so she encourages you to go. It doesn't matter what the agenda is; we all have reasons for what we say and do and how we communicate to others, even if it is as simple as wanting another person to be "happy." This can underlie the guidance offered and lead us down a path that may not be for our highest good.

Extending this further, how often do we make our own decisions based upon lies we tell ourselves? We often look for someone to blame for our lives not running the way we want, or we look to others to fix our lives for us. This is a culturally accepted way of not taking responsibility for who we are, but deeper than that, it is a reflection of our disconnection in our relationship with ourselves. It seems to be a vicious cycle.

The relationship with the self is the most fundamental of relationships and is what all other relationships are based upon. If there is not a solid relationship with the self, then how can we create strong relationships with others and with the other aspects of our lives? Building and growing this self-connection is a way to truly know who you are and to know your heart center intimately. From this place, anything is possible. From this place, you have access to your higher self, the highest expression of your soul force and spirit, and you will be able to discern the self-guidance received. This aspect of you does not contain an agenda and holds no judgment, and it is precisely where your heart-centered intuition occurs. Your heart-centered intuition will guide you to the best place, in the best way, with the best people and in the manner that is perfect for you.

As a professional intuitive, this is how I see my role: to help you establish, encourage and nurture your connection to your own higher self and heart-centered intuition, building your relationship with yourself, until you are able to do this on your own. This will give you back the power of you.

Remember, you are your own god, goddess, angel, and guide, all rolled into one beautiful, heart-centered human package. You are your own higher self and your own teacher. You are your own star, galaxy, and universe. The moment you know this to be true is the moment you know—truly know—who you are and what you are capable of.

Exercise

As you read those words, how did you feel? Write your response in your workbook, noting feelings, emotions, thoughts or ideas. Do you perceive your intuition differently? How? Why?

Instinct versus Intuition

I think it is important to explain here the difference between intuition and instinct. These two responses or reactions to an environment, person, or event are often misunderstood and confused by people.

Imagine that you are at a party with friends. There are many people at this party whom you have not met before, but you are still feeling relaxed and confident. A man approaches you to chat, and instantly your body reacts to his presence. Perhaps this man appears nice and polite on the exterior, and yet you are acutely aware of a feeling of dread in the pit of your stomach. There is no obvious reason for your body to react this way to this man's presence, and yet you are experiencing an increasing level of anxiety and nervousness. Your body has firmly reacted on a fight–or–flight level of response. This is where your physical body responds to a potential survival threat, which then signals the brain, through the endocrine system, to flood your body with the hormone adrenaline. While all this is happening on the physical level, your ego is trying to decide whether to run away or to stay and fight. This instinctual response is what every human being carries within them. What is happening is this. Your body is having a cellular memory activated by the presence of this person because someone has actually threatened you with the same energetic signature in the past. Your body realizes this not intuitively but instinctively. Perhaps you had an abusive ex–husband, father, or boyfriend and you have experienced a traumatic event, physically, emotionally, or mentally. This experience and trauma will then be locked into the cellular memory and may lay dormant within the body until a similar situation presents itself and the instinct then kicks in to warn you away from that person, place, or thing. This cellular memory may be from a past life, or it may originate from this lifetime. As the soul and spirit are eternal, it makes no difference as to when the original event took place.

Coming back to the scenario at the party, your body has responded on an instinctual level to a perceived threat. Whether or not the man you are speaking with poses an actual threat to you is, in a way, irrelevant. This man holds the same or a similar energetic signature that you have experienced before, and this will trigger and activate your body memory or cellular memory into its instinctual fight-or-flight response. All this may occur within a few seconds of interaction.

We are often, in our society, taught to mistrust this response, particularly as women. People say often, "I just knew that person wasn't good for me, but I ignored what my gut was telling me! I should have listened!" This is your instinctual response, and it originates from a trauma or wounding locked into the cellular memory that is triggered by a person or event.

Your intuition is a reaction or a response from a higher aspect of yourself—from your spirit, not your soul. Your spirit is the eternal aspect of you, and this is the place where your divine wisdom resides. This is brought through your heart center and then processed first by the right side of your brain (the intuitive side) and then by the left side of the brain (the analytical and logical side) to define what is the best way to handle the situation and to determine if you are at risk. This reaction tends to be subtler in nature but is still as potent a way of communicating as your instinctual response, if you are open and listening to what is being communicated to you.

If we continue with the situation above, when presented with the man at the party you may hear a warning in your mind, you may see an image in your mind's eye, or you may feel a physical response as a feeling or an inner knowing rather than an intense physical reaction. The spirit is giving you direct information without a direct physical cellular reaction. As you continue to read and experience the set exercises, you will be able to strengthen your own intuitive communication, learning to hear, feel, or see what your spirit is communicating to you.

Self-Care

Forgive yourself of any unhealthy relationships that you have been involved in. Love yourself enough to listen to what your intuition is telling you and understand that you already have everything you need within you and in your heart to guide your life forward. You are amazing!

CHAPTER EIGHT

———◆———

The Three Levels of a Human Being

How is it possible that a being with such sensitive
jewels as the eyes, such enchanted musical instruments
as the ears, and such fabulous arabesque of nerves as
the brain can experience itself anything less than a
god?—Alan Watts

The concept of perceiving each human being from three
levels of experience can help you to learn more about
yourself and those around you. Asking yourself some
questions while also observing others in relation to you and your
interactions can be very helpful. From what level do you regularly
respond? When you are awake, you will always be receiving
information through your body. Notice the times, however, when
you may be responding from the level of soul or spirit. Can you
differentiate your responses? Use the questions below to help you
understand from where you are primarily responding. Ideally, the aim
is to have most of your responses occur from the level of your spirit.
Realistically, this may take years of focused attention, awareness, and
self-actualization to achieve. Start at the beginning, without placing
too much pressure on yourself. Simply being aware of the level from

which you respond and interact in your life allows you choices and potentially different outcomes.

This simple concept is the foundational structure for your intuitive development. When you are working with your intuition, it is important to understand at what level you are working and receiving information. This process can, of course, cross all three levels and often does. Your job is to address what is most present in your life at this time, not to go digging to uncover all of your skeletons at once.

Of course, issues will float to the surface as you continue to develop, but it isn't your job to get in there and wake things up unnecessarily. There is nothing wrong with taking things slowly.

Notice how you respond in your daily life when you are interacting with others.

Body

This includes any and all physical, emotional or mental aspects of you, including your cellular memory in your physical body.

Soul

This aspect includes karmic patterns, life lessons, soul contracts, and ancestral encoding. It is programmed into the body at a cellular level through incarnation. Your soul is what chooses to reincarnate into a physical body to learn, evolve, and have more physical and dualistic experiences. The memories from other lifetimes are then downloaded into the physical body, creating the cellular memory. The soul can get stuck in limiting patterns and karmic contracts with other souls and through events and experiences.

Spirit

The spirit is the god/goddess aspect of who you are. Your spirit is the divine and eternal essence of you that transcends time, space, drama, trauma, contracts, and the physical and soul experience. It is eternal, omnipresent, and the core of your being. This is where you will find unbiased and truthful answers to your life.

When working with these three levels, be aware of how they will connect to and cross over one another, as one is never separate from the other. By developing your intuition, you are creating a deeper connection between all three.

This should give you a conceptual understanding of the three levels of a human being.

Below are some questions to ask yourself during an intuitive exercise or development process. They will give you clues as to where you may need to place your focus or if there are any hidden limitations or blocks bubbling to the surface of your awareness.

When you are accessing and developing your intuition—and also in your everyday life—ask yourself the following questions and begin to take notice of the wisdom you are being shown.

Body

What is your body language telling you?

How are you sitting?

Where are you looking?

Are you fidgeting?

Are your legs or arms crossed?

Language

What words do you repeat, if any?

How is your stream of communication?

Do you finish sentences?

Do you make sense?

Are you jumping around to multiple topics?

Are you avoiding the questions?

Emotions

Are you reacting to the questions? If yes, note which ones.

Are you calm?

Are you fearful?

Are you openly emotional?

What can you feel?

Thoughts

Do you understand the concepts being brought through to you?

Are you displaying self-understanding?

Are you testing your reality against the process?

Are you stuck in a limiting belief?

Can you perceive a sabotage mechanism at play?

Soul

Are there karmic patterns influencing your life's experience?

Can you detect your own poverty consciousness?

Can you detect any patterns of victimization?

Are you in alignment with any certain type of archetype, e.g. martyr, prostitute, healer?

Does the issue originate in a past life?

Is it genetic or hereditary?

Are the people around you karmically influencing you?

Does a karmic contract or agreement influence you?

Do you have any agreements of entrapment?

Is there an incomplete karmic agreement that has been activated?

Spirit

What is your purpose?

What is your ray? (Ray will be explained in later chapters)

What is your medicine?

Exercise

Over a month, notice on what levels you are interacting with your world. Make three columns titled "Body," "Soul," and "Spirit," and place a score within each column, each time you feel a response from one or more levels. As stated, you will receive most of your information through your body, but also notice the following:

Am I emotional?

Am I argumentative?

Am I stuck in a karmic relationship?

Do I know and do I trust my heart to guide me forward?

Am I connected to my intuition?

Can you detect a pattern within your responses? We are multileveled and multifaceted beings, so you won't be confined within one level. This exercise will give you the realization that perhaps you get stuck on one level or other.

Think over your life and observe how you grew up. How did your parents and siblings interact with the world? Do you carry an imprint from them? Are your responses your own, or have they been conditioned? Please journal as much as you can around this topic.

Self–Care

Acknowledge and contemplate the immense wisdom and beauty that you have experienced through the way you uniquely interact with the world. If you feel you are able, give thanks to the wisdom and the gifts that have been handed down to you from you family.

If you would like to interact on the secure Intuition On Tap Forum through the Heart Centre to discuss the topics and exercises in this chapter and the opportunity to interact with Heidi and with other readers, please go to http://www.heidisvision.com/community and become a member of the VIP forum. After you have joined you may follow the topic heading to this and every other chapter.

Part Two

Understanding Your Universe

CHAPTER NINE

The Universal Structure

It was much pleasanter at home, thought poor Alice, *when one wasn't always growing larger and smaller, and being ordered about by mice and rabbits. I almost wish I hadn't gone down the rabbit-hole—and yet—and yet …*—Lewis Carroll

There are other life forms in the universe, which you may have difficulty understanding and accepting. Here I will explain to you from my understanding and experience the other realms of consciousness that extend down to the first and second dimensions and out to the furthest regions of the universe and beyond. This is what is referred to as the Universal Structure. I have seen many different models of this, and so I will share with you the one that I find easiest to understand and work within.

We are multidimensional beings. This means we are capable of accessing multiple dimensions at any time we choose, whilst our bodies, or physicality, remain in the third dimension. A dimension is a level of consciousness, existence, or reality. It is also important to note that there are both negative and positive life forms, consciousness, and beings on each of the four lower dimensions. Duality,—or dark and light, positive and negative—life forces tend not to exist in the fifth dimension and above.

First Dimension: This is where the elemental and mineral realm exists. On this dimension we are able to access the wisdom and consciousness that is held within the deva or spirits of the mineral world. This also includes the elemental energies, such as air, fire, earth, water, and ether, or spirit. This dimension holds the elemental energies or spirit of the natural world, such as

- undines, water spirits,
- gnomes, earth spirits,
- sylphs, air spirits (often known as faeries), and
- salamanders, fire spirits.

All of these forms of consciousness can access other dimensions, like us, but this is their home or where their soul naturally resides.

Second Dimension: This is where animals, birds, and other creatures exist—along with the third, physical dimension, of course. The physical bodies of some mystical creatures, such as dragons and unicorns, can be found here. Plant and tree spirits can be found here and are wonderful to work with. Tree spirits are called dryads.

Third Dimension: Obviously, this is where the physical body and realm of existence reside for human beings, animals, plants, and minerals. This is also where our consciousness resides and where we can interact with one another on the physical plane or reality. A good rule of thumb to remember is that forms of consciousness with a physical body in the third dimension are safe to work with.

Fourth Dimension: This dimension has many, many layers of other dimensional planes within it and is often referred to as the astral realm. One of these layers is a reflection of the collective consciousness of humanity, often reflecting fear, rage, or trauma. This is also where I will be a little different in the information I share with you compared to the New Age principles and teachings. Within the fourth dimension, or astral realm, is where a great many beings, entities and life forms live. These would include what people commonly know as entities, attachments, fallen angels, ghosts, demons, ascended masters, spirit guides, vampires, werewolves, and earth-bound souls, to name a few. These life forms are constantly interacting with human beings, often through deception and deceit, appearing as helpful and well-intentioned. They are not supposed to interact with us, and their accessing the third dimension via human beings is a violation of universal law. This is also the place where the religious concept of God resides. I will explain this in more detail shortly.

Fifth Dimension: This is where our passed-over loved ones cross over to and where our consciousness goes when we meditate and go to sleep. If you have a nightmare, your consciousness hasn't moved through the fourth dimension during the process of sleep. This can be clearly seen in children who experience night terrors.

There are a great number of beings that live within the fifth dimensional plane, often referred to as light beings. The fifth dimension is where we can access our higher selves and our souls, although they are present at other levels too.

Sixth to Eleventh Dimensions: The higher aspects of consciousness can be found here, as can a great number of benevolent beings. It is thought that human souls enter a portal through the seventh dimension to be incarnated or reincarnated, moving down through the other dimensions until they reach the third dimension and the physical realm.

It is important to note that there are an infinite number of dimensions, universes, and planes inside and outside of this universe. The planes of existence outside of our universe are sometimes referred to as the multiverse and omniverse. It can be a bit overwhelming when you begin to consider all the realties and places that exist. It is important, however, to understand the basics or fundamentals of the dimensional rules.

Some souls or forms of consciousness from the higher dimensions (fifth and above) are often referred to as divine light beings, with the exception to this being angels. As stated, there are an untold number of dimensions and types of light beings in the universe. A lot of intuitives report independently similar experiences of certain light beings.

On earth, we are all born into a particular culture or country. Imagine that it is the same in the other dimensional planes, that there are many different cultures or "countries" that light beings can originate from. Light beings are often associated with a stellar constellation, which can be seen in the night sky. This of course does not mean that if you were to look through a telescope, you would see these beings waving down at you! They are on another dimensional plane that cannot be seen by the naked eye.

Scientists working with the Large Hadron Collider in Switzerland in 2012 released to the public a statement that they had found proof of more than three dimensions. They had achieved this by bilocating particles in different dimensions at the same time using the Large Hadron Collider. Perhaps the technology to see interdimensional beings through a telescope isn't far away! For now though, you will have to be content to use your intuitive abilities.

There is a race of light beings from the Pleiades known as the Pleiadians. The same is true for Cassiopeia, Sirius, Orion, Arcturus,

Antares, and Andromeda to name a few. Just as in your human life you originate from a particular culture, your soul may have originated from a particular soul family or soul group connected to a constellation or star system. These light beings are often happy to oversee you in your travels, as they are members of your soul family and can add to your healing, teaching, and evolutionary pursuits. These members of your soul family are helping you to understand the concepts and lessons that you have come here to master. They do this because they are also able to evolve through your growth. You learn; they learn. You grow; they grow. It is a beautiful symbiotic relationship that has been in place since earth life began and even longer.

It is extremely important to mention here, though, that light beings are bound by universal law and can only oversee rather than actively engage with human beings. If they did so, they would become caught in the third-dimensional time track, which is not where they belong. In other words, they become trapped. The way our soul family work with us is to communicate with the level of our consciousness that resides in the same dimensional plane as theirs. For example, fifth-dimensional light beings and members of your soul family would be able to communicate and offer assistance or advice on the fifth-dimensional level of you, which is your soul level. If they were from a higher dimensional plane, they would be communicating to your spirit. They cannot and will not relate to you on the third-dimensional plane. It can be hard to understand the concepts that they pass on, as the information comes in at a higher level than your human mind can often understand. Through developing your intuition, you will be able to understand these communications as they filter in through the fifth-dimensional aspect of your heart and then into your conscious understanding. You can then translate this information into very real and practical ways to move your life forward. Following are diagrams of how we as human beings connect to the different dimensions.

Body

The body includes our mental, emotional, and physical aspects.

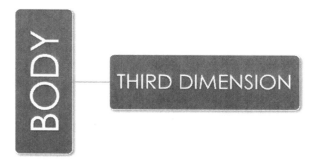

Soul

The soul is the aspect of ourselves that carries memories from this lifetime and other lifetimes, including past lives. It can hold a great deal of trauma or wounding, setting up cycles of time throughout our lives. This can imprint upon our body at a cellular level and create our life experiences in each incarnation. This is where contracts and agreements are made, prior to incarnation, with other souls.

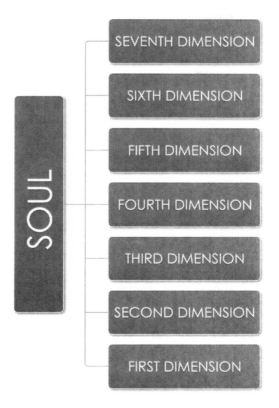

Spirit

Spirit is the aspect of us that is all-knowing and ever-present. It is our higher self, our sovereignty, and our god/goddess aspect. It knows exactly what we need at any given moment and is there to guide us through our lifetimes. It can access all dimensions, past, present, and future, throughout all space and time

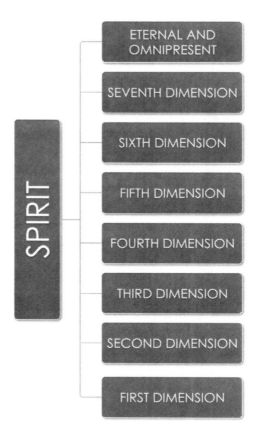

Self-Care

Go to a place in nature and sit still. Wonder how many dimensions are interacting as you sit in this beautiful, peaceful place. Contemplate how you relate to these.

CHAPTER TEN

Interdimensional Interference

Monsters are real, and ghosts are real too. They live inside us, and sometimes, they win.—Stephen King

Some forms of life in this universe have no issue breaking universal law by interacting with humanity in the third dimension. These life forms carry an agenda and can and do interfere with the evolution and development of human beings. A great number of psychics, channels, and mediums working today have been misled, misguided, and misinformed regarding these life forms. Often they will appear as benevolent and helpful, but when they are unmasked or are commanded to reveal their true nature, you will find a very different picture indeed. This includes, but is not limited to, those life forms that call themselves ascended masters, angels, the brotherhood of light, spirit guides, and the hierarchy of light. Please understand the concept of universal law, which involves the understanding that human beings have free will and choice upon this earth and that no one and nothing can interfere with that free will and choice without creating karma and becoming entrapped. That is why the truly benevolent and helpful members of your soul family will only observe or pass on impressions of how you can evolve as a human being. They will never interfere in your life—ever.

The other life forms that hold an agenda will play this out through drama, war, famine, global economic crisis, homelessness, religious fundamentalism, hatred, racism, addictions, murder, rape, sexual abuse, religion, and governmental control mechanisms within cultures, society, and people. Their doorway into this third dimension is through human beings.

These life forms can be referred to as interdimensional interference. They exist in another dimension of time and space, within a layer of the fourth dimension, and the only way they can have access to the third dimension is through human beings. This is done via an agreement of entrapment. These can be promises, contracts, and deals made with humans. Some humans make these agreements consciously through initiations, soul contracts, and rituals, but mostly they are made without an understanding of what is actually taking place. A few ways this can happen is during a trauma, by using drugs or alcohol, or while begging outside of yourself for help and also by praying to God. When you are open and you have your defenses down, these interdimensional beings can access your body.

It is important to note here that this can also happen through channeling or by using trance mediumship. Someone who is channeling any being from outside of themselves or their higher self is giving an open invitation to any interdimensional being that wants to access the third dimension through their body. These beings have no other way to interact on the third dimensional plane. Be conscious of any channeled teachings from beings outside of this dimension, no matter how evolved or benevolent they may appear. If you are very astute and allow your intuition to guide you, you will probably pick up their lies and perceive how they can very subtly entrap humans into their way of thinking and their agendas. If at any time you feel less than or are belittled through these messages, then you are not dealing with who or what you may think, regardless of what the channel tells you.

It is your responsibility as a conscious intuitive to understand how the universe works and to ensure that you do not walk into agreements of entrapment without knowing. Unfortunately, ignorance is not an excuse.

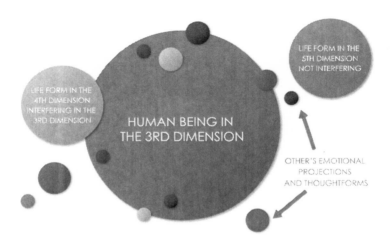

A few years ago I used to work during my reading and healing sessions by connecting my consciousness into my clients' guides and angels. By the end of the day I was depleted, exhausted, and sick. I was only able to see a maximum of five clients a day. What I came to understand was that when I set my intention at the beginning of my reading session to connect with my clients' guides and angels, I was allowing these other life forms to feed from my life force and vital energy. I was giving them permission to snack on me!

For years I could not understand why, if I was balanced and doing the work of spirit, I always felt so sick and tired. When I finally understood what was actually going on, I instantly changed my intention and refused to work with anything outside of my clients—only their own bodies, spirits, and souls. I can now comfortably give at least ten readings a day with little or no effect on my health and well-being. I now understand that I was giving my full permission to these life forms to feed from me. When that realization hit home, I made it very clear that I would no longer allow anything to invade my energy or to drain my life force.

Here are a few of the life forms that I'm referring to as interdimensional interference.

- reptilians
- draconians
- dragons
- winged serpents
- thought forms and life forms
- entrapped human souls
- aliens (These beings are not necessarily interdimensional, as some races can have access to the third dimensional plane without the need of the human body.)

If you have ever heard people refer to a race of beings commonly known as "reptilians," you will understand what I am speaking of here. These beings are soldiers, coming from a warrior race and are interested in creating, being involved in, and sustaining universal conflict. I have met a number of these beings, at different times and often when I am on the precipice of further spiritual development. They attempt to threaten, scare and bully me, to prevent me from evolving and so through my experience, I can see where this greater understanding has come from. These beings have no emotional body and can be compared to crocodiles or reptiles in our human experience. Their presence is very intense and heavy, and they are very tall and imposing, often wearing full body armor.

I am not sharing this information with you for any reason other than to give you awareness and understanding that there are certain rules to be guided by and adhere to when developing your intuition and engaging in spiritual work. There is no reason to be afraid; simply be informed, and then you can make a choice as to what you would like to experience. At all times you have a choice, and often the simplest concepts are the most powerful. Learn to say no, have clear boundaries and an understanding of universal law, and then set your clear and strong intention to work in alignment with your spirit, the divine aspect of you.

Exercise

Look over your life and contemplate if there have been any times when you have felt the presence, influence, or energy of any interdimensional beings. Write down what you have experienced or become aware of throughout your life and spiritual journey.

Exercise

How do you feel as you explore the universal structure presented here? Are you confused? Does it push your buttons? Please record any reactions you experience. Can you remember experiences, books you've read, or sessions you've had that fit into what has been offered in this explanation of universal structure?

Working with your higher self and spirit is about working with freedom and openness, not dogma and constructs. Paradoxically, it is also helpful to have guidelines to work from and within. These guidelines may include integrity, truth, honesty, love, balance, and power. Remember that you are far better off following your own truth and what rings true to your heart. With that in mind, I am also one for the KISS rule: Keep It Simple, Stupid!

You can become very quickly overwhelmed with often-conflicting viewpoints related in different teachings and books. Let me be clear: these are not wrong, nor are they right. They are simply another's expression of information they have received regarding the subject matter. It is up to you to discern your own truth.

I feel it is important to note here that authors or teachers who talk about concepts based in fear or lack, without a solution or potential for transformation, are not working from their higher selves. Rather, they are working from their egos or have interdimensional interference online. Are they asking you to open yourself to the light, to invite in your angels and guides? Do they tell you that you don't know as much as their guides do or that you are less evolved? If, when you read a text or listen to a teaching, you feel uneasy, sad and fearful, you know that your soul is communicating a message to you through your body. This is a very different sensation to when you are trying to understand a new concept that may challenge your current belief structures.

Check through your heart center, not your head.

Self-Care

Become aware of what you read and see on television and of how other spiritual people portray themselves and the language they are using. Do you recognize any interference? Be very gentle with yourself and meditate, connecting to the earth mother often, as you are unfolding and shifting your understanding of our world and your place within it.

CHAPTER ELEVEN

———◆◆———

Spiritual Boundaries

The most important thing in life is to learn how to give out love, and to let it come in.—Morrie Schwartz

As you move through this book, you will become more and more aware that the work you do is taking place on a deeper than intellectual or conceptual level and that feelings, thoughts, and realizations may be coming up. Great! That's the plan! Please continue to journal and complete the exercises.

During this chapter, you will be observing any challenges you may have with establishing boundaries. In my experience, boundaries are essential for accessing your intuition and improving your health and well-being. If you do not have clear boundaries, then you will become depleted very quickly, energetically, physically, and emotionally. This is not just when you are dealing with spirit but is also very valid in terms of your daily life. If you don't have clear boundaries, then there is a real risk that you will experience feelings and thoughts belonging to other people and that you will have difficulty in discerning what belongs to you and what does not. This can then lead to feelings of confusion, resentment, and anger and being overwhelmed, and this obviously doesn't help anyone, especially you!

Boundaries in Relationships

Continuing along with the concepts from "As Within So Without," it is valuable to look at your personal relationships. Particular relationship patterns often have threads that run through a few areas of your life. If you have difficulty establishing boundaries within your birth family, your marriage or intimate relationship, or with colleagues and friends, then you will have difficulty upholding your boundaries with spiritual energies.

Exercise

Part One

Make a list of your family members, close friends, and work mates. Beside each of their names, write down two to three words that describe their relationship with you.

Example

Mum—loving, demanding, guilt
Dad—absent, distant, good provider
Sam—accepting, fun, open

You get the idea. When you have completed the list, run through it, noting the people with whom you may have struggles. This is simply to bring your awareness to any unresolved issues, particularly around how you relate to each other. As you are working, also note feelings as they arise and any sensations or pain in your body. Write these down too. Particularly note those people around whom you feel a loss of power or energy. Does your body have an instinctive response? Are you noticing any physical sensations, signs, or emotions rising in your body? Note these down too.

If there are a few of these people in your life, you may have challenges establishing boundaries and that this will need continued attention, understanding, and compassion. For some people, establishing and continuing to uphold boundaries may be a lifetime's work. Don't pressure yourself to be perfect straight away; rather, be open to learning more about your patterns of interaction and relating to the world around you.

Part Two

Create an image, picture, or artistic work that expresses you regaining your personal boundaries within these relationships noted. This can be done with whatever medium you feel comfortable using. It is not about artistic excellence but about artistic and creative expression. Wax crayons and paints tend to work well. Again, as you are working witness what comes up for you. You are welcome to create more than one image. When you are finished, place this work of art in a spot where you can see it easily so that you are reminded of the boundary you are creating and intending to maintain.

Regaining power and establishing boundaries may take a great deal of work if these patterns have been established for much of your life. On its own, this book is not designed to heal the past. It will, however, give you an understanding of where to focus your healing journey. I believe that if we are still breathing, we still have work to do. Please be gentle with yourself, showing the same compassion you would to a friend or loved one.

There are a few fundamental truths that I will share with you here. You have already decided on the soul level to experience what you have experienced and are yet to experience in your life. If you don't want someone/something in your field and choose to have a clear boundary on every level of your being, then it is up to you to say no.

- You are not responsible for another's suffering.
- You are not responsible for another's happiness.
- You are a sovereign being.

When you remind yourself of these truths often, you will gain freedom and boundaries in your life.

Spiritual Boundaries: Learning to Say No to Spirit

Often when people begin to develop their connection to their intuition and their higher self, they are so excited that they are happy to feel, hear, and see anything spirit can throw at them. It's new and exciting and can feel a bit like falling in love. What you've intuitively known for years is being validated with your senses, which feels great, especially now that you know you weren't making it up and going a bit mad! When this honeymoon period settles down, it is very, very important to establish some rules. If you don't, all the information you are receiving may make you feel overwhelmed. This can lead to exhaustion and sometimes, in extreme cases, to mental illness.

I am often asked whether I can turn off my abilities, and the answer is yes, absolutely. I am able to be in close contact with other

79

people and get no information at all. This is because it is one of my rules. I don't want to know about other people's lives or hear their thoughts, unless they are my clients, and certainly not without their consent!

(Important note: It is a violation to read a person's energy, thoughts, or feelings without their knowledge or permission. If you feel drawn to do this, please take some time to consider why.)

I have another rule that has been tested time and time again. This has to do with earth-bound souls, or souls who are stuck between the third and the fifth dimensions. When you increase your life force through intuitive work, these souls tend to become attracted to you, as they see your light and are drawn like moths to a flame. It can be very uncomfortable physically and spiritually when these energies are around.

There are many intuitives who have dedicated themselves to what is termed "proof of survival mediumship" and perform a great service to humanity by helping these souls to pass over to the fifth dimension, or, as many people call it, heaven. They also bring through messages from these souls to the living, proving that the soul still exists after physical death, hence the name "proof of survival". After much consideration and meditation, I know that this is not my primary work. You must find your own truth and decide whether this work interests you.

It is unacceptable to me to have passed-over souls standing in my bedroom at three in the morning. I wouldn't allow a complete stranger to wander around my house at night, so why would I allow earth-bound souls to?

I do have, on occasion, "visitors" or earth-bound souls who come into my house at night. They turn on radios and lights and air conditioning units to wake me up, or they wake up my children instead, who invariably come to me to sort it out. For me, this is unacceptable. I have a right to sleep every night undisturbed, with my children and animals unaffected. I will not allow these energies into my house. They are only able to visit if I am unwell or overworked, as my boundaries are not as clear at these times. The last time this happened, I had been at a family member's funeral, and I picked up three hitchhikers! I made them wait outside until the next morning after I'd had my coffee, which is when I was willing and ready to help them move over. I am tested time and time again with this boundary or rule.

Exercise

In your workbook, create a list of rules that you feel are important to establish regarding your intuitive development. Try to make this as long as you can, including the different aspects that have been discussed.

Examples

- I won't tolerate abusive or rude behavior from people around me.
- I won't allow earth-bound souls into my house.
- Don't show me information that I cannot share with people and never without their permission.
- I won't allow anyone or anything to drain my energy or access my life force.

When you have your list, notice if there are any people, events, or experiences that appear in your life to test what you have stated.

You may have to state a certain rule over and over again to ensure that the universe is hearing you. You may also like to add more rules to your list as you develop your intuition.

Self-Care

Allow yourself to receive offers of help, assistance, and love. Receive these openheartedly and without guilt. You may even like to buy yourself a small gift or perform an act of self-love.

Give yourself permission to say no to social invitations or requests for help from the people in your life, if you don't feel like saying yes. Say no without guilt, and avoid the desire to beat yourself up mentally or emotionally. It is one thing to say no; it is another thing to say no without guilt.

Practice this as often as you like. This does not mean you are selfish but rather that you are creating a balance in your life of both giving and receiving, which will help to strengthen your boundaries.

CHAPTER TWELVE

Energy Vampires

There are only two ways to approach life: as victim
or as gallant fighter. You must decide if you want to
act or react.—Merle Shain

N ow we will look at some certain types of people you may
come across in your life, especially during your intuitive
development, and how they relate to your boundaries
and reflect what may be hidden for you. Before we proceed, it is
important to note that I am not forming judgment around any
of these characteristics in people. I do know, however, that it is
important to be aware of who and what you may be dealing with so
you are not caught off your center or with your defenses down.

One particularly difficult type of person is the energy vampire.
These people have a lack of life force and so carry the deluded belief
that they need to draw from others to gain more energy and power.
They don't realize that they will never feel full and that they cannot
energetically utilize another's life force for their own advantage. The
problem is that this does not stop them.

In my experience, there are two types of energy vampires. The
first is the type that draws unconsciously from others, often through

conversation and personal interaction and in social situations. Perhaps you have had the experience of feeling drained every time you spend time with a particular friend or family member. Such people will often talk at you, rather than to you, about how terrible their life is and how much drama there is. They are not interested in listening to you or any solutions you may offer. These people have an underlying pattern of victimization and don't actually want your help. They enjoy being the victim, as this has become a crucial part of their identity. I advise you to limit contact with these people, as they will continue to drain your life force, time, and energy.

The second type of energy vampire is the conscious type. These are not people whom you would not necessarily choose to spend time with, and yet ironically they often tend to be in perceived positions of power, with many people who act like followers around them. I will share with you about a man I encountered in my life during my spiritual development, many years ago, and the damage this person caused to those around him.

This man put himself forward as a spiritual teacher and surrounded himself with women who were at vulnerable stages of their lives—for example, recently separated from their husbands or going through relationship breakdowns, and often with a history of sexual and emotional abuse. He would draw the life force from these women as if drawing blood, often sexually seducing them at the same time and encouraging "sex magic" or "sex rites" as a way to spiritual evolvement. This vampirism would take place over a period of weeks or months until the women would become utterly disempowered and, in a sense, under his spell. They were incapable of stopping him or saying no to his false charm and charisma. Many of these women ended up with serious physical and mental health issues after having sex with him as the sexual act created an energetic link between him and his victim. Through this link he was able to continually draw from them even when they were not in his physical presence.

Such people are very dangerous and often have serious mental health and energetic challenges of their own. At this stage of your development, I recommend you have no contact with a conscious energy vampire, especially if they present to you as a teacher. They are often very charming, and yet you will have a sense that something is not quite right with them. They carry with them a strong sense of darkness, and if you are clairvoyant you may also see entities around them and within them. I like to describe people like this as "not driving the bus." What this means is that the personality is evident but becomes overshadowed by the entity's energy. The person is, in effect, on the back seat of the bus of their consciousness, with the entity at the wheel. The man I mentioned is still to this day continuing to vampirize women and is seen as an expert in his field of spirituality, having written many books and been interviewed by many publications and media outlets! Remember, it is up to you who you choose to work and spend time with. It is your divine and sovereign right to say no.

Psychic Attack

This can sometimes occur with people who have low self-worth or low self-esteem. As the recipient of psychic attack, the victim may experience strong and distinct physical, mental, and emotional symptoms. These may include depression, anxiety, stress, nausea, restlessness, inability to sleep, indecision, and a feeling like there is someone or something in their energy, mind, or body.

Social psychic attack can occur when a group of people gets together and spends time gossiping or complaining about another person who is not present. If you have ever seen a group of women sitting together having coffee and talking about their friends who aren't there, you will know what I mean. This creates an energetic link to the target, and they can experience a sense of anger, depression, or fear. This usually dissipates once the energetic link is broken through the cessation of the gossip. It can still have quite strong effects if it occurs often enough.

Conscious psychic attack is not actually that common, but when it occurs the effects can be debilitating. Fundamentally this attack happens when victims allow others to be in their field through surrendering their power to another, especially if these people have been in a position of power, such as bosses or teachers. I have seen this take place when the student outgrows the teacher and the teacher does not want to let them go or to progress. To stop this from happening, they commence a psychic attack, disempowering the student.

A person may be singled out within a group setting and made to feel wrong or out of place. This is different from bullying, yet it looks the same. Victims feel ostracized and may start to question their points of view, conceding to the teacher or attacker. They will begin to believe that what is being said about them is true, and their perspective of themselves and their opinions will begin to change. From this place, attackers begin to control the targets' thoughts and ideas; they may make them question what they believe and value. Attackers may also make generalized statements and direct them at the targets. For example, I was told in a group setting that to use intuitive abilities was a misuse of power and would align the user with the masculine, controlling energies of the planet. I was the only person in the group doing intuitive work, and so even though it appeared to be a general statement, it was directed at me.

If social psychic attack has already taken place, the victim will be in a weakened and vulnerable state. Interestingly, this is also the first step that takes place when a person joins a cult.

It is important to understand that this does take place and to understand what you may be intuitively picking up when you see this happen. You may be surprised at what you see.

How Can You Help Yourself?

The best way I know of counteracting any form of attack is to understand what is happening and develop one's torus field, as explained in the next chapter.

When working to end psychic attack, it is important that the energy of the attacker be sent back to them, as it is an aspect of their shadow self, and therefore their consciousness, which is doing the attacking. Again, the target needs to energetically say an emphatic *no* to the attacker as a first step of healing.

A good visualization technique is to imagine that mirrors surround the person being attacked. Whatever energy is sent to them is instantly and automatically reflected straight back to the sender. You may also like to state the following: "I send all that does not belong to me back to the source of its original creation."

Karmically, attackers will be taken care of. It is also important to address the issues that may have allowed this to happen in the first place.

Self-Care

Embrace yourself as a wonderful being that has the ability to say no in your life. It is up to you what you experience.

CHAPTER THIRTEEN

Torus Field

You shall not pass!—J. R. R. Tolkien

The torus field is simply an electromagnetic field or circle set around your energy with intention and strength. This emanates from your heart center and flows out to surround your auric field and your physical body, not allowing anything negative to enter this space or affect you from outside of it.

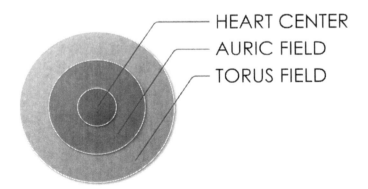

HEART CENTER
AURIC FIELD
TORUS FIELD

Through your intention, you can set a torus field to surround yourself, your house, and your property, stating that nothing negative may enter your space. Strengthen this whenever you need to.

Setting Your Torus Field

Exercise

- Sit quietly in a comfortable place.
- Close your eyes and take three deep, cleansing breaths.
- On the exhalation, let go of any cares or worries. On the in breath, allow your lungs to be filled with life-giving oxygen and life force.
- Then allow yourself to fall into the natural rhythm and cycle of your breathing.
- Bring your awareness into your heart center.
- Each time you take in a new breath, imagine that you are filling your heart with love.
- As you feel your heart expanding with the increasing amounts of love, on an out breath, allow this love to start to flow out of your heart center and begin to surround you.
- In your mind, ask that you embody your own spirit, feeling this beautiful connection take place.
- Do not call in light or any other energy from outside of yourself to do this! Use only your own spirit or higher self and your breath and feelings of love.
- Allow your own spirit to flow out of your heart center along with the energy of love and then set this in a circle around you.
- You may like to state, "It is my clear and strong intention to create a torus field around my personal space. No thing, energy, or person that wishes to harm me or create negativity in my life may enter my torus field."
- Imagine in your mind's eye a force field surrounding you.

- Next, expand your energy and spirit out a little further to envelope your office or house and then state, "It is my clear and strong intention to create a torus field around my home/ office. No thing, energy, or person that wishes to harm me or create negativity in my life may enter my torus field."

- Then expand your spirit and energy of love out to surround the boundary of your property and state, "It is my clear and strong intention to create a torus field around the boundary of this property. No thing, energy, or person that wishes to harm me or create negativity in my life may enter my Torus field."

- Sit in this energy for a few moments, imagining in your mind's eye the three layers of your torus field surrounding you.

- When you are ready, gently open your eyes. Take a few breaths and then continue with your intuitive exercises or whatever else you have planned for your day.

As you do this process a number of times, it will ultimately become like a habit for your soul. Eventually, you will only need to take a few moments to set your torus field using your intention. Generally when your torus field is set often enough, you won't need to do it every day. When you are starting off, however, it is a good idea to get into the habit. I use this technique most days when I am working, traveling, or at shows with many people. This allows me to get on with what I am there to do with as little interference as possible.

When you set your torus field correctly, it will prevent people from harming you or taking something from you. It will ward off interdimensional interference, including entities, astral beings, and anything else negative that may be attached to a human. I have found that sometimes clients cannot find my office, even when they are on the same street and after I've given them directions over the phone. I know then that my spirit and my torus field are preventing them from finding me. I literally become invisible to anyone who wants to harm me in any way. This can include people who simply want to take my energy. When this happens, I know my torus field is doing its job!

I want to mention here a very common thing I see over and over again when working with people intuitively. They are often told by well-intentioned psychics or others in the new age industry to surround themselves in a "bubble of white light" to protect themselves from negativity. This will not work, especially if you are an empath, which we will discuss shortly. Please do *not* ever call in white light to protect yourself. If we go back to the understanding of the universal structure and interdimensional interference, you will see that just because it is so-called white light does not mean it is positive. Where does the white light come from, and why do you need to call in anything from outside of yourself to protect you? I invite you to question what you have previously been told. If nothing else, look at the results you are getting. Ask yourself, is it working? If not, then why not? Just because everyone else does it doesn't means it is healthy for you. In my experience, this is another form of entrapment.

It is my intention to give you an awareness that difficult situations may happen when developing your intuitive abilities. It's also important to remember that the majority of people are amazing, loving, and compassionate beings who will bring untold joy, love and pleasure to your life.

Self-Care

Be gentle and loving with yourself regarding difficult relationships that you may have encountered in the past. Give yourself a big pat on the back for understanding that dynamic and making a different choice from here on in. Well done to you!

CHAPTER FOURTEEN

— ◆ —

Meditation

Your sacred space is where you can find yourself over and over again.—Joseph Campbell

Meditation is one of the most effective ways to develop your intuition and your emotional, physical, and mental health. It is a very important tool to keep your energy and your mind clear as you do increasing amounts of intuitive exercises. It is the best way to check in with your spirit and higher self, giving them an opportunity to communicate with you and giving you an opportunity to hear, see, and know what is being communicated to you. Especially when you are starting out, your mind becomes very active and can have a great deal to say about what you are doing. Limiting beliefs and patterns may start to emerge. Meditation is a great way to get to the heart of things and give you a clearer understanding of where you are in your development and what is going on in your life. Meditation allows you to bypass the sometimes-constant mind chatter and find your inner space of peace, wisdom, and tranquility. It is a tool that you will come back to time and time again and that is invaluable for both spiritual and personal growth.

People often say to me, "You must know everything that is going to happen in your life." No, I don't. I am emotionally attached to the outcome of my life, and this can alter and influence the information I receive through my intuition. I generally have a good idea or sense of what's in store, but if I want details and clear, comprehensive answers, I simply meditate. I use meditation at the times I feel blocked or confused or have an important decision to make. Through meditation I can bypass my mind and my emotions and get clear impressions, understandings, and directions from my spirit. I also meditate when I work with clients or students, to create a clear set point from which to work. I meditate when I am in nature, when I am at home, in my office, or on a plane, and whenever I feel I need some clarity, peace, and openness. With a little practice, this is what you can achieve also.

There are many types of meditation, and if you are not very practiced, I recommend you start with a guided visualization. The reason for this is simple. The Eastern style of meditation is effective, without doubt. However, living in our Western culture, being bombarded by noise and images from the television, radio, phones, computers, and billboards, your mind experiences and comes to expect stimulation. It is very hard to master the Eastern style of meditation (i.e., sitting still and clearing your mind completely of all thought) when you have been trained to become hyper-vigilant to and overstimulated by your environment. Without intensive training, this is very difficult. I have seen many clients give up or say they can't meditate because the first time they try it they are not able to quiet their mind. Like anything, the more you practice the better you will become.

Imagine wanting to run a marathon. You would certainly need to train more than a couple of times to build up your physical fitness. If you intend to use meditation as a tool in your intuitive development, then give yourself the opportunity to practice and practice. The more you do, the easier it becomes. I promise.

With a guided visualization, your mind is given a storyline or a point of interest to hold on to. There may be times when your mind still wanders, but it is easier for the Western mind to relate to and master a guided visualization. If when you are following a guided visualization, your imagination creates another landscape or scenario than the one offered, that is perfectly fine. The mind has been taken out of the picture, giving the soul and the higher self a channel to communicate with you. This may come in the form of pictures, feelings, knowledge, sounds, or visions of people in your mind's eye. The ways spirit will communicate to you during meditation seem endless.

Imagination

"Imagination is everything. It is the preview of life's coming attractions."

—Albert Einstein

Your imagination is one of the most powerful tools you have at your disposal. It is truly your intuition at work, creating images or pictures of possible realities and outcomes for you and your life. Your thoughts become realities of time and space, actual dimensions in which your life and your consciousness exist. You are then able to empower these realities with your intent and your imagination, so be aware of what you create and sanction with your imagination. You just might get it!

Your imagination originates from the right side of your brain and is directly linked to clairvoyance, clairaudience, and clairsentience: your intuitive abilities. Within guided visualizations, you are able to stimulate your imagination, opening up wonderful new opportunities, new understandings, and new realizations through the worlds, experiences, and souls you interact with. Allow your imagination to create wonderful places for you to have adventures in.

A great way to keep your energy in check and to make sure you not only look after your emotional and mental health but also develop your connection to your spirit and your intuition is to set up your own meditation area in your home. This will give you a sacred space to use anytime you feel you would like to meditate and access the wealth of knowledge and wisdom you have within yourself. You can also use this space to write in your journal and reflect upon your development and your spiritual and life journey. This is your space to be with yourself, uninterrupted and at peace.

Creating a Sacred Space

Exercise

- Find a space in your home that no one else in the family uses and that is quiet and out of the way. If you have only a small house or apartment or share your living area with a number of people, you may create this space in your bedroom.
- If you have a massage table, this is ideal; if not, you can use your bed or a comfy chair in your sacred space.
- If you have some crystals, place them under the massage table, chair, or bed, or around you in your space. Please use

your intuition as to what crystals you need and where to place them. It is always a good idea to cleanse your crystals before and after use, using white sage, running water, and pure sunlight. Stay away from overstimulating crystals such as amethyst, clear quartz, moldavite, and lapis lazuli. When you begin, stick with yellow, red, brown, and orange-colored crystals that will keep you grounded, otherwise you may end up with a headache and feeling sick and ungrounded. Crystals amplify your energy, so please use your intuition when choosing what is right for you. Sometimes less is more.

- Whenever you would like to meditate, go through the following process:
- Find yourself a scarf or eye pillow and plenty of beautifully colored blankets if it is cold, as your blood pressure and body temperature will drop. Use pillows under your knees and head if you are lying down on the massage table or bed.
- Hop onto the massage table or bed, or sit comfortably in your special chair. Plug in your headphones, place the eye pillow on, and wrap yourself in your warm blankets.
- Set your torus field around yourself, as outlined in chapter 6.
- As you are beginning to relax, set your very clear and strong intention that your higher self and spirit join you. Now you can set whatever intention you choose, and ideally it will be different each time you are in this space to meditate. If you need some healing, ask your spirit for that. If you need some guidance or clarity around a situation, ask your spirit for that. Or perhaps you may simply want to go on a journey or adventure led by your soul family. Whatever the intention, allow yourself to experience what comes to you.

You can use guided visualizations, uploaded to your iPod, to take you on these journeys and access a deeper understanding of your life. I have developed four wonderful guided visualizations called "The Heart Series" to assist you with your journey. Each is aimed at a different aspect of your evolution and development:

1. Heart Breath Healing
2. Heart-Centered Intuition
3. Heart of Avalon
4. Heart of the Earth Mother

You may purchase these through my website, http://www. heidisvision.com/audios, in MP3 or CD format.

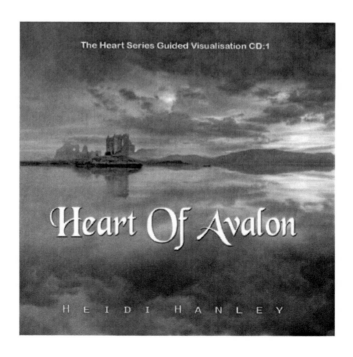

Guided visualisation CD:2

Heart of The Earth Mother

H E I D I H A N L E Y

Heart Series Guided Visualisation CD:3

Heart Centered Intuition

H E I D I H A N L E Y

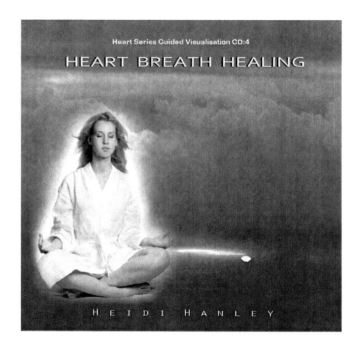

Heart Series Guided Visualisation CD:4

HEART BREATH HEALING

H E I D I H A N L E Y

Have fun setting up your sacred space, allowing your intuition to guide you through the process, from where to sit to the colors and what you place around you. Don't necessarily follow other people's opinions but rather let your heart guide you to create a special and blessed space.

I invite you to meditate at least twice a week from now on in this manner, recording your adventures, epiphanies, and experiences in your journal. You may also like to use this space to read this book, to create spirit art, or to engage in any other form of developing your intuitive abilities.

I encourage you not to bring in any light or anything else that lives outside of yourself during meditation. You are very vulnerable at this time, as your defenses are down, and so be very picky about who and what you invite into your sacred space. Once they're in, you may not be able to get them out so easily.

It is important to mention here an occurrence that can take place all too often when you are developing your intuitive abilities and begin to meditate regularly. You may experience people around you who become blissed out on spirit or meditation and become what one of my students refers to as "cosmic trippers." These people can become so overrun by interdimensional interference and their state of induced psychic ecstasy that they become incapable of having a healthy, functioning life. They think they are evolved, enlightened, and spiritual but can't pay their rent, take care of their children, or hold down a job. Using the excuse of spirituality to check out of your life and your human responsibilities has nothing to do with being spiritual or enlightened. If you would rather sit in a room all day and meditate than consciously interact with the world around you and the people in it, then I would be seriously questioning what is going on.

We are here on this earth in these physical bodies to experience all that this world has to offer in the third dimension. This includes loving one another, having beautiful, consensual sex, eating wonderful, nourishing foods, creating abundance and wealth in all of its forms, and taking care of children, animals, and the earth. This involves being active in our physical lives, which is the quickest but sometimes the most challenging way to evolution, not using spirit as an excuse to disassociate from your life. All intuitive development must be achieved through balance and self-responsibility, not by giving up and blissing out. If you have a balanced approach to meditation and spiritual practice, then you are being a responsible human being. As Buddha has said, "The way is not in the sky. The way is in the heart."

Take a moment to contemplate the physical reality of this world. You have a body to use and enjoy, and this is an integral part of your journey and soul's experience. If you were not here to experience the physical realm, your soul would still be in spirit.

Walking Meditation

A great way to combine the spiritual and the physical world is to do an active or walking meditation. This is very simple and can initiate quite a deep and profound state of grace and connection to your higher self and to the world around you.

Walk in nature in a place where there are not many people around. Near the ocean, in a park, or in a forest are all wonderful places to practice this technique. As you are walking, direct your entire attention to focus on each step that you take.

Your eyes are relaxed, but your entire vision and sight is directed at each foot as it moves forward. Walk slowly and intentionally, and feel your mind clear and your heart begin to open. Open your awareness to the sounds of nature around you. Can you hear birds, trees, water, and the wind? What are you truly present to in this moment? What can you smell or sense? How does your body feel? Can you feel your breath? Are you relaxed? Can you sense the energy of the earth traveling up through your legs as you move? Allow yourself to receive the experience of nature, and give yourself permission to be truly present during this wonderful practice.

You may do this for as long as you choose, but starting with about ten minutes and then adding time to this is the best idea when starting off. Journal all that occurs, as even the smallest occurrence can be profound.

Self-Care

Meditate three times this week as suggested, with the intention of deepening your connection to your spirit. Spend time simply sharing with spirit and feeling, hearing, and seeing it in your field of experience.

If you feel you need to, please ask for a healing during these meditations, to help release any blocks or resistance to the connection with your spirit.

CHAPTER FIFTEEN

Discovering Your Ray

Today you are You, that is truer than true. There is no
one alive who is Youer than You.—Dr. Seuss

What Is a Ray?

In my experience we all hold a unique energetic blueprint, a
little like our spiritual DNA. We, as souls, have all chosen to
bring our own unique and different gifts to the earth plane
to help and interact with those souls with which we have contracts.
This is true for each soul, not just a chosen few. Whether you
decide to fulfill your contracts or not, is up to you. If you have read
through the completion exercise in chapter 2, you will understand
this concept more deeply. There are people in your life with whom
you won't be able to complete your contract unless you use the
completion exercise to do so. You will not be punished or create
karma for yourself. There is no right and wrong choice for you
as a soul. You have chosen to experience what you have chosen
to experience. I have found that depression, disconnection, and
disassociation from life can occur when you have difficulty coming
to terms with the decisions you have already made or are yet to make

on a soul level. If you truly understand this concept, then half the work is done.

You have already made every decision about everything you will ever do in this lifetime. Wow! That's huge. When your ego stops struggling with that concept, you will find an ease and a flow come into your life that are truly profound. I would assert, that is exactly why you are reading this now: to learn to let go and let flow!

A ray fundamentally carries the energy, theme, or blueprint of your soul's purpose and what your divine spirit is anchoring into the earth plane through your physical body. Your ray will help you to discern what you have come here to help others with and with self-evolution. I like to see this as every human being bringing a certain ray of energy and infinite grace, particular to them and their divine spirit, and grounding this into their bodies through the expression of their life.

Discovering your ray can be a very helpful step forward on your journey to develop your intuition and can help you to focus on a particular way of expressing your intuitive ability. The concepts and exercises in this book are here for you to discover who you are to the core of your being and how you can best live and express this knowledge in alignment with your personality, your decisions, and your life. Rays, when discovered, will also unfold a theme for your life's lessons. We teach what we most need to learn!

It is very common for your greatest challenge to be the polarity of your ray. Let me give you an example of this. My ray is power; I am a warrior of the heart. I facilitate powerful transformation in others, through my words, my presence, and my teaching. Within that, I have, during my life, often experienced the lessons of power. This came to me through my parents, my older brothers, friends at school, my ex-husband, former business partners, interdimensional interference, and my work with clients. Interestingly, I tend to draw people to me who struggle with their own power or, conversely, who use their power to take advantage of and bully others. Because this is my ray, I can trigger people who hold limiting patterns or beliefs around power simply by being in the same space with them. These people then respond both verbally and energetically, projecting and directing their fear and anger toward me. Through my personal journey, I am learning not to engage with this projection, and in fact, I feel very passionate about helping people move through various states of victimization and bullying whilst empowering them at the same time. That is the warrior of the heart! I am aware that this can be a tough ray to be and to live with, and I am often tested on a personal level to stay in my own power. Through this learning, I can really allow my ray to flow down onto the earth and help humanity. At this time in world's history/herstory, power is certainly a relevant issue!

Often within your ray, you will be challenged by and experience both sides of the coin, or the polarity within. For example, I am comfortable with owning and standing in my power, and yet at times throughout my life I have given my power away to others, or they have taken it from me. This is one of the polarities of my ray.

Exercise

Sit in a comfortable, quiet place with your workbook and allow your mind to wander over your life. Look at the different experiences you have had and the people who have featured and see if you can begin to see a common thread or theme running through your life.

Answering these questions may help you:

- Do you or those around you have issues with your integrity?
- Do you or those around you have challenges with love, or are you exceptionally loving and open to giving and receiving love?
- Do you or those around you tend to speak your truth, or have you had challenges with lying, betrayal, and deceit?
- Is your life balanced, or out of control, or overly controlled?
- Do you or those around you have a deep sense of compassion, or have you had challenges feeling shut off from or closed down to others?
- Do you or those around you have issues with your own power, or are you comfortable using your power and owning your warrior aspect?
- Do you or those around you have a strong sense of justice, or have you had challenges with injustice? Do you stand up for others or turn a blind eye when you see an injustice being perpetrated?

See which question resonates or really stands out to you, which ones strike a chord. Write as much as you would like about this.

It is normal to find that you feel a response to more than one of the questions above. What you want to do though, is weed out what may be personality traits, patterns, or ways of being. Using myself as an example again, I am a deeply loving and compassionate person, and I cannot tolerate injustice. These are certainly strong aspects of my way of being but are not the totality of my ray. They have an influence, certainly, but they do not define my ray. As I look over my life, I can see that my experiences of abuse from birth define my ray.

What ray do you think King Arthur was? Take a few moments to contemplate this question.

For many he is the embodiment of justice. He led the British people forward through compassion and a higher truth. He sat equally to his knights and did not see himself above anyone. King Arthur opened himself up to different points of view and different experiences, desiring to know the entire story or truth before making decisions. King Arthur was a champion of the Divine Feminine and liaised directly with the priestesses of Avalon. King Arthur's ray was justice, and this defined his life and achievements.

If you are unsure of your ray, that's normal. You are not expected to know your ray straightaway. It is an unfolding process, and when you know your ray as truth, you will have discovered an aspect of your divine presence, what is called the I-am presence. I can assure you that when you experience your life from this place there will be no doubt about your abilities, your work, or how to go about anchoring your heart center and soul onto the earth plane.

Exercise

Set an intention for this week to be shown your ray by your higher self, through the people you meet and interact with and also through the experiences you have. Write down anything that really stands out to you at the end of each day, before you go to sleep, and take special notice of your dreams.

When you are ready to hear what you already know be true within the higher aspects of yourself, your ray will be as clear to you as your own name. Your ray is what you have come to experience in this body, as an extension of your highest aspect of self, your spirit. It is one expression of the whole of the sovereign being that is you and is fundamental to learning more about who you are and how to develop your intuition. I also invite you to contemplate this during a meditation, entering the meditative space with the clear and strong intention to be shown your ray.

Self-Care

Wear the color yellow, eat yellow fruits and vegetables, have yellow crystals around you. Spend time sitting in the sun and contemplating the element of fire.

Continue to journal. Smile as often as you can, and do one thing every day to experience the feeling of joy.

CHAPTER SIXTEEN

Working with Your Medicine and Animal Totems

Some people talk to animals. Not many listen though.
That's the problem.—A. A. Milne

Your medicine is an animal spirit that is dedicated to your soul's purpose and your spirit's journey. This is also known as your totem animal or power animal in other traditions, but for the sake of continuity, I will refer to this consciousness as medicine throughout this book. Your medicine holds a vast array of information, inspiration, and knowledge that directly relates to your life's journey.

The theory behind medicine is this. During our lives it is said that an animal spirit chooses to work with us and through us. They dedicate themselves to us throughout our lives. It is very rare for a medicine to change, but that is possible during a time of huge transition such as a near-death experience, divorce, work change, illness, or breakdown. It is widely held in traditional cultures that your medicine will sometimes leave you at this time, sacrificing itself so that you may survive.

When you discover your medicine you may begin to work more closely with this beautiful energy, integrating it in all areas of your life. Let me give you an example. Say your medicine is the wolf. Wolves in nature hold particular characteristics and ways of interacting with each other. They live within packs and are very social creatures. They have a hierarchy within the pack, and each wolf has a valuable role to play within the pack's infrastructure. They are loyal, tenacious, intelligent, and hardworking and tend to be natural leaders. They enjoy family and see the importance of play, joy, and fun in their lives. Wolves can be fiercely protective and yet touchingly gentle. They tend to travel long distances to find their prey (reach their goals) and eat a variety of vegetable and protein sources. Wolves are connected to the moon and the night and are also associated with intuitive abilities. They know the value of—and in fact, their survival depends upon—working together as a team. As you can see, if your medicine were wolf, you would hold all of these characteristics but in human form, displayed in your human experience.

Knowing the food your animal would naturally eat, how many offspring they have, in what terrain they live, and whether they mate for life or have multiple partners can all give you a great insight into your natural tendencies for health and harmony in your life. This animal is what you would be if you were an animal.

There are many meanings for each animal via the physical, emotional, mental and spiritual realms and the medicine, or teaching, they bring to our lives. I have found that if I live in accordance with my medicine's teachings, my body is stronger, and I am happier on all levels. It is no coincidence that my ray, power; warrior of the heart, has the same teaching and signature that my medicine holds, and this will be the same for you.

We do also have what I will refer to as animal totems that come in and out of our lives at different times to lend support or teachings to us. These can often be found at the different directions of the medicine wheel, adding their particular energy to that area of our consciousness. The value our medicine and animal totems have in our lives cannot be overstated, and we can utilize their wisdom to our advantage.

Finding Your Medicine

Often you may think you know what your medicine is, but in fact, it can be a great surprise when you discover the animal actually working with you. I encourage you to approach this with an open heart and mind, allowing the truth to come to you rather than trying to get it right.

Exercise

Here is an exercise to help you find your medicine.

- Go to your sacred space that has been set up for meditation (see above).
- Sage the area with the intention of clearing the space.
- Make yourself comfortable and ensure you will not be disturbed during this process.
- Put on some music through your iPod if you would like.
- You may also like to do the Heart of the Earth Mother meditation for this process.
- Begin by closing your eyes and breathing deeply and evenly, imagining your breath is like the gentle tide at the ocean's

shore, rolling in and out. Take as much time as you need to relax and let go of your day and any worries or concerns you might be holding on to. Starting at the top of your head and moving down through your body, bring your awareness to each place or area where you may feel discomfort or stagnation. Using your breath and intention, breathe into that place and feel it gently releasing and dissipating. Continue this process until you feel your body is fully relaxed and open.

- Call in your spirit, soul family, and higher self, asking them to assist you in this process, taking your time to feel their presence and support. Then set your intention for this meditation. You may like to state something like, "It is my clear and strong intention to meet my medicine during this meditation, and I ask that I will be clearly shown the animal spirit that is working with me in my life as my medicine. (Add anything else that you feel is relevant or important to you.) I ask this in alignment with the highest good of all, with my divine will, and I ask that this happen with ease and grace."

- Visualize in your mind's eye that you are standing in a very beautiful and peaceful natural landscape. As you look around yourself, you can see the colors and features of the place you are in. You feel the sun gently warming your body and a gentle breeze caressing your face. You feel very peaceful and safe in this beautiful landscape. As you are standing here, in your mind, state your intention, repeating it three times.

For instance, say, "I am here to meet the medicine animal that has a specific soul contract with me. I am here to meet the medicine animal that has a specific soul contract with me. I am here to meet the medicine animal that has a specific soul contract with me."

Then allow yourself to be open to what appears before you in the landscape. Perhaps you would like to walk along the landscape, taking in the sounds and smells as you go. All the while, keep your awareness open to any animals that may appear. You may see quite a few different animals; this is normal. During this meditation, you must see the animal three times. This can be in its natural form, as a cartoon, or as a name written in words. Note how it presents to you. Once you have seen a particular animal three times, then approach this animal and ask it three times, "Are you my medicine animal that has chosen to work with me? Are you my medicine animal that has chosen to work with me? Are you my medicine animal that has chosen to work with me?"

Wait for the answer. You must ask it three times, and then if the animal says or indicates yes three times, it is your medicine. (Note: Any animal that bares its teeth to you is not an animal that can be your medicine.)

Once you have discovered your beautiful animal, spend some time connecting to it, speaking with it, and generally experiencing it. It may offer to take you exploring, on its back or similar. If you are comfortable, then allow yourself to enjoy this blessed experience. Spend as much time as you feel comfortable with your medicine in this landscape, thanking it for all that it shows you. When you feel ready to leave, go to the exact spot where you entered the landscape. Slowly, begin to deepen your breath into your belly as you feel yourself coming back into the room. Take your time to come back very slowly by wriggling your fingers and toes, stretching out your arms and legs, and then gently opening your eyes. Have a drink of water ready, and take a big sip after you have sat up, slowly, to help ground yourself. Have your journal close by and write down all you have experienced.

- Take your time to integrate this experience, as it can be very powerful. You want to ensure that you feel good about the experience, thus deepening your connection to your medicine.

Another great way of deepening the connection to your medicine animal is to have images of them around you, to watch movies or shows featuring them, or to wear jewelry with their likeness. I know a number of people who have had their medicines' images tattooed on their bodies. Invite them and honor them in your life in whatever way you can.

It is important to note that respect must be shown at all times toward your medicine. In some traditions you would never tell another person about your medicine in case they ridiculed it, showed it disrespect, or made fun of it. This was said to dissipate its power. I will share with you a story that a shamanic teacher shared with me many years ago.

The shaman had taken a client through a process similar to the one above to discover his medicine. Now, this man was very large and heavyset, and he had a rather intimidating presence about him.

After journeying into the lower world, the shaman found this man's medicine and "blew" it into him (a traditional shamanic technique). She then took the man on a journey to connect with and experience his medicine. The man was clearly surprised at his medicine when it appeared, as it was Mouse. This animal did not fit into his egoistic idea of who he was and of his own strength, size, and importance. After the process he was heard saying that the shaman must have got it wrong, that he had no use for such a small, weak animal.

A month later the man returned to the shaman, complaining of illness, lethargy, and confusion. The shaman did a process to meet the man's medicine and explore the cause of his upset, only to discover that his medicine had left him. After much persuasion, Mouse spoke to the shaman. Mouse told her that the man did not respect it or want to work with it, so it had decided to leave. Unless, Mouse stated, the man changed his attitude, it would not be returning. The shaman brought this news to her client and spoke strongly of the importance of respecting and honoring our medicine. Eventually the man realized that his arrogance and his ego had caused his medicine to leave and hence brought disruption and illness into his life.

After the man agreed to change his ways and attitude, the shaman then petitioned Mouse to return. She was told that the return was conditional. Mouse stated that if it felt disrespect or dishonor again it would leave for good and that no amount of persuasion or promises would bring it back to this man. It is said that the man accepted his poor behavior and has learnt much from his medicine, Mouse.

Exercise

What do you think this man's lesson was with his medicine, and what teachings do you think Mouse may offer such a person?

I encourage you to research your medicine, along with other animals and their meanings, although the information that you receive from your medicine itself will be far more relevant and powerful to you and your life.

Working with Your Medicine

> [The Sun Dancers] also put rabbit skins on their arms
> and legs, for the rabbit represents humility, because
> he is quiet and soft and not self-asserting—a quality
> which we must all possess when we go to the center
> of the world.—Black Elk

Now that you have discovered your medicine, it is very important to continue to work with its energy. I encourage you to take time every day to talk to it, feel it, and build your relationship with it. If you have ever seen the images of shamans wearing animal skins and skulls and dancing in trancelike states, then you understand one extreme of this concept. The shaman would have been working with that animal spirit by shape-shifting into it, intending to bring healing, wisdom, insight, or a good hunt for his or her tribe. This was also a way to honor and respect the spirit of the animal. This is not what you need to do to strengthen your relationship to your medicine, although dancing and moving like your animal may help you to understand it further. Research where the animal would live and, if appropriate, visit this environment and experience it as your medicine would. Eat what it eats, see as it sees, feel as it feels, and think as it thinks. Building a respectful, intentional connection with your medicine will return you great results. Your medicine will acknowledge and recognize this effort and will happily work with you when asked and instinctively when needed.

Self-Care

If you are very sensitive and have a great deal of trouble in crowds or working closely with people, you can use the energy of your medicine to wrap around your body like a shield or blanket. Its energy will protect yours from your environment.

It can also be important to study the prey of your medicine if it is a carnivore. The energy of its prey will also be relevant to you and your work.

CHAPTER SEVENTEEN

———◆———

Empaths and Highly Sensitive People

Am I too much for the world, or is the world too much for me?—Kelli Jae Baeli

Simply put, empaths are people who naturally, and often unintentionally, merge their emotions, thoughts, feelings, and souls with the energies around them. Different from psychics or clairsentients, empaths not only connect to but also merge with their environment and with whatever is in that environment. This includes people, animals, trees, nature, land, houses, crystals, and spirit. Through this merging they become one with the target, person, object, or surroundings. They experience the thoughts, feelings, and physicality of another as if they were that person, thing, or place. They are similar to chameleons, in a sense, with the ability to change to suit their environments.

Empaths are born; they are not made. This is not an intuitive ability that you can learn. Having said that, if you are an empath, then you can definitely learn how to master this unique way of experiencing and interacting with the world. You are a very old and evolved soul that has incarnated upon earth at this time to do what you can to assist humanity and its evolution. Unfortunately, empaths are the ones who feel, know, sense, and experience everything that happens on this planet, and this knowledge can be debilitating and overwhelming if not handled well.

If empaths are conscious, balanced, and aware of their abilities, they will be able to utilise their skills for all manner of intuition. They tend to be able to achieve all of the spiritual abilities, including mediumship, clairvoyance, clairaudience, and clairsentience, and can use whichever one they like to suit the conditions. They can also master any other concepts, areas, and theories of human endeavours fairly easily. This includes science, philosophy, psychology, medicine, mathematics, language, business, and any other subject they desire to learn. They absorb the concepts into their consciousness and can then understand these very well. Often empaths have many qualifications and skills, never really being able to settle on one thing. This is, in part, because they are influenced by the conditions and the people around them. They do, however, have an unconscious drive to help and to fix and are often found in caregiving roles.

Empaths are natural shape-shifters and will start to shift their physical, mental, and emotional bodies to mirror the people around them. For example, they may start to put on weight if they are living with someone who is overweight. They may start to like a particular food or music or book just because a person close to them does. Empaths who do not know themselves very well tend to become confused and unable to make clear choices, as they seem to be constantly at the mercy of their ever-changing environments. This can lead to depression, anxiety, and a sense of constant uncertainty regarding their own choices. It can also lead to a desire to withdraw from people and sometimes from life altogether.

I used to have an assistant who spoke with a stutter. After a few days of working with her closely, I realised that I had begun to stutter also. I was empathically and unconsciously mirroring her way of speech.

An empath might commonly be referred to as a "highly sensitive person," but empaths are more than simply sensitive. An empath is a person with a very unique energetic makeup. These people often have difficult childhoods and experience trauma during adolescence. They often find it difficult to fit in and have a sense of being different to others. This sense can affect the way they relate to other people, and it can be difficult for an empath to create healthy relationships with others.

Empaths often experience a love-hate relationship with the people around them. If empaths are unbalanced, unconscious, and unhealthy this can lead to deep resentment toward the people in their lives and people in general. An empath will naturally absorb other people's feelings and emotions and thought forms. Struggling with discernment and boundaries leaves them feeling overwhelmed and physically and psychically exhausted, which can lead to mental illness.

Empaths in relationships with other people will, by their very nature, be able to merge with the other person on the deepest level of their soul. This can leave them exposed to manipulation, abuse, and control issues. Empaths in balanced and healthy relationships will experience an utterly deep and profound loving connection and will often stay for life. But empaths who do not have self-understanding, boundaries, and the ability to say no run a very high risk of depression and a need to withdraw from the world. Not all codependents are empaths, but most empaths struggle with codependency.

Empaths also have a deep connection to the animal and natural world. Empaths often possess the ability to communicate energetically and also telepathically with the animals around them. This can be a pleasant respite for some empaths, and they are often found working closely with animals. Interestingly, they tend not to work as veterinarians or in animal rescue shelters. These environments are far too traumatic for an empath to experience. The empath would experience exactly what the animal is feeling and thinking. This ability can be helpful in communication, but if there is fear, panic, or pain present, then it is very difficult to receive a clear communication from the animal.

Are You an Empath?

Please answer these questions to discern whether you may be an empath. You can also use these to help you assess whether the people in your life may also be empaths.

1. Do you have sensitivity to food additives and colouring?
2. Are there particular foods that you are unable to eat, such as wheat and dairy?
3. Are you oversensitive to bright lights and noise?
4. Do you feel overwhelmed when you are amongst a large group of people, such as shopping malls, concerts, or in the middle of a large city?
5. Do you have difficulty in discerning boundaries?
6. Are you able to feel other people's emotions without them saying anything about how they are feeling?
7. Can you often hear people's thoughts or know what they're about to say?
8. Have you struggled with depression, anxiety, or resentment throughout your life?

9. Do you react badly to violence on television and in movies as if you were actually experiencing what you are viewing?

10. Do you become confused with your own emotions and thoughts when you are in the company of other people?

11. Have you ever been called oversensitive by others and told to toughen up?

12. Do you have an unconscious directive to want to "fix everything for everyone"?

13. Are you highly emotional, perhaps crying often?

14. Do you have a tendency toward food, alcohol, or drugs to make the feelings go away or to numb yourself?

15. Do you feel drawn to work in a caring or service-oriented position such as in the healing industry, with animals, or for the environment?

16. Do you experience intense feelings of emotion for other people?

17. Do you feel you are "here to do something big" but don't know what it is?

18. Do you feel like you don't really fit in?

If you have answered yes to two-thirds of these questions, then you are more than likely an empath.

How Can Empaths Live Happily in This World?

Empaths have a tendency to be ungrounded, flighty, and not present in their bodies and their lives. On some level, they believe that if they are not in their bodies, they won't have to feel. This is the opposite of what actually happens. The less grounded you are, the more you feel. If you are an empath, this is a habit that you have probably learnt from childhood, and so you will need to retrain yourself to stay present, even when you are in a highly charged emotional space or state.

- Grounding is one of the most important things you can learn.
- Meditating often and using Heart of the Earth Mother guided visualization will teach you to become more connected to this planet and to your physical body.
- Wear the colors red and brown in clothing and crystals.
- Sit with your legs crossed upon the earth every day for at least ten minutes.
- Swimming in the ocean or taking showers and baths will help to clear the excess emotional energy in your field.
- Sit in the sun to charge up your life force.
- Limit exposure to violence on TV.
- Eat protein at every meal and stay away from foods with high sugar or carbohydrate contents.
- Practice saying no and creating boundaries in your life.
- Consciously connect to the earth throughout the day.
- Use the energy of your medicine to protect you from other people's energy.
- Get plenty of sleep and rest.
- Laugh and feel pleasure.
- Picture all of the excess energy, emotions, and thoughts draining out of you and into the earth.
- Build healthy relationships.

As outlined, empaths will try to withdraw themselves so they don't feel as much. Try to understand that the more you resist other's energy, the more you will be negatively affected. As an empath's natural flow of energy is like a sponge—i.e., it draws inward—a defensive mechanism would be to try and shield yourself.

Empaths are here on this planet to assist in the earth's evolutionary processes and to raise human consciousness. Empaths are like human vacuum cleaners, sucking up all the human and environmental waste and transmuting it into light. Just by being alive and breathing, empaths are providing an amazing service to humanity. Within this context, they must also learn to allow the waste to flow into them and then let it go. Visualizing this energy flowing down through their central channel into the earth is a good way to train their consciousness to achieve this. Every time they are aware of taking on someone else's waste, they can allow their breath to release it into the earth. There is no need to worry about harming the earth, as the empath has already done most of the work!

The Human Dowsing Rod

If you feel you are an empath, then I would like you to do the following exercise.

Exercise

Go into an environment where there are at least a few people.

Sit or stand quietly and observe what happens within. You are *not* reading other people without their permission; you are simply observing your own reactions and responses. Can you feel the other people in your body, your emotions, your mind? Do you have an urge to adapt yourself to fit in? What are you feeling? What are you thinking? Do you feel yourself become defensive? Are you open?

Record your responses.

Next, go out in nature where there are no humans around. Do exactly the same thing as before, observing what you experience within your own heart, mind, body, and spirit.

Record your experience.

Notice if there are any differences in the way your body and soul responds to the two different environments. Remember it's not about reading others, it is an exercise to become aware of how your body and soul respond so you know whether or not your are reacting defensively or not.

There are many ways to live and prosper as an empath. Empaths who are balanced and grounded can achieve spectacular results in their lives. Oprah Winfrey, Caesar Milan, the Dalai Lama, and Sir Richard Branson are all great examples of highly evolved and achieving empaths.

Exercise

Reflect upon what you feel you are here to achieve as an empath. Do you feel you are here to do something big? If you knew what it was, what would it be?

Write these answers in your workbook.

Often when you discover who you are more deeply, you can start to connect the dots of why you react and respond the way you do to people and to your environment. This can help you to feel more "normal" and less like there is something wrong with you that needs to be fixed. If you are an empath, embrace your uniqueness, your difference, and your gift. If you can do this, then others will too.

Self-Care

Journal daily. Embrace your beauty and uniqueness. Spend time lying on the earth, feeling the sun's rays fill your body with its golden, warm light. Eat organic and healthy whole foods. Exercise by walking outside every day for a week. Deepen your connection to the earth mother.

If you would like to interact on the secure Intuition On Tap Forum through the Heart Centre to discuss the topics and exercises in this chapter and the opportunity to interact with Heidi and with other readers, please go to http://www.heidisvision.com/community and become a member of the VIP forum. After you have joined you may follow the topic heading to this and every other chapter.

Part Three

Turning on the Tap

CHAPTER EIGHTEEN

———————

Intuition and Clairsentience

The best and most beautiful things in the world cannot be seen or even touched. They must be felt with the heart—Helen Keller

We are going to start to discover your strongest intuitive ability, in terms of clairvoyance, clairaudience, or clairsentience, through your connection to your heart center. Again, as we move through, observe what you feel naturally drawn to and what feels easiest to use.

Clairsentience is the ability to discern and receive information intuitively through your feeling, sensing, smelling, touching, and knowing. This can also be explained through "feelings" and "just knowing" something. On many occasions in your life, you have probably known whether someone was telling you the truth or lying to you. This is your clairsentience at work.

This is a very useful ability to develop and can be utilized within your life, bearing great results. Clairsentience can also be used to connect more deeply with your higher self through the physical world.

If you have been accessing your intuition, you will perhaps be aware of different energies around you or visiting your workspace or home. Perhaps you've had the experience of feeling like you are being held and protected at a moment of danger or personal concern. Maybe when you were driving and found yourself lost, you "just knew" which way to go. Whatever your experience, it is important to build upon that connection with your intuition and your higher self, and it is great fun to do this through your clairsentience.

Exercise

- Sit quietly in a warm room where you won't be disturbed or bothered. Take the phone off the hook and close the door.
- Begin to breathe, slowly and gently, filling your belly on the inhalation and completely emptying your lungs on the exhalation.
- Do this deep breathing for a count of ten and then fall into the natural rhythm of your breath.
- Ask from your heart for your higher self to gently make its presence known to you.
- Wait until you feel your higher self is connecting to you through your heart. If you are unsure, then strongly intend to be connected to your higher self.
- Using your clairsentience and your body to feel your higher self, ask in your mind to be gently shown a sensation in your body that confirms this connection.
- Very slowly, ask your higher self to connect with you on your right side. All of the movements should be done very slowly; it will feel uncomfortable for you if your higher self moves too quickly.

- Feel all the sensations you can. Then ask your higher self to move to your left side.

- When you have felt sensations on your left side, ask your higher self to stand at the side it normally connects through you.

- Allow yourself to feel the sensations. These may include warmth, tingling, buzzing, or waves of energy.

- Ask in your mind to be given a sign in your physical body every time you are connected to your higher self. This could be a touch on the hand, a sensation on your cheek, or whatever else you feel comfortable with. Then whenever you feel that sensation in the future, you will know that you are connected.

- Take this opportunity to ask about your own energy and if there is anything your higher self wishes to demonstrate to you, through your body and your feelings.

- Take your time with this process, and enjoy the very special experience of connecting to your higher self on a physical level and feeling the wonderful sensations in your body.

Please write your experiences in your book directly after the exercise to keep them fresh in your mind. Use this exercise as often as you like to deepen your connection with your magnificent higher self.

Exercise

- Find a guinea pig who is willing to work with you. This can be a family member or a friend; it's up to you.
- Ask them to relax and sit across from you.

- Quieting your mind, breathe slowly and rhythmically until you feel quite relaxed.
- When you feel ready, begin to expand your heart energy to connect with the person in front of you (you can have your eyes open or closed).
- Feel yourself beginning to merge with their aura, their bioelectric field. Once you feel connected, begin to receive impressions, feelings, and information from them in your body, without speaking to them.
- Take your time to really feel the sensations of being connected to another person at this level.
- Then see if you can pinpoint what they are feeling emotionally, if they have a health issue or disease, and how they feel energetically—e.g., tired, overwhelmed, stressed, etc.—and how their life force is flowing.
- When you have gained the information, very gently pull your heart energy back, take a few deep breaths, and slowly open your eyes.
- Ask the person how they felt during this process, and don't worry if they didn't feel much.
- You may share with them what you have found.

I will take this opportunity to impress the importance of sharing from a positive perspective with the people you are practicing with, whether they are a family member or a friend. If you discover that they have an illness, repressed anger, or a spouse who is having an affair, please ask your heart to give you the most positive and healing words to use to share this information with them.

You can imagine how you would feel if someone said to you, "Oh my God! You are such an angry person. I can feel a ball of rage sitting in your belly! You really need to deal with that!" It wouldn't make you feel very good about yourself, would it? I would assert that not much healing would take place! It is important that the people around you are made to feel "normal" and that your interaction with them provides an opportunity for them to grow. If you hear yourself using words that are not positive, take a step back and take stock of yourself and what is going on for you. Remember the filters that we hold in place with our own judgments and experiences? Work on and be conscious of your filters, all the time, to ensure you are bringing through the highest information possible. In other words, if the communication is judgmental or fearful, you are not connected into your heart center; you are connected into your ego.

Write in your exercise book what you discovered about this person. You may ask them if what you felt makes sense to them. It's good to get feedback and confirmation.

Please continue this process as much and as often as you like. It may only take about ten minutes each time, but don't rush yourself through the process.

Continuing with Developing Your Clairsentience

Working with different energies will help to increase your spiritual vocabulary. Your understanding and abilities will deepen as you familiarize yourself with the energetic vibrations of different forms of consciousness. I invite you to connect with the following energies and document your experiences in your workbook.

Crystals: Choose a crystal that you feel drawn to. After asking the deva or nature spirit that lives within the crystal whether it is happy to work with you, place it in your hand. Begin to receive information from the crystal, feeling this through your body. How do you feel when you are holding it? Can you feel it in a particular place in your body? Record your findings in your workbook. Experiment with different colors and types of crystals. See if you can determine any differences.

Animals: Find a cat or dog, or whatever animal may be around you, and ask permission to work with the animal in your mind. If you receive a yes, then you may gently connect to the animal's energy through your heart center, opening yourself to receive its information and communication. Dogs love to talk to us energetically. They seem absolutely thrilled to have a person connected and listening to them. Their energy can be quite high or hyper and excited sometimes.

Most cats will allow you to work with them, but usually on their terms, as they tend to be very shy and very, very self-conscious. Cats are often misunderstood as being arrogant, but it is usually that they are extremely shy.

Horses may be a bit trickier, but if you're game, give it a try. They may make you work for it.

Record what you felt when you were connected to each animal in your workbook. What were the differences in energetic quality? Where in your body did you feel the connection take place?

Trees: Here is a great opportunity for all of you closet tree huggers! Go to a park, out in nature, or in your backyard and find a tree you feel drawn to. Ask permission and then expand your heart center to connect with the tree. Feel what it feels, and open yourself to the connection fully. You may be surprised by what you discover. The spirit that lives within a tree is called a dryad. They love to work with humans, although sometimes initially they may be a bit shy. I can assure you that once you feel connected to a tree, you will want to spend a lot of time with it. Sitting at the base of a tree with your back resting upon its trunk is a great place to do spiritual work, meditate, and write in your journals.

If there have recently been trees cut down in the area, you may find that the dryad, or tree spirit, is trying to show you about this event. Please be compassionate and understanding toward this spirit, as they are very sensitive and tend to hold on to what they witness, especially if there was trauma.

Try this exercise with a few different types of trees and see if you can discern a difference. Record your experiences in your workbook.

When you are working with clairsentience, is it common for transference to occur. You are connecting with another's energy on such an intimate level, feeling what they do within your body and your auric field, that you may retain some of their energy or even pain. At the end of each exercise, please intend that you be completely disconnected from that consciousness, before you move to the next task or person. Otherwise, at the end of the day, you may be feeling very overwhelmed and unhappy. If a feeling persists, it is more than likely showing you, like a mirror, something about yourself. If this is happening, ask your higher self to show you what you need to know and then ask to have it taken away. Please remember your boundaries.

Psychometry

Psychometry is the art of discerning information from a piece of jewelry or other physical item belonging to a person, living or passed. When we wear a ring, for example, that ring is imbued with our vibration, our feelings, thoughts, and experiences. An intuitive person who holds that ring can receive the information held within the object. This can be a useful tool to use to access your intuition.

Exercise

Give a short reading to a friend using psychometry. Holding the object to be read in your hand, open yourself up to receiving the information and see what comes through. Remember to share this information from a positive perspective. When you are finished, ask for some feedback from your "client." Write this experience in your exercise book.

As you can see, there are many ways to discern and receive information using your clairsentience. We will continue to explore other options in later chapters, so for now, please practice these skills set out for you and complete all of the exercises.

Self-Care

Take time to contemplate the element of earth and how it relates to you as a human being having an earthly experience. Lie upon the earth and feel how she has the same feelings as you. Imagine for a moment that you are not separate and that the earth mother is teaching you how to communicate more deeply using your body.

CHAPTER NINETEEN

————•••————

Intuition and Clairvoyance

It is a terrible thing to see and have no vision.—
Helen Keller

Developing Your Clairvoyance

In the last chapter you looked at ways to develop and experience your clairsentience. Now you will be exploring the intuitive expression of clairvoyance. Clairvoyance is a way to experience your intuition through your mind's eye or third eye center and perhaps, after some development, even with your waking eyes.

This information is displayed through visual impressions, images of words, colors, faces, and forms, and other various visual expressions from sprit. These visions are very similar to dreams. Like dreams, clairvoyant visions use symbols, impressions, and archetypal images as their form of communicating messages. Archetypes, according to Jungian psychology, are inherited memories represented in the mind by a universal symbol and observed in dreams and myths.

Some clairvoyants create a whole symbolic language based around the flashes of insight they receive. For example, an apple may have more meaning then simply being an apple. The picture of an apple may mean good health to the clairvoyant receiving the image. If that is the meaning or interpretation they place onto an apple, then every time they see an apple using their clairvoyance, it will mean good health for their clients or for themselves.

Clairvoyant images can also be literal in their communication. If you see a lovely house with a view of the water, then that can be a literal place that your intuition is showing you. As you get used to working with your clairvoyance on a regular basis, you will understand more deeply what is being communicated to you and your particular way of receiving information through this intuitive gift. It is much easier for the subconscious mind to relate to symbols and archetypes than to literal meanings, as we are often attached to the outcome of the information we are viewing.

Clairvoyance is probably the most popularized form of intuition, and many people understand what a clairvoyant is or have at least heard of clairvoyance. I encourage you not to get too caught up or disappointed with yourself if you have difficulty with this intuitive sense, as for some it is difficult to develop. Your intuitive skills will often be stronger in one form than another. Some people are very visual, being able to see pictures in their minds. Others feel deeply and are natural clairsentients or are very auditory and have a natural propensity toward clairaudience. Again, we are aiming to develop a balanced approach to intuition, not to make one skill better or worse than the other.

It is quite common that as you continue to develop and work with your intuition, your other abilities will begin to unfold. When I first started using my intuitive abilities, I was very clairsentient and clairaudient with not much clairvoyance. Now I use my clairvoyance every day, and it is quite easy and natural for me to do so. My clairvoyance has unfolded at a healthy and natural pace for me, so try not to get frustrated if you are not seeing everything you want to straight away. Trust that this will unfold for you at exactly the right time, in a healthy, balanced manner.

Exercise

Write in your workbook your own definition of clairvoyance. Consider its benefits and also the challenges it can bring to your intuitive guidance. List the ways in which you may use clairvoyance within your life. How will you experience your clairvoyance, and how can you apply this in real and practical ways in your life?

Feeling Sight

Sometimes when your intuitive ability is predominantly clairsentience, intuitive feelings through your body, you may have what I call a feeling sight. Say you are being shown intuitively the color pink. You may not be able to see the color pink in your mind's eye as a vision, but you can feel through your clairsentience that it is the color pink. This can be the same for other "images" you receive, such as what people look like. For example, you can't see in your mind's eye that a person has brown hair, but you can feel that they have brown hair. Naturally clairvoyant people have a difficulty understanding the concept of feeling sight, so unless you have experienced this yourself it may be hard for you to grasp. Those who have feeling sight often find a sense of relief when they understand that it is actually the way they work with clairvoyance. This feeling sight may develop over time to a clear clairvoyant sight, or it may not. Regardless, it is just as effective and valid a method of receiving intuitive information.

Exercise

- Sit quietly in your sacred space.
- Begin to notice all of the colors and light in the space around you.
- See if there is anything that stands out to you as you relax your vision.
- Does there seem to be energy surrounding and within objects, plants, or animals? Record this in your workbook.
- You may like to try this in different environments.

Seeing a Person's Aura

The aura is the bioelectric field that surrounds every living thing. It can contain many beautiful colors but may also have tears and holes.

- Ask a person who has agreed to work with you to stand against a light-colored, plain wall.
- Relax your vision as you soften your gaze and look around the edges of the person.
- What can you see? What do you notice?
- Record every impression, no matter how small, in your workbook. (When starting this exercise, please be gentle with yourself and stay relaxed, as you can feel nauseated if you strain too hard. It can also be more difficult to see clairvoyantly if you are trying too hard. Relax and surrender.)

Your Future Exercise

Create an image around your future. You may choose any aspect of your life for the exercise. After you have chosen one, allow your mind's eye to create an intricate and detailed image of what you would like to happen in the future regarding this aspect of your life. Write down all the details through story, describing the richness and details that you can see in your mind's eye. You may also like to transfer this into an image through drawing or painting.

Soul Family Exercise

Just as you took the opportunity to feel your higher self through clairsentience, now I invite you to ask a member of your soul family to stand before you.

- Using your clairvoyance or your mind's eye, look at their face, the way their hair falls around their face, the colors that surround them, and what they are wearing.
- Notice their clothing and how it drapes or falls around their form. Notice if they are wearing any type of jewelry or anything else that stands out to you.
- As you gaze into their face and their loving eyes, notice any features here.
- Take as much time as you need to see your soul family member. When you are complete, thank them. Then gently bring yourself back into the room and ground yourself.
- Using wax crayons or colored pencils, now draw what you have seen with your clairvoyance on paper.
- You may do this as many times as you like.

Remote Viewing

This is a skill that can be a great ability to master. As the name suggests, it is the ability to clairvoyantly view people, places, and objects that are in a different location to the person viewing it. This can also be used to see objects in boxes or envelopes but has been primarily used to access other locations.

It is interesting to note that governments around the world, including the USA and Russia, have dedicated programs within their espionage and military arms to research and develop this ability. They often recruit gifted clairvoyants, who are then given drugs to heighten this ability. These men and women are then used as psychic soldiers to gain information regarding the opposite forces' positions, intelligence, and movements. Obviously this is not why you are learning this technique, and it is important to remember that it is *not* appropriate to read a person without their permission.

This is an advanced technique, so don't worry if you feel that you are still finding your intuitive sight during this exploration. Some find this difficult and don't use it again, and others have a natural talent and skill for this type of ability.

What can you use remote viewing for?

- helping police to locate lost bodies
- locating lost objects, e.g., jewelry, personal papers
- locating lost people, including children or teens who have run away
- locating lost animals
- assisting police on past or current cases

These are a few examples of when remote viewing can be used with success and in situations that are far more relevant to you. People always want to know how to locate lost objects, such as keys, documents, or jewelry, and you will be able to help find them. You can of course also use this for your own purposes, too.

The Process

The process to use your remote viewing is to sit quietly and clear your mind as effectively as possible. When you are comfortable and relaxed, clear your mind of any thoughts or images. Set the intention to connect remotely with the object, person, or place and then open your mind to see what begins to drift in. You may like to record verbally or written what you see and experience.

- Are there obvious details?
- Can you see colors?
- Are there distinctive landmarks?
- What type of environment is it?
- Are there any people there?
- Are there any animals there?
- What does the landscape look like?

These questions give you a guide to what to be looking for, but open yourself to whatever you are seeing. When you have received the information, relax back into your space, take a few deep breaths, and then slowly open your eyes.

Please do not practice this too often at first, as you may end up with a psychic migraine. It is also very important to only do this process when feeling fully grounded and present; otherwise, you may feel nauseated and light-headed afterwards.

Advanced Exercise

Get a helper to place an object in a location and see if you can find it or collect as much detail around it as possible. Check with your helper for feedback.

Self-Care

Throughout the week I invite you to stimulate yourself visually by watching uplifting movies, going to an art gallery, watching the sunrise or sunset, and observing your surroundings and the people in them. Don't read anyone without his or her permission, though!

The more neural pathways you create, in terms of visual experiences and frames of reference, the better equipped you will be to use and strengthen your clairvoyance.

CHAPTER TWENTY

Intuition and Clairaudience

So when you are listening to somebody, completely, attentively, then you are listening not only to the words, but also to the feeling of what is being conveyed, to the whole of it, not part of it.—Jiddu Krishnamurti

Whose Voice Is It Anyway?

Being able to hear and discern the different voices in your head is a very valuable gift to master when you are developing your clairaudience. It can be difficult knowing what is your inner voice and that of your intuition. Let's take a step back, however, and look at the ability of clairaudience.

This is the ability to hear, psychically or intuitively, the messages being sent from your spirit or higher self, other forms of consciousness, including crystals, trees and animals, and even people who have passed over. Clairaudience can often be the trickiest skill to master and one of the most rewarding to attain. I encourage you to spend time over the next week listening to all that surrounds you, including music, birds, people, and everything else in your environment.

Exercise

Sit outside quietly with your eyes closed for at least five minutes. Open your awareness to the surrounding environment.

- What can you hear?
- What sounds are you aware of?
- How far away are they?
- Is it people, wind, waves, animals?
- Take your time to listen to all that is around you. When you are ready, gently come back and write what you found in your workbook.
- Do this exercise in various settings over the next week, noticing the different qualities in sound.
- Try these for suggestions: ocean, mountains, forest, your backyard, near a school, at a mall, and near a playground.
- Write down all that you can hear.

Clairaudience can be experienced as hearing information occurring from outside of your mind, but not with your physical ears. In other words, the thought, idea, or concept can often seem like it is "dropped in" and may be a concept, idea, or word that you do not necessarily use. This can happen even when you least expect it. When you are vacuuming, doing the dishes, and driving the car, you may receive clairaudient messages from your higher self. This is because both sides of your brain are working together. This tends to get your ego mind out of the way, which then opens the space for inspiration and messages to flow through.

If you do receive information clairaudiently, check to see if you feel you are connected to your intuition and contemplate whether you have asked for an answer to a bothering situation or question or have been worrying over circumstances in your life.

There is sometimes a phenomenon that takes place when your clairaudience begins to open. This can seem like you can hear spirit with your physical ears. When my clairaudience was opening, I would hear my name being called all the time. I would hear children speaking to me, and I would hear knocking on my front door and on the walls of my house, to the point that I thought I was going a bit crazy! You can only answer the door so many times with no one there before you start to question yourself. It got to the point that my children got very used to me asking them if they had called me or if they could hear what I was hearing. As I began to embrace my clairaudience, the noise began to dissipate. Spirit no longer needed to "turn up the volume," as my spirit now had my full attention.

This seems to be quite a common occurrence when you are developing your clairaudience, so don't worry if you have had any similar experiences. It seems to be quite a normal part of the process.

Exercise

- Make a list of five questions that you would like answers to, relating to anything in your life. These questions can be spiritual or about your life in general. For example, you may want to know about your work, your relationship with a family member, or what is your most dominate intuitive ability.

- Look at what you would most like the answers to and start from there.

- Once you have formulated your list, relax and call upon your spirit.
- Ask spirit to stand on the side that you have established with it in earlier exercises, and begin to ask your questions.
- Open yourself to what comes through.
- You may like to write down the answers *after* you have received them.
- Look through your answers and begin to discern what you feel spirit has answered and what has, perhaps, come from your mind.
- Notice how it feels and decide if you can discern any differences while you are receiving the answers to your questions.
- Try to be as honest with yourself as possible. Remember, you are not expected to get it perfect starting out.
- Repeat this exercise as much as you like.

Listening

Being able to listen is a gift that cannot be overstated, particularly if you want to develop your clairaudience. If your mind is constantly full of chatter, it can be difficult to hear spirit talking to you! Likewise, if you are constantly speaking, you are not really listening. This skill often needs to be developed to encourage your receptivity from spirit.

Next time you are having a conversation with someone, check yourself to see whether you are really listening. Often when we think we are really listening to another, we are simply thinking of the next thing *we* are going to say, not hearing what is being communicated to us. If you are not really listening, your friend or partner will know, and the interaction will be limited at best. This is how most people live their lives.

Exercise

During your conversations and interactions, intend to be really present with your listening.

- Set a goal to be able to repeat exactly, or at least the main points, of what the other person has said to you. This is a great counseling technique that sets the space for people to feel more comfortable with you and open themselves even more deeply.
- You may start this with, "What I heard you say is ... Is that what you meant, and is that correct?"
- Conversely, notice when you are speaking if the other person in the interaction is listening to you or not and how that feels for you. If you have ever tried to have a conversation with a person who is watching television at the same time, you will understand what I mean.
- Write down your experience.

As you develop and continue to fine-tune your listening skills, you will open yourself more strongly to communicating clairaudiently with your spirit. Continuing to meditate is also a very important key to this, as it helps to center you and gives your higher self and spirit the chance to speak.

Self-Care

As you strengthen your intuition, you will continue to increase the level at which you receive information from spirit. You will also increase your health and well-being on all levels. To increase the receptivity of your clairaudience, eat blue and indigo fruit and vegetables.

CHAPTER TWENTY-ONE

Your Ego Mind, Ego Voice, and Emotional Addictions

Of course it is happening inside your head, Harry, but why on earth should that mean that it is not real?—
J. K. Rowling

What is your ego voice? This is the little, or sometimes very big, voice in your head that will give you instructions, directions, comments, judgments and opinions regarding the choices you are making in your life or the thoughts you are entertaining. The ego voice also has an important role: keeping you alive. It is the voice that will say "don't hold the knife that way" or "watch out for that car." So as you can see, it has a value to your life. If you think you can get rid of it, think again. The ego voice is what makes us human, and the only time it stops is when we are dead. That is not to say, however, that we can't get a handle on this often-disruptive voice. What you need to ask is, who is in control? Is it your higher self and your consciousness, or is it your ego voice? If it's your ego voice, then more likely than not you are also addicted to your emotions as a direct result.

What happens when we have a negative thought? Neuropeptides are released in our brain, which then travel into our blood stream as hormones and attach themselves to our cells, which have, over time, built specific receptors to hold these peptides or hormones. If you have been having abusive or negative thoughts for a long period of time, it is difficult for these cells to receive much else, as the receptors have been conditioned to only receive the hormone that is released by the negative thought. This can even lead to the point of decreased nutritional uptake from our food, because there is no room left on the cell to receive and utilize the nutrients. In other words, we are not getting the vitamins and nutrients from our food because our cells are blocked from the result of self-abuse and negative thoughts! It is a sobering thought for sure. We become addicted to the feeling we receive as a direct response from our thought-hormones, even though that feeling is often unpleasant.

Exercise

- Track your thoughts and feelings during the week and any emotional responses.
- What where you doing at the time?
- Were you triggered somehow?
- Was there a person you were interacting with?
- Was it a thought straight from your ego mind including a judgment?
- Write what you find in your workbook.

When you are developing your clairaudience, it's very important to understand that your ego voice may have quite a bit to say about the process. It will pipe up and add its opinion to the mix. This can be confusing and disconcerting, to say the least. This voice will also tell you that you can't succeed and may say things like, "who do you think you are" and "maybe you're crazy hearing these voices." The best way to deal with this voice is to be really clear with your own interaction. It is also very helpful to name your ego voice, giving you some distance from its influence on you. I have two names for my voices, as they offer me different types of "advice." One is "Moaning Myrtle," as she loves to whine about how hard everything is and how much she has suffered. The other is "Safety Sally," as she gets really scared and creates avoidance when there is an important decision to be made. As you can see, these two aspects of myself are there to teach me but can also limit my experience and the opportunities that come into in my life, if I allow them.

Name That Voice

Exercise

Give your ego voice a name and begin to interact with it as if it is *not* in control but rather you are in control of it. Notice that when you tell it to shut up it may get louder and more vocal, thinking you are not listening.

Respond gently and firmly using it's new name, and see what results you have. I like to say to mine, "Thanks for sharing, but I'm going to do this anyway." The ego voices are acknowledged, and still I am in control.

Continue with your thought journal. Track how many times your ego voice has something to say about what you are doing and what others are doing. Notice whether there is anything in particular that it likes to focus on. Is it very judgmental, scared, limited, angry, anxious, hysterical, resentful, hateful, or obnoxious? Simply observe what you find, not allowing yourself to feel these same states of being but acknowledging they are a part of you and are there to show you more about yourself.

Exercise

Watch the news and notice how your energy responds to it. Notice also how many stories during the news or current affairs shows are negative compared to uplifting and inspiring. Write in your book what you observe regarding your physical response, emotional response, and mental and energetic responses.

Then for the following week don't watch the news or read the papers at all, and record how you feel after that week. Are you aware of a difference in your energy, particularly in the back of your neck and head? This is where other people's thoughts, judgments, criticisms, and telepathic energy can get stuck.

Exercise

Make a list regarding the driving force behind your choice to open and develop your intuition. Please be honest with yourself, as you may be surprised at what comes up. List everything, even if it includes desires to be famous, special, or recognized as different. Helping others and a desire to empower may also be on the list. Be as comprehensive as possible.

Self-Care

As you develop your intuition, limit your exposure to the television, newspapers, and other forms of media. These can have a numbing effect on your brain function and your consciousness. The fact that you are being bombarded by negativity does not help to keep you anchored in your divinity. It will put you in a place of fear, and this will influence your choices and your intuitive connection. I can't remember the last time I watched the news, and why would I? It would only leave me feeling down and sad. There is nothing wrong with being informed, but don't allow yourself to be inundated with negativity! It will lower your vibration and thus make it harder for you. Having said that, I love watching movies. They are a great respite from work and a vehicle to have a laugh or a good cry. I use movies to access any stuck emotions or concepts and get them flowing and out.

CHAPTER TWENTY-TWO

Embodying Your Spirit

I have decided to stick with love. Hate is too great a burden to bear.—Martin Luther King Jr.

As you have been traveling along this path, you will have noticed many changes and transformations occurring. These may have manifested in obvious and overt ways, or they may be working under the surface, waiting until the perfect moment to be made manifest in your consciousness and your life. All that you have experienced within relationships, including the relationship you have with yourself, will be transformed and rewoven. All the shifts and challenges that you have experienced so far are spirit's way of preparing you to develop yourself more deeply.

"Know thyself" is the most important lesson at the moment and must be adhered to, within the best of your ability. This means always checking in with your feelings and thoughts. What is your body telling you, what are your emotions telling you, and what are your thoughts telling you? Use these tools as a compass to ensure you stay focused and on track.

Ask yourself the following questions:

- How are my relationships?
- How are my finances?
- Do I have enough time to achieve what I want?
- Is my body healthy?
- How is my spiritual connection?

Your answers will give you some insight into the areas that perhaps need a little extra work at the moment.

If you believe you don't have enough money, guess what: you don't. If you believe we are in a global economic crisis, guess what: we are. If you believe you don't have enough time to achieve your goals, guess what: you won't have enough time to achieve your goals. What you may not realize is that your state of mind is of paramount importance in creating your life the way you would like it to be, especially when you are becoming increasingly spiritually aware and able. The flow of your energy goes both ways, and it can affect your thoughts and emotions as well as the experiences and manifestations in your life.

Exercise

What emotional states are you addicted to? Fear, anger, drama, victimhood, sadness, powerlessness? Chart your emotions over the week, observing the dominant emotional state during all seven days. At the end of the week you will gain a clearer picture of how you may be controlled by your emotions and not the other way around. Notice if there are any stand-out triggers related to your emotional state of being. This could include a person, place, or event. As has been stated throughout the book, the external world is a reflection of your internal world.

Gratitude

One of the most important ways to maintain a clear connection and to embody your heart energy is to incorporate a gratitude practice into your daily life. Every morning, start the day going through a list of all the things you are grateful for in your life and remembering them throughout the day. This will increase your vibration and make it easier for you to connect with spirit, which directly flows through your heart center.

Building Bridges

"Invisible threads are the strongest ties."
—Friedrich Nietzsche

When you are embodying your spirit, you are building a bridge from yourself to the realms of your spirit and higher self and back. This is bringing through the vibration of that particular energy, intention, or ray. It is a great way to receive answers for yourself and your life by simply connecting to your spirit and asking the right questions. The quality of your questions often determines the quality of your answers so be precise and clear not general and vague. By connecting to your spirit you have a library card to the stars!

Exercise

Here are some suggested questions that you may like to ask your spirit:

- Tell me about the past relating to ...
- Tell me about the present relating to ...
- Tell me about the future relating to ...

Please try at least two of these questions relating to yourself or two other questions of your own choosing, and record what you receive.

When we think about how strongly our emotions can affect our bodies, we should also think about how objects around us will contain the bridge of information our consciousness is connecting to. An example of this would be if you have a piece of jewelry that you really love and wear all the time. If someone were to pick it up and hold it, they would probably smile. This is because you are constantly channeling the energy of love into it, and so the energy of love is anchored into the object. If it were an object that you hated, then when they held it they would most likely feel uncomfortable and want to put it down, as it would contain the vibration of hatred.

Water is an awesome conductor of energy and will hold the vibration of the energy surrounding it. I have included some images from Dr. Emoto's work *Messages from Water*. This man is a Japanese scientist who took microscopic cellular photos of water droplets in their original forms, drawn directly from their source. He then programmed or channeled a concept or word into the water droplets and then took another microscopic photo of the same water droplets to see if there were any molecular changes in its cellular structure. What he found was quite amazing!

I have included some of his results below so you can see for yourself.

For a moment, think about any negative self-talk that you engage in and the fact that your body is made up of at least 70 percent water. It might make you stop and think next time you are engaging in negative self-talk and filling your body's cells with that energy!

Exercise

Build a bridge to your water by placing a word under the water container. Notice if you can taste a difference. I would recommend positive words so you don't make yourself sick! You may also like to try this with your food.

Spirit Art

Another very beautiful way of building energy bridges is through spirit art. You are not required to be an artist; in fact, you can have absolutely no artistic ability whatsoever and still be a great bridge or connection. You can ask your spirit exactly what you can draw and how to draw it. For example, if you don't know how to draw a flower, then ask at each part, "What next? How do I draw that shape? What color shall I use?"

I highly recommend that you go to an art shop and buy yourself a box of soft pastilles (these are better than oil pastilles) and some smooth paper. You may like to also buy some fixative spray, although hairspray works too. For some reason the medium of the soft pastilles works beautifully to bring through the vibration of spirit onto the page.

If I want to manifest something, I will do spirit art and then hang that image in my meditation space to connect into that bridge associated to my intention. I may also even hang it in my bedroom so that the energy of what I want to create flows to me as I sleep.

This can be a very powerful manifestation tool if used correctly, and of course the best way to achieve this is to set your very clear and strong intention before beginning any work. Just to reiterate, by embodying your spirit through spirit art you are connecting into the place in the universe that holds vibrations, information, and wisdom that you can access and bring through into the third dimension and your life. It is an incredibly rewarding experience and can be loads of fun!

Exercise

- Gather your pastilles and paper and set yourself up in your sacred space where you won't be disturbed.
- Set your intention for the process (see suggestions below) and then go through the process of connecting into your spirit.

- You may at times feel like your intuitive connection drops in and out whilst you are working. Simply stop and reconnect to your intention and then continue.
- You will know the difference between this sensation and the sensation you feel when you are complete, as you won't be able to reestablish the connection with your spirit.
- It is always a good idea to then stand back from your drawing and really look at it. See if it feels complete, ask your spirit if it is, and then pat yourself on the back for creating a wonderful bridge from your spirit to you.
- Hang it in your space so you can connect into the wonderful energy that you have made manifest.

Some suggested intentions to play with:

- Show me how to draw my life in the next year
- Show me how to draw my I-am presence
- Show me how to draw my future partner (if you are single!)
- Show me how to draw my medicine
- Show me how to draw myself in another lifetime

You may really enjoy this process, and I encourage you to practice it as many times as you like. Have fun with it but also really feel the emotions that are in your body as you are bringing the image through. Spirit art comes through your heart center, so you will feel the energy through your body. The healing energy you bring into your body can also help with whatever process or intention you have set.

The stars are the limit (literally) when you are embodying your spirit, and I encourage you to explore and experiment with this very beautiful and very rewarding expression of your intuition.

Self-Care

I highly, highly recommend you do the Heart Centered Healing and Heart of the Earth Mother meditations daily over the following week. Please keep up with your journaling throughout the process of the CDs, as there will probably be things coming to the surface of your awareness.

Spend time outside to help clear yourself and eat healthy fruit and vegetables. It's the best way to heighten the vibration of your heart center.

CHAPTER TWENTY-THREE

Past Lives or Concurrent Lives?

Who are we really? Combinations of common chemicals that perform mechanical actions for a few years before crumbling back into the original components? Fresh new souls, drawn at random for some celestial cupboard where God keeps an unending supply?

Or the same soul, immortal and eternal, refurbished and reused through endless lives, by that thrifty Housekeeper? In Her wisdom and benevolence She wipes off the memory slates, as part of the cleaning process, because if we could remember all the things we have experienced in earlier lives, we might object to risking it again.

—Barbara Michaels

Past Lives

Much is said about past lives and how they can affect us in the present. Before we continue into this topic, however, it is important to have a true understanding of the term itself.

If we look at the concept that the past is a third-dimensional linear construct, new possibilities begin to emerge. What if we are living all of our lives concurrently, throughout all distance, time, and space? What if you were able to access anything and everything that you have ever experienced from any lifetime? Wow. You could really develop your superpowers!

It is a common misconception that what we have experienced from other incarnations has all happened in the past tense, that it is somehow our history or herstory. But what if we were still experiencing these other lives right now? Well, that gives us a wonderful opportunity for healing, learning, and growth.

I understand that the average person is often still trying to get his or her head around the whole concept of past lives and whether they are real or not, let alone dimensionally concurrent lives. This is the message my spirit has brought through my consciousness to explain this concept.

Dimensionally Concurrent Lives

Open your mind for a moment and imagine that your spirit is in the shape of a great tree. This tree has strong roots and firm branches holding it to the earth. You see these branches extending up and out from the trunk, reaching into the universe. Upon these branches are beautiful green leaves. Of course these leaves and these branches are both a part of the tree, intrinsically connected to one another. What the leaves feel and experience, the tree feels and experiences. Each leaf would have a different experience upon this tree, yet they are all still connected to the one, the whole. What one experiences, the whole experiences. Now imagine that the trunk is the whole of your spirit and that each of the branches and leaves on this beautiful tree is an aspect of your soul. Each of these aspects, leaves, and branches is having a different experience at the same time. Some may feel the breeze and some may feel the sunshine, for example. The information is stored within the leaf and within the tree, and it would be freely accessible to any of the other leaves or branches that desire it. Each time one leaf has a new experience, the whole tree grows, strengthens, and learns. Each branch reaches to a different plane or dimension and yet is still connected to the trunk, which is connected to the roots, which are connected to the earth.

This metaphor is what spirit would like you to imagine when you are thinking about past lives. As you can see, you are able to access vast volumes of information regarding your soul's journey and the lessons you have agreed to experience.

In my experience if you master a concept or learn a lesson, then that benefit flows onto all of your other soul aspects that may not have mastered that lesson for themselves yet.

Have you ever wondered why some people have no trouble manifesting money but really struggle at forming healthy, long-term relationships? Of course, you could apply the tenets of psychology, behavior, life experiences, and conditioning to explain this dynamic, but as I am focusing on the concept of past lives I shall continue to explain in those terms. Imagine that in one life you have absolutely mastered and learnt all that you need to in relation to manifesting money and wealth. Well, this would then certainly be easy for you now, and you would experience the results of this not only on the physical plane but also within your soul. You probably wouldn't give money much thought or worry, as you would just "know" it would always be abundant. You may also have a great skill at manifesting money by being very successful in business or attracting great windfalls. You may, however, struggle to find a person to accept you for who you are, to love you unconditionally, and to build a healthy relationship with. This may weigh down your soul with a longing and a yearning for this intimate connection. You may find yourself in one disastrous relationship after another.

When you master this lesson around relationships, however, and learn the lessons that you need to, then all of the aspects of your soul experiencing the same challenge may in fact find that they too are able to form healthy, loving relationships. This lesson then integrates within your soul and your spirit, and the next lesson unfolds. It may take many, many incarnations to master a particular lesson, where many of your soul aspects are working on the same lesson at once. The moment one of those aspects has mastery, it then flows out to all the others, which in turn opens up another new opportunity for growth and a new level of self-mastery.

Exercise

- Make a list of all the lessons that you continue to struggle with. It may include topics mentioned above or completely new ones.
- Choose one of those lessons that you would like to receive mastery over.
- Prepare yourself for meditation in your sacred space.
- Using your imagination, go to a comfortable landscape in nature in your mind's eye and ask the soul aspect that is helping you achieve mastery to step forward in your energy.
- Have a conversation, asking to be shown all the steps, tools, and skills that you can use to attain this mastery.
- Ask this soul aspect to help you with this, like a team working together to achieve the same goal.
- Come back, writing the information and insights you have been given in your workbook.
- Take the steps in this lifetime, including creating a plan, to help you implement what you have been shown.
- Check back with your spirit or soul aspect, whenever you feel stuck, to ask for more help.
- Track your progress with this.

Self-Care

Contemplate the concept of the tree as a reflection of your spirit and soul. How do you feel about this? Sit outside amongst trees and allow them to teach you this lesson though their open-hearted communication.

CHAPTER TWENTY-FOUR

Reincarnation

The enlightened can recall their former lives; for the rest of us, the memories of past existences are but glints of light, twinges of longing, passing shadows, disturbingly familiar, that are gone before they can be grasped.—Peter Matthiessen

M ost souls have had numerous lifetimes on the earth plane. They continue to reincarnate into this dimension, as perhaps they have not yet completed all of their lessons or tasks. They still need a physical life to be able to learn what they need to. Often we think it is to experience wealth or fame, but more likely it is to understand concepts such as forgiveness, love, compassion, control, and power. Some souls choose to reincarnate to help others or have a certain task to achieve. This can be grand or small; it doesn't matter the size, as every experience is sacred and important. It is said that the earth plane has the greatest possibility for growth and that souls line up to have an experience here. Because of this realm's physicality, its dualistic nature, and the free will and choice for its inhabitants, the earth offers an abundance of lessons to be experienced and opportunities for growth.

Often people will feel a certain draw, pull, or affinity to one particular culture or epoch. You may feel a draw to Celts, Egyptians, Native Americans, or Africans, for example. This is a reflection of a lifetime you have had in those cultures. I have also found that you will feel drawn to a particular culture based on your own developmental stage in this lifetime. For example, you will want to study and immerse yourself in Native American lore as you are re-embracing the gifts and lessons you learnt in that lifetime. Once you have remembered all you need you, will then gain interest in another culture or period in time. Similarly you may feel repulsed by a certain culture or country. Perhaps your lifetime didn't end up so well there and you have trauma locked into the soul and your cellular memory in this regard. Alternatively, you may have learnt all you can learn from this culture, so there is no pull or need for your soul to revisit the past.

Exercise

Think over your life to see if there are any particular cultures, epochs, or times in history/herstory that you feel drawn to or have studied in the past. Write these in your workbook.

What about these cultures do you love or are you interested in?

Are there any cultures you feel repelled by?

Are there some countries that make you feel uncomfortable? Write these in your workbook too.

This exercise may give you an understanding of where your soul's strengths and accomplishments are and conversely where your soul's wounding may lie.

Lives on Other Planes, Planets, and Dimensions

All souls have also had lifetimes in other dimensions and in other worlds. You are a spiritual being having a human experience, this time around. It is logical, then, to think that you may not even originate from the earth plane but from another dimension or place altogether.

If you look at the spiritual history/herstory of the planet, it is accepted to believe that we are a hybrid race or a mixture of extraterrestrial DNA and humanoid DNA, with the Aboriginal race of Australia being the original and the oldest human race on this planet. This DNA mixing allows us to be sustained and to have a connection upon the earth plane but also to be multidimensional beings, able to access all dimensions at once if we choose. Remember, anything that has a physical body in this third dimension has the right to be here.

It is also interesting to note that modern Hollywood movies are attempting to relate this concept to us. Examples of this are *Avatar, Prometheus, Lord of the Rings, The Knowing,* and *Men in Black,* to name a few.

I would like you to note how you are feeling whilst reading this. Do you notice a resistance to this concept, or does it seem to make perfect sense?

I have vividly recalled other lifetimes in other dimensions on the earth plane and also upon other stars, realms, and planets. This is a list of some of the lifetimes, cultures, and places I have lived.

- Antares-angelic realm
- Elven-earth plane
- Pleiades

- Cassiopeia
- Atlantis-earth plane
- Lemuria-earth plane
- Andromeda
- the original moon/Diana
- Avalon-earth plane
- Tuatha Dé Danann

As you can see, some of these lives are on the earth plane and some are not. It is interesting to note that I can recall physically, emotionally, mentally, and spiritually these lives and the bodies my soul and spirit inhabited. I remember having wings and being an angelic warrior. I remember living as an elf and speaking fluent elvish, and I remember being a Pleiadian and an Atlantian. These are not simply fantasies but full body memories that I have reexperienced.

Exercise

- Do you feel you have had a lifetime in another realm or place?
- If yes, write this in your book with as much detail as possible.
- What were your talents?
- Who were you?
- What did you look like?

Doing All the Work

I have been shown that sometimes one soul aspect of a spirit tends to take on board more than its fair share. For example, they are busy learning everyone else's lessons for them. I invite you to feel into this and decide whether you would like to take this on board. Of course you are all one, but this imbalance can make for a very challenging life for one soul aspect. Why not share the load? It certainly makes it easier for you all!

Similarly, you can also call on skills you have already mastered and integrated. Perhaps you would like to experience financial abundance. Call to yourself the knowledge and mastery in this regard. If you would like to call in the spiritual gifts that you have already mastered and are not utilizing, then do this. The sky's the limit with this, so get very clear about the challenges you face this life and how you may achieve your goals.

Journeying into Another Life

After gaining clarity over what challenges you are currently facing or issues you may want some clarity on, set you intention to view a past life that directly relates to this concern.

Go to your sacred space and do the following:

Sit quietly with your eyes closed.

Use relaxation techniques, including slowing your breathing and feeling your body become heavy. Memorize the following process or record it before you do this exercise so that you can play it back to yourself.

1. Imagine in your mind's eye that you are in a plain white room.
2. In the middle of this room are three steps that lead down to a sunken area.
3. In this sunken area is a very comfortable lounge.

4. Slowly walk down the three steps and sit down on the comfortable lounge. Explain this in as much detail as you wish.

5. Imagine that on a wall just in front of the lounge is a large screen, like a TV.

6. As you look at the screen, you see scenes beginning to appear. You are viewing another life, just like watching a movie. It is very important that you simply view and observe what is happening. It is not necessary to experience these things again, especially if there is trauma. Keep reminding yourself of this.

7. Observe any details, including people, places, and events. Note what you looked like and the relevance this has to your life now.

8. When you feel you have received enough information, then come back, see the TV images stopping, get up from the soft lounge, and step back up the three steps into the white room.

9. Slowly deepen your breath. When you are ready, open your eyes.

10. Write your experience and what you were shown in your workbook.

11. Relate these concepts to your life in terms of how this may help you to master your lessons.

12. Often the realizations and the understanding of the pattern can be enough to shift you out of your old ways.

You may also use this technique to discover your gifts and what you have already mastered in other lifetimes so that you may embrace and embody this in your present lifetime. You may also use this technique to access your lifetimes in other planes and realms. Remember, it is not necessary at any time to reexperience trauma. You have already experienced it once, so there is no need to feel it again. If you feel yourself connecting into the trauma or drama of a particular lifetime, then stop, disconnect emotionally from the images, and take a few deep breaths. Remind yourself that you are just watching the movie of your life, not reliving it! Another-life exploration is simply a tool that can be used to help you move through blocks and release limiting beliefs while enabling you to master lessons and challenges you are currently experiencing.

Self-Care

For a period of time, immerse yourself in a particular culture that you feel very connected with. Eat their foods, wear their clothes, listen to their music, and see how your body, soul, and spirit respond.

CHAPTER TWENTY-FIVE

Soul Family

I live my life until I start the cycle of my dreams, then I leave and search for you until I die. When I come back, I live to remember, I live to find you—Molly Bryant

On earth, we are all born into a particular culture or country. Imagine that it is the same in spirit; there are many different cultures or "countries" from which we originate. As mentioned above, these races are often associated with a stellar constellation from the night sky.

Just as in our human lives we originate from a particular culture, our souls originated from a particular soul family or soul group connected to a constellation or system. These soul families or groups are often happy to oversee us in our travels and can add to our healing, teaching, and evolutionary pursuits. These soul families can work with people here on earth to understand the concepts and lessons that we have come to master. They do this because they also are able to evolve through our growth. When we learn, they learn; when we grow, they grow. It is a beautiful symbiotic relationship that has been in place since earth life began and before.

Throughout your life you may have had the experience of feeling a connection and a reaction, either positive or negative, to certain people that come into your life. These people may be members of your soul family. This is a group of souls that have agreements, contracts, and understandings to reincarnate with one another to facilitate learning and growth.

Before you are born, you make agreements with certain souls in your soul family or group to create certain experiences that will give you the opportunity for the most growth. These can be positive or negative experiences. For example, you may agree that one member of your soul group may incarnate as your abusive father so that you can learn the concept of forgiveness. (It is important to note here that abusive behavior is in *no* way condoned from a member of your soul family or anyone else! There are always many ways to learn our lessons, and they do not have to be through trauma.) Another may choose to be your husband or wife to help you and support you to achieve what you have set out to do within a loving relationship.

It is important to understand that one or another soul may decide not to uphold its part of the agreement. This can leave you stuck in relationships with members of your soul family, finding it difficult to separate or finish the connection. I see this time and time again in my clients' lives where they are stuck in a pattern or loop with a soul and feel they can't break out of it. This is because on a soul level they still want to fulfill their side of the agreement. This can lead to a deep drive to fix or stay in a dysfunctional relationship, hoping that it will get better. Sometimes souls change their decisions, and it is important to accept that such decisions result from that soul's free will and choice, and you cannot violate them without creating karma for yourself. You may perform the completion exercise mentioned earlier to end any unfinished business.

You will also have members of your soul family that are not incarnated with you. You may ask these members for assistance in your life and for guidance if you choose. These are the only souls or forms of consciousness, apart from your medicine, that may help you on your journey. When asking for help, please remember to be very specific about whom you are asking. For example, you may state, "I call upon my soul family to give me guidance and assistance with the issue of ..."

Exercise

Listen to the Heart of Avalon guided visualization to meet members of your soul family. Record your experience.

Members of Your Soul Family

When you are developing your intuition, members of your soul family will assist you by

- protecting your energy from other people,
- offering you information and guidance,
- relaying information from your spirit,
- connecting you into your I-am presence,
- helping you to deal with any feisty earthbound souls,
- stabilizing your energy,
- anchoring you to the earth plane,
- opening your heart center, and
- bringing through concepts that will help you understand the information received intuitively.

Continue to expand your awareness of the possibilities of the immensity, wisdom, and experience of your soul family and your spirit. Utilize these lessons to help you along your journey.

Self–Care

Watch the *Our Journey Home The Movie* DVD, which can be purchased at **http://fillim.com**. I am featured in this documentary along with other leading spiritual teachers. This movie will give you an understanding of some of the concepts in this chapter.

CHAPTER TWENTY-SIX

Intuition on Tap

> Spoon boy: Do not try and bend the spoon. That's impossible. Instead ... only try to realize the truth.
> Neo: What truth?
> Spoon boy: There is no spoon.
> Neo: There is no spoon?
> Spoon boy: Then you'll see, that it is not the spoon that bends, it is only yourself.
>
> —*The Matrix*

You have been given the tools and have had some experience with the fundamentals of accessing your intuition using the various processes in this book. You have been shown how to build the relationship with yourself, perhaps learning things you didn't know you didn't know. You have begun delving into the deeper and sometimes darker side of your nature, coaxing these characteristics to light and awareness, and giving yourself the opportunity to heal, complete and to move forward, to evolve and grow.

You will now know your medicine, your ray, and who you are as a divine and sovereign being. These understandings, realizations, and inner wisdoms have given you the means to access your intuition at any time you choose, in any way you choose, and for whatever reason you choose. You know the boundaries, the rules, the guidelines, and the parameters from which to work. You understand the universal structure and the part you play within it. You understand interdimensional beings and the need for boundaries and discernment when working with your intuition and opening your awareness to other worlds and other realms. You have learnt that you are always in charge of your life and the creation of your experiences. You know that the people in your life—past, present, and future—are all in one way or another gifts of education and ultimately self-realization. And after all of these lessons, experiences, epiphanies, and developments, you know the very simple, yet profound way to turn on the tap of your intuition. You simply say yes. Yes to life, yes to yourself, and yes to the possibility that this is in fact your birthright as a spiritual being, to have the awareness of and direct connection to your own divinity, grace, and power.

Throughout the book you were asked through the exercises, journaling, and practices to determine your natural way of accessing your intuition. If you have taken the steps to do this, then you will easily and sometimes effortlessly be able to turn this tap of intuition on and off at will. I know this to be true because I am able to do it, after going through all of these exercises throughout my journey and developing the framework for you. If I can do it, you can do it. This was created based on my own experiences, my own learning and lessons, my work with clients, and also my personal life. This is my gift to you. I have been there, I have done that, and I have come through the other side. I offer this book, this knowledge, to you from my own experiences, not from external concepts or dogma that don't relate to me or resonate with my heart. This is the way that I have maintained my integrity, even when the status quo of the spiritual and new age industry does not agree with many of the concepts I have shared with you in this book. That's okay, though, as I've never been one to follow what everyone else is doing. It is my ray to empower you to find your own pathway, your own road, and to own, completely and to the core of your being, who you are as a gorgeous, divine, powerful spirit and soul having a very human experience. We all have access to our divinity at any time. All we need to do is choose yes. What will you choose?

Self-Care

If at the completion of this book you find yourself wanting to learn more about developing your intuition for both your personal and professional use, please go to www.heidisvision.com to find out more details about Internationally Accredited Intuitive Dynamix™ Training with Heidi.

If you would like to interact on the secure Intuition On Tap Forum through the Heart Centre to discuss the topics and exercises in this chapter and the opportunity to interact with Heidi and with other readers, please go to http://www.heidisvision.com/community and become a member of the VIP forum. After you have joined you may follow the topic heading to this and every other chapter.

CPSIA information can be obtained at www.ICGtesting.com
Printed in the USA
LVOW11s2326240315

431825LV00001B/131/P

ALW
THE B/

An autobiography

Shane Briant

DEDICATION

This book is dedicated to the women in my life. My mother, Elizabeth Nolan, my fairy godmother Kit Adeane, my first theatrical agent Adza Vincent, my literary agent, Laura Blake Petersen,

and Wendy, my muse.

ACKNOWLEDGMENTS

I'd like to include in this book the names of people I've met on the Internet and who are now my cyber friends. Michael Christian, Elba Cruz, Melinda Villalobos, Russ Lanier, Ian Jennings, Jeffrey Cryer, Leslie Suzie Cryer, Santiago Villalobos, Jackie ONeal, Andrew Satmer, Deborah Clinger-Vacano, Andrew Ralton, Mike Chinea, Manuel Ballesteros Gimeno, Cynthis L. Watson, Jane Considine, Uwe Sommerland, Steve Thompson, F.H. Tocho Canales Jr, Christopher Philip Olivas, Brett Wright, King, Jane and Mark Thompson, Jake and Ruby, Autumn Caro, Ian Ashley Price, Annalisa Bastiani (Miss Tiggy-Winkle) Jeffrey Simon, Brett Ashworth, Kristen Hall, Christian 'Perry' Salicath, Tara DeVries, Beverly Anne Thompson, Neil Fulwood, Jeffrey Simon, Melissa Para Adedeji, Molly & Robert Kenchington. Amanda, Josef and Beau Nalevansky.

I'd like to thank Scott for helping me. He's a wonderful designer.

I love you Giblet and Freddy – sit on the keyboard any time you want!

Love to Marnie, Tash, Rosie, Nick, Tom, Toby, Theo, Jonah, Jessica, Olivia, Harriet, Beatrice and William.

CHILDHOOD

WHY BAD GUYS?

Why write my memoirs at all? Good starting thought. I'm hardly Daniel Day Lewis, Peter O'Toole, Richard Burton, Alec Guinness or any other celebrated actor. I think of myself as an actor who has managed to make a decent living solely by acting – a rare thing these days. When Brad Pitt walks down the street people stop and stare. When I walk down the street possibly every thousandth person thinks to themselves, *'Hey, haven't I seen that face before, somewhere...'* That's good enough for me. I hope people will see this biography for what it is – a book that gives some insight into my personal life; one that features all manner of hopefully funny anecdotal stories about the fascinating people I've been lucky to work with.

I've been cast as dangerous people all my life, and I've always been happiest playing them. On the odd occasions I've played 'good guys', I've had to dig deep into my imagination to come up with an interesting character. Does this suggest that I am at heart a bad person? I hope not. I consider myself a pussycat at heart. I run at the very prospect of immediate violence and am overly kind to anything that moves on the earth – other than mosquitoes.

I think that 'bad guys' rule. They're a better bet than 'nice guys' to win Golden Globe nominations. The number one award-winning genre involves mentally challenged people. Very politically incorrect to suggest this, but I think it's a fact. If you ever get a chance to nail a mentally challenged role, grab it; you know you're on a winner. Just look at the stats. Cliff Robertson for *'Charly,'* John Mills for *'Ryan's Daughter,'* Jack Nicholson for *'One Flew Over the Cuckoo's Nest,'* John Voigt, for *'Coming Home,'* Dustin Hoffman, for

'*Rain Man,*' Daniel Day Lewis for '*My Left Foot,*' Tom Hanks for '*Forrest Gump,*' as well as countless others. If there isn't such a challenging part, then settle for being a 'bad guy,' but give him a twist. Or find an outstanding part where you can play a gay role – they always attract critical comment. Physically or mentally challenged or gay, always give him or her one redeeming feature.

I've had, and continue to have, an amazingly blessed life. By the time I was thirty, I knew I'd had so many lucky breaks it didn't seem possible my good fortune wouldn't end soon. A novel based on my life wouldn't have been credible. I'm not saying for one second that I'm rich or famous – far from it. But somehow things have always fallen into place just when I was thinking they'd turn awry.

For instance, just when I thought I would have to give up all thoughts of a tertiary education so I could become the bread winner and look after my asthmatic and troubled mother; recently divorced and suffering badly from the '*Black Dog,*' along came a fairy godmother named Kit Adeane, a magnificent woman who paid for my education and set everything straight at home. And just when I thought I'd have to knuckle down to grown-up hard work to work as a barrister, along came a play that catapulted me into London's West End; an event which translated into the movie career that's kept the wolf from the door for nearly forty years. And when I hit fifty years of age and thought I was going to have to settle for the 'old fart' roles, along came directors of the caliber of Roger Spottiswoode and Roland Joffe; directors who made me feel I was back in the loop, about to be a part of the major league film world again; saved from television soap operas and commercials for Viagra and Cialis.

When I look back on my career, I've mostly have great memories. How I managed to avoid working with all the pain-in-the-arse directors and actors of the world amazes me. Everyone works with a few actors who think they know everything but in reality are as wooden as a park bench, as well as directors who believe they know how to direct feature films but have a television mindset. Yet for most of my career I've been lucky enough to work with some of the most accomplished actors in the business, and have been directed by the best directors imaginable. All my anecdotes have up till now only been shared with my closest friends at dinner parties, so now is my chance to see if I can remember a few and put them down on paper.

MY FIRST THEATRE ROLE – AGED SIX!

Was I born with the 'acting gene'? Maybe. If you think it's possible that a career choice is based on genetics.

My mother, Elizabeth Nolan, starred in London's West End opposite Rex Harrison.

My Mother, Elizabeth Nolan.

It was a time before the Second World War when Londoners were fond of light-hearted comedies. There was always a gorgeous young ingénue to delight theatergoers. My mother was one of these gorgeous actresses. Not only stunning looking, she was a fine actress (yes, I still like to use that word!) But alas, the war came and ended her career abruptly and she went on to become a journalist for the News Chronicle newspaper as a celebrity interviewer, lunching with the likes of Enrico Caruso in the Savoy Grill. I still have all her scrapbooks and I am amazed by how beautiful she looked in those days. As I grew up, she seldom talked about her acting days nor ever encouraged us to embark on a similar career path.

My mother in my grandmother's arms in the Blue Mountains. 1917.

Born in Queen Charlotte's hospital in August of 1946, I was soon living in Bad Oyenhausen in Germany. My father, Keith Briant, a former editor of the Oxford Isis, an author and poet before war broke out, had ended the war as a Lieutenant Colonel in the Irish Guards tank regiment, and was soon appointed Public Relations Officer for the Army on the Rhine.

So mum and dad, older brother Dermot and I packed our bags. Actually, my mum packed mine, as I was one year old. We went to live in a big family house the British conquering army had requisitioned from a German woman by the name of Frau Riedel. She was given the task of running it for us. She was more than happy to do this as Germany at this time was in a very poor state indeed; food was difficult to find outside of the confines of the Allied Army NAAFI, and starvation was endemic. So most Germans were very anxious to have their houses requisitioned, as they no longer faced starvation.

I grew up a little *German* boy, speaking German as my first language, chatting with my German nanny Anna-Marie, reticent to speak any English at all, something that soon proved an embarrassment to my father. Each time he entertained his fellow British army officers at home he used to say to me: *"Speak English, Shane."* I'd usually be hovering greedily close to the canapés (I was a fat and gluttonous child.)

Christenening at the Guards Chapel with my Godmother June Ross and my father, Colonel Keith Rutherford Briant.

"Nein! I will nicht," I'd shoot back. *"Ich bin ein kleiner Deutscher!"* No, I will not. I am a small German!

My Aunt Margaret recently told me that apparently the first sentence I ever spoke in English was addressed to my father at a cocktail party after I'd been brought down from my bedroom by Anna-Marie to be shown off to the officers' wives.

"Vot you vont?" I enquired of my father, stone-faced. The British officers' wives were horrified – possibly the war had taken the edge off their sense of humour.

Each Christmas Dermot and I would have a delicious *Knuspenhaus* made for us, fashioned out of biscuits and other sweet things. Our fresh *tannenbaum*, the Christmas tree, would be decorated with lighted candles. Today's safety-hounds would shudder – but back then I found the smell of pine and candle wax absolutely intoxicating. And to top it off, one of Frau Riedel's friends, a man we called *Der Holzschnitzer* because he carved delightful nativity items from wood, would give us some beautifully carved wooden toys.

I loved those years in Germany and when we had to return to England I missed the fabulous rose garden at the rear of the house. If ever I went missing, my mother would know where to find me. In the garden, my head buried amongst the petals of some flower, sniffing like a deranged bloodhound!

A dedicated flower-sniffer.

When I was five, we returned to England and moved into a big flat belonging to my brother Dermot's celebrated godmother, the wonderfully eccentric pioneer of birth control, Marie Stopes Roe. This lovely apartment was spacious, had lovely gardens back and front, and overlooked Kew Gardens.

Marie Stopes had a wonderful way with children. She never cooed and patted our heads. She treated Dermot and me as adults and discussed all manner of things with us as though we were grown-ups – religion, aliens from outer space, politics… everything! I think children appreciate this kind of behaviour – they loathe being patronized by grinning adults.

Marie Stopes lived on an estate near Dorking called *'Norbury Park.'* We'd visit for the weekend every now and then. Marie would send her vintage black Rolls Royce (driven by a vintage chauffeur) to pick up mum and my father, then Dermot and me at our school in Richmond, and we'd all cruise down to her big house. There were always chocolates in our bedroom when we arrived, and fresh cream for dinner – cream she'd made herself from the milk of her twin Jersey cows.

The reason Dermot and I found her so much fun was not just because she treated us both as equals, but also because she was so subperbly different from other adults. For example, on one weekend at *'Norbury Park'* she showed us a new addition to her family – a baby crocodile she was looking after for a friend. On another occasion, just before we went to bed, she recounted the story of how she'd been abducted by aliens from outer space, and had spent a whole day inside a UFO chatting to little green people, finally being delivered back to her home in the evening. We sat agog.

She firmly believed she'd live forever. Fitness and the right diet were fundamentally important to her. She'd swim around the lighthouse she owned at Portland Bill each day she was there, and then drink a pint of seawater. She was a powerhouse of a woman, but sadly died in 1958 aged seventy-seven after a long illness. Incidentally, my father wrote a splendid biography of Marie Stopes, which I highly recommend.

Aged six and a bit, I started my prep-school days at Kings House in Richmond, and it was there I came to love the stage. So, possibly it *was* in my genes, since my mother had never shared her London theatre memories with me nor even showed me her scrapbook. When the opportunity arose to play a part in the end of term production of *'Little Miss Muffet'* I knew I simply *had* to play the bad guy – *The Spider.'* My mother made me a brown costume that had four extra 'bits' to give me eight legs. I then scuttled around chasing *Little Miss Muffet* on stage. So, even then it seemed to me that the bad guys had the most fun.

I'd say that almost fifty years down the line more than ninety per cent of the roles I've played have been dodgy people; murderers, hired assassins, deviants, sociopaths, twisted serial killers. I love 'em all!

During my years at Kings House I was blissfully unaware that my parents were, in essence, practically separated. My father, Features Editor at *Newnes & Pearson*, a company that published amongst many other magazines *'Woman's Own,'* would leave for work before Dermot and I got out of bed, and would return when we were back in our beds. As we lay in bed each night we'd fool around until we heard a key in the front door. Then we were quiet as mice. So, close to my father I was not then, nor later – he never showed much interest in me. A shame, but a fact of life.

When I think of my father I think of driving through the night in Germany in his classic vintage Rolls Royce, while my mother cuddled me in the back seat. I remember very clearly looking out the window and seeing the dawn rise on the outskirts of Lindau and the Bodensee. It's funny what things are burnt into your brain.

I also remember that when I was six, and Dermot was nine, my father Keith would take mum and us boys to the refreshment bar at Kew Gardens Underground Station. He and mum would have drinks while we'd chugalug Vimtos (an old-fashioned English soft drink) as we sat on the platform. The game we were told to play (to keep us quiet, I think) was to correctly predict whether a red train or a green train would arrive next. Not exactly the most fun a kid can have on a Saturday morning, eh?

Playing 'Le Chef' in 'Le Café Crème' aged eight.

Kings House had a rich tradition of end of school entertainment. Each year they'd construct a stage in the main hall and three plays would be selected for production – one for the 'littlies', one for the middle age group, and one for the final year. I well remember my favourite role. It was a short French play produced when I was aged nine called *'Le Café Crème.'*

I played *'Le Chef '*– the head of a band of criminals. I dressed up in my mother's clothes, and smoked a cigarette in an overly long cigarette holder. It's interesting to note that in 1954 no one at prep school took issue with a nine-year-old smoking, so long as it was on stage. The entire play was performed in French, and I worked long and hard on my accent. Each year after the play, my father would take us to an early dinner at an Italian restaurant named *'Valcheras.'* I was only to see my father once after he finally moved out of our Kew Gardens flat. It was odd living without a father, but I'd seen so little of him up until then that it didn't affect me too dramatically. Yet, despite the fact that mum disliked my father Keith with a vengeance after he left her for another woman, I know she led a lonely life from that moment onwards – she'd also become the bread winner, and there was precious little alimony granted to her in the divorce settlement. She had a quirky sense of humour. An example of this was when she visited me in Sydney aged seventy. She walked into a shop in the Rocks run by Aboriginal Australians and asked if they had a *'pointing bone,'* for sale because she currently had a grudge against the man who delivered her newspapers. When you *'point the bone'* very nasty things happen to the pointee!

Dermot and I loved growing up in the mid to late 50's. We were very close brothers. Because he was four years older than me he usually called the shots and I liked to imitate nearly everything he did or said. I certainly picked up his very dark and tasteless black humour! Probably inherited from my mother.

This was the time of coffee bars such as *Pronto* and the *Wimpy-burger*. My music heroes were Guy Mitchell, Lonnie Donnegan, Bill Haley and, at a pinch, Tommy Steele. Dermot's heroes were composer Arnold Schoenburg (Pierrot Lunaire, was his favourite rather creepy piece) and philosopher Freidrich Nietzsche. While I was an average kid who wanted to play the guitar, he was happiest reading existentialist poets. I well remember one year, when he couldn't have been older than eleven, he began sticking sheets of paper on his bedroom walls. One I remember word for word – it was stuck above his bed. *"The sclerosis of objectivity is the annihilation of existence.'* I'm NOT kidding. I asked him what it meant – I was seven years old – he replied simply that I'd find the answer *'too depressing.'*

There wasn't much violence in Kew, nor Richmond. If there was a murder in London it was headline news. Whatever drugs were to be had, they weren't easily available to the average young boy or girl, so drug abuse wasn't rampant. Generally, Richmond and Kew were safe to grow up in.

My mother had to watch every penny, though I never felt deprived of anything other than a father's affection. We ate well, even though mum would often cook up delicious dishes, then days later would divulge the ingredients. *'Heart stew.'* *'Tripe à la mode du Caen.'* Ugh!

We'd holiday at Deal in Kent for a week each year. That was

great. I loved the seaside. As did Dermot. So I was doubly delighted when my mum told me that my father had asked if I'd like to spend a few days with him at Bognor Regis. Dermot was still at boarding school so couldn't join me.

Since Keith had access to me in the divorce settlement there wasn't much mum could do about it, so she asked me if I would like to go or would prefer *'to have nothing to do with that cruel man.'* I replied I'd take my chances with *'the cruel man.'*

My visit to Bognor proved to be my debut as a cabaret singer! At the time I was a huge fan of Lonnie Donnegan and his skiffle group. I'd learned to play the guitar and had formed my own skiffle group at Kings House. I took the Underground to Kensington where my father was now living, and when he met me and saw I was carrying a guitar, he suggested he might ask the manager of the 'Royal Norfolk Hotel' whether I might 'jam' with the three tuxedoed middle-aged musicians who played 'musak' every night in the formal dining room.

When we arrived in Bognor, Keith was true to his word and the manager thought it a great idea. I met with the three musicians and we played some songs; *'Cumberland Gap,'* and *'Puttin' on the Style,'* amongst others The professional musicians were good sports and up for anything, so we had a ball, despite their knowing diddlysquat about rock and roll, or skiffle. After an hour or so the manager of the hotel joined us and suggested I might like to sing in the dining room that evening with the band! I was ecstatic! The dining room was a huge room that seated over three hundred people. I wasn't in the least nervous, immediately insisting my father buy me some green fluro socks to match my green short-sleeved shirt and khaki shorts.

"Bright green socks? What on earth do you think you'll look like?" my father objected.

"It's what all cool people are wearing," I replied.

That night I played my first 'gig,' and felt like a real rock star. Many years later Bob Fosse would let me know how good I was as both a singer and a dancer – but that embarrassing episode comes later.

The interesting thing about my French play, *'Le Café Crème'* was that all these years later I still can recite the exact lines, and it's proven very useful throughout my career when casting directors ask me how fluent my French is. Instead of lying by stating I'm fluent, I simply launch into my long childhood speech as *'Le Chef.'* Invariably, the casting director waves a hand after five sentences, quite satisfied. It's a good tip – learn a short passage in French, Italian and German. Incidentally, it was my fist 'drag' role – it wouldn't be my last!

PUBLIC SCHOOL AND MORE THEATRE.

Of course as a child a career on the boards and in television and film were far from my thoughts; everyone was telling me I should do something sensible, such as become a lawyer since my father had studied law and was a member of the Middle Temple. But as it happened, the next school I attended was, like Kings House, well known for its school theatre productions. It even hosted European tours of Shakespeare.

The school was Haileybury & Imperial Service College. My father had been to school there, my brother was there already, yet I'd been concentrating so much on skiffle and sport, that I actually failed my Common Entrance exam.

Much to my mother's chagrin, this gave my father the perfect opportunity to suggest to the Family Court judge that a public school education would be wasted on a dullard such as me and that I should go to a secondary modern school instead. He argued his case in court. *"Shane's not very bright,"* he said in court. *"Coombe House secondary modern would suit him well,"* My mother was furious. A State School? No way!

In the fifties, England was incredibly class conscious. When I was thirteen it was expected that upper-middle class children would, as a matter of course, go to public schools rather than mingle with the hoi polloi at State Schools – this was unthinkable to my mother and grandmother. Grammar Schools were *kind* of okay because it proved the child in question was 'brainy.' However, since my father was thinking of remarrying, the prospect of saving on public school fees was uppermost in his mind.

However, my steadfast mum wouldn't have a bar of this. The judge summed up mum's case as follows. *"The father went to Haileybury. Shane's brother Dermot is currently studying at Haileybury, so providing the boy can pass the Common Entrance at his second attempt, he will go there too!"*

And while on the subject of English snobbery I can admit now that one of the chief reasons I chose to live in Australia was to escape this ghastly English trait.

As it turned out, when she heard of my plight, Kit Adeane, the wife of my mother's childhood friend Sir Robert Adeane, offered to pay all my school fees. This was a huge relief for mum. Kit thought I'd make a good friend for her son, James, who was three years younger than me and needed someone to bond with since his elder sister, Rose Mary Poppy (everyone called her Dobbie) was his senior by almost five years.

During the following eight years I spent most of my holidays with the Adeane family in their beautiful estate in Essex named *'Quendon.'* Also at their huge farm in Bawdsey, Suffolk. To me, both estates were somewhat akin to Alain Fournier's *'Lost Domain,'* the best thing was that I was no longer on the front line as far as family problems were concerned.

It was the most wonderful altruistic maternal gesture of mum to virtually 'lose' me to Kit for all my holidays from then on – she always thought of my welfare first. I know how much she missed me during the following few years even though I went home every now and then to check on her.

Hunting, shooting and fishing? I was too young to hunt, and

the Adeane's, despite having two fine horses in their stables, didn't care to hunt. But I certainly fished on the Spey in Scotland, and shot pheasant and partridge in Suffolk and Essex, as well as duck at Hickling Broad in Norfolk.

The shooting parties often included the finest shots in England, such as Aubrey Buxton, the Duke of Edinburgh, Angus Ogilvy and Charles, Prince of Wales – then aged twelve.

My first salmon caught on the Spey in Scotland. 1959.

On the Queen Mary. Kit Adeane in black. Dobbie 2nd from left. James far right.

However, while I was being looked after and pampered by very rich people in lovely surroundings, my brother Dermot was not so lucky. I constantly felt guilty about this but could do nothing. Dermot never appeared jealous. Yet I was living the life of Riley and he was struggling to make ends meet.

Of course there was no reason that Kit should have looked after my brother as well as me. Besides, I was thirteen and the right age to be a friend to James while Dermot was seventeen. So my elder brother was left to look after mum, and consequently his holidays were not exactly the same as mine. I'd take the Queen Mary to New York, first class, and then on to their mansion in Barbados, waited upon hand and foot by George the Barbadian butler and the two Barbadian girls Mary and Pearline.

Dermot would simply mooch around Richmond, and in the evening prop up the bar at the *Three Pidgeons* pub in Richmond.

During the years 1960 to 1968 Dobbie, James and I had such

happy holidays. Quite often James and I would be joined by Francoise Gilot's children, Claude and Paloma Picasso. Claude was one year younger than me, but about ten years my senior when it came to sophistication. He chained smoked, drank wine, and looked super cool the way he handled cigarettes – very adult. Paloma was a sweetheart, aged ten to my thirteen. Quiet yet fun. Very dark and striking.

Playing vingt-et-un with Paloma, aged 10 in Scotland.

On one occasion I was sent by Kit to visit Francoise and her children in Neuilly – to brush up on my French. I can't recall why James didn't join me.

It was the week before Christmas and Claude and I were chatting in his room when the postman called at the door. Claude returned with an annoyed face and a huge envelope. *"It's from Papa,"* he told me. *"I told him. I want a bicycle, and this is what he gives me."* I apologize to Claude if the exact words are not correct, but I've never forgotten this incident because he then slit open the envelope and pulled out a Christmas card. It was a gouache of a Santa Claus with *'Claude'* and the date at the top, and signed at the bottom – not *'Papa'* but *'Picasso.'* He tossed it into a corner. I wanted

SO much to do a 'deal, 'a bicycle for the card' was my idea, but I realized it was soooooo incorrect to suggest such a thing.

Before I left on this trip Kit had given me money to buy some tortoiseshell combs. She told me to buy twelve – she never did things by halves. I was handed a wad of fivers because these special combs cost around one hundred and ten pounds each at the time. Imagine what they cost today. Before I returned home to London I visited the upscale shop in the Rue de Rivoli where I'd been told to go and asked the stitched-up salesman how much a Morabito comb might cost. He looked down at me – I was thirteen – and smiled the most horribly patronizing smile.

"Six mille francs, Monsieur," he told me and looked away and yawned.

I stared at him for three seconds.

"Alors…J'acheterai douze, s'il vous plait, Monsieur," I replied.

I'll take twelve then.

I pulled out my wad of notes and began riffling through them. You should have seen the man's expression as he wrapped the combs. He would have liked to throttle me. I was thrilled. The best fun I'd had for many years! I'm not sure I'm exact about how many francs – but it was a total of well over a thousand pounds.

Over the years, I've seen less and less of Claude and Paloma. I miss them both. But that's the way the world revolves.

Years later, Claude took Wendy and me out to a fabulous restaurant in Paris, a swimming pool that had reinvented itself as a restaurant. I shall never forget the pâté de fois gras I was served that night. The slab was five inches by four, and half an inch thick. I no longer eat goose liver because of the cruel force-feeding, but back then I thought little about it. To my shame. Now Claude spends much of his time at his Place Vendôme offices where he works tirelessly on organizing, collating and looking after his father's works worldwide. If you have to work, try to find an office in the

Place Vendôme!

As most people know, Paloma became New York's society queen and a magnificent designer of jewellery!

The last time I met her was when she came to Australia to showcase a new *parfum*. She was only fifteen when I'd last seen her, and now that she was close to forty, I had no idea what to expect.

She was staying in a suite at the Sebel Townhouse in Sydney. A butler opened the door and asked me if I'd care for a drink while I awaited Mademoiselle Picasso. I had a gin and tonic. When she walked in from the bedroom I was stunned by the look of her. She was darkly *very* beautiful and her wide intense eyes were magic! Though I don't know much about couture clothes, her exquisite dark green dress had to have been a Coco Chanel vintage classic. All the jewellery she wore was of course designed by herself. Was this the young girl I'd played rummy with in Scotland when she was ten? We sat and talked for about an hour. It was like talking to a childhood pal; Paloma had no airs and graces whatsoever. Finally, she told me she had to go to some television studio to be interviewed. She handed me several different bottles of the new 'Paloma' scent to give to Wendy, who happened to be working that day and couldn't join us. Then I left. I haven't seen her since. I hope I will again soon.

PUBLIC SCHOOL DAYS, TOURING EUROPE.

Haileybury is a very different institution now to what it was when I went there in 1960. Thankfully there were no longer cold baths, but it certainly had an austere atmosphere, and the senior prefects still thrashed the new boys as and when they felt like it. These were still the days of 'fagging' – the younger boys shone the shoes of the senior boys and made their beds, as well as cooking them breakfast, fetching them goodies from the tuck-shop, and generally waiting on them hand and foot. I was determined not to be humiliated by any casual thrashing, so kept my nose very clean indeed. I didn't enjoy my first year there at all. I couldn't come to terms with other boys treating me like an unpaid servant, yet I didn't rebel for fear of the cane. The worst thing about Haileybury as far as I was concerned was that none of the lavatories had doors. Staff members who professed to know a thing or two about 'young boys' were of the opinion that they'd get up to mischief anywhere they could lock themselves away from the prying eyes of masters and prefects.

There was a vast lavatory block in those days called *'The White City'*, called that because it contained about a hundred white Twyford's lavatory stalls – all without doors. I was so embarrassed by this lack of privacy that I took a heap of Imodium tablets and ended up very uncomfortably bunged-up for the best part of a week!

The best part of the day was after sports when we had an hour or so to go down to the tuck shop, buy biscuits and make a cup of tea in someone's rooms.

Teatime at Haileybury & I.S.C. 1960.

The school had a rich theatre tradition, and each year a Shakespearean production would be mounted. During my first year the chosen play was Shakespeare's *'Richard II.'*

My brother Dermot played Richard II, I was Queen Eleanor.

It was the first Shakespeare play I had ever taken part in and Dermot gave me a great deal of coaching as to how to speak the lines properly.

We took the school play to Sweden and Denmark. Stockholm and Alkmaar were my favourites as I stayed with some stunningly beautiful girls there. On one occasion I stayed with a family who owned a milk farm an hour from the theatre. I would spend the day on the farm with the cows, then return to play Queen Eleanor.

Dermot, a naturally talented actor as well as being ten times cleverer than I was, was cast as Richard and I was cast as his queen – Eleanor. Looking back, I am amazed at the quality of these productions. All the students took the theatre very seriously, as did the master in charge.

The tours abroad served to introduce us school boys to other languages and cultures. One year, just for a change, we took the

Mikado to Denmark. As my voice was very strong and hadn't yet broken I played *Dame Carruthers*. This wasn't the last time I dressed in women's clothes – as an actor, I might add! Two up and going strong.

"The Yeoman of the Guard." That's me in the dress as Dame Carruthers.

Aged sixteen, at Haileybury, a house prefect entered my study during 'prep' and told me that Mr. Harris, my housemaster, wanted to see me. This was a summons similar to being told *'Granny's on the roof,'* so I knew something was up. On entering Mr. Harris' study, he looked up, met my eyes, and said: *"I am afraid I have some bad news for you, Briant. Your father died last night."*

I stared back at him, unsure what I should say or do. You have to realize I had seen my father only twice in the previous ten years, so I simply had an empty feeling. Yet clearly some tears were expected. Or perhaps a tiny internal shriek?

Harris waited some moments then asked me if I needed some time alone in his study, or might prefer to go back to my studies. I chose the second option.

"Jolly good show, Briant," he replied, beaming.

A week later Dermot came to take me to my father's funeral. Arriving on a Saturday at midday he was informed by Harris that it'd be appropriate to stay and watch the school rugger match before leaving for the Finchley crematorium. *"Haileyburians should support their school team,"* he observed, and this was, after all, the 'Uppingham match.' *"Besides, the funeral isn't until four, is it? You should have plenty of time to get there,"* he observed kindly.

THE SIXTIES AND TRANSITIONS.

For me, the sixties were even headier than the fifties – if that were possible. When I wasn't at Quendon or at school I'd be in Carnaby Street buying skin-tight velvet jeans, walking around Soho looking at photos of semi-nude girls outside the Raymond Revue Bar and listening to the best music in town at the Marquee Club or at Ronnie Scott's jazz club.

I'd found I quite liked alcohol. Mostly anything that was either sweet, such as cider, or could be sweetened, such as gin and lime juice. I was hardly a binge drinker – kids weren't in the sixties, but I did get pissed occasionally and always threw up. I was unaware of 'binge drinking'. Back then if you drank a bit and smoked cigarettes one felt rather adult. (I actually hated smoking but forced myself into the habit – one I would find almost impossible to kick forty-five years later. The folly of youth!) But if you could persuade pretty girls to have a few drinks, the chances of some heavy petting in the back seat of a Mini Minor shot up dramatically.

These were the days of the Beatles and the Rolling Stones. Lonnie Donnegan? Bah, he and Cliff Richard were now old hat. And here's a strange and wonderful story. Kit's husband, Sir Robert, was a board member of Decca at that time, and on one particular day attended a meeting where one of the points on the agenda was to decide which of several pop and rock groups the Decca label would sign. That particular month, amongst the contenders were both the

Beatles *and* the Rolling Stones.

Sir Robert was in his sixties at the time and was hardly a rock and roll enthusiast, so he asked for the opinions of those at Decca who knew a thing or two. They chose the Beatles. The Rolling Stones were discarded. Quite an interesting day at the office, eh?

After five years at Haileybury, I began thinking of University, despite having always been told by my masters that I wasn't *'University material.'* I'd been a very late starter – as my Granny used to say. I'd failed my Common Entrance once, and entered Haileybury in the D grade. In my second year I moved up to the C grade, then up to the B and then the A grade by the time I was a senior. But University? The teaching staff didn't see me making it. However, I surprised them all when I was offered at place at Trinity College Dublin having achieved some quite 'tasty' A-level results.

Kit insisted I study something useful. English and Fine Arts were out of the question – utterly useless! And since she was paying the fees, Legal Science it was! I knew I wanted to pursue an acting career, but in the meantime was resigned to be groomed as a barrister – a solicitor 's life was deemed to be a little too vulgar.

I knew I'd little chance of making a financially viable career as an actor – after all, how many actors succeeded in the 'biz'? One per cent? The other 99% chose to *think* of themselves as actors, while waiting on tables until they gave up and went into business. So when I was offered a place at TCD, I was ecstatic!

My rather too serious school headmaster wrote in my final report; *'He has the air of the dilettante. He will not go far.'* Quite why he'd written this blunt one-liner on my report I couldn't fathom, and quite what he hoped to achieve by voicing this miserable opinion baffled me. Dilettante? Me? Because I enjoyed the arts? When I read my final report, I thumbed my nose at him and laughed. As did my mother *and* Kit.

"Let's see how far I can get," I muttered to myself.

HALCYON DAYS AT TRINITY COLLEGE DUBLIN.

I am a firm believer in karma. How else can one explain the serendipity of the strong tradition of theatre existing not only at my preparatory school, but Haileybury *and* at Trinity College Dublin?

Yet again, it was due to Kit Adeane's generosity that I was able to study there. I was given an amount to live on by her lawyers, a man who was always referred to in a somewhat Dickensian way as *'Mister Phillips,'* and she provided in her will that if anything should happen to her, her estate would pay for any future studies I should care to take.

I was also given a Mini Moke car, which was the coolest thing around at the time. I would drive all my acting chums into the Wicklow Hills or down to the beach. It was heaven. And in my first term I enrolled in the University Theatre group, named the Trinity Players.

This was the most blissful time. I was soon to experience everything for the first time – personal freedom, living in my own flat, studying law, falling in love with the girl everyone was in love with but very few managed to end up naked with, behaving badly in pubs, and learning how to become a professional actor.

In the mid sixties the snobby thing was to try to get into Oxford and Cambridge. But if you weren't quite up to that mark you did your best to squeeze into TCD. The alternative was to either go to Scotland – far too cold and austere – or put your name down for 'a red brick university.' 'Red brick' was the phrase that made most elitist public school boys shudder in those days – it was Oxbridge or nothing. Well, with the exception of TCD, the college of choice of Wilde, Goldsmith, Yeats, Swift and Beckett.

Things have changed a lot now at TCD – non-Catholic Irish students are in the majority there. In my day it was the first choice of Englishmen and women who had failed to secure a place at

Oxbridge. But don't get me wrong for me it was a *huge* honour. TCD was then, and still is, a stellar University famous for its medical and law schools. And not only did it have similar scholastic integrity to Oxbridge, it also had a tradition of theatre very similar to OUDS at Oxford, and the Footlights at Cambridge. When I arrived in Dublin in 1967 it was a very different capital city to the one we know today. The standard of living was a shadow of what it would be when the European financial institutions decided Dublin would be the new Zurich, and the city became expensive, boutique and so decidedly hip. Back then the majority of Dubliners living anywhere other than the privileged suburbs were barely able to put meat and two vegetables on the table. Yet despite that, all Dubliners drank like fishes and smoked in a somewhat frenzied way. The pubs were always packed like a sardine tin, and you had to fight your way through a dense fog of cigarette smoke to get to the bar. I loved this fantastic atmosphere reminiscent of J.P Donleavy's *'The Ginger Man.'* Sadly, all that is now a thing of the past. Maybe we're all healthier and less likely to die of lung cancer, but as far as I'm concerned, pubs have maybe ten per cent of the atmosphere they had when I was living in Dublin. The Irish Republican Movement was still very much in evidence at that time. There was a pub called *'The Brazen Head'* where the English TCD students were not at all welcome. Of course this made having a few pints there a challenge. But each time I sampled a *'Smithwicks'* or two in *'The Head,'* I'd feel eyes boring holes into my back, and this made my companions and me very uneasy. The last time I returned there I again visited *'The Brazen Head.'* It'd changed its name to *'Ye Olde Brazon Head'* for the tourists. There were charabancs outside ready to pick up Japanese and American holidaymakers, and inside there was a small Gaelic band playing rather obvious Irish music. I left, depressed.

As I write, Ireland is undergoing a downward economic trend. Thanks to the hedge funds, Freddie Mac and Fannie Mae, Ireland has become an unwitting, innocent victim. I hope things get better; after Australia, my heart remains in Ireland, the Irish are a wonderful people.

'Legal Science' was a superb subject to study at TCD because it required little more than turning up for lectures, making notes,

learning them by heart, then spewing them out at exam time. No conceptual thinking was either encouraged or thought useful. So when I enrolled, I looked forward to spending four wonderful years doing exactly as I liked. It was four years at TCD as opposed to three at Oxbridge – another plus for the Irish University! I well remember my first lecture. It was Company Law. By then I had bonded with one of my fellow Law students, John McBratney. As we entered, I nudged John, pointed to the benches in the huge lecture hall and said, *"John! Just as I thought. These are de shares and those are debentures."* For those unfamiliar with legal terms, I was making a pun on shares and debentures & chairs and the benches." Years later John reminded me of my quip. I was pleased.

Although I made certain I never missed a lecture, my heart was always elsewhere – either in the university theatre or falling for beautiful young students, very few of whom returned my advances. In my first year my dreary expectation was that in four years time I'd be following in my father's footsteps at the Middle Temple, becoming a barrister in the depths of Dorset, ending my days as a Judge at the Bristol Assizes.

However, I'd lived a charmed life for some years now and although I didn't know it, it was to continue.

My first role at the Players was Cassius in a production of *Julius Caesar*. Martin *'News at Ten'* Lewis, played Mark Anthony and I secured the small role of Metellus Cimber.

It was not to be my best moment on stage. On the first night, the conspirators walked on stage and lined up. Each of us was asked our opinion of Caesar until, after a good three minutes of sweating and waiting to speak for the first time, Mark Anthony turned to me and asked the question, *"What says Metellus Cimber?"*

My heart was beating like a jungle drum. I'd been mouthing my first line for the three minutes I'd been on stage. As Martin stared at me, I took one step forward, my tongue turned to plastic, and several seconds of silence followed.

"Line?" I mumbled weakly.

Hey ho, I still wince when I think of that moment. Mercifully I was not to dry again for around thirty-two years.

In my first year at TCD I had digs north of the city near to the abattoir. I shared a room with my late and dear Haileybury school friend Andrew Tozer. Two other young men occupied the bedroom opposite ours on the first floor. Our landlady reminded me of the famous landlady I'd read about in George Orwell's *'The Road to Wigan Peer,'* where our hero decides to decamp from his rooming house after seeing his landlady carry a chamber pot down the stairs moments before preparing breakfast *'with her thumb well below the level of the urine.'*

During my first year at TCD cult legend director Roger Corman came to Dublin to shoot *'Von Richthofen and Brown.'* The average age of the German pilots was very young indeed. I met with Roger and he cast me as one of the Red Baron's pilots. The Baron was played by John Phillip Law. Gene Corman produced. I looked about twelve years old.

The filming was plagued by terrible accidents. On one occasion the chopper containing the D0P and four other crew members flew into the wing of a bi-plane and all died. On another occasion a bi-plane plunged into the costume trailer – fortunately no one was in inside. However, the pilot died. I remember being on set when the news of the loss of the aerial director of photography was delivered to the producer, Gene. I didn't know what was being said, but I could see by the expressions it was very bad news. I moved closer. The aerial photographer was a Belgium, the finest in the world. I heard Roger say, "Find out who's the next best. Get him over here. Fast!"

My other best friend at University was another Haileyburian by the name of Anthony OBrien. His father was an eminent physician and the family owned a vast Georgian house in Fitzwilliam Square, in the centre of Dublin. When I was hungry I'd show up at Anto's house and together we'd raid the fridge. Anthony was a brilliant student, yet gave up Medicine to concentrate on becoming a potter. He's the kind of man who can do anything. One time he decided he'd make a violin. Not an easy task, but when finished it was a joy to play. Another time he fashioned a beautiful replica of a medieval crumhorn. Perfect in every way.

That first year was a thrill a minute. Never before had I been the master of my own destiny – there'd always been some adult telling me what to do. Now I was on an allowance to do with as I pleased; not only that, I had a sea between me and my somewhat aberrant family.

Probably at this point it might be helpful to give some family background. When Dermot left school he turned down a place at Merton College Oxford because he thought my father's mother Alice had 'fixed it' somehow, and he disliked her hugely. In fact such an arrangement *had* been made, but only on the basis of Dermot's outstanding A-Level results. Nonetheless, he turned Merton down, waited to get a Scholarship to Cambridge, and missed out on everything.

I believe the lack of a university education was the catalyst that turned a hugely bright young man into someone who had a grudge against the world in general and he felt he could wreak his particular brand of revenge against society by taking advantage of certain people he referred to a 'smart alecs.' He genuinely thought he could get away with all manner of 'dodgy' deals. More often than not, he did. I'll give one amusing example and then move on.

Dermot bought a book *'The Three Pigeons,'* for just two weeks. That's when he felt he knew as much as any London dealer in Egyptian and Roman artifacts. He probably did; as I said before, Dermot was very intelligent indeed. He did very well for three years until he made his first mistake. He'd bought a first rate Roman marble statue that was so perfect that none of the London dealers would touch it – the piece was just too good to be true. However, Dermot was adamant that it was genuine. Frustrated, he took a hammer to the statue one night and broke off one foot. He then took it to Hamburg and sold the torso to a delighted German dealer. But Dermot could not let things rest the way they were. No. The foot was sitting around in his flat in Richmond serving no useful purpose, so he decided to sell that too. After dipping the damaged ankle in various acid solutions to make the patina seem plausible, he had me take it in to the Folio Society. We rehearsed everything I had to say. Dermot was convinced that so long as Mister Eade was convinced that I was a gullible idiot, he'd buy it from me. I dutifully played the stooge to please my big brother. Mr. Eade bought it for forty quid, believing it was worth hundreds.

It goes without saying that Mr. Eade at the Folio Society then happened to sell the foot to the very German who'd bought the torso from Dermot and at once the game was up. It was the end of Dermot's career as a dealer in antiquities – no one would deal with him again.

My first University year flew by like the Concorde in better days. And contrary to my hopes and inflated expectations regarding sex with gorgeous fellow students – a love affair every five minutes – I found it virtually impossible to interest any of the girls in doing more than hold my hand. I was far too shy.

I remember the *'Freshers Ball,'* an occasion where the first year students get together and make friends. I asked about fifty girls to accompany me but only with a day to go locked in a date; a lovely Northern Irish girl called Gillian, whose surname I cannot for the life of me recall. I apologize to her now. I informed her I was attending the costume ball dressed as Henry the Eighth. *"Perhaps that might give you an idea as to who you might come as,"* I said. When I picked up my date on the night of the ball, she was dressed in black tights and a black and yellow top. I looked at her confused.

"I'm a bee!" she told me delightedly.

With Gillian ("I'm a bee!") at the Freshers Ball.

At the start of my second year, I moved into 'digs' in a slightly more salubrious part of Dublin–a delightful house in Ballsbridge that I shared with a philosophy student by the name of Stephen Remington, and Bob Collins, a floor manager at *Radio Telefís Eireann*, the national television company. Bob had the look of one of Éamon De Valera's revolutionaries. The girls? They just loved him. He played Bossa Nova on his guitar, and could charm them to the bedroom in minutes. He definitely had a way with girls.

By contrast I was gawky. Bob and I shared one vast bedroom (with two beds, I might stress) and Stephen Remington had the single room. Bob had such a 'free' attitude to his sex life that quite often I would wake to hear low excited moans in the bed opposite. And frequently there were knickers and bit's of earrings scattered on the bedroom floor as I made my way to the kitchen in the morning. To this day I can't really understand his huge charisma – he wasn't exactly an Adonis. But that's not the point with the ladies, is it? I think it was his confidence; he had no fear of being turned down because no one ever did. Me, I could never bring myself to make the first move. I well remember taking out a gorgeous girl for many weeks and finally stopping my Mini Moke, looking at her, doe-eyed, and asking, *"Would you mind very much if I kissed you?"*

She replied *"Yes, I would.'*

I asked, *'Er...why?'*

'Because you actually asked my permission."

I learned from that mstake.

During the four years I spent at TCD I appeared in any number of theatre productions. The production I was most proud of was Michael Bogdan's (I believe he now calls himself *Bogdanovic*) production of *'Under Milk Wood'* in which I played *'First Voice'*. This production was so well received by the critics – they reviewed Trinity Players as a professional theatre – that it transferred to one of the most celebrated professional theatres in Dublin, the Gate Theatre, made world famous by Michael Mac Liamoir.

Subtle (Shane Bryant), Dol Common (Cathy Roberts), in a scene from "The Alchemist", which opened at Players last night.

With Cathy Roberts in the Players production of 'The Alchemist.'

Amongst a host of other plays I appeared in were *'The Glass Menagerie'* with now famous Sorcha Cusack, daughter of the legendary Cyril Cusack, as Laura, *'The Importance of Being Ernest,'* *'The Alchemist,'* where I had such great fun playing Subtle, and *'Romeo and Juliet'* in a production that alternated night by night between two Romeos and two Juliets. One of the Juliets was my girlfriend – not my Juliet, the other one! Incidentally, Sorcha played Brad Pitts mum many years later in the film *'Snatch.'*

GOING PRO.

IRISH TELEVISION AND THEATRE.

Luck is everything in setting a career alight, isn't it? Of course – that's always been true. In my case luck came to me in the form of someone who had seen quite a few of my Trinity Players' productions. He suggested to a director at *Raideo Teilefis Éireann* that I might be suitable to play a young Hamlet opposite the legendary Irish actor Maureen Toal in a television series titled *'Shakespeare for Schools.'* This was to be my first stab at acting for a camera – albeit a television camera.

A well-known Irish television director by the name of Louis Lenton who saw my television Hamlet when it aired then sent me a telegram asking if I would be available to play the young Andri in Max Frisch's *'Andorra.'* Again it was for RTE.

I accepted at once. Milo O'Shea played my adoptive father – one of the very few people I have ever met who has bushier eyebrows than me.

But it was being cast by Nora Lever as Hamlet in the theatre production that was the biggest stepping-stone yet.

Nora used to mount productions of plays that were featured in the school curriculum of any particular year, and since her funds were limited, she needed young talent who would accept the basic minimum wage – actors who didn't much care for the financial aspect of the work, but were looking to be discovered. So in her professional production of *Julius Caesar* at the Eblana Theatre, I played Cassius – another glorious 'bad guy,' and in *Hamlet* I had a stab, for a change, at being a good guy.

My close friends from the Trinity Players came to see both shows and most were rather snooty. *Shane? Playing Hamlet?*

Professionally? I don't think so. I was actually a tad hurt that they could be so less than supportive. Maybe they were jealous, as it was a major professional theatrical role and they had yet to turn pro. Anyway, who wouldn't kill to play Hamlet? Nevertheless, I was a little disappointed that the friends I had acted with in *'Under Milk Wood'* could so easily pooh-pooh the production.

'Hamlet' at the Eblana Theatre Dublin. 1970.

However, I was relieved to find the Dublin theatre critics were more generous. *'Teenage Hamlet alive and original,'* was my favourite quote, in the Irish Times.

Although it was hardly in the same league as the Royal Shakespeare Company, I felt our production had *some* merit and it certainly went down extremely well with the kids. That had been its purpose – not to impress the theatre cognoscenti. The Dublin Evening Press went even further. *'I have seen twenty-six interpretations of the role, and Briant's Hamlet may well have caught that little-boy-lost quality that has eluded at least one of our leading actors... this is the real Hamlet of our day and age.'* I liked this man immediately and drew his sage words to the attention of all my pals at the Trinity Players, but few were impressed and all professed not to have seen the review.

There were three matinées a week of Hamlet. Each afternoon, the theatre would fill with around four hundred children aged between eight and seventeen, all of them clutching bags of sweets and crisps bought at the concession shop in the foyer (some way had to be found of making enough money to mount the production, and Nora reckoned sweets and crisps were 'it'.) All had copies of the text balanced on their knees. And since they all had the school edition, the page turning every minute and a half sounded like a small plane flying through the theatre.

My favourite recollection of this production of Hamlet was when Claudius knelt very close to the edge of the stage and began his speech *'My words fly up, my thoughts remain below: Words without thoughts never to heaven go.'* The kids closest to the sage would invariably play a game to see who could bounce a boiled sweet off Pascal Perry's bald head.

My second favourite moment was one afternoon as I lay in Horatio's arms. As he said, *"Now cracks a noble heart. Good night sweet prince, and flights of angels sing thee to thy rest!"* I distinctly heard a child sobbing somewhere in the stalls. Seconds later a tiny voice called out to me. *"Oh jez! Don't die, Hamlet. Don't feckin' die!"*

With the end of the run, a few more people in the Dublin theatre biz knew who I was. And quite a few young Irish actors had taken a dislike to the marauding Englishman who had arrived from London and snaffled the role of Hamlet. But there was another bonus in playing my first, and up till now my last Shakespearean lead. The manufacturers of a new heater called the *'Hamlet'* enquired whether I would agree to having a life size cut out of me in my Hamlet black velvet costume mounted in the window of the gas showrooms in Stephen's Green. I asked for and received a hundred pounds, and for the following six months was ridiculed by *all* my Trinity friends.

After my *'Shakespeare for Schools'* stint, I went back to the Players Theatre and several productions later was asked whether I would like to play the role of *'Cowboy'* in a production of *'The Boys in the Band'* in the vast two thousand seat Olympia theatre. I agreed at once, though I was concerned that my lack of 'hunkiness' – I was a snake-hipped lad weighing in at just under eleven stone – might be a drawback, as *'Cowboy'* was a gorgeous *'American hustling hunk.'*

Three weeks into rehearsals the producer took me to one side.

"I'm afraid I'm going to have to fire you, Shane."

I responded *"Why?"*

"Because you are not hunky enough."

I was shattered. *"But I'm the same size now as I was three weeks ago."*

He studied me. *"Maybe. The thing is I never really looked at you then."*

I was mortified. It was the first time in my pro life I had been fired before, and more importantly I was going to miss the eleven pounds weekly wage I'd been offered.

My producer could see my disappointment, so he came up with a novel idea. *"Hey, Shane. Tell you what. You become our understudy and I raise your money to seventeen quid."*

Although this helped assuage the embarrassment of having to tell my Trinity colleagues that I had been fired, I was still pretty glum. *"Who do I understudy?"* I asked.

"Everyone," was the swift reply – our producer was not a generous man at heart.

Luckily for me, no one fell sick, but on the final Saturday the cast played a nasty trick on me, telling me with only fifteen minutes to go I would have to fill in for Michael, the lead character, played by American, Doug Lambert. As the five was called I was still vomiting into the loo, clutching the text. The entire cast finally burst into the toilets and surprised me, shouting, *"JOKE!"*

Some joke.

In my last year at TCD, the Players Committee put me in charge of organizing Sunday evening entertainment. It was normally a very roughly cobbled together variety show giving everyone a chance to show what they could do; the emphasis being on amusement, music and humour. I remember one Saturday being asked by a fellow Trinity Player if he could possibly have 'a spot' because he wanted to showcase his talent for singing and playing the guitar. This was a problem that particular week as I already had a full list of attractions. But he wouldn't drop off, so I said, *"Well, all right Chris. But make it just two songs. Okay?"* As he left the theatre I called after him, *"Oh… and please - not your own shit if you don't mind. Can you make them Beatles songs?"* The young singer involved was Chris de Burgh. A fat lot I knew about talent and songs. Three years later he opened at the King's Road Theatre in Chelsea as the opener for 'Supertramp.' We're still good friends.

Variety night at Trinity Players. Anto plays trombone.

KEEPING MY FINGERS OFF YOUNG ACTRESSES.

I've always found that the shows you think will lead somewhere wonderful seldom do, and those that seem insignificant at the time prove to be the ones to propel you in the right direction. And so it was with my next professional production of Kevin Laffan's *'It's a Two-Foot-Six-Inches Above-the-Ground World.'* I was back at the Eblana theatre, and although this frothy comedy about the pill was well received at the time, it was also to be a stepping-stone to London's West End and the beginning of my real career. The reason? It had nothing to do with the acclaim the play received – which was okay, but no big deal – but rather because it just happened that the actress who played my girlfriend in the play was the daughter of Irish theatre legend Vincent Dowling!

Bairbre Dowling. A temptation!

But before I explain this serendipity, let me make a case for myself being one of the world's great gentlemen. Well, almost. In the play Jacqueline, my girlfriend – played by the eighteen-year-old Bairbre Dowling – and I exit stage left during the first act and don't appear again for twenty minutes. For reasons I could never quite fathom, the set designer had failed to provide an exit to the wings the other side of the door we passed through. So when we left the stage we walked into a small box the size of a porta-loo. Bairbre then sat on my lap. We were then in darkness for the following twenty minutes.

At this point I have to point out that Bairbre was extremely pretty, had a perfect body, flawless skin, long, thick, lustrous red hair and full lips. She also smelled absolutely intoxicating every night; a very alluring mixture of perfume and youth.

At the time I'd been going out with my then girlfriend Jane Dillon for two years so I knew I had to grin and bear it. I was also very aware Bairbre was the young and very innocent daughter of one of Dublin's most influential theatre directors. All in all it was like being offered a glass of Krug champagne every night, forced to inhale the heady bubbles, yet not taste a drop.

I never made a move during the entire run. But I couldn't help teasing myself just a teeny bit. Because let's face it I'm no saint!

When she sat in my lap and wound her bare arms around my neck to get comfortable, we could only talk to each other in the barest whispers. At the beginning of the second week, my fingers seemed to stray, of their own volition of course, down the inside of her arm towards her perfect silken left elbow. I noticed that her entire body tingled. So in a whispered aside, I explained that I had inadvertently chanced on what I referred to, erroneously, as an erogenous zone. She whispered back that, whatever it was called, it felt '*lovely.*' So from then on I would run my fingers so very lightly up and down the inside of her arms each time we were in 'the box'. Why I put myself through this teasing torture I have no idea.

During the final week of the run Bairbre whispered into my ear. "*Do you know of any more of those erogenous zones? You know, places where when you stroke them, it feels nice? If you do know, you can touch them now if you like?*"

OMG... somehow I toughed out the following ten minutes.

As a footnote to this sexual torture I might add that this innocent, divine girl, who I thought knew nothing much about sex, chose to elope with an Italian film producer, almost twice her age, less than six months after we closed. She went to live with him in Rome and I am certain knew more about bedroom fun and games than he did!

I was not to see Bairbre for close on thirty-five years, when we met up again in a bar in New York. At that time she explained she'd definitely had a crush on me during that play. I managed not to attempt to stroke her 'zones.'

My first love, Jane Dillon, and my first cat, Trophy.

BREAKTHROUGH! 'CHILDREN OF THE WOLF.'

It was not long after this that I was asked by Vincent to audition for a play he was about to direct at the Dublin Theatre Festival, titled *'Children of the Wolf.'* Just as well I restricted my fingers to Bairbre's arms!

Written by a young Englishman by the name of John Peacock, it was a play that the critics referred to as *'Grand Guignal.'* I'd never heard of this genre before. As I researched I found *Le Théâtre du Grand-Guignol* was founded in 1894 in Paris by Oscar Metenier. With 293 seats, the venue was the smallest in Paris. The plays were in a variety of styles, but the most popular and best known were the horror plays, featuring a distinctly bleak world view as well as notably gory special effects in their notoriously bloody climaxes. These plays often explored the altered states, like insanity, hypnosis, panic, under which uncontrolled horror could happen. John Peacock's play, which was a modern day Greek tragedy in style, fitted very nicely into this genre.

With Yvonne Mitchell in 'Children of the Wolf.'

Basically our play concerned the calling to judgment of a nymphomaniac mother who abandoned her twin children at birth. On their twenty-first birthday the twins lure her to a derelict mansion. Their 'interview' with their mother becomes an interrogation, and leads to a torture so cruel that one's sympathy shifts from persecutor to victim.

I was desperate to be cast as Robin as I knew that screen legend Yvonne Mitchell, BAFTA winner with *'Woman in a Dressing Gown,'* was to play the mother, and Sheelagh Cullen, a very up-and-coming young Irish actress was to play the twin sister role.

With Sheelagh Cullen in "Children of the Wolf" at the Apollo Theatre, Shaftesbury Avenue.

The reason Vincent thought of me was because he had come to see Bairbre in the 'condom' play, unaware I was fingering his daughter's erogenous zones every night, and twice on Wednesdays and Saturdays.

The long and short was that Vincent cast me, and the play was a huge hit at the Dublin Theatre Festival of 1971.

"Yvonne Mitchell is superb as the woman, and so is Shane Briant as the boy. Sheelagh Cullen is equally good," said the Irish Independent. The Evening Press said, *"There is flawless acting throughout."* The Irish Times said *"Children of the Wolf is probably the strongest meat of this, or any other festival."*

The reaction from both the Dublin and the London critics was great. I couldn't have been happier. It was a fantastic role for me, incredibly emotional.

The result of so many London critics giving the play such accolades was that a representative of the Bernard Delfont organization approached Vincent with an offer to transfer to the West End. Our new home was to be the Apollo Theatre in Shaftesbury Avenue.

"Vincent Dowling has established himself as a director par excellence," said the Dublin Evening Press, *"And Shane Briant is a formidable new star."*

Me? A star? This was the stuff of dreams.

So, only a matter of weeks later, Sheelagh and I climbed into my car and we motored from Dublin to London via the Holyhead Ferry and the M1 motorway.

Neither of us could disguise how thrilled we were – it was like being on speed for days on end, while drinking iced tea rather than consuming drugs. When we arrived in London, I drove directly to Piccadilly Circus and up Shaftesbury Avenue. Then I slowed my Mini Moke to a crawl as we passed the Apollo. All the photos and front of house 'stuff' was up reviews and all! It was the biggest thrill Sheelagh and I had ever had. So heady was it that we turned left and left again, so we could crawl past the theatre three times!

It had been a roller-coaster ride from Metellus Cimber to a three hander in Shaftesbury Avenue in just three years. And the most extraordinary coincidence was that my mother, Elizabeth Nolan, had played the Apollo for over two hundred performances in a play called *'The Housemaster'* in 1934. Here I was, thirty-seven years later about to tread the same boards – amazing serendipity.

But I digress briefly – for one amusing event that occurred during the refresher rehearsals at the Apollo. Yvonne, Sheelagh, and I were into the last few extremely emotional moments of the play when a man appeared stage left and knocked hard against a post to gain our attention. We all stopped and stared. Vincent strode down to the stage from his seat in the stalls.

"I gather you maybe want to buy a door slam?" ventured the suited intruder.

It was true, we did need one, it was a pivotal audio effect in the play; word must have gotten around the theatre scene. This man had a selection to offer.

"I got a big door, a small door, a toilet door, a double door..."

Vincent held up a hand. *"Come and see me in an hour – you just sold a heavy front door."*

The first night was the most thrilling moment of my life up till then.

The Apollo is not exactly an intimate theatre, seating almost eight hundred patrons, so it wasn't really the most suitable theatre for an intimate three-hander. But at short notice, it was the only one available in the West End. As far as I was concerned the bigger the better, though I did have some reservations about being able to project to the back of the balcony – the Apollo has stalls, dress circle, upper circle and balcony.

The final few moments of the play are a gift to any young actor. Robin, completely under the thrall of his cruel vindictive sister, is given two choices; kill his own mother with a knife handed to him by his sibling, or be left to fend for himself in a cruel world devoid of the only human he has ever known – his twin, Linda.

This is true modern day Greek drama, no?

Robin's mother, desperately remorseful for what she did to her children and for the first time feeling a violently strong bond for her son, attempts to make things easier for him by guiding the knife to her heart as Linda looks on. *"Be brave for me,"* the mother says. But Robin cannot bring himself to kill the mother it has taken him all his life to find. His sister turns and leaves. Crying out *"I'm sorry!"* in a high-pitched scream, he stabs his mother many times. The final stage direction in the play is: *"He continues screaming with terror as the curtain falls – quickly."*

The effect on the audience each evening was magical. Stunned silence for a few moments, then applause. Yvonne and I would rise and Sheelagh would join us on the proscenium. I was always in a state of emotional turmoil at this stage, with tears flowing like a gusher. I could scarcely speak. The three of us would hug, and then the curtain would come down.

What more could a young actor want?

After the rapturous notices we received in Dublin, the reaction in London was somewhat of a disappointment. The headline in the Daily Telegraph was *"Yvonne Mitchell grips the audience"* while Cecil Wilson of the Daily Mail said, *"Yvonne Mitchell crumbles under the weight of her sins with enough harrowed dignity to keep the situation just this side of ludicrous."*

As I read this I wondered if he was familiar with any Greek tragedy. *The Medea*, perhaps? *Oedipus*? Who was Peter Wilson anyway, I mumbled. After all, the revered Herbert Kretzmer of the Daily Express called our production *"A lesson in the art of terror,"* and called me *"An Irish actor of whom more will one day be heard."* My new agent, the incredibly wonderful Adza Vincent, who had taken me on at the Dublin Festival, liked the quote in the Guardian. *"Yvonne Mitchell marvelously projects a sense of terror and is balanced by a wonderful performance of a half-retarded semi-stammering twin Shane Bryant (sic) whose disheveled unease helps lift the play into better regions."*

Another critic whom I admired from afar in Dublin, John Barber, said, *"As the stammering male twin, Shane Briant could not be bettered."* And the New York Herald Tribune predicted I was an actor *"destined for great fame."* Nice of him to suggest this might be the case, but he was to be proven not *entirely* accurate. Shame.

One thing I learned was that if everyone in a city other than London says a play is brilliant, it will always encourage the London critics to take issue with their comments. It's the same with films, I think.

The play lasted four weeks. I think the theatre was simply too big for us and we couldn't fill it. Although J.C. Trewin had said the play *"should undoubtedly stay in Shaftesbury Avenue,"* and Bernard Delfont had sent each of us a telegram to that effect, Delfont had already made arrangements to end our run. I understood then that business was business, and actors were in the hands of a few important critics. It was a salutary lesson.

But the most ironical twist was to come two weeks after we closed. Harold Hobson, doyen of London theatre critics, who had not been able to attend the opening night because of ill health, had come to see our final performance. In the Sunday Times Weekly Review he said, *"If Bergman reduces an Eastern myth to the greyness of an off-form unimpassioned Zola, John Peacock, a writer of considerable promise, is much more successful in re-interpreting the story of Electra and Orestes in his play, 'Children of the Wolf'."*

I had to smile when I read this. A sad smile, but a smile nonetheless. At last a critic had said something intelligent and 'got it.' This review could have saved us, but it came too late. *"Yvonne Mitchell gave a memorable performance of haunting beauty and Sheelagh Cullen and Shane Briant showed how rich in acting talent Ireland is."* Again I was dubbed Irish – but I didn't mind at all.

There was a great cartoon in Punch that month, one that featured our play. To be in Punch? Wow!

Punch 1971

Strangely enough, many months later someone told me I had been nominated for the London Theatre Critics' *'Newcomer of the Year.*' I hadn't won it, but just to be nominated was fantastic. The odd thing, though, was that no one had informed me; a shame, as it was the first and last nomination for a theatre award to date! Mind you, I'm not dead yet!

Those four weeks at the Apollo were sheer magic. I had a wonderfully spacious dressing room and somehow managed to refrain from going over the top and buying silk dressing gowns à la Noël Coward. I did, however, organize a pretty good bar in the corner for any friends who might drop by after the show. There was a decent selection of spirits, wine and bubbly – no French champagne as Delfont's wages scarcely covered what I was advised was a decent weekly tip for the aged doorman (about ten per cent of what I had left each week after Adza's commission). I can see that dressing room in my mind's eye quite vividly even now. And one more nice touch was to come. J.C. Trewin was to include *'Children of the Wolf'* in his annual volume, *'Plays of the Year.'* We were in good company that year with David Story's *'The Contractor'* and William Douglas Home's comedy *'The Jockey Club Stakes.'*

In 2010 I visited Vincent at his home in Chester, Massachusetts. He is a very sprightly eighty-two years old and has just completed a wonderful full length play titled *'The Upstart Crow.'* The thrust of his play is this; months after Shakespeare's death his daughter meets his favourite actor, Richard Burbage on the stage of the Globe and they talk of her father and his friend. Great reading – should be performed soon.

Vin owns about three hundred yards of delightful trout fishing at the end of his garden and he casts a mean fly.

MY LEGENDARY AGENT, ADZA VINCENT.

Despite *'Children of the Wolf'* closing far earlier than we had anticipated, I knew that I was in the very safe representational hands of Adza, an agent who handled just the few special clients that she really believed in. One was Yvonne Mitchell, another was Michael Crawford. Adza was the lifelong close friend of Anthony Asquith, son of English Prime Minister H.H. Asquith, and director of many famous films in the '30's such as *'The Winslow Boy,'* *'The Browning Version,'* and *'The Importance of Being Ernest.'*

Adza was far more than a theatrical agent; she was also teacher and mother figure. Every Sunday she'd invite Jane and me to lunch at her small home in Ivor Place, a home she shared with three wonderful lurcher dogs who had the run of the house (inside *and* outside of dinner hours) and the run of the kitchen when it came to Sunday lunch. The board was always groaning, and it was she that taught me how to make the crispiest roast potatoes and the most heavenly Peking duck. She was also a stern pseudo-mother. I had to do what I was told – her 'advice' was more like an order.

So it was that one morning she telephoned me and told me I was to attend a 'cow-herd' audition for a forthcoming big West End Musical the name of which escapes me.

"But I can't sing and I don't dance, so what's the point?"

This immediately got her hackles up. *"Don't be ridiculous! I've heard you singing Sweeney Todd the Barber. Not bad at all. And anyone can dance. I expect you to be at the Prince of Wales Theatre at 2 p.m. Sharp!"*

She rang off.

So, at two o'clock that afternoon I was waiting in the wings with about fifty other 'wannabes' – terrified. When I reached the head of the queue I heard the stage manager call out loudly. *"Mr. Shane Briant!"*

I stepped forward and was immediately asked for my sheet music by the pianist – the rest of the vast stage was bare.

"I don't have any, I'm afraid," I replied.

"What are you singing, young man," he asked.

"Er... Sweeney Todd the Barber," I responded.

"I know it well, I don't need any sheet music," he said.

"I'd rather sing it without accompaniment, if you don't mind," I ventured.

"Do get on with it," someone called from the stage right wings.

I did as I was told and finished two minutes later. Several moments of silence followed. I didn't quite know what to do. Was I expected to shuffle off stage right?

I'd taken one step in that direction when I heard footsteps at the back of the stalls. I stopped. Five seconds later I made out the features of a man. My heart sank. It was the legendary Bob Fosse. He was kind enough to smile up at me from the far side of the orchestra pit.

"Hey, Shane. How about you give me some kind of a dance routine. Suit yourself. Something with a bit of a kick. Whaderyousay?"

I stared back at him; the only dancing I had ever done was to the Kinks at the Marquee Club.

"I'm afraid I don't dance," I croaked.

Fosse's smile practically split his face in half. *"Well, that's a damned shame,"* he replied, *"'Cos sure as hell you don't sing!"*

It was the first time I died on stage. Now I tell the story all the time. I think it's hilarious. At the time, with fifty young actors roaring with laughter, it wasn't exactly a fun experience. I never told Adza the truth. *"How did it go,"* she asked that evening. *"Really well,"* I replied, hoping she'd believe me, but never send me for another musical.

Talking of musicals, I did appear in one and great fun it was too. It was shortly after I had worked with Yvonne.

In those days The Bush Theatre was one of London's most interesting fringe venues. The musical was called *'The Greasy Spoon.'* The musical comedy was the hilarious story of a takeaway restaurant. However, in this musical it wasn't the food that was delivered, but the restaurant itself. It was written by Richard Fegan and Chris Langan, and had some great songs. Chris and Richard were to go on to write several comedy series for the BBC.

My role was that of a Hollywood movie producer, and my best song was *'How'd ya like to be on Broadway, baby!"*

"How'd'ya like to be on Broadway, Baby?"

I had a ball singing that song. As I finished, the script called for a special effect. *'His teeth light up.'* I asked Chris how this might be achieved, and was told simply to *'make it happen.'* So I manufactured a fake cigar that one could smoke and had a pencil torch down one side. When I sang out the last line I'd withdraw the cigar from my mouth and flick a switch halfway down it, so that the battery made contact with a tiny bulb that was directed at my open mouth. My teeth actually lit up.

Yvonne came with her daughter Cordelia to the opening night. She told me she found it thoroughly enjoyable. Her favourite line? *"No matter how hard you shake it, the last drop always goes down your leg."*

As with all great theatrical agents, Adza could arrange anything and so immediately found me, her new client, a reasonably priced yet wonderful flat in Pimlico. A duplex above a branch of the Sunlight Laundry. Four huge rooms and a vast stairwell where it was rumoured the last occupant had hanged himself. I put in a bathroom and kitchen and lived there with my lovely Jane for many wonderful years.

Incidentally, I forgot to mention something that most likely should remain unmentioned. But I like to think I'm reasonable modest and frank, so here goes.

I did get my Honors Degree in Legal Science at Trinity. Not only that, I came top of the law school that particular year! The year before, Mary Robinson, who went on to become President of Ireland no less, topped the list. But here's the thing I've never mentioned in any press release. The year I topped the law school was one of the most inauspicious in living memory. I came top with a 2-2. There! I have come clean at last! What a catharsis. This only goes to prove that there are many other dummies at University. And they most probably all go on to become judges. A sobering thought.

It was around this time that my wonderful grandmother passed away. I'd always had a strong bond with Doris and my Aunt Margaret. Mum, Dermot and I used to spend every Christmas Eve at granny's. Dermot and I would dress in the Gordon tartan (sporran and dirk to boot) one we were allowed to wear since my father was a Gordon. The adults dressed in black tie. When we'd finished our Christmas pud and Dermot and I had extracted every sixpenny bit, Conway, my Grandpa, would always ask the *'ladies'* to *'repair'* to the living room so that the men could drink a glass or two of port. Then he'd lock the door and sit with Dermot and me sipping an aged port while we sipped soft drinks in port glasses. It was the tradition that was important to Conway. He was delightfully old fashioned, and during the half hour we remained locked inside the dining room he'd talk about politics and world affairs. We were six and nine years old at the time.

When Doris died Margaret my aunt was the executor. Since she appreciated that my brother Dermot was at heart a chancer, she nevertheless allowed him to dispose of the less valuable furniture in the house, while the 'nice' pieces went to Bonhams. Needless to say, the pieces that Dermot stashed in the huge van he hired for the day disappeared without trace. But here's the funny part. Granny had given me the baby grand piano – a Steinway – in her will, and I had yet to transport it to my flat.

"How about I put it in the van with the other stuff and take it to your flat now? It'll save you hiring another van," he said.

Naïve as I was, I never suspected his motives. Not a smart move.

"Great idea! Thanks," I replied.

A week later, no piano. So I telephoned my brother.

"Hello, little brudder," he said.

"Where's the piano?" I replied sternly.

There was a long pause.

"How would you like an upright?" he said.

"Where's the baby grand?"

"How would you like an upright," he repeated over and over again.

I never saw the piano again, nor did I receive an upright. He was a consummate rogue at times.

We both loved our maternal granny. We weren't so close to Alice, our paternal granny. I think it was because mum hated her, so we didn't warm to her either.

Two years after her son Keith died, Alice decided to dig him up from his resting place in Burford, Oxfordshire and re-bury him in Scotland. So she called mum and asked if Dermot and I would travel up with the coffin in the train to Scotland. We'd never seen Scotland before so we persuaded mum to let us go. It felt very odd to sit in a railway carriage knowing that our father was in the goods van behind us in a spanking new coffin. We both felt very confused to be standing at his graveside for the second time.

When Alice passed away, many years later, Dermot and I were

invited up to Dumphries for the reading of her will, to be followed by her burial.

First up was the reading of the will. We were the only ones present, as well as being the sole relatives, so we were anticipating some, er… 'mention' in her will. After all, she was very wealthy, and we didn't own a red cent.

The solicitor then informed us she had given her entire estate, barring her huge diamond ring, to a religious charity in Luxembourg. The diamond ring was left to a Church of Scotland minister, who later married my late father's second wife.

We listened with poker faces. Not so much of a twitch from either of us. Finally the solicitor told us that Alice had left us a hundred pounds each. To give you some idea of Dermot's very dark sense of humour, when we left he immediately visited the town florist and bought a two-pound bunch of flowers – the cheapest bunch he could find. We then attended the burial in a very bleak churchyard.

When it was over, Dermot told me we'd go and have some lunch and then return later. He went to an off-license and bought a cheap bottle of red Argentine wine, that he always referred to as *'the old infuriator.'* Then we bought some sandwiches. Why? Dermot wanted to drink a bottle of red wine while sitting on Alice's recently filled-in grave. She had been a staunch advocate of temperance all her life – so this was my brother's form of payback. So we ate the sandwiches and drank the wine leaning against granny's headstone. To this day I can't think why Alice should have wished to disinherent us boys.

THE HAMMER FILM YEARS

THE LAST CONTRACT PLAYER AT ELSTREE STUDIOS.

What I didn't know when the curtain fell on *'Children of the Wolf'* was that Michael Carreras, head honcho of Hammer Films, had seen the production and had me in mind as a possible anti-hero for a new film he was about to produce titled *'Straight on Till Morning.'*

It was to be directed by Peter Collinson of *'The Italian Job'* fame. Rita Tushingham had been approached to play the female lead. I suppose one of the reasons Michael thought of me was because in *'Children of the Wolf,'* Robin was a trifle brain-damaged (lack of oxygen when he was born – anoxia.) The character he had in mind for me was a very psychologically disturbed young man with a Peter Pan complex. I hoped this would be the start of a string of 'crazy-guy' roles, and I was not disappointed.

Adza called me one day and told me that Hammer had made an offer. The idea was to put me under contract to the film company for two years. I would, during those years, make four films, all in leading roles. Sounded great to me.

"But what films do they have in mind, Adza?" I asked.

"A re-make of 'Lorna Doone,' with you as the handsome John Ridd. Then 'The Man who Imagined Too Much,' the life story of Bram Stoker. You know, he wrote Dracula. Those and two other films—he doesn't exactly know which they will be."

The fee for these two years was a spectacular two thousand pounds; a fortune in those days.

"Count me in," I replied, excitedly. *"But can I have a parking spot at Elstree Studios, Adza,"* I asked.

"I wouldn't have it any other way, dear heart," she replied. And so my career at Hammer films began.

I was the last contract player at Elstree Studios.

'DEMONS OF THE MIND.'

My first film was *'Demons of the Mind.'* And guess what? I was to play the brain-damaged son of Robert Hardy – the Baron Zorn!

I recall wondering if I would ever play sane people again, and thinking it wouldn't matter if I never did, providing the crazies were well written roles. And so it came to pass I was invited to Elstree to meet the cast – lunch in the executive dining room with director Peter Sykes and Michael Carerras.

I was incredibly excited at the prospect of meeting the girl who was to play my sister – Marianne Faithfull.

Mick Jagger's girlfriend and me, twins? Whoooaaahhhh! I couldn't wait to wrap my arms around her… in a brotherly way, of course. Not. She looked so incredibly sexy. And that wasn't all the good news. The good guy was to be played by Manfred Mann aka Paul Jones. But you can forgive me for thinking I could now *really* impress my TCD friends. It was to be one of the most prestigious casts for any Hammer film. Never had so many big stars assembled for a gothic horror piece. Yvonne Mitchell, Michael Hordern as an insane priest, Patrick Magee as an insane medic by the name of Falkenberg, Robert Hardy, insane father, Paul Jones, not insane, Kenneth J. Warren as the burly enforcer, and the lovely Virginia Wetherell as the innocent victim I strangle early on in the piece.

However, the casting process didn't go at all smoothly. Marianne Faithfull arrived in the dining room looking and behaving in a very 'tired and emotional' fashion and failed to either eat or utter one word during the entire lunch. Possibly she'd had an argument with Mick – I was never to find out, as she didn't speak to me at all that day. I think it was because of her behaviour that Michael Carreras rethought the casting. I was later told that it was a question of insurance; the entire major cast had to undergo a medical and it was feared that Marianne at the time was unwell. I was very sad indeed when I heard I was not to play her brother and clasp her to me in scene after scene. However, it wasn't all bad, as her replacement was the incredibly delicious Gillian Hills. Not that I was having lustful thoughts – as I was living in Pimlico with Jane. But if I had to hug anyone, and kiss them passionately it was bloody good to kiss and cuddle a girl like Gillian – one who seemed to me a shoe-in to play Lolita one day! It was like holding molten gold!

I studied my contract avidly, wondering what had become of *'Lorna Doone'* and *'Bram Stoke.'* I quizzed Adza and she told me not to worry – it was simply that they could not legally commit to the *exact* projects two years from then.

This was to prove a mistake. On the plus side I noticed in the small print that I was to have my own parking spot at the studios with my name on the wall in front. Very appealing to a young actor. What else do actors dream of? Personal trailers, parking spots with a name on them, personal stand-ins, drivers, endless cups of coffee, lunch in the executive dining room at Elstree and Pinewood!

I was living in the fast lane at last – my cup was running over!

What I remember most vividly working on 'Demons of the Mind' were these words from my director Peter Sykes. I paraphrase, of course, but this is what I recall.

"Just push the girls down on the ground, over there between the roses. You can see the marks. Then leap on them, pinning them down with your knees. Then rip their blouses down on the right hand side so we get a clear view of their right breast - nipple and all. Okay? We've got five gorgeous girls to get through today so... let's get on with it, eh?"

Peter Sykes, my director, smiled. *"Enjoy the day, Shane."*

You're probably wondering *'what on earth...?'* Well, this was just ten lovely hours work on the set of Hammer Films' *'Demons of the Mind,'* the entire day allocated to 'jumping' young Gothic maidens and ripping their clothes off.

A good way to spend the day? Well, yes. But only in a way. Because along with grasping and holding the sexiest young girls in the world, at the same time as tearing their clothes off, comes the task of doing this in a professional manner. As an actor – a very different thing. You see, there are so many things you have to get right. And by that I mean, do it perfectly for the camera every time.

Firstly, on the cue '*Action!*' you have to wait for the gorgeous village lass – 'Magda,' or 'Heidi' – to run ahead of you until she arrives at an exact mark, then call out to her so as to make her look over her shoulder, see you, and look suitably terrified. One microsecond late, and the luscious prey will have run too far and you'll hear the director's annoyed voice. "CUT."

Then, you have to make certain you run forward and grab the lass so that your body does not mask her face. Not only that but you have to slow down the entire process so that it's not simply a blur across the camera, and the audience can see everything. This means slowing it down without making it look fake. Not easy. Then you have to push the girl down so that it looks as though it's violent and rough, but you have to do it so you don't hurt the actress. Again, not so easy.

Finally, the breast!

Have you ever tried ripping a shirt? It doesn't rip easily. It needs some help. Stitching has to be loosened in all the right places by the wardrobe department.

Of course the stitching on *these* maidens' blouses were 'loosened' very expertly. Nevertheless, I had to, in my frenzy, grab the three-inch fold I'd been directed to exactly and tug. Anywhere else and the stitching would hold fast.

My wife Wendy and I became great friends with Virginia Wetherell who married Ralph Bates in 1973.

With Wendy and the perfect couple, Virginia and Ralph Bates, at the premiere of the film 'Roar.' London.

Ralphie was a Hammer films stalwart in his early days and later on starred as Warleggan in *'Poldark.'* Every Christmas he and Vig would entertain all their friends who had no family to spend the holiday with. My task was to bring the bread sauce. Very tasty it was too, though I say so myself. Ralphie died in 1991 aged just fifty-one, of pancreatic cancer, and Vig set up a charity in his name. I encourage everyone to give as generously to her charity as Ralphie gave happiness to his friends during his life.

Most people think acting is a glamorous profession and has to be the most amazing fun. Most of the time it's a job that I wouldn't change for the world. However, let's not forget the very hard work that needs to be put in even before you start in on a film project.

Natalie Portman in *'The Black Swan'* is a good example. They say she trained for one year as a ballet choreographer. The result – she looks totally believable and, instead of her concentration being directed to her feet, she could allow her feet do the dancing almost on autopilot, while her mental focus was free to concentrate on the emotional nature of the scene.

Another example – possibly even more dramatic – is how Charlize Theron managed to make herself look the way she did in *'Monster.'* For one of the most spectacular beauties of our age to morph into the character of Aillen is almost beyond belief. And what about Christian Bale in *'The Fighter'*? Haggard? Gaunt? Amazing.

Over my career in films, theatre and television I have been asked to play so many different people that, looking back, I am amazed by the diversity. The majority of roles I was offered centered on my being an evil or mentally challenged young man. Why? Because that's how I made my name, onstage at the Apollo Theatre in the West End of London, playing the anoxic youth Robin in *'Children of the Wolf,'* a boy who stabbed his mother to death. From there Hammer Films spotted me, and I played another two mentally challenged youths in *'Demons of the Mind,'* and *'Straight on Till Morning.'*

Two years down the line the die seemed to be cast. Casting directors saw me as an androgynous crazy guy, killer, manipulator, gigolo – the fact was that I was young, a trile too androgenous and had long beautiful blonde hair. The thinking was that whomever I played would be the least suspicious member of the cast when it came to spotting the murderer. Nowadays this kind of thinking is old hat. Back then, tall dark and very mean looking actors were cast as murderers. Obvious? Yes. But that's the way it was. I like to think in some ways I broke the mould Hammer.

'Demons of the Mind' was my first foray into film. I hardly knew a thing about acting in front of a camera, so I determined to watch everyone else like a hawk and take every morsel of advice I was offered.

Peter Sykes was such a friendly man and nothing was too much trouble for him – he taught me a lot.

I mentioned before that there were some stellar acting luminaries in the line-up, but I was totally unprepared for the attitude most of the stars had to portraying roles in a Hammer horror movie. It was clear from the start that most of the male cast, the exception being Paul Jones, thought the Hammer genre should be hammed up quite a bit. After all, surely one didn't take gothic horror movies that seriously?

Robert Hardy, who played my crazed father, was a fine actor, yet I felt his portrayal of Baron Zorn just fell short of a Madame Tussaud's figure. His voice was loud and harsh sounding, as though someone had slowed down a tape recording of his natural speaking voice. Patrick Magee was clearly of the 'Hardy' camp too. Magee's fabulous sonorous tones knew no boundary in this film, and though he played a demented psychiatrist, he acted more like a psychotic medico.

Don't get me wrong, I'd always admired Patrick Magee greatly, but I simply didn't understand how over-the-top the acting was becoming. And a guest appearance of Michael Hordern, a splendid actor who has always been one of my very favourites since I saw him in M.R. James' 'Whistle and I'll Come to You,' played a wild priest on steroids.

Yvonne headed up, what for want of a better term, the 'realism camp', which included Paul Jones, Gillian Hills and myself.

Although I knew little or nothing about film, I had always been of the opinion that no matter how different the genres might be, the portrayal of any role should be real. Believable, rather than veering towards 'pantomime.' Film is a much more intimate medium, and this means less dramatic make-up and little or no projection. This suited me perfectly as I never much cared for having to project a hundred and fifty feet to the back of the dress circle. So much more relaxing to think and act more inwardly.

On the first morning of filming my call time was 5.30 a.m. At the studio I was directed immediately to make-up.

Hardy and Magee were already in their chairs and Eddie Knight, one of the last make-up supervisors of the old school, a man with an accent that surely had its origins at Eton, was opening a two foot by three foot leather case. I was astonished to note it contained three gloriously antique cut-glass decanters – one containing gin, the other two filled with vodka and whisky. There was a decent selection of mixers to one side.

Eddie must have already ascertained Robert and Patrick's tipple, because as he poured Robert a G & T and served Patrick two generous fingers of Scotch whisky, he turned to me.

"Can I interest you in a choto-Peg or burra-Peg young man?" the seventy-something make-up supervisor enquired. Both were Indian names, the former a short drink such as a neat Scotch, the latter a long drink such as a gin and tonic.

Not wishing to be obtuse, I settled for a gin and tonic. And very nice it was, though I wasn't in the habit of quaffing strong liquor before lunch. But, hey, that was Britain in those days, as was hitting the bar pronto the moment lunch was called. Pinewood had a delightful bar, but the one at Elstree was not quite as old fashioned and gracious.

Of course I was to find out many years later that drinking during working hours is anathema in Australia and New Zealand, while getting stuck into a bottle of *vin rouge* or *vin blanc* is *'de rigueur'* in France.

I learned a great deal from watching Yvonne. She told me all her secrets. *"Watch the director of photography closely as he is lighting you, that's the key. Find your key lights. Don't be too fussy with gestures – they'll come back to haunt you when it's your time for a close-up. Most importantly, listen to what you fellow actors are saying as if it's the very first time you've ever heard these words. Don't be like so many so-called actors who simply wait for the other actors to stop speaking, then speak themselves."*

I promised myself I would always know my dialogue well in advance so that I never had to worry about forgetting lines. In my early career I hardly ever tripped up over my words, and this made me feel great, as the crew never treated me as a new boy. As the years passed I came to know it's absolutely paramount to gain the respect of the crewmembers. I believe I can pretty accurately gauge what the crew thinks of actors within a few days.

Most crew members respond well if you are courteous, friendly, know your lines, hit your marks accurately every take and can act adequately. I've always found the nicest and most self-effacing actors are practically always those who have nothing to prove. My favourites in this department were Paul Newman, James Mason, Olivia de Havilland and John Hurt. Mark Harmon and Geoffrey Rush are also wonderfully solid professional actors with no attitude whatsoever – something that made working with them a pleasure. Here I am dropping names? Why not?

On the third week of the *'Demons'* shoot a whole day was set aside for the scenes where the incestuous Emil is set free by his lunatic father to find young maidens. He's actually looking for his cherished sister, but when he discovers they simply village maidens, he kills them very violently. Back in Castle Zorn, in some kind of a trascentendal trance, his father gets his various kicks out of his son's murderous rampage.

So, on that day six beautiful young amply endowed blondes – yes, all blondes – were costumed in 'maidens from the village' costumes. One by one we were to shoot the scenes where I came upon them and grasped their slim and lovely necks, pushing them roughly to the ground where I suffocated them.

Once one was dispatched, it was on to the next wench.

Funnily enough they all seemed to expect the 'ripping.' I'm sure it was in their contracts. I remember asking the wardrobe supervisor how it was possible that each girl's shirt would have the same ripping pattern. She replied, *"It's like a serial killer's 'signature'."* I actually bought this. Fool.

James, Kit Adeane's son, came on set as my guest the day the ripping began. He wanted to know what acting in Hammer Films was like, so I simply told him that this was an average day on set – *I have to run after gorgeous girls, wrestle them to the ground, tear off their flimsy blouses, then strangle them."* I told him with a poker face, and then went to work.

James watched the entire morning's shoot. As soon as lunch was called I offered him a drink in the bar.

"My GOD! That's what you do every day?" he asked.

"More or less," I replied, with my best casual look of sangfroid.

Before I go any further into the territory of juicy asides, may I draw the attention of the reader to the words of one of my oldest friends, Jeffrey Bloom, American screenwriter and accomplished director. I'd emailed him, asking what I should do if I suddenly remembered some, shall I say, raunchy episodes. The fact is, I've never had much respect for 'kiss and tell' stories, as they often causes division amongst friends, and lead to *"You never told me about THAT!"* from loved ones. Upsetting.

You'd think that events that occurred thirty years ago wouldn't be too important, but to some people they definitely are. So, as I started writing, I was toying with simply omitting *all* the fun stuff.

This is what Jeffrey said. *"I'm telling you, if you DON'T put in the sexy, dirty, crazy, zany, and perverted stuff (no animal sex, please), it's a complete waste of time and energy, and will never be published, and even if it is, will never sell."*

With the delicious Gillian Hills in "Demons of the Mind."

Okay. At the end of the third day's filming on '*Demons,*' I was asked by an actor if I would kindly do him a favour and give Gillian Hills a lift home to the apartment I was house-sitting in Ovington Gardens. (Incidentally, it was apparently two doors down from Ava Gardner's flat, though I never spotted her.)

I didn't ask why, but I knew that had this cast member been seen with the actress, he would have been snapped by the paparazzi. The idea was that he would pick her up at my place, later.

I am not suggesting for one second that any hanky-panky took place after this lovely Lolita was whisked off from my pad in Ovington Gardens, so please don't jump to any conclusions. Ahem.

However, one evening something happened that I have never forgotten.

We arrived at my flat, and I gave Gillian a glass of something or other, and we sat down on the huge sofa, looking out onto Ovington Gardens.

I couldn't take my eyes off her – she really was perfect. I remember being amazed by her flawless skin. Not one single wrinkle or blemish; it was as if she had had the skin of a newborn infant grafted to her face. I felt a certain natural stirring below the waist as we toasted each other and Gillian tucked her long legs underneath her on the sofa. Of course I knew I could do nothing. I had my own girlfriend – but it doesn't stop your mouth watering slightly, does it?

We chatted for fifteen minutes when the conversation took a turn towards famous screen love scenes. Then it focused on things more personal.

"You know, Shane. I have never had a satisfactory…."

My pulse quickened. I was intrigued. I prompted her to finish her sentence.

"Well, you know what I mean?" she continued quietly. *"I've never had a nice one."*

Though I had an idea what she was referring to, I knew I could be dead wrong. Then how foolish would I look? One cannot assume that when a girl says, *"Let's do it,"* she means leap into bed. In my experience it normally translates as *'order that pizza.'*

Was she sending me up just because I appeared a bit naïve? Or could it be…? Nah, surely not!

So what did I say? This will amaze you as much as it amazes me today.

"That's terrible, Gillian," I croaked. *"Absolutely… er… terrible."*

Big intake of breath.

"Have you seen a… gynecologist?"

I seem to remember her eyes glazed, she looked away, and she took a sip of *Sancerre*. Whether or not she had been making an advance was debatable. Most likely not – she was probably playing a joke on me, one she'd rehearsed with my fellow cast member, and she'd hit the bull's eye!

To this day I wonder why I didn't offer to help her with her 'problem.'

'Demons' was to my knowledge the first Hammer film ever to be made entirely on location. It makes sense that if both the interior and exterior of a location is perfect, why build sets at Elstree, Pinewood or Bray?

Castle Zorn, alias Wykehurst Place, was a magnificent Gothic Revival Mansion designed in 1871 by Edward Barry. Situated near Bolney in West Sussex, it looked more like a chateau in the Loire Valley. Its turrets, arches, conical roofs, and many architectural devices give it the appearance of a fairy-tale mansion. The massive black entrance gates looked wonderfully forbidding, made as it was of wrought iron.

Just to be working inside and outside of this atmospheric mansion made acting very easy. It had seen parts of Richard Attenborough's 'Oh What a Lovely War' filmed there, as well as two other Hammer films and 'The Eagle Has Landed.'

Each day, from breakfast onwards, as I stepped into the clothes and skin of the tortured Emil, I could well understand why he should be madly in love with his sister and consequently revile his Father and Aunt.

I'm not saying I was the kind of actor who literally had to be the character in question. As Olivier once said to Dustin Hoffman on the set of 'Marathon Man.' "Can't you simply act it?"

If I'd been a method man it would have spoiled my wonderfully catered lunches – can't just switch off and tuck in, can you?

With Patrick McGee and Robert Hardy in 'Demons of the Mind.'

The way I operated was simply to inhabit Emil's world for the moment at hand, so as to make him both a real person and absolutely believable.

When I saw the première of the film, I remember thinking that my character didn't appear half as crazy as Hardy, Magee or Hordern. Yet it was I that was the brain-damaged assassin.

It was rumoured at the time that the Wykehurst estate belonged to one of the Great Train Robbers. This intrigued me, as at that time it was the biggest daylight robbery in British History. So keen was I to find out if this was true that I left a letter in the study one weekend addressed to Ronnie Biggs. I suggested that we meet sometime for a game of backgammon or canasta – I'd bring the drinks. Sadly, it was still where I placed it when we went back to work on the following Monday.

The fact is, I've always been intrigued by bad guys simply because I was playing them, one after another, so I wanted to get a proper understanding of their mind set.

Paul Jones, producer Frank Godwin, Patrick Magee and director Peter Sykes.

The ones I did meet socially, via a good bit of research, seemed rather normal. I can't mention any of their names here as some of them promised to do various things to me if I did – inter alia, make a handy bag to keep small change for the Sydney Harbour Bridge out of the skin of my testicles. You'd never believe they'd think nothing of beating a complete stranger to pulp for five hundred dollars into the hand.

I've often been told that as far as most 'crims' are concerned, if you don't get on the wrong side of them they make good friends. When I hear this I always think, *'Really?'* It's said all the time that they're usually very loyal until crossed, and love their families; their mothers in particular. Everyone else is a target.

One of the most interesting aspects of the *'Demons'* shoot was how old fashioned the filming seemed to be.

For instance in the early seventies we were still using limelight, also known as calcium light. An intense illumination is created when an oxyhydrogen flame is directed at a cylinder of quicklime which can be heated to 2572 °C before melting. The light is produced by a combination of incandescence and candoluminescence. Nowadays no one uses this manner of lighting, it's all electric, but the term has nonetheless survived, as someone in the public eye is still said to be *'in the limelight.'*

I miss it – call me old fashioned, but I found it exhilarating when the cylinder was placed in the big light such as a 10-K with iron tongs, and then fired up producing a violently strong and brilliant light.

Another thing we used was real blood – Kensington Gore,' the mainstay of modern day horror pictures, was still to break into movies. On *'Demons'* and *'Frankenstein and the Monster From Hell,'* we usually used human blood from a blood bank that had reached its 'use-by date.' It was the real thing (the colour was a very deep delicious red) and the joy was that it would congeal on my hands! Also on the breasts of young maidens! Oh, and it also gave me the creeps, so that helped my performance immeasurably too!

Working alongside Yvonne again was magnificent. She was the most gifted, generous and professional actress I have ever worked with. Her way of working always involved ensemble work – she would workshop a scene with you for as long as it took to make solid sense. She'd imbue every line with the back-story of her character as well as mine. I'd look into her eyes – she played my aunt in the film – and I'd see a depth of caring and sensitivity I had only seen before in my mother's eyes. With such intense feelings coming back at me it was incredibly easy to become completely involved in the personal tragedy of Emil. All the other cast members I worked with, while being solid actors, seemed to be doing it by the book – acting. There's a big difference.

I've experienced this higher level of intense commitment to acting in only a handful of actors I have worked with – Rosemary Harris, Olivia de Havilland, John Hurt and Sheelagh Cullen spring to mind.

Working on a first film is a very exciting experience. I had no knowledge of how to connect with a camera. Nor did I know how the most basic things were done, what marks were, that there would be a master shot then two-shots maybe, and then close-ups. I did know you had to present the same level of performance in both wide and close shots, yet bring down the facial expressions to accommodate such close shots. I didn't know a thing about focal lengths or key lights. Yet despite this lack of knowledge of the very basics of acting for film I was expected to start work on day one and simply 'do it.' That's where the senior cast members helped me enormously. I could ask questions of the cast as well as the director and as each question was answered I'd file away the answers. I'd also quiz the camera operator and the DoP for tips – after all they was lighting and filming me and I wanted to make his job easy while ensuring I looked my best.

I also got a big kick out of being chauffeur driven to the set each day. It made me feel special. I enjoyed having a director's chair with my name on it every kid likes that, and I was no different. I liked the catered lunches very much indeed. And when we moved to Elstree I enjoyed having my own parking space with my name on the wall. Ever the child at heart.

'STRAIGHT ON TILL MORNING.'

I started in on principal photography of *'Straight on till Morning'* a few months later.

At the time I remember thinking that this was very cool – my future lifestyle would be making movie after movie in quick succession.

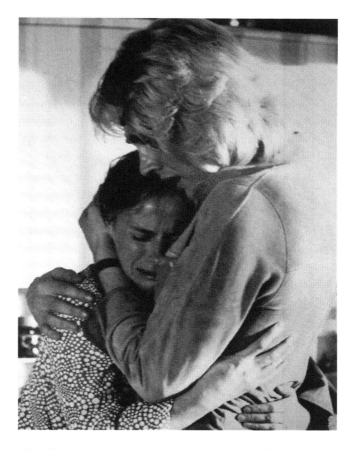

Rita Tushingham as Brenda in 'Straight on till Morning.'

I met Peter Collinson for the first time at Elstree, hugely impressed by his film *'The Italian Job.'* I'd seen it a year or more previously. It starred Michael Caine and Noel Coward, and both were heroes of mine.

I was soon to find Peter quite difficult to work with; the kind of person that insists on getting his own way. His style was to tell the actor what he wanted, listen attentively to what the actor thought he might bring to the feast, negotiate with the actor for a very short period, then TELL him what to do.

The moment I met Rita Tushingham, I knew I'd met a friend. She was warm, and had no ego despite having a huge body of great work behind her. I loved her at once. In the nicest of possible ways.

I believe John had wanted *'a real star'* to play the lead, rather than an *'up-and-coming-nobody,'* but I fully understand. If I had one of my novels made into a film and the choice was between Daniel Day Lewis and a newcomer for the lead, I know who I would choose, even if the newcomer was a pal.

John Peacock and I drifted apart and I haven't seen him for about forty years.

As most people are aware, films are not shot in chronological order because it's seldom financially convenient. For example, it's best to shoot all the 'scenes in the forest' on consecutive days even though they appear spaced throughout the movie. So it's always a toss-up which scenes you'll be asked to shoot first day of principal photography. Scheduling is all about budget and saving money – little thought is given to the feelings of actors, they're expected to be ready for anything.

For those unfamiliar with the film, Peter finally realizes that he must test his new love, Brenda, played by Rita Tushingham, by sharing with her his grizzly history of murder and mayhem. If she can accept the fact that he's made a few mistakes in the past – killed up to ten females – then possibly she might love him sufficiently not to rat him out to the cops. Oh, and I forgot, she is, by now pregnant with his baby. So he plays her his favourite audiotapes – recordings of the various final horrific echoing screams of his previous victims.

This doesn't go down so well with Brenda, who begins to lose it in a big way and adds to the recorded manic screams. Peter leaves the bedroom, sits down on the stairs and starts to sob.

So, on the first day of the *'Straight on Till Morning'* shoot there I was, standing on a gantry at 7.30 a.m. about to film the final 'breakdown' scene of the movie.

I was to come out of the bedroom, close the door behind me, sit down and weep uncontrollably. Peter told me maybe just one full minute of wracking blubs would do.

"Okay! Let's do it, Shane. Up you go," Peter said.

I climbed the stairs and opened the door, only to notice there was no actual room there – just a plank where I was supposed to stand.

My heart was hammering. I was so terrified of failing to get myself to a fever pitch of emotional turmoil, with tears flowing freely, that I froze.

The seconds passed.

Then I heard Peter call out loudly and angrily. *"Hey! I said everyone keep quiet! So shut the **** up! Shane's concentrating."*

You could have heard the proverbial pin drop.

First scene of first day at 8 am at Elstree Studios. 'Straight on Till Morning.'

Then I heard Peter Collinson from way below calling up to me – this time more warmly: *"Take your time, Shane. No hurry."* Then he shouted VERY loudly indeed. *"EVERYONE QUIET, FOR GOD'S*

SAKE!!!"

I knew I had to get those tears flowing. Somehow. The silence was so palpable, I was sure I could hear the blood pumping through my veins.

I thought of tragic moments of my youth. No good. I thought of people I loved who had recently died. Nah. Dry eyes. I imagined my pet cat being run over by a car; a *bit* more successful, but not nearly enough.

What the hell was I going to do? Would I have to simply confess I couldn't do it naturally, and ask make-up for menthol crystals?

The shame! My career was over. I'd failed. This was it!

Immediately the tears began to flow. I opened the door, sat on the steps and sobbed like a green girl. One minute later, Peter called 'cut,' walked up to where I was sitting, wrapped me in his arms, and hugged me. I never told him that my emotional space had been many miles from my character's – that it was the fear of humiliation that saved my bacon that day!

In a way it was odd to be working on what was Hammer's first modern day film having just completed the Gothic horror of *'Demons.'*

Looking back at the style of the film; my clothes, the skin tight velvet trousers from Carnaby Street, tightly fitted colourfully spotted shirts, as well as the E-type Jag, the buzz of the Earl's Court Road, the hip house I lived in – it really was such a seminal early seventies film.

Peter was a friendly man, but could turn in an instant if he didn't get his own way. I always did my best to accommodate his every whim, and when I radically disagreed with anything, I would pretend not to understand and play it my way as much as I could, knowing that the cost of film stock was paramount. You see, I looked so young and innocent that most people would look at my big blue eyes and believe any lie that came forth.

During the shoot there was one very difficult moment for me. I'm sure there was a power struggle going on between Michael Carreras, who had just taken over from his father, Sir James Carreras and was asserting his authority, and Peter who saw himself as the major cheese. I don't think Peter had much time for Michael – he was a naturally arrogant man and he expected to always be top dog. Of course, Michael was the studio head and he employed Peter – not the other way around.

Anyway, one day on set I walked over to Peter and told him I had to meet with a journalist who was going to interview me. I'd be half an hour. Peter told me to sit down – I wasn't going anywhere.

"This is my set. Do as you're told."

Fifteen minutes later Michael Carreras stormed in, strode up to me and told me very firmly so that everyone could hear; *"I told you earlier today to be in my office at 11.30 for an interview with Screen International. What the hell are you doing sitting here?"*

I replied, *"Peter told me I was not to leave the set."*

Michael looked at me, furious. *"I am telling you to get your arse in gear and get over there. Now!"*

He pointed to the studio door then walked off. As I stood, Peter, who had been watching this entire scene walked up me and shouted at me. *"Stay where you are! Do as you're told."*

I didn't much care for being called out in this way in front of everyone, so I replied, *"I have to do what Mr. Carreras says, I'm afraid. My contract is with him."* Peter looked daggers at me. *"I'll handle Carreras,"* he replied, *"You stay there – we're trying to make a feature film, not accommodate some stupid journalist."*

He then followed Michael outside. I sat down again, wishing I could vanish. Ultimately Peter returned. I never gave that interview. Somehow he had managed to get his own way yet again. But from that moment onwards I never felt that Michael saw me as a friend –

they had both challenged me and I think I made a poor decision.

Apart from that day, the shoot went really well. I got on famously with Rita, not so much with Tom Bell, who I think needed the work but wasn't too excited taking part in horror films. He was, I thought, sulky and distant. But it had been his choice to accept the support role so he had to live with it. That was how I felt. As nearly all my scenes were with Rita, all was fine.

I remember almost killing a pedestrian outside Earl's Court tube station. I was supposed to pull out suddenly into the traffic in my white E-Type and the street had not been adequately 'wrangled' by the assistant directors.

I believe there were two major glitches that spoiled what could have been a decent film. One was the way they dressed Rita. She was supposed to be 'an ugly ducking.' That was simply supposed to mean she was not too glamorous. Yet Peter and the designer went completely over-the-top and gave her incredibly dowdy clothes, and a ridiculous blonde wig – one her character buys to make herself look beautiful for my character. Funny how some small point such as this can ruin a film.

The critics had a ball making fun of those two facets. The other big 'no-no' was to have our hero butcher his pet dog. Not only was such a thing so completely anathema because it turned off the entire audience (except for a handful of sociopaths) but it was the manner in which it was supposedly done – slashed to death with a Stanley knife – that appalled everyone. Adza told me at the wrap party I'd have to seek representation elsewhere if I ever killed an animal again on film.

We had a great wrap party at Elstree. Always the joker, Peter played a practical joke on me that ended up going very awry.

The party was a sit down affair, and all the cast and crew were invited.

Sitting at our table were Rita, Peter, Jane and I, and a great looking woman who might nowadays be referred to as a 'cougar.'

She must have been around thirty-five and had fire-red hair in a ponytail falling down her bare back. She wore a very tight-fitting dress. She was definitely very curvaceous – the French have a word for her cleavage; *'tout le monde au balcon,'* (the whole world on the balcony!) The fact was she actually *was* very gorgeous. A red-haired 'Mrs. Robinson.'

As she was sitting across the table from me, I didn't have a chance to chat with her, but our eyes did lock a few times – I couldn't resist sneaking occasional looks, and I have never been exactly subtle when I try to sneak peeks at gorgeous beauties in the high street or in a restaurant.

I was to get a shock an hour later.

I was at the bar ordering a drink for Jane when this voluptuous woman sidled up to me. We hadn't even been introduced, but she whispered something in my ear that took me completely by surprise. She asked me very casually when I intended to become intimate with her. The actual words she used were, *"So when are you going to **** me?"*

I was so surprised, I was temporarily lost for words. What to say? Something witty? I couldn't think of any clever repartee. I said, *"Let's see. Next Thursday at all convenient?"* I was joking of course, but she seemed to take me very seriously.

"Thursday it is," she said, handing me a slip of paper with her address on it. She then returned to the table.

When I sat down, Peter avoided all eye contact with me. Every time I looked across at *'Red'*, and then at Peter he always seemed to be chuckling.

He never came clean that night.

Thursday came and went. During that entire day my thoughts strayed frequently towards *'Red'*, but I stayed put at home. I often wondered if Peter and a few of his friends had waited for me to arrive at the address she'd given me in Lancaster Gate, hoping I'd knock on the door.

It was just as well I didn't, as I found out later that she was 'an extremely very close friend' of Michael Carerras, and only months previously had been the girlfriend of Barry Spikings, one of the biggest English studio bosses in the seventies.

What an escape!

When the film premiered in England and America it received mixed reviews. A few critics were put off my 'killing' Tinker the dog – and quite rightly; it was completely gratuitous.

My favourite review was in the Sunday Times written by one of London's all-time finest reviewers, Dilys Powell. She drew attention to my *'steely arrogance'* and *'goldilocks good looks.'* It didn't seem to be too bad a notice; *'Mr. Briant deserves a better film.'* Then came the crushing blow. *'So does Miss Tushingham. So, for that matter, does the dog.'*

Hmmm. You can't win them all.

One last footnote, my great cyber friend Melissa Brooks emailed me out of the blue a while ago saying, *"I watched 'Straight on Till Morning' last week, and then discovered you are married to a girl called…Wendy. Spooky."*

Incidentally, a few months after *'Demons of the Mind'* was released I suddenly realized I had a stack of Hammer film fans. They seemed to appear from everywhere, wanting to shake my hand, ask for an autograph, and bring me gifts. It was a new and amazing part of being a film actor.

One such fan would quite often knock on my door in Pembridge Crescent hoping he could have a chat with me. This didn't bother me in the least, although I often wondered quite where the appeal lay in chatting with a complete stranger for ten minutes. However, this fan came around frequently.

To give some background to this story, my great uncle, Sir Dudley Colles (not actually a blood relative – my grandmother remarried after my grandfather, Morven Nolan, was killed in action in The Great War) was what was referred to as an Extra Equerry to the Queen. When he retired he went to live in a Grace and Favour House in Kensington somewhere. As a consequence my grandmother would often ask me if I'd like to see any concert at the Royal Albert Hall, as Sir Dudley could let us have seats in the Royal Box, which were of course the best seats in the house.

A week before a concert called 'Film Harmonic 74', an evening of film soundtracks played by the Royal Philharmonic Orchestra, I was delighted to hear from my granny that Dudley had obtained two tickets for Jane and me.

It was the same evening that my friendly fan arrived on my doorstep, carrying a bottle of red wine. *"This is a present for you, Shane,"* he said, adding, *"I happen to have some seats for 'Film Harmonic' on Saturday. Would you like a couple for yourself and your lovely girlfriend,"* he asked.

Rather than show-off about the Royal Box, I thanked him kindly and told him we couldn't make it because we would be in the country that evening.

Come the night, Jane and I dressed appropriately for the Royal Box and made our way to the Royal Albert Hall.

However, on entering the box, who should we see sitting in the front row but my fan and his partner. Our eyes met and I smiled weakly, embarrassed.

My 'fan' turned out to be Prince Charles' dresser.

What an ass I felt that night.

'CAPTAIN KRONOS VAMPIRE HUNTER.'

In my third Hammer film, *'Captain Kronos Vampire Hunter,'* I was cast as a red herring – the character everyone thinks is the bad guy, but isn't.

With John Carson in 'Captain Kronos Vampire Hunter.' (Plus silly hat!)

When I first read the script at home I recall thinking that it was a very original idea, one that could easily translate into a whole series of *'Captain Kronos'* films. But what was I doing in it? Not a great deal – that was for sure. To put it mildly I was annoyed at suddenly being asked to play such a nothing role after starring with Rita. What had happened to the films that Michael Carerras had promised me – the re-make of *'Lorna Doone'* and the biography of Bram Stoker? In *'Kronos'* I was little more than the unwitting son of two filthy rich titled vampires, a character too stupid to ever realise the fact that mum and dad were blood-lusting vampires draining the blood of innocent virgins every night.

Was this payback for getting on the wrong side of Carerras? Maybe my character slept too soundly and never heard the terrible screams? I was extremely disappointed, but as Adza observed *"don't rock the boat, we can't do much – I've had a lawyer check out the contract and strictly speaking you are under contract so you have to accept what you're given."*

I replied, *"But what about good faith?"*

She smiled at me. *"You've still got a lot to learn about show biz, Shane.'*

'*Kronos*' starred the wonderfully good-looking German actor Horst Janson as the Captain. His entourage consisted of the mouth-wateringly sexy Caroline Munro and the late John Cater. The idea was that as a team they ride furiously from place to place, exterminating vampires.

While Horst, Caroline and John Cater had all the fun cavorting around the countryside, Lois Dane, Wanda Wentham and I were mostly stuck in the interior sets. Someone also had the brilliant idea of putting me in a wig that made me look like Harpo Marx. Why anyone would want to put a wig on someone with as much lustrous hair as me was a mystery. I'm surprised they didn't give me eyebrow extensions!

Since I was playing the 'cypher,' I had few decent scenes. This meant I went to work most days with little enthusiasm. I'd also do my best to avoid bumping into Michael Carerras as I was afraid I'd let him know exactly how I felt about my role in '*Kronos.*' Fortunately Lois was such great company the days flew by. We joked around on the set while the heroes were busy with their swordplay. Lois always had me in stitches, and as I remember she was always having boyfriend problems. Wanda was equally good company – she enjoyed life immensely and didn't take a lot too seriously. She was always smiling and sending me up if I got too serious.

I enjoyed all the carriage scenes. Where other kids liked to go to drive fast cars, I enjoyed riding in antique horse-drawn carriages. The smell of them was heady and took me back to a time I'd never in fact experienced.

I was happy that '*Kronos*' wasn't my last Hammer film because, good as it was and a great vehicle for Horst, it did me no favours as I was hard pressed to make anything of my character

With Lois Dane as we realize mum and dad are actually vampires. Surprise!

Lois with a crop, eyeing my grapes.

'FRANKENSTEIN AND THE MONSTER FROM HELL.'

My fourth and final foray into the heart of Hammer was to be in *'Frankenstein and the Monster from Hell.'*

With Peter Cushing on 'Frankenstein.'

At last, a classic Hammer tale! And not only was I going to star with 'Mr. Hammer' himself, the indomitable Peter Cushing, the film was to be directed by Terence Fisher, veteran of 69 feature films at that time – the King of Gothic Horror!

This was my *'Dream Team.'*

Fisher had begun his film career very late and had finally made a name for himself with the film *'The Curse of Frankenstein'*, a film that broke box office records. In so doing he shocked a lot of film critics with *'propensity towards ample bloodletting.'* Most film buffs agree that his *'Dracula'* was possibly the best Dracula ever. He was a natural master of the genre, and I couldn't wait to meet both Cushing and Fisher.

Both were charming and professional gentlemen of the old school. I can't recall one moment when I glanced at Terry and he wasn't smiling. He was seventy years old when I met him, but had the most incredible vigour. He loved his work and was happiest when on the set directing. He had such a happy demeanour, while Peter seemed to be perpetually putting on a brave face to the world while trying to keep his all-abiding sadness at the death of his wife Helen to himself.

Terry was a workaholic – he was happiest on set. I never saw him in the dining room, he was forever working on the next scene in some quiet spot on set, such as a cell or cage.

Terry Fisher working through lunch.

Many people have told me that when Helen died Peter lost a great deal of his will to live and threw himself into his work. We were the best of friends almost at once – that was the way he was, friendly, outgoing and generous to a degree, as well as fiercely proud of his professionalism, which was prodigious.

Each day he'd come to work completely secure in his lines, alert, and ready to see what the other actors had to offer, so he could put that into the mix and we'd all end up bouncing new ideas off each other.

With the enchanting Maddy Smith in 'Frankie & the Monster from Hell.'

One thing I remember most about him was his ability to make things work on the day. His portrayal was never set in stone – it changed with the moment. If I delivered a line a trifle differently his reply would adapt.

This was a salutary lesson to me, and I now pass it on to other actors. If you are REALLY listening to your fellow actors, they often change either their tone, their expression, or the way they bear themselves. So if your portrayal is the same each time, you're not really listening and your response will make little or no sense.

Madeleine Smith was the female lead. She was brilliantly cast by a man who later became my friend, James (Jimmy) Liggat.

Maddy was the sweetheart playing a sweetheart.

As Sarah, the Baron's assistant, she was supposed to be dumb – speechless, that is. Only at the very end of the film, when she has to speak to save lives, does she say anything. Yet, she acted her heart out throughout the film and the audience's heart went out to her character. Again, it's not the *lines*, it's what you do with *silence*.

The Frankenstein story was this time set in an insane asylum where, Simon Helder a young imprisoned surgeon, discovers that the Baron is piecing together a monster from his dead inmates. Of course eventually the monster goes mad and has to be killed – being torn asunder by the crazy inmates. Classic horror stuff!

Dave Prowse played the monster from within a latex monster suit. I well remember seeing it for the first time. I was being made up and Dave entered. All I could hear were some muffled words from inside the suit.

"What do you think, Shane?"

I looked at him from head to toe. I have to say I thought the costume was way over the top and looked like a hairy plastic Halloween suit. But since it couldn't be changed and I didn't want to disappoint Dave I tried desperately to think of one redeeming feature – in the same way as people say after a play *'I loved the costumes.'*

Finally I looked at the feet. They were huge, gross and very ugly – almost deformed. At least the feet were good, I thought to myself. I told him so. There was a long pause, then he said, *"The feet are my own."*

As most film aficionados know Dave and James Earl Jones went on to play Darth Vader.

We had a great supporting cast – actors who were only too happy to come in and perform cameos just to be part of Terry Fisher's horror circus. There was Bernard Lee who we all know as Bond's *'M,'* Patrick Troughton who everyone in England will know as a 'Dr. Who' played a body snatcher, Philip Voss, who played the lead in 'Keane' at the Globe Theatre just months before was a jailer. Charles Lloyd Pack was a crazed Professor.

I noticed that Peter had a trick to make sure he never stumbled over his words. Exercise. It's vital. Start off by being in decent physical shape – can't look relaxed if your body is as stiff as a board. Then, the brain. Can't do your best work if you are pissed or suffering a hangover. Then the voice – make sure you exercise that properly so it's in the best possible shape and you're capable of giving whatever 'colour' to your voice you think is appropriate.

Peter's trick was to thoroughly exercise his facial muscles before every take. I noticed it on the first day. Before every take he would silently go through his dialogue for the scene hugely exaggerating the words as they came out of his lips – it was as if he were screaming the words silently. When it came to the take, his lips had been nicely stretched and were ready for work. He rarely stumbled over a word.

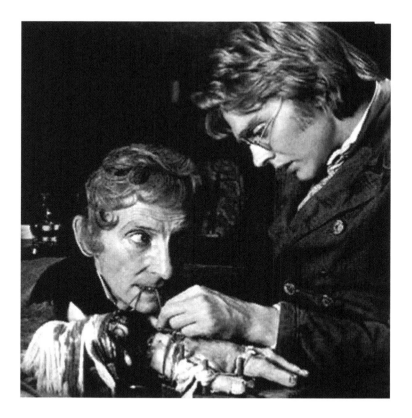

The Baron's hands were useless, so he used his teeth.

I am often asked about the 'hose scene' by Hammer devotees. In this scene the guards punish me by hosing me down with a fire hose. Yes, another time I offered to do my own stunt work! But I had no idea how strong the force of a fire hose was. I thought it might be just a bit stronger than a garden hose.

There were no rehearsals, I just stood there and did it. When the hose was tuned on it hit me like… a fire hose. It took both Philip Voss and Chris Cummingham, the jailers, to hold the hose steady. I was supposed to dance about, slip and fall down, get up, be knocked down again, gasp for breath – the whole box and dice. It was easy! I actually *was* knocked flying, got up, was knocked flat again, time after time. If you ever see the film, look for the red welts on my back; you can see the bruising appear during the thirty second take. It was painful.

Shower for Shane

Shane Briant was one of the young people we tipped for stardom as soon as it became apparent that Hammer was taking a keen interest in him. When we saw his performance as the blond psychopath in the thriller **Straight on Till Morning** we were doubly sure. Now Shane has a couple more Hammer films under his belt—**Kronos**, which he describes as "a mixture of bounty hunter and vampire killer. Captain Kronos hunts vampires for the price on their head", and **Demons of the Mind**, a Gothic Horror directed by Peter Sykes which was originally titled **Blood Will Have Blood**. The film will be released in a double bill just before Christmas. Now Shane is hard at work down at Elstree on his fourth successive Hammer film, **Frankenstein and the Monster From Hell**. He plays a young anatomist who refers constantly to the textbook of Frankenstein in his attempts to create life. Arrested and brought to trial, he is committed to an asylum for the criminally insane where he meets up with his mentor, Baron Victor Frankenstein (Peter Cushing) who plays the role for the sixth time). This powerful hosing-down (for which Shane refused a stand-in) is his introduction to asylum life, but it isn't long before he discovers that the Baron hasn't been exactly idle during his stay. Terence Fisher makes his directorial comeback and Roy Skeggs produces.

Photograph by RONNIE PILGRIM

The hose sequence in 'Frankenstein and the Monster from Hell.' It HURT!

In those days a Hammer film normally took eight weeks to shoot. This hasn't changed much. Of course major motion pictures can take months, even years, but modern day pictures with budgets under thirty million dollars are shot quite quickly.

In *'Frankenstein and the Monster from Hell'* there were naturally quite few scenes where I performed the surgery while Peter watched me (in the film his hands were crippled). The hands of a violinist were grafted on to an arm, the best and sharpest eyes transplanted, the brain of a genius inserted, and so on.

On the second week we were to extract the brain of the monster and put in the perfect brain of the 'Professor.' It was Friday afternoon and the art department had made up a wonderful head for me to work on. Inside the cranium they had placed a fresh sheep's brain. They had then sealed it but forgotten to put it in the fridge. However, things didn't go as planned. We took far too long on another scene and never got around to the brain transplant. So we went home for the weekend and returned on Monday to start off with this scene at eight in the morning. With scenes such as this you really only have one shot at it because it's so difficult and painstaking to make up a second head.

Moments before the stench hit the air!

We rehearsed the dialogue and Peter, as usual, made his exaggerated lip movements. Then we started shooting and I began to saw through the cranium.

As I lifted off the top of the skull, a bubble of the most incredibly fetid air burst upwards into our faces. I have a strong stomach but I thought I might vomit it was so bad. However, I knew I had to continue for the reasons I gave before – one shot! So we grinned and bore it and I lifted the ghastly brain from the head and placed it in a dish. If you look at the footage of this scene you'll see not one single sign from Peter that he has just inhaled *'The Stench from Hell.'* He just watches, as if fascinated by the surgery. Then when Maddy brings in our breakfast moments later, in the same shot, he looks at the food she's presented and says, *"Kidneys! How delicious!"* I was hard pressed not to laugh aloud, as his delivery was so perfect. I did smile – that was all right, it worked.

That was to be the last time I saw Peter. As actor's do, we kept in touch for a short while, then didn't. He went on to make a further twenty-nine films, 'Star Wars' amongst them. There was no one quite like Peter Cushing, and his fan club is testament to that. I don't remember Peter receiving any honours in the Queens Birthday list. He should have, and probably has.

Doctor Helder in 'Frankenstein and the Monster from Hell.'

'Frankenstein and the Monster from Hell' was my fourth film for Hammer and it proved to be my last. So far, anyway! Sadly

Hammer went into a decline from 1975 onwards. They produced just one film in '76, *'To the Devil a Daughter,'* and from '79, when they made again just one film, they produced no more features until their renaissance in 2010 with the very chilling *'Let Me In,' 'The Resident'* and *'Wake Wood.'* During these lean years Hammer concentrated on television series productions such as *'Hammer House of Horror,' 'Hammer House of Mystery and Suspense,'* and *'The World of Hammer.'* I was hugely sad that this iconic company should have ceased to make feature films, so I shouted aloud when I heard that Hammer were back with 'Let Me In,' especially when it received such great reviews. *Vive le Hammer!*

Peter sent me a lovely card a week after the shoot ended. He was NEVER a 'nuisance.'

Peter was the most thoughtful man imaginable.

EARLY U.K. TELEVISION WORK.

CASTING DIRECTORS OF THE OLD SCHOOL.

While I was waiting to begin work on my second Hammer film, I went back to television. Adza was the most wonderful agent, someone who could sell ice cubes to polar bears, probably vodka too, so there was always work to be had.

In the early seventies there were about seven famous casting people. Four of them were women, the most respected being Maude Spector and Miriam Brickman. There were also two or three men, the most famous being Budge Drury, his son, Weston, and Dyson Lovell, who always seemed a bit terse. For instance, I had just returned from filming *'The Picture of Dorian Gray'* in America and had been waiting for thirty minutes in the corridor outside Dyson's office when I heard him call out for me through the closed door. I entered and sat down opposite him. He was busy shuffling papers. Several minutes passed – he didn't look at me but simply continued to shuffle the damned papers. Finally he looked up, studied me closely, and said, *"You look terrible. Are you ill?"*

I told him I felt fine. That was that. Oddly enough, I never much cared for him from that moment on.

Miriam Brickman cast such wonderful movies as *'Oh, What a Lovely War,' 'Far from the Madding Crowd,' 'Straw Dogs,' 'Oh, Lucky Man,'* and *'A Bridge too Far'* to name but a few huge movies.

The fabulously warm and friendly Maude Spector always had a soft spot for me – we got on famously. In fact if I had to wait in her office for more than five minutes before being sent in to meet a director, she would invariably pop a bottle of Moët and share a glass with me.

Maude's career began in 1946 and her films were always cast

impeccably. *'Lawrence of Arabia,' '55 Days at Peking,' 'For Your Eyes only,* 'and *'The Big Sleep.'* Casting a film in those days was handled very differently to today. Casting directors then were highly respected by all directors and producers. If Maude said you were a capable actor, everyone took her word for it. Instead of being obliged, as Australian actors have been since the invention of the video camera, to prove you have talent to speak, open doors and chew gum while smiling, Maude, Budge, and Miriam would simply study the list of characters that were to be cast and then make suggestions to the director in question. Of course very often producers and directors had already made up their minds about leads such as Sean Connery and Katherine Hepburn.

However, during my time in London I was called to meet many celebrated directors, and not one of them asked me to prove that I could act. I chatted with the very engaging and highly intelligent Lindsay Anderson, the sometimes testy Michael Winner, the very easy going John Boorman. Of course, if such directors were searching for a young man to play a major role such as the lead in *'Young Winston,'* a film with a massive budget, a whole selection of actors would usually be asked to screen test at Pinewood; on 35 mm film. That was fair enough.

On my arrival in Sydney in 1982, I found myself having to 'put down on tape' everything I was up for – my past body of work was of no relevance to anyone, nor who I had worked with. But more of that later.

'NOTORIOUS WOMAN'. THE BALZACS!

One of my most favourite television performances was as Alfred de Musset in *'Notorious Woman,'* a 'Play of the Month' for the BBC.

Rosemary Harris played the lead, Georges Sand, and the support cast was stellar. I was delighted to be amongst such fine actors.

George Chakiris played Chopin – when I met him at rehearsals I couldn't stop seeing him leaping around as Bernardo in 'West Side Story.' Alan Howard was Prosper Merimée, Sinead Cusack was Marie Dorval, Brian Blessed was Albert Gryzmala, Joyce Redman was Sophie Dupin de Fancueil and Jeremy Irons played Franz Liszt.

I felt a million quid at the read-through, although at the time my friend Jeremy was yet to become a star, so I was much more impressed by the other cast. Working with Rosemary Harris was divine.

The divine Rosemary Harris in 'Notorious Woman.' BBC.

I've been incredibly lucky to work with some of the best actresses of the past fifty years; Rosemary, Olivia de Havilland and Yvonne Mitchell to name just a few. I can only say that when you work with such gifted people it's like being caught up in a kind of transcendental state of grace where can give your all to the other actor. Cuddling up to Rosemary in those bedroom scenes and sharing a laugh between takes is something I shall remember to my dying day – she was the most beautiful woman.

There were two incidents during the filming of 'Notorious

Woman,' that I remember, and both were hilarious.

The first was a moment in rehearsal. Jeremy Irons as Franz Liszt was supposedly sitting at a piano (in fact a bench in the rehearsal room) with one hand on a dummy keyboard, the other was supporting his head in an extremely serious fashion. Liszt was supposedly composing his famous Concerto in E flat, idly tapping fingers on the keys. When he got to the fifth note he'd shake his head and start over again. He did this maybe four times, stopping each time at the same note – one everyone by then had screaming in their heads. There was a long pause, then Liszt smiles knowingly and plonks the fifth note. Here, the script was, I thought, too obvious. Yet it made me laugh.

Having a laugh between takes!

The second clanger was a line of Rosemary's dialogue. In the script I was in the throes of some kind of epileptic fit. Georges Sand was unaware of this since she was in an adjoining room, unaware of my state. As I writhed on the floor she called out: *"Hurry up, darling. The Balzacs are due at eight-thirty!"* Too good, huh?

Warris Hussein was our wonderful director. I've been directed by many very talented people, as well as less than talented people. My personal ratio has been till now probably eight percent superb, sixty-two per cent very talented and the rest average.

I wish I had the original script of 'Notorious Woman' but I don't. So forgive me if I try to recollect one passage. It was the stage direction, cum writer's note, in parenthesis at the top of a scene that begins with Alfred de Musset falling to the floor screaming that he has demons in his head. Georges Sand scoops him up and hugs him as he rants and raves.

This is what I remember being in brackets – *'Alfred de Musset suffered from terrible epileptic seizures, madness and brain syphilis – the playing of the following scene is left to the discretion of the director and actor.'*

So what the hell was I going to do in the first read through, I wondered, as I read the script for the first time at home? I knew I would have to go for it, rather than wimp out - I wasn't one of those actors of the opinion that you didn't take readthroughs too seriously. As far as I was concerned you put your heart into it.

On the day, the other cast members were somewhat unprepared for my tirade. *"I HAVE DEMONS IN MY HEAD! MY BRAIN IS ON FIRE!"* I screamed so loudly that I could be heard in the BBC canteen several miles away. I then deliberately fell off my chair to the ground.

As I paused for breath, silence reigned. No one said anything. Then Warris muttered, *"Very interesting Shane. Let's move on, eh? This is just a reading. Give us the gist from now on, what do you say?"* I was embarrassed, clearly I had a lot to learn about read-throughs.

From the English T.V Times.

As a footnote to this episode, I might add that when I told my mother I was to play de Musset, she recalled an Ogdon Nash poem about him – *'Alfred de Musset, called his cat 'pusset', it was somewhat affected, but only to be expected.'* Here I was, about to star in a BBC mini series with a lot of luminaries, and all she could think of was this poem. It was both apt and very funny, but I was concentrating on more serious matters. But that was my wonderfully eccentric mother to a T – she would always ask if I would be wearing 'nice clothes.' If I'd told her I was to play *'Fool'* in *'King Lear'*, or the tramp in Egon Wolf's wonderful play *'Paper Flowers,'* she'd have said the same thing.

My one final memory of that month at the 'Beeb' was visiting the club every evening after work. It was usually packed with actors, journalists, directors, and producers. One of my acting friends had this great idea of paging himself at least three times every Friday evening so that everyone would hear his name mentioned loudly. *"A call for *****! Will ***** please pick up the nearest red telephone?"*

The night we finished recording I was in the BBC club and on my third gin and tonic when I heard someone behind me mutter. "I say, who the hell is *****? Well, they were soon to find out! Even more so when he won an Oscar! He was a dedicated actor with heaps of chutzpah, and that idea of announcing himself was pure genius. I believe it became very popular in later years. Wish I'd thought of it.

ARMCHAIR THEATRE AND COSSACK HORSES.

In 1972 I starred in my first television play in the UK. It was a play in the Armchair Theatre series for ITV called *'Franklin's Farm.'* Written by the very talented Guy Slater, and directed by a man who became a great friend, Peter Hammond.

It was a very sensitive and lovely play that focused on a young man and his aged grandmother played by Maureen Prior. The third major character, granny's gardener Rienhardt, was played by the comic legend Max Wall. It was Max's first foray into acting from stand up comedy, and I have to say he was wonderful. He brought tears of laughter to my eyes when he was kind enough to do a routine or two from the fifties and brought tears to my eyes again with his heartbreaking performance in *'Franklin's Farm.'*

Peter always brought out the best in people, certainly the best I had to offer. He'd say to me just before we started filming, *"Shane, you can be magic...but only if you want to."* This always made me try like hell!

I believe the play was a big success – the notices were great.

With iconic comedian Max Wall in 'Franklin's Farm.' Thames Television.

Incidentally, it must have been around that time that Adza called me and asked me if I'd do my bit for the National Film and Television School. This is a funny story – I hope!

Equity members are often asked to help out students in their final year NFTS production. As a favour. No money. And it's always the young poverty stricken actors who are approached, never the rich ones.

Being the generous philanthropic woman that she was, Adza told me I had no choice in the matter – I'd take part in John Lind's short film, *'The Reprieve,'* the following Thursday. She told me she'd informed Lind that I was 'a very fine horse rider.'

"Why," I countered.

"Because you will be playing a Cossack. The lead!" she replied quickly.

"But I hate riding horses," I said. *"I've had nightmares about being crushed by horses ever since that time in Dublin where a horse lost it's*

footing and crash landed on my leg."

"Well, you're going to enjoy riding on Thursday. Good free practice. Only a matter of time before you are asked to play Ghengis Khan's son in some film."

On the day, I was helped up on a horse at eight o'clock in the morning and rode the highly excitable young filly (one that galloped like the wind at the slightest touch of the heels) till the sun set. As if that wasn't enough, all the riding was done through wheat fields so mature and high that I couldn't see the horses legs, nor the lie of the ground. It was a miracle none of us fell and was killed.

At six o'clock I was helped off my steed and immediately pleaded with the stable girl to be laid down flat on my back – I was in such incredible pain. This condition lasted several days.

Adza was right, as ever. I needed experience, since many years later I was to play Sir Clifford Chatterley, a Master of the Hunt. And that involved one of the most hair-raising stunts I've ever performed. But that's a story to come.

SHYSTERS, TOYBOYS AND STALKERS.

I'm not sure which television play came first, but during 1973 Adza worked like fury for me, and I was involved in all manner of wonderful television plays.

Fortunately for me, the seventies were a great time for television plays. The BBC produced *'Play of the Month'* with generous budgets, while the ITV Network made plays such as 'Armchair Theatre.'

Nowadays there has been quite a significant cut back in filming plays for television, because reality TV came winging in quite a few years ago. However, while there are many more cable channels today, it's still the BBC and the ITV Network that make the more serious and intelligent content, while the cable channels fill their daily quota with cheap American re-runs (trying to persuade us all we actually want to see *'Gilligan's Island'* and *'I love Lucy,'* over and over and over again) There is also a glut of 'Celebrity' this, and 'Celebrity' that; how to survive in a jungle, how to sell your house, how to do everything. Because they're a part of the 'cross-promotion phenomena,' they're here to stay.'

Here in Australia our commercial channels haven't produced a television play as far as I can remember. They preferred the 'mini series' in the eighties, and now it's the 'Underbelly' phenomenon – the huge hit crime series.

I was extremely lucky to be resident in Australia in the seventies when the mini-series was at its most popular. Sadly, now it hardly exists. The ABC still make great intelligent series, but they are strictly speaking 'series' rather than a one-off two part mini-series. *'Rake'* with Richard Roxbough was one of the best series of 2010.

Channel 7, 9, and 10 all produce a decent amount of home grown material, but with the Aussie television stations buying American series cheaply in bulk, most evenings Australians are watching last seasons American crime thrillers.

Of course we are blessed with our multi-cultural channel SBS which has World News in the evening, as well as news in many languages direct from overseas, and wonderful foreign films.

1973 was a bumper year for me, if the Internet Movie Database is accurate. I played a gloriously arrogant shyster in *'Crown Court,'* the daytime series Granada Television produced.

I don't think modern daytime television is nearly as good now as it was then. It lacks character and intelligence. There are shows that buck the trend, but back then 'Crown Court' was a clever series that cost very little and was completely unusual in concept.

It ran for thirteen seasons. An incredible six hundred and fifty episodes! My episode was written by my friend Guy Slater and was directed by Bob Hird, who I was later to work with again in John Buchan's 'Huntingtower' for the BBC.

Cult leader in 'Crown Court.' Granada Television.

Each episode stood on it's own, and was an individual criminal case that took place in a Crown Court somewhere. The one I was in was called *'The Inner Circle.'*

Naturally, all the characters were played by actors, but the jury was made up of people who showed up on the day at the Granada studios. So the fun part of appearing in these episodes was that the actor could try to influence these jury members with his/her performance.

Naturally, all the dialogue was scripted, so performance was everything – you couldn't deviate from the words on the page. Nevertheless, you could 'charm' certain members of the jury, and attempt to manipulate their emotions – which is what I tried to do in spades.

My character was the leader of a religious cult named *'The Church of the Open Box.'* The group took money from naïve people. The box, as you can imagine, served as an offertory – a box forever open to receive money from suckers.

I'd been given some most unforgiving dialogue. I was arrogant, self-centred and clearly guilty. Yet it was also written that I was an intelligent, fun, and generally likeable guy. So I played my character as warm, amusing and a little bit devilish.

I singled out several women on the first day, and each time I had a good line I'd fix them with a very intimate glance.

Occasionally, I'd hit the jackpot, and they'd smile back at me. The more they smiled back at me, the more sensual my glances.

Sadly it didn't work. I was found guilty. The 'cougars' in the jury smiled their expressions of *'sorry.'* Too bad, these men and women off the streets clearly took their television job very seriously. I'm sure it'd be different in real life! Bad guys can *always* wheedle and charm lonely women.

I always thought the series should be revived. Cheap as chips to make, and we all know everyone loves courtroom drama. Add to that the element of a studio audience and you have another remake that would surely be a winner. Now the ABC has made a courtroom drama series called *"Crownies,"* and the initial reviews have been good. I played a Supreme Court Judge in one episode.

As a footnote, I've noticed that this small inexpensive series has attracted quite a cult following. On *YouTube*, a short sequence of me in the dock has had the most 'hits' of anything I've ever done.

Curious.

I never lost sight of the possibilities that lay the other side of the Atlantic, so one morning I rang and asked Adza if she could find me someone in America to represent me. She didn't appear to have any strong contacts there, so I decided to fly there and see who I could come up with.

One of my first choices was Marian Rosenberg, because she represented so many fine European actors. However, during our very brief chat she told me she never took on anyone who didn't earn less than a quarter of a million dollars a year. Bear in mind this was over twenty-five years ago. Never mind. Next choice?

I had meetings with William Morris, Triad and a few others. They were all very polite and charming.

I soon discovered that that's their default mode during meetings with actors. One major agent shared the secret with me. *"It's a breeze to get rid of people you never want to see again. Just tell the actor he's hugely talented, and that you're 'very excited.' Then say good-bye. When they call again, you're never in the office. Easy, Shane."*

I eventually signed with an agency called Contemporary Artists. The reason? I liked the name, their premises were conveniently situated in Santa Monica on 3rd Street Promenade, and the agent who'd be looking after me had the wonderfully apposite name of Gary Fuchs (yes, I *know* how it's pronounced). Many years previously the agency had been owned and run by a well known agent called Ronnie Lief, but when I signed up it was a trifle on the skids. It no longer exists today.

For years after securing an agent, I'd fly over to L.A. for the 'pilot season,' and each year I'd stay for a month or six weeks and wait for Mr. Fuchs to call me. He never did. I stayed in a great apartment on Horn Avenue in West Hollywood, just up from the famous Spago's Restaurant. It belonged to a good friend, Paul Ibbetson, an Aussie producer of wonderful commercials who was now making commercials in California as well as in Oz.

It was a fun time, and I did my best to network and schmooze my way into some big job or other. Nothing seemed to pay dividends.

Every now and then my old friend Steven Nalevansky, then a producer at Paramount, would invite me to lunch in the commissary and I'd feel a real part of the action. He is the most genuine and amusing Hollywood guy I have ever met. He has wonderful children and is married to Marti now. She sings wonderfully. And Wendy and I are god parents of Josef and Amanda's son Beau. He's a stunning boy.

But all these lunches never amounted to a job, and so I had to be content to view the pilot season as a holiday, during which something *might* happen. I'd always pack and go home and see what work Adza had found for me – and she'd nearly always have something tasty waiting.

Every inch the Hollywood producer, Steven Nalevansky.

1973 was also the year I went to Europe with a great detective series called *'Van der Valk.'*

It starred Barry Foster and the late Michael Latimer as the two lead Dutch cops. *Every* English actor wanted a 'gig' on that show because it was a free holiday to Amsterdam. I was no different, and asked Adza what she could do.

Almost immediately I was cast as, guess what, you got it, a long-haired bleach blonde gigolo.

I wore a white linen suit and open-necked shirt and white casual shoes. It was recently suggested that I pre-empted John Travolta in the white flared suit brigade – that I was strutting my stuff in '73 and Travolta didn't for another four years. Mind you, he did it *way* better than me.

I was to become the best of friends with Michael Latimer years later in Australia – we both took flight for Oz at about the same time, but we never worked together on this episode. He died in June 2011 – he was one of my heroes.

The single funny anecdote I have of my time on the set of *'Van der Valk'* was during a scene where I'm lounging around near a swimming pool. Mike Vardy, the director, asked me to casually amble to the pool, then dive majestically into the water and scythe my way at speed to the far end. The problem was that I didn't dive, and was a hopeless swimmer. I told Mike and he simply heaved a sigh and replied, *"Just get in the water, Shane, and I'll speed up the film come the time."*

With Lisa Daniely in 'Van der Valk.'

Another play I was cast in that year was a play that Anglia television produced called *'Fixation.'* It was a bizarre yet amusing story of a young man who develops a fixation about an older married woman and begins stalking her relentlessly. Eventually she and her husband, played by the lovely Mary Peach, and T.P. McKenna, board a cruise ship to get away from the pain-in-the-arse-kid, only to find he's a fellow passenger. Eventually T.P's character becomes so fed up with the ridiculous boy, he simply throws the young lad into the sea and he's drowned.

Wouldn't it be wonderful if we could all get rid of pesky stalkers in this way? I loved playing my character, Dennis Wilson, because he was so acutely annoying. I wanted the audience to cringe every time they saw him and cheer when he was tossed into the North Sea. I think I achieved it!

When it came to shooting the on-board scenes, we had to board the ferry from Harwich to the Hook of Holland.

The weather was filthy, with gales and rain and high seas, while it was supposed to be somewhere calm and lovely – like the Mediterranean.

Our director, Alan Seymour, had to be very inventive, since the cast were all sick as dogs and found the only thing that helped was brandy – somewhat too much of it, as far as I was concerned on more than one occasion!

We sailed back from the Hook of Holland at night. The weather was particularly bad and again we were all ready to throw up. The cold buffet dinner provided in the ship's dining room featured a far too graphic display of cold pickled fish. Only a few travellers ventured near the food because of the heady herring odour, and the moment they actually saw the groaning seafood board they ran for the hills.

By contrast T.P. was in fine form and tucked into a huge selection of everything. After ten minutes I left him to it and made my way to my cabin.

In the early hours of the morning there was a knock on my cabin door. It was one of the production team – she looked very worried.

"Just checking he's not with you. We can't find T.P! We've searched the entire ship! There's a possibility he fell overboard."

There were tears in the young girl's eyes.

"Have you alerted the Captain?" I asked.

"Of course," she replied, wringing her hands. *"He's had all his people walking the length and breadth of the ship."*

Of course no one thought of the engine room. Why would they? T.P was eventually found there, in the bowels of the steamer, chatting to the below decks engineers. He was clutching a bottle of Irish Whiskey. Because T.P. knew that none of the crew were allowed to drink, he took a bottle with him and passed it around.

When he was finally discovered, he was stunned to hear of his death and laughed a great deal.

At breakfast next morning he wasn't laughing so heartily.

I became great friends with Mary Peach who later married my great buddy, writer and Hammer director Jimmy Sangster.

'THE SWEENEY.'

I think there are two prerequisites to becoming a successful actor. By that I mean being able to survive entirely on income generated by acting without having to moonlight as a neurosurgeon, male prostitute or CIA operative. They are talent and intelligence.

Everyone thinks they can act, and most are right. They can. But the successful actor has to be able to act better than most people. Maybe better than 98% of them. Then he/she has a chance.

As for the intelligence, let's face it not all actors are too bright, and that shows in performance. Of course, it's normally the stupid actors that stick at it longer than anyone else, because they never get the message that they're hopeless. But there's no harm in that, is there? Let them enjoy themselves.

More seriously, if you look at any of our major/famous stage or film stars I challenge you to find someone stupid. My favourite movie actors are the most obvious, I'm afraid. I don't think one can go past Pacino, De Niro, Walken, Hepburn (Katherine and Audrey) Anna Karina, Johnny Depp, Daniel Day-Lewis, Cary Grant (at his best with humour) and of course Newman.

That's just off the top of my head. But my point is this. If you love it, stay with it and risk being poor. Never start a career after the age of twenty-five (girls especially – sorry to be sexist!) and if you can't get an agent initially, don't be despondent, get on with cobbling together a show reel. *Then* get an agent.

There's no limit to what you can do if you set your heart on it, so don't be depressed. Just when you think you're washed up, along comes something wonderful.

When you're in the film business, always respect the film crew, and never act the 'star.' Newman and De Havilland are two of my role models. A little modesty goes a long way. It'll make you happy, and gain you a great many friends. When I'm rich and famous I hope I'll still be able to spend an evening drinking with my butler and treating him as an equal ('joke, Joyce' – as we say in Oz.)

In early 1975 I got a shot at playing a role in the hugely successful *'The Sweeney,'* cop series starring John Thaw and Dennis Waterman.

With the utterly captivating Leslie Ann Down in 'The Sweeney.'

Created by Trevor Preston, and written by Trevor and Ted Childs, it was one of those hugely popular shows that everyone stayed in to watch. Consequently it was a TV show that Adza targeted to advance my television profile.

The episode I was in was called *'Chalk and Cheese.'* I was again blessed with a high profile guest cast. My girlfriend was to be played by Lesley-Anne Down, who incidentally is now working on *'The Bold and the Beautiful'* and looks every bit as beautiful as she did when I clapped eyes on her at rehearsals.

Some people stand the test of time; Audrey Hepburn, Lesley-Ann and my wife Wendy. After *'Chalk and Cheese,'* Lesley-Anne went on in 1978 to win the Evening Standard *'Best Newcomer'* award and was nominated for a Golden Globe in 1986 for *'North and South.'*

Also guesting was my old friend Paul Jones – it was great to hook up with him again. He and I were fellow 'crims' – he was the working class lad, and I was the 'toff'. It was a great story and fun to shoot. I had just one short scene with Thaw and Waterman (when they 'nick' me at the end) so I never got to know either of them. The bulk of what I did was with Paul and Lesley-Anne.

One incident stands out in my memory and makes me laugh to this day. First of all you have to remember that Lesley was exquisitely beautiful and in her early twenties, slim perfect figure, lovely flawless skin, fabulous eyes. She had been voted *'Most Beautiful Teenager'* at the age of fifteen, and was even lovelier aged twenty-two. She had everything. Yet my character, Giles Nunn, treated her in a very offhanded fashion. He was a very arrogant bastard – I seem to have been singled out for these roles at the time!

Every man on the set thought she was the most beautiful girl they had clapped eyes on in years, so when in one scene her character tried to impress him by opening her fur coat to reveal she was topless, the whole crew moved forward to watch – everyone seemed to have something really important to do at that precise moment. Even the runners and the art department!

They were all outsmarted. The director, Ian Kennedy-Martin

organized matters so that I was sitting on a sofa with my back against the wall, and when Lesley-Anne came in, she stood in front of me, and then took off her top. All you could see from behind were her shoulders and the obvious lack of bra straps. Some days an actor's life can be hard work. This was *not* one of them. But there *was* a catch. In the script it is very clear that the super-arrogant Giles Nunn pays scant attention to this striptease – He doesn't look,' the script says so, despite my bad intentions, I only caught a blur of milky soft loveliness in my peripheral vision.

One of the perks of being an actor. Leslie Ann undresses.

Later than day, I suppose about a dozen members of the crew asked me the obvious questions. *"Hey, nice, huh?"* Every time I was asked I'd put myself in Giles Nunn's character, look bored and say, *"Come on, seen one, seen them all."* They found this extremely annoying, so it was great fun.

With Paul 'Manfred Mann' Jones in 'The Sweeney.'

'SHADES OF GREENE.'

In the autumn of 1975 I appeared in another play directed by one of my favourite directors, Peter Hammond. *'A Chance for Mr. Lever.'*

It was one of a series of plays written by Clive Exton, based on Graham Greene's short stories. I was especially happy to be in this series as I had once met the man himself at Quendon Hall in Essex, the home of my fairy godmother Kit Adeane.

I was thirteen, so I didn't engage in any erudite conversation with him, but I did study him closely all evening because he was who he was. I'd just read his novel *'Brighton Rock'* and thought it outstanding. My impression, just from that evening – and this was almost a boy's impression – was that he was a very sad and withdrawn man. I believe it comes across in his work – a certain sadness and Catholic guilt.

Freddie Jones played Mr. Lever. He was also a client of Adza. A fine actor who was five times nominated for BAFTA awards. I found him absolutely charming, eccentric to the point where eccentric borders on bonkers, but a wonderfully gifted actor.

This short play was one of his tour de forces. If you get a chance to see it, do. Freddie's character, Mr. Lever, is a machinery sales representative down on his luck, who is offered a chance to improve his situation by making his way through the Liberian jungle to find a buyer.

Of course he gets malaria and dies. Freddie's performance was heart-wrenching – Lever does it all for his wife at home and has such courage. I played a kind of 'Gordon Gekko' type – young and ruthless.

BETWEEN THE SHEETS. MARIA MARTIN.

I didn't know it at the time, but *'Maria Martin or Murder in the Red Barn'* was to be my last production for the BBC. I'd go back tomorrow if asked, it goes without saying!

It was a fun show – I'd been in a production of the same play at University. It's been done to death yet people look forward to yet another version.

I have absolutely no recollection of any event other than lying in bed next to Pippa Guard waiting for the sparks to light our love scene. It's always a bit confronting when the assistant director says, *"Okay, why not take your robes off and hop into bed."* Nearly always, the actors keep their pants on, so for males it's a piece of cake, but the poor girls are often embarrassed at going topless. Pippa and I didn't know each other very well, and it seemed like an inordinate time we had to lie in bed with a sheet over us while they lit us.

I find bed scenes rather enjoyable. I think of them as 'sleep-overs' rather than a time to get hot under the collar and choke back a 'stiffy.' So, on this occasion the conversation soon became somewhat stilted. Eventually I thought I'd lighten the atmosphere with a joke.

"Is this your first bedroom scene," I asked Pippa.

"No," she replied, *"I had one with Peter Firth."*

I smiled *"Tho, I'm the thecond?"* I said, with a strong lisp.

She laughed, thank heaven's. It wasn't much of a gag. But it did lighten things up. Pippa was a real sweetheart.

HOLLYWOOD!

CULVER CITY STUDIOS AND DORIAN GRAY!

One of the most fabulous things that happened to me was to be cast as the name role in *'The Picture of Dorian Gray.'* As ever, it was the wonderful Maude Spector who called Adza to summon me to her offices in Mayfair. American producer Dan Curtis was looking for a Dorian Gray for his *Movie of the Week* for the American Broadcasting Company. It was to be a two-part three-hour production. Very prestigious. I was thrilled.

Maude and I shared a glass of bubbly before I went in to meet Dan. The many times Emmy-Award-winning director Glenn Jordan had left the casting to Dan. When I say 'left' the casting, this was more probably a question of Dan saying, *"I'll cast him. You direct the sonofabitch."*

Dan knew what he wanted and he always got it. Scared the hell out of me on more than one occasion. You didn't mess with Dan, or answer back.

Later in 1983 he would direct the award winning series *"The Winds of War"* with Robert Mitchum, Ali McGraw, and a heap of other heavyweights. It would win him an Emmy, and a PGA Award as producer that year. The series was also nominated for a Golden Globe for Best Mini Series or Motion picture made for TV.

I met with Dan on a Wednesday in London, heard from Adza that I'd landed the role on Thursday, boarded a British Airways flight – first class no less (those were the days) – on Friday, with the peerless Nigel Davenport who was to play Lord Harry Wooton, and met up with Glenn at a read through at the famous Culver City Studios on Saturday morning.

It's a series of events that young actors dream of – and I am here to tell all you struggling actors that it CAN happen. Just when you least expect it.

Nigel and I had a great flight over, one I'll never forget. I can remember the seats in which we lounged as if it was last week.

In the seventies there were no beds of course, but the food was even more spectacular than it is today (my opinion only).

The first thing I was told when the plane took off was that I could ask for anything my heart desired and they'd probably have it ready in a matter of minutes.

Nigel started off with several orders of Beluga caviar while I had some lobster. As the champagne – *Bollinger* of course – flowed, I voiced the opinion that possibly I shouldn't arrive in Los Angeles with a hangover.

"Nonsense," Nigel barked with a grin, *"It's the only way to arrive!"*

Lord Harry Wooton to a T!

The wonderful Nigel Davenport as Lord Henry Wotton in 'Dorian Gray.'

As luck would have it, I was the victim of an isolated skin problem the night before I flew, and by the time I checked into the gloriously old fashioned Montecito Hotel in North Hollywood, I had a nasty red boil on my nose.

I stared at myself in the bathroom mirror, wondering what on earth I could do – the livid red pustule was growing by the second. I knew I 'd be in trouble when I walked into the studios to meet Glenn the following morning, looking like Pinocchio in a clown's costume.

A car came to collect me at the Montecito at ten-thirty next day. I'd just returned from the breakfast joint I'd found close by called *'The Golden Cup.'* Everyone there was extremely friendly as I sat up at the bar and ate a full breakfast. One young man even suggested we should meet up later in the day for a few drinks. I was so impressed by the friendliness of these Californians that I mentioned the experience to my driver. He smiled wryly.

"The Golden Cup on Highland?" he asked.

"Sure," I replied.

"It's a twenty-four hour gay pick up joint, Shane," he told me. I cast my mind back – that's why there were no girls in the short order bar.

Half an hour later we arrived at the Culver City studios and I entered the vast rehearsal room. Glenn walked over from the 'coffee and sugared donut' table. He shook my hand warmly, and then stared at the fiery pustule on my nose. No smiles. Just concern.

"Oh my God…" he said in an undertone, *"I was hoping to meet the most beautiful man in the world – Dorian Gray. Yet here's a young man with the biggest pimple known to man on his nose."*

He then called out to someone behind him, a man helping himself to an iced donut.

"Sam, come over here and look at this."

Sam, head of make-up, came over.

"What do you reckon, Sam – we lance it now?"

Sam suggested leaving it for a day or two. It was only then that Glenn smiled, looked me in the eye rather than the nose, and welcomed me to the reading.

"Had to get that sorted out first, Shane. I'm sure you understand. Now come and meet the cast."

Over the years I have watched several of the cast members I met on that day become rich and famous. Fionnula Flanagan went on to win Emmys for *'Rich Man, Poor Man,'* and be nominated for *'How the West Was Won.'* She's starred in just about every television series that has been made since 1970.

Linda Kelsey, who played Dorian's wife (an addition to Wilde's story) was nominated for five Emmys and three Golden Globe Awards for the series *"Lou Grant."*

John Karlin snagged the role of Detective Cagney's husband in the hit series *'Cagney and Lacey'* and surely could have retired many times since then.

The beautiful Vanessa Howard, who played Sybil Vane, married celebrated producer Robert Chartoff (they had the most gorgeous house in Malibu with the bedroom literally hanging over the high tide mark – what romance!) the late Charles Aidman was Basil Hallward, and we all know that Nigel Davenport is one of the best actors England has ever produced (*'A Man for all Seasons,'* *'Chariots of Fire.'* and *'Mary Queen of Scots'* are just three of his forty-eight films)

Dorian Gray. Culver City Studios.

Dan put us all on a very tight schedule. We had twelve rehearsal days, then had to shoot the entire one hundred and eleven minute mini series in four days on a beautifully crafted set constructed in two vast studios in Culver City. This translated into two one-and-a-half-hour episodes of prime time *'Movie of the Week.'*

It was hard, grueling work, but I feasted on collaborating with Glenn. He was a master, I could see that almost immediately. He's won four Emmys and has been nominated for ten more. My favourite Jordan productions are *'Barbarian at the Gate,' 'The Long Way Home'* with Jack Lemmon, and *'Les Miserables.'* And on the subject of *'Les Miserables,'* Glenn told me a great story.

He was originally approached to direct the piece, but the script he was given was about five inches thick and weighed more than a fat cat.

"Can you give me... say a hundred and twenty pages on Monday, Glenn?" the producer asked. Surprised, Glenn enquired how he could possibly shave three hundred pages over the weekend. In true Hollywood fashion, the producer replied, *"Tear pages."* I have to add that it is possible Glenn was exaggerating. If so, I apologize to the producer in question. Incidentally, I heard from another source that some studio people were concerned that the American television viewer would be unfamiliar with Victor Hugo's masterwork. Not only the story, but also the title.

"People are going to think this is a darned depressing movie. The miserable people? What do you think?" someone was said to have muttered in the ITC offices.

"Why don't we give it a title our audience can identify with," someone else suggested.

"Such as?" yet another exec asked.

After a pause, someone offered. *"'Tough shit'?"*

Everyone laughed loudly.

Maybe this story is apocryphal.

After twelve days of rehearsing, several massive trucks arrived at the studio lot where the sets had been built, and four 1970's television-style video cameras were brought inside.

The idea was to film the show in a film studio, with film lighting and film sets. Everything was to be exactly like a movie set except for the cameras, which were to be video.

I think the idea worked well. Of course anyone who is familiar with movie-making can immediately see that it was not shot on 35-millimeter film. In view of the fact it was made for television, why not use video? I think it had a really good 'look' because Robert Cobert photographed it in such a wonderful way.

First shoot day in Culver City.

Those intense four days flew by. One evening I hosted a drinks party at the Montecito. All my new Los Angeles friends came. I ordered in catered nibbles and canapés and a great deal of wine, beer and spirits. Nearly all the booze was gone within an hour or so, and my new friend, screenwriter Jeffrey Bloom, was kind enough to telephone Turners on Sunset for more booze. Every hour until 2 a.m.

As the hours passed he kept on phoning for more and the same young Mexican would arrive with more supplies. Each time Jeffrey would give him a huge tip – Jeffrey's always been the über-tipper, and I sometimes think his tip amounts to more than the cost of the meal.

Jeffrey had written the great 'caper' movie, 'Snowjob,' starring Jean-Claude Killy (another of my heroes – I love skiing) the year before, as well as the cult hit, 'Blood Beach,' and was in the process of working on a movie script '11 Harrowhouse,' that was to have a stellar cast—Candice Bergen, Charles Grodin, Trevor Howard, James Mason and John Gielgud.

In those days Jeffrey had long dark hair, great taste in clothes, and a very dry sense of humour. As I write I can tell you he still has the same sense of style, and a great sense of humour. He's remained one of my best friends now for thirty-seven years. He's a big talent and has written, directed and produced some wonderful films.

**SHANE BRIANT
BLOND, BEAUTIFUL
AND BRITISH!**

Give your eyes a treat and feast them on sensationally sexy Shane Briant in costume for his role in the ABC-TV presentation of *The Picture of Dorian Gray*. Shane is a sleek six-footer, with blond hair and blue eyes, who lives in the Pimlico section of London. He won this role over hundreds of other young Englishmen and Americans because he was the most perfect person to play the bad and beautiful Dorian. Shane worries about being typecast as a pretty boy so in his next film, *The Mackintosh Man*, in which he co-stars with another sizzler, Paul Newman, he plays a super-tough guy, someone you wouldn't want to meet in a dark alley. It's hard to imagine not wanting to run into this gorgeous guy any.

This always makes me laugh! T.V Guide in L.A.

I am reasonably fearless when it comes to hard work and memorising dialogue. We started filming *'Dorian'* each of those four days at 8 a.m., had one hour for lunch, and wrapped at 6 p.m.

I was in practically every scene enjoying the bulk of the dialogue, but this didn't bother me at all. I was a very hungry actor. Each day I came on set completely prepared, and I made very few gaffs. It was exhilarating.

Two weeks before, I had been at home wondering what Adza had in mind for me, and here I was now playing one of the best roles a young man can ask for in one of the oldest and most famous Hollywood film studios, working with dedicated and talented people.

Each evening I'd be driven back to my hotel and order up some fabulous food – I never went out on the town because I wanted to be sure I didn't get pissed or have any late nights. It was always home to the Montecito, ordering in food and studying the script. Nigel thought I wasn't having nearly enough fun, and was forever suggesting we hit the clubs. He must have thought me very dull – either that or very dedicated and green.

On one occasion the press lady arranged for the late Hurd Hatfield to come on set, so that the first screen Dorian – he played Dorian aged 28 – could be photographed with the latest.

I was delighted to meet Hurd. He looked extremely dapper, dressed like an Edwardian gentleman. He didn't look too happy to see a new Dorian, and was probably aware that he was now fast approaching sixty and I was still so young. I only say this because he never cracked a smile – he kept staring at me sadly.

On the penultimate day of filming we started late so that we could film night exteriors. These scenes were mostly scenes featuring nighttime London with horse drawn carriages and darkened laneways. They were filmed on the old 'Gone with the Wind' exterior street sets, made to look like London.

It was quite eerie to wander up those empty streets and wonder whether I was walking in the same footsteps as Clark Gable or Vivien Leigh.

Very early one morning – it was around 3 a.m. – I skipped on dinner so that I could have a good look around these magnificent sets before returning to filming. I'd just taken a right hand turn from one street into another when I heard a low moaning sound that gave me real goose bumps – I had no idea what it could be since the street was completely deserted. Three or so seconds later the entire glass front of a barbers shop fell forward into the street and shattered. I think I was the only person who heard the sound, as I was a good two hundred yards from where the crew was enjoying dinner. To me it was a very sober reminder of the passage of time. Gable and Leigh were long since dead. These period back lots were falling down and dying, and the days of the big studios with their lots containing entire streets would soon be a thing of the past. That wailing sound was to me like a sad call from the past. One day, I thought as Dorian might have, that sometime I too would be old. It didn't bother me at all at that moment – I was going to act until I was a hundred.

On my sixtieth birthday I recalled that sad scream as the windowpane fell and was dashed into a thousand pieces. I didn't feel immortal then. I spared a thought for Hurd.

When the First Assistant Director called the wrap at a few minutes to six the evening of the last day, I felt a huge surge of sadness. The whole experience had lasted less than two weeks, and I would soon be on a plane home.

However, I was consoled by the fact that Fionnula Flanagan had organized a wrap party hosted by herself and her larger than life husband Garrett O'Connor somewhere in the Hollywood Hills.

It was a great party, and I only realized at around midnight that I'd left the actual portrait used in the film (the one given to me by the art department) in the cab that had taken me up into the Hollywood Hills.

While Adza called the various cab companies – yes, she'd flown over from London for the entire four-day shoot – Fionnula came up with a brilliant publicity idea. *"Take out an ad in tomorrow's Daily Variety! LOST: one portrait of Dorian Gray. That's all you say. Then the next day you take out another. This time it's: FOUND: One portrait of Dorian Gray. But...it's changed! Horribly."*

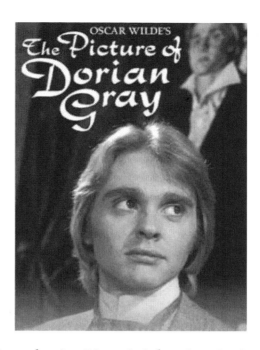

I often look back on the day I boarded the plane back to London. It never occurred to me that I could remain in America and build a career for myself there. How many young English actors were so lucky to have such a launching pad as playing the lead in a two-part *Movie of the Week*? My problem was that I had little money stashed away in the bank, and I knew I'd have to hire immigration lawyers, and then find somewhere to live and risk being unemployed for who knew how long. So I settled for the safe risk free alternative, and hurried back to working at the BBC and the Independent Network, appearing in plays at the Haymarket Theatre, Basingstoke Theatre and the Thorndike, Leatherhead. I didn't regret it at the time, and in truth I don't regret it now. Had I stayed, I might well have made far more money than I have now. I might even have become a 'TV Star,' or made a few American movies. But I wouldn't have lived the life I did back in London, and I would most likely never have met my future wife, Wendy, nor moved to our new home in 1982 – Australia.

As I was lounging in the rear of a startlingly long stretch limo taking me to LAX, idly wondering what I was doing returning so quickly to the U.K., the driver told me he'd just received a call from base.

"There's been a change of plan, Mister Briant."

Curious, I asked, *"Who changed the plans? I have a plane to catch."*

The driver replied *"Mister Curtis. He's asked me to tell you your flight is now a later one and in the meantime he needs you at Glenn Glenn Sound right away."* I leant back and wondered what Dan had in mind for me today.

Dan was waiting for me in one of the sound stages.

"We're gonna do all the narration again. Right now. If you want to catch a plane at all today, you'd better move fast," he told me without a hint of warmth.

It wasn't Dan's chill attitude that bothered me. Where was Glenn Jordan, I wondered? *He* was the director who had brought out the best in me. Was I the victim of another power play?

"Will Glenn be here soon?" I asked.

"He's not coming," Dan replied, looking at his watch. *"Go on, get in there,"* he said pointing to the small booth that housed the microphone. *"I'm telling you. We re-do the narration. All of it. Now."*

That was it.

I put down the entire narration in three hours grueling work. What Dan wanted was a much more vibrant narration. Much more colourful and florid. I gave him exactly what he wanted, though at the time I felt it was far too OTT. As it turned out I feel now that he was absolutely right, my original narration had been too internal.

Three hours later I was back in the limo. I decided not to call Glenn; I'd learnt my lesson about fuelling the flames of internecine quarrels.

I've been back to Los Angeles many times since that day, but never to act in such a huge role. Maybe sometimes you play the best roles early? Such as Hamlet in Dublin aged 22, and Dorian aged 27. It's altogether possible – and I am hoping it'll be the case – that the best is still to come!

I don't remember flying home. I didn't have Nigel as my companion as he had to return early for the birth of his son with Maria Aitken.

London seemed very cold and windswept when I disembarked at Heathrow. But it was my home, so hey, I was happy enough.

The portrait is now in our Sydney home. Sadly, it never changes.

THE MAJOR LEAGUE!

HUSTON, NEWMAN, MASON, SANDA!

In 1973 I scored a role that I'll never forget as long as I live.

Nowadays, if you tell an actor that he's going to be in a film directed by Sam Mendes or Quentin Tarantino, starring Johnny Depp, George Clooney and Angelina Jolie he'll be jaw-heavy for some time. Same with me when Adza told me to go and see casting giant Weston Drury for a role in John Huston's upcoming film, 'The Mackintosh Man,' which was to star Paul Newman, James Mason and Dominique Sanda.

I chatted with Drury and we got on famously – I never got to meet Huston or the producer John Foreman prior to the shoot. I did know that Ossie Morris, one of the legends in photography was to be Director of Photography, and Maurice Jarre was to compose the score.

To my amazement I was offered a juicy role as James Mason's enforcer later that week. I was ecstatic! I was to fly out to the set in Malta in ten days! I couldn't help thinking I'd been touched by a magic wand – Newman had been my hero since I'd watched him play Rocky in 'Someone Up There Likes Me.' That was when I was ten. As for being directed by Huston? Well, he was a God, wasn't he? I mean, 'The Maltese Falcon,' 'The Asphalt Jungle,' 'Key Largo.' As well as all the others. I was buzzing at the thought of being directed by 'God'.

However, all would not go to plan.

Wolf Morris, Peter Attard and I arrived in Valetta, the de facto capital of Malta, in time for lunch ten days later. By this time the Irish shoot was finished, and they were beginning the Maltese filming before finishing off at Pinewood just before Christmas. It was my first 'big' movie.

There are small, medium and seriously major films, and this was one of the latter, a thought that set my pulses racing.

An assistant director met our car and walked us to a huge space where the cast and crew were eating lunch, out of the blazing sun. As we entered, one man got up. He was unmistakable. Newman. He'd been sitting on a bench with members of the crew and when he saw the three of us arrive he immediately stopped eating and came over to welcome us to the set. Amazing.

"Hi, I'm Paul. You the actors from England?"

As if he had to introduce himself. But that's the way he was – the perfect gentleman and modest to a degree.

"Yes," I replied shaking his hand, instantly amazed by the blue of his eyes and his unblinking stare that hits you like a shaft of lightning. Here was the star of stars, for heaven sake!

"Why don't you go grab some food? I have to do stuff. See you guys later."

With that, he was gone.

We ate a great lunch and then were driven to the Hilton Hotel where we signed in and went to our rooms. Within five minutes I received a call. My bubble was about to burst, but I didn't know it then. It was Weston Drury, the casting agent, who was now traveling full time with the production. *"I'm in room 506, Shane. We need to talk. ASAP, you know."*

Weston's room looked just like mine, which showed he was a decent guy and not too fond of himself. He asked me to sit. Suddenly I felt something wasn't exactly right.

"Look, we've been having some major re-write problems, Shane. You may as well throw away the script we sent you—it's changed completely."

All I could do was nod, as if I understood that this was perfectly normal.

"John, Paul and a few writers are rewriting day by day, every evening, so you're going to get your pages – whatever they are now – under your door not later than nine each evening." He added, *"May be no pages at all."*

I was later told that 'The Mackintosh Man' was made as a money-spinner rather than one of Huston's labours of love, such as the wonderful boxing film he'd made the previous year called 'Fat City.' The idea had been to shoot this espionage film as quickly and efficiently as possible on the understanding that Paul Newman could go skiing at Christmas. I was so incredibly disappointed that I probably looked like Lot's wife from the bible. I couldn't speak; so Weston went on to fuel my disappointment some more. *"You may like to sign a form releasing us from your screen credit. I only say this because you came here to play a decent role and it may not exist at all in the final cut, in which case it'd look pretty silly if you had 'with Shane Briant' in the credits."* I've no idea why I did it – maybe because I was desperately trying to curry favour with Weston; maybe because I believed him. Anyway, I signed away the nicest credit I had had without even calling Adza. You can imagine what she said on the telephone when I told her later. It was akin to being a howitzer battery commander at Stalingrad, listening to her tirade.

That was the nadir of my week in Valetta. From that moment on, things started to get better. That very night the pages were slid under my hotel room door. I grabbed them as Scott of the Antarctic might have grabbed a ham sandwich if offered one when he left his ten comrades to say, *"I am just going outside, I may be some time."*

There I was, 'Cox', in a big scene to be shot the following day at Valetta harbour as James Mason, *numero uno* bad guy, finally arrives from Ireland in his yacht. I didn't have much if anything to say, but that didn't overly bother me. As Jack Palance had told me, *"I had seven lines in 'Shane' and it made me a star! Lines don't mean a damned thing."*

Tomorrow I was going to work with the greats!

My role was to be Mason's right hand man – his 'fixer,' if you like. So, despite my losing the bulk of my role in the re-writes, I was still there, in most scenes. I tried to make the most of them by squeezing into the best spots during rehearsal – if any of the stars were speaking, I'd be there, very close-by.

To my surprise, I found that Huston liked to sit in a director's chair a good thirty yards from the action. I had to presume that he'd told Mason, Newman, Sanda and Ian Bannon what he wanted from them beforehand.

My boss, James Mason in 'The Mackintosh Man,' in Malta.

He normally read a paperback while the crew set up, and then watched the rehearsals on a small screen set up by his chair. This was a bit of a disappointment for me since the only direction I received from him was via the First Assistant Director, Colin Brewer. There'd be messages such as *"Mister Huston thinks that's fine, Shane, but could you angle yourself more to the left?"* I'd then look out at the directing legend, and see him reading a novel and smoking one of his signature Cuban cigars. *"Sure, no problem, Colin,"* I'd reply.

The yacht that supposedly belonged to Mason's character was exactly the kind of yacht I would buy if I were a billionaire – thirty years old, gracious, about a hundred and twenty feet long, with a crew of maybe ten. The sun shone all morning and it was fun to be a part of my first big film. I often chatted with Mason in his trailer, asking all the questions any young actor would want to ask. Mason was patient enough to answer all of them.

My favourite 'Mason *bon mot*' was this: *"Never crave to be the top star in a movie. Don't do it. I've managed to be second or third in line nearly all my life and I'll tell you why it's important. If you are number one and the film fails, it's down to you. It's your fault. But no one remembers who was the support. I've never been blamed for the failure of a movie in my life, but when a film is a big success, I make damned sure everyone knows it was one of my films!"*

I found them both delightful. Mason and his wife Clarissa often invited me into their trailor for snacks and a chat.

On the afternoon of the first shoot day in Malta everyone was milling around preparing for a shot of Newman looking down from the top of the cliff that overlooks the harbour. We must have appeared like ants from up there. I was lounging around on the rear deck of the yacht, relaxing, wondering what all 'the poor people' were doing that moment, when we heard Newman call out to us. Everyone looked up trying to spot him. At that instant there was a long high-pitched scream as he fell over the edge. During the four seconds it took for the body to fall to the concrete, there was complete and utter silence. All I could hear was the gentle rocking and creaking of the yacht. Then there was a dull thud and one woman screamed. Then everyone joined in. The assistant directors rushed to the body. That's when we heard another delighted shout from up above. It was Newman. *"Hey, up here!"* He laughed hugely as the crowd gathered around the dummy that was splayed out on the concrete dressed in the same clothes as Newman.

It was an excellent prank! Of course, Paul could have stopped the hearts of quite a few people with this stunt. I know I was buzzed.

Later that afternoon I shot my first scene with Paul.

I'd been looking forward to it. In the scene, I am in the radio room of the yacht, the *'Artina'*, and Newman swims across the harbour, climbs up the anchor chain, enters the radio room, clubs me on the back of the head, grabs me by the scruff on the neck, and begins to interrogate me, asking where Mason is hiding. It was a long complicated sequence.

First up we shot Newman diving into the filthy harbour, fully dressed. Then came the shot where he climbed the anchor chain – boy, my hero could do anything! Finally the camera was in the radio room and we were about to shoot there. I was wearing the radio headset with the mouthpiece in front of my lips, as it should be. Huston, as ever, was a hundred yards away smoking a cigar, watching what the camera was seeing on his video screen. I heard a lazy *"Aaaaaand... action,"* from Huston's director's chair. This translated into another *"Action!!!"* from the First AD. I pretended to raise someone on the FM ship radio.

I waited a full ten seconds passed, then I became aware of someone entering the radio room. I waited for Newman to fake the slap to the back of my head with his gun. I was supposed to fall to the ground and Paul was supposed to whirl me around and start the 'hard talk.'

That's when I felt a very hard blow to the back of my head. I didn't have to act; I fell to the floor, stunned. Being the consummate pro, Newman carried on, stepping over me and grabbing me by my shirt, turning me around to face him.

I stared at him. He stared at me. The seconds passed. Then Paul turned to camera and shouted out. *"John! Shane's got blood all over his face!"*

With Paul Newman. After the blood had been washed away. 'The Mackintosh Man.'

The reason? He'd inadvertently made such a strong impact with my skull that my head had made violent contact with the glass table in front of me and my mouthpiece had split my bottom lip open. Blood was spattered everywhere and was dripping onto my shirt.

There was a few seconds silence, and then I heard Huston call loudly from his director's chair, in his signature deep booming voice. *"Tell the boy to keep it there. We'll go again."*

Later on we posed for a publicity shot. The blood had caked and I looked a tragedy so they cleaned me up.

But that wasn't my only mishap during the filming. At Pinewood, we filmed the moment where Cox kills *'The Mackintosh Man'* himself, played by Harry Andrews. In the script, Mackintosh travels home in a commuter train, and as he crosses the road outside the station a car accelerates into sight and mows him down. Cox is the driver.

When you read this kind of thing in a script, you take it for granted that you will get the lead up shot and a close up, while a stunt man will do the driving. Not so in this case.

I was approached in my caravan by the stunt co-coordinator, an American by the name of James Arnett.

"Hi Shane. Look, John likes his actors to do as much of the stunt work as they feel comfortable with. I've checked everything and I don't think this is in any way dangerous. How about it?" He hesitated as he saw my expression. *"The thing is, we get to see that it's you driving the car and not a stuntie, so that's great for you,"* he cooed.

I thought about it. If it wasn't dangerous and I would get to seem 'cool', then why not? And not only that, I'd get in Huston's good books.

"Sure, I'll do it," I replied.

Advice for young actors here. Never volunteer to do work that should be done by a stuntie – you take work from them, and put yourself at risk at the same time. It may make you look like a hero, but it may see you dead or crippled.

The stuntie who was to work with me that evening was world famous Nosher Powell.

Half an hour later I was sitting in a rather old Rover car. Arnett explained exactly what I had to do. I remember his words almost word for word. *"Nosher will come out of the station and walk at a forty-five degree angle across the road. When you see me drop my hand, accelerate to nineteen miles an hour and drive in a straight line at that constant speed. Nosher'll do a roll across your bonnet. When he's over and in the ditch the other side, accelerate like hell. Okay?"*

"Sure... fine," I replied, uneasily.

James looked satisfied with my reaction. *"Right! Now, we're going to do a rehearsal. But this time in slo-mo, at five miles an hour. Just to show you exactly what's going to happen."*

I saw Nosher, dressed as Harry Andrews, exit the station, and Arnett dropped his hand. I drove off, trying to keep the speed at a constant five miles an hour (rehearsal speed), but as the car was an old one, the speed indicator was all over the place from four to eight miles and hour, despite my best efforts. At the exact spot that had been designated, Nosher arched his torso upwards, and while still keeping his feet on the ground, rolled over my bonnet. I then accelerated away. Arnett then came over to me. *"That's great! Now we shoot one okay. Huston loved it!"* The car was returned to its starting point, and I waited to do the real thing. My heart rate was now nudging 180. Just before we were about to shoot, Arnett again approached the car. He was carrying some heavy-duty leather gloves.

"Hey, Shane. Take these and put 'em on. You won't need them, but I'm a firm believer in safety."

"Actually, James, I prefer not to wear gloves," I replied. *"I feel I have a better grip on the steering wheel with my bare hands."*

James made a face. *"Look, it's not going to happen… But if Nosher should make any contact…and I repeat it isn't going to happen…with the windscreen, you just punch through the crazed glass so you can see where you're going."* He mimicked someone punching.

At that moment my heart rate skyrocketed to 250. But I had no time to argue the toss, as James was already hurrying back behind the camera and someone was calling for 'absolute silence.' There was nothing else to do—I was now in the expert hands of Nosher Powell.

"Aaaaaaaaaaand….ACTION!" came the scream through the loudhailer.

I accelerated, doing my best to keep the car between eighteen and twenty miles an hour. Then in my peripheral vision I saw Nosher just five feet from my car. That's when he was flipped by the front left bumper bar, flew up into the air and exploded headlong through my windscreen. I could just make out his head hanging down inside and his body still on the bonnet. I swear I thought I'd killed him. Nosher was dead!

Instinctively I drove on, figuring that if I braked hard, the motion would propel Nosher out and under my wheels. Not so bad if he *was* dead, but not so good if he were simply crippled.

Eventually I stopped, and immediately looked down at Nosher. His hair was a mass of tiny shards of glass. He immediately looked at me and grinned sheepishly.

"Sorry, mate, I caught my foot in the bumper bar. Shouldn't have been there. Won't happen next time."

By this time James was at the car pulling my door open and helping me out.

"You okay, Shane? You come with us and we'll make sure there's no glass around the eyes."

George Frost, the head of make-up, dusted my face for glass with a make-up brush. *"Got to make sure no glass gets into the eyes—it can lodge there and creep around, severing the nerves at the back. We're not going to let that happen,"* he said with a reassuring smile.

That's when Arnett entered the make-up truck. *"Anything I can get you Shane?"* he asked.

"A brandy?" I replied.

"Nice one, Shane. Not allowed. Safety thing."

I remember thinking, 'safety?' I can't have a brandy because of *safety* regs? Just ten minutes after a near-death experience?

Arnett brought me out of my stunned reverie. *"Look, Shane. We may have to go again. I just looked at the footage on the video screen and you seemed to hesitate when Nosher came through the windscreen."*

I stared at the big American. *"No ****ing way, James. But I would like a brandy."*

"Fair enough," James replied and left me.

I did get a large brandy.

One night back at the Hilton in Valetta, 'Wolfie' Morris and I decided to 'fine dine' in the hotel restaurant. Our per diems – the money we got to feed ourselves in the evening – were not overly generous, but we'd had enough of taxiing down to the 'Gut' for some bistro fare. So we dressed in what we thought was appropriate – shirt, pants, jacket – and made our way to the dining room.

As we got there we saw Paul enter, dressed in a one-piece air force jump suit. He looked great. But surprise, surprise, as we walked in we were stopped inside the door. *"I'm afraid you have to wear a tie, sir,"* the maitre d' told us. I pointed to Newman's table. *"There's a guy over there, wearing paramilitary fatigues,"* I replied.

The maitre d' simply shrugged. *"That's Mr. Newman,"* he said. What else was there to say or do? He was right. We fetched our ties.

In the middle of the first week we had a night shoot scheduled.

The crew call was midnight. Yet at 1 a.m. there was no sign of Huston. Calls were made to the hotel, but we weren't told what the problem was. We waited around until almost 3 a.m. when Newman decided he'd take matters into his own hands. He marched up to the doors of the best restaurant on the waterfront and knocked loudly. The bleary-eyed owner came to the door. Newman then asked him if he'd open his restaurant for a couple of hours. He wanted to buy everyone drinks, because Mister Huston was unwell and couldn't make it down to the waterfront that night. The proprietor beamed, and fifteen minutes later the cast and crew – about a hundred and fifty people – were having a party. Newman paid for everything. It was a great evening. Paul only stayed an hour, but as you can imagine most of the crew stayed much longer. As Paul said goodnight to the patron of the restaurant and thanked him for opening up, the man pulled out a small photo. It was a head shot of Paul. I could see the patron wanted an autograph, but couldn't understand why Paul was so reticent to sign. The next day I asked him why and he told me. *"The last time I signed an autograph was around ten years ago. I was peeing in a urinal in New York somewhere and this guy comes in, sees me and pulls out a piece of scrap paper and a ballpoint pen. Then he asks me to sign my name while I'm still pissing. I ignored him and he said I was a spoilsport. I made up my mind then to quite signing my name altogether."*

On the last day of the Malta shoot the final scene of the film was scheduled. But since the script was still being hatched night by night, no one knew what would happen when we got to Pinewood, so Huston decided the answer lay in covering all bases. The denouement was to take place in *'The Church at Marsha Schlaack'* in Malta. Would Newman triumph? Of course he would. But who would die? And would his love affair with Dominque Sanda stand the test of time? They filmed every possible permutation. Firstly, Newman came out of the church door looking very sad. Then he came out looking very happy. Then he came out looking triumphant. Then he came out holding Sanda's hand and they kissed. I watched them all, thinking they'd go with a happy ending with all the bad guys dead. It was the obvious choice. I was right.

In the preamble to the scene that we were to film later inside the church, Newman forces me to drive him to where Mason is hiding with Ian Bannon. The car I was given to drive was a huge old Mercedes. This was problematic because I had to maneuver the clunker between a whole bunch of fishing boats. There was about an inch leeway one side and a foot the other.

I was shown a mark for the front right wheel of the car. It was a slice of gaffer tape about two inches wide.

"I want you to cover that piece of tape with the tyre, okay?" I was told.

"Sure. No problem," I replied easily.

Newman slid in the back and we backed up into our first positions. I was acutely aware it would be like parking a Hummer in a Mini parking spot, but I wasn't about to argue the toss – Newman had seen what I was being asked to do and he clearly had no problem with it. We set off on *'action'* and I wove my way through the fishing boats and stopped the car right on the tape. Phew. I was delighted. Then the First AD walked up. *"We have to go again, you left the engine running."* I was disappointed. *"But I have to put the hand brake on first,"* I countered. That took time. Then I heard a voice behind me. Newman. *"Pop the clutch."* I hadn't thought about that. But he was right. Just as I reached the gaffer tape the second time, I took my foot off the clutch and the car stopped suddenly. Success.

One last memory of *'The Mackintosh Man.'* The interior shots of the church in Valetta took place weeks later at Pinewood. The last minutes of the film are a standoff between the good guy; Newman, and the bad guys; Mason and Bannon. Oh, and the girl who couldn't quite make up her mind what she should do – Sanda.

Newman brings me in with a gun to my back and the scene begins. As the sparks was lighting us, Newman nudged me slightly to my right saying, *"Hey, I don't need this scene. Why don't we make you look good, what do you say?"* He then made sure that I was in the best spot while he was lurking somewhere behind me. That was the kind of man he was – generous and aware of what it was like when he started out as an actor.

Maybe someone had been kind to him when he was beginning his career – I don't know, he didn't say. Yet here I was, in the forefront of the shot, well lit thanks to Paul, and the lead was standing just behind me. This was the ideal time to make the most of an opportunity – and here's a word of advice to young actors. Never be overwhelmed by the stature of the actor you're working with. If you think his or her performance will outshine you, it will. In front of the camera every actor is just that, an actor – it's up to you to step up to the plate. Never be cowed. Over the years I've played scenes with many big names, but I've only been nervous prior to meeting them – never while I was acting. The reason? Because it is the best experience imaginable to look and listen to a great actor and hear the dialogue always as if for the first time, despite it being take thirty-four. There's always so much coming back at you. The best actors bring out the best in other actors. Suddenly you have movie magic.

The final scene in John Huston's 'The Mackintosh Man.'

So here I was in a long scene standing in the best spot with Newman at my elbow, without one word of dialogue. I had two choices; stand there like a rock, or do some hard work. I decided on the latter. I listened like fury to every single word that was spoken by all the other actors in the scene, and I listened to the silences that followed every statement. I watched their faces as they spoke and as they listened, debating, in character, who was going to live or die, who was believing who, who knew they were beaten and most importantly, whether I was going to die.

I expect everyone who watches the film will be glued to Newman. That's understandable. For those who glanced at me, I was acting every microsecond – and by acting, I mean I was thinking!

During rehearsal I decided that Cox was such an arrogant bastard he wouldn't be scared – he'd be working out the odds against Mason getting away with things and then nailing Newman.

We all learn 'stuff' till the day we die. Actors worth their salt keep learning every day, while those who think they know it all never progress to the next level. From Paul Newman I learnt a lot of things, not the least of which was to treat everyone on the set with the same respect, be they the director, director of photography, the so-called stars, those with the supporting roles, cameo players, fifty-worders, extras, and the entire crew. This not only guarantees a happy and productive atmosphere, but also gives the film its best chance of being a great one. Newman treated everyone the same and had time for every man and woman working on the film. The result was that everyone loved him – I doubt if he had an enemy in the world.

You may think this is the way everyone behaves on a set, but it's not true. I have seen many an actor behave very differently depending on whether he or she is talking to a director or director of photography, or talking to a runner or grip.

When I'd finished my last scene I went to say good-bye to John Huston. He was standing talking to Ozzie Morris, in a haze of cigar smoke.

He smiled broadly as I approached, holding out a hand. I said, *"That was my last scene, Mister Huston, I'm off back to London. I greatly enjoyed being a part your film."*

He took a massive puff of his cigar and replied; *"Paul's been saying good things about you, Shane. Says you're going places."*

I drove back to London on cloud nine. Paul Newman had told Huston that I was going places! Of course I now know what he meant. Somehow he must have felt in his bones that I was going to emigrate to Australia in 1982!

HAWK THE SLAYER,' PLAYING JACK PALANCE'S SON!

When I'd finished filming the American television movie, *'The Flame is Love,'* with Linda Purl and Timothy Dalton, I flew back from Dublin to London to start in on a medieval drama titled *'Hawk the Slayer.'* The most exciting aspect of this project was that it was to star the incredibly larger than life Jack Palance! And I was to play his son, no less – *Drogo, son of Voltan!'*

My screen 'dad,' Voltan, in 'Hawk the Slayer.'

The other star was an up-and-coming American actor called John Terry – every inch the tall dark and handsome hero – and the great thing about John was that he could act as well as look good! He went on to star as Felix Leiter in *'The Living Daylights,'* had a leading role in *'Full Metal Jacket,'* and has appeared in just about every television production in America – *'E.R., '24,' 'Las Vegas,'* etc.

John's character, *'Hawk,'* is bent on revenge on his older brother *'Voltan,'* played by Palance, for killing his father and fiancé. With him he takes his 'mind-sword,' and a motley band of warriors: a giant, a dwarf, a one-armed man with a machine-crossbow, and an elf with the fastest bow in the land. It was the perfect pilot for many movies to come, but while it still has a cult following, these films were never made.

When I met Jack Palance for the first time on set I was astonished at how big the man was – six foot four inches tall, and wide as a small car. Not one once of fat. He was in full costume at the time, wearing a heavy leather and metal jacket and a black metal helmet.

He looked terrifying. I'm six feet tall, but I felt about a foot shorter. I shook his hand, and then waited for him to release it so I could work some blood back into it. Not only was his presence something to experience, his voice came out of a black hole. Just when you think Lee Marvin has a deep voice in *'Cat Ballou,'* along comes Jack and it's an even lower growl. He knew the effect it had.

Never annoy Jack between takes!

"Good to meet you, Shane," he said, while burning a hole through me with his black eyes. He loved the effect it had on young actors like me. Disorienting. I knew then that I'd have to come up with a HUGE performance to match him.

During the rehearsals, I became aware of an odd thing about Jack that I hadn't come across before in other actors. Either he didn't care to much about rehearsals because he knew exactly what he was going to do in the take – regardless of what the actors around him had in mind – or simply found them boring. The result was that in rehearsals his volume was very light and his performance was a shadow of what was to come in the take. Hence I found it difficult to know how I should respond to him, and had to wait till he dumped his portrayal on me in the actual take, and then take my chances to respond in the moment. I found this perplexing. Don't get me wrong, I had the greatest respect for Jack and found him great to work with – a great pro. However, there are some actors who like to wait for the take, and some who like to rehearse with the other actors and see what they can come up with as a whole. Jack preferred the former approach, and once you're aware of a fellow actor's technique, you can adjust.

By contrast, John Terry's strength lay in his expressive eyes and understated acting. He was the quintessential American heartthrob to look at, and one of the nicest and most intelligent people I've met.

On the first day of the shoot, Jack and I worked together for several hours, with me trying to match hissteely portrayal. When lunch was called, I thought I'd see what Jack was up to; possibly he was on his own and may have forgotten where the dining facilities were at Pinewood.

"Are you going to lunch, Jack?" I asked.

He looked down at me (six foot four stares at six foot!) fixing me with 'the look.'

"Why? Do you want me to buy you lunch?" he growled in 'über-base.'

I was taken completely by surprise. Was he serious?

"Er, no. Not at all. I simply wondered if you had friends here at Pinewood," I replied.

He studied me even more intensely, then growled even deeper.

"Why, do you want to meet my friends?"

I had no idea how to respond. We stood there for a good five seconds. Neither of us blinked. Then he broke into a wide grin, and slapped me hard on the shoulder.

"Just kidding, boy!" he said, and strode off to the dining hall.

It was an honour to play the son of one of Hollywood's greats;

occasionally, if I feel depressed, I still growl the words, *'I am Drogo son of Voltan!'* to the winds. It still makes me laugh.

I watched Jack's one-arm push-ups at the Oscars some years later, and was again amazed at his physical power.

Jack is remembered also for his one-liners. One was *"I'm amazed people read this crap about us – about me most of all."*

When I read this recently I knew I'd have to tread carefully when I wrote about our time together. He'll rise from the dead and say, *"What a load of crap, boy!"*

My second favourite was *"I used to be six foot four. Now that I'm old, I slouch. So, I'm six foot three."*

One last thing. Jack told me this, and I think it's something every aspiring actor should know. Never ever flip through an unread script and count the lines.

"The amount of lines means nothing, Shane," he told me once. *"It's what you don't say that counts. You understand what I'm saying?"*

He was one major bad guy! One of the best. He inspired me.

As a footnote, when the film opened I well remember taking my two beautiful nieces to the Odeon Marble Arch for a matinée. It wasn't a Hammer Film so they were allowed to see the film with an adult. Tash was about nine, and Rosie about seven, and both were excited about seeing 'Uncle Shane' in a movie. When we arrived, I bought the best seats and went up to the dress circle, which I immediately saw was empty – not one patron to be seen. As we sat in the front row, Tash and Rosie took a look downstairs. I shifted awkwardly in my seat – there were perhaps just fifty people in the entire cinema. The girls couldn't have been nicer, or more adult about it – I'm certain they felt my embarrassment. This is what Rosie wrote in a school essay, titled 'My Favourite Relative.'

Ice cream with Tash and Rosie after the cinema. Heaven!

'*Once we went to one of Shane's films in a huge cinema near Marble Arch. It was virtually empty and as we went down the steps, we pretended it was really full saying things like, "Gosh, I don't think we'll be able to find a seat! And "What a sell-out!"'*

Tash and Rosie are the best – I love them to death! And now I'm reunited after many years with my nephew Toby. Racecar driver and financier – good combination. So now I have seven great nieces and nephews.

One last thing about Jack Palance. He said something once that I have always found funny because over the years I've worked on many very ordinary films.

"I go see maybe seven films a year at the most, and since I only go to see the best, it follows that I rarely see my own."

Riding again in "Hawk the Slayer."

'LADY CHATTERLEY,' 'EMMANUELLE,' MEL BROOKS & PARIS.

'Catalyst' is a wonderfully expressive word. There are moments in everyone's life where something happens that'll change your life. You usually meet your soul partner by sheer chance, and years later you can't imagine what life you would have lived if you hadn't met them. In my mother's case the catalyst that changed her life was the onset of the Second World War. No WW2, and I doubt she would have married my father in such a hurry. Although I still know very few of the intimate reasons for their personal unhappiness, there's no doubt that many people made snap decisions during the war years because they were afraid they or their partner might die soon.

I've had three personal catalysts; being introduced to Kit

Adeane when I was thirteen – without her love and help I would have stood no chance of making anything of my life; meeting Wendy on a tennis court in Battersea – we've stood the test of time and are still so happy to be together; and finally, landing the role of Sir Clifford Chatterley in the film of D.H. Lawrence's novel in 1980.

"Lady Chatterley's Lover," was the brainchild of the two famous Israeli producers, Menaham Golan and Yoram Globus; executives in charge of The Cannon Group. They made over two hundred films over the years. Their strategy was to make a serious film, follow it with a couple of money-spinners, then assemble another stunning cast and produce another serious film. One such film was 'That Championship Season,' with Bruce Dern, Robert Mitchum, Martin Sheen, and Paul Sorvino.

I admit this is pure gossip, but I heard from various sources that 'Chatterley' came about because of the following idea. Golan and Globus looked for a sexy classic script, and then hired the current sexist woman in movies, engaged the director of the sexiest film made during the past decade, looked around for the sexiest Englishman around – not me – and then topped up the cast with English actors who knew their craft.

So they came up with 'Lady Chatterley's Lover,' the most shocking novel of its time, Sylvia Kristel was hired to play Constance as she'd acquired an incredibly huge fan base after her 'Emmanuelle' films, Just Jaeckin was hired as director because he had directed 'Emmanuelle,' and finally they hired Nicholas Clay, fresh from worldwide accolades for his performance of Lancelot in John Boorman's film 'Excalibur,' and finally, they cast some reputable English-speaking actors to make it all work. I was lucky enough to be one of them, together with Ann Mitchell and Elizabeth Spriggs. The finishing touch was to re-voice Sylvia, because she had a pronounced Belgian accent and didn't sound much like Connie Chatterley at all.

How could they lose money, provided the screenplay was good – and it was. Golan and Globus thought they had the perfect exotic movie cocktail, made even sweeter by hiring Stanley, 'The Deer

Hunter,' Myers to compose the score.

During the weeks between being cast as the crippled Clifford and the start of principal photography I did my best to lose as much weight as possible so that my legs would look like match sticks when out of the wheelchair. I think I lost over a stone and a half by the time we began filming. Part of the rehearsal period was devoted to learning how to drive the period-motorized wheelchair that I would use in the film. To put it bluntly, it was a bastard. The motor was far too powerful. The engine had several gears as well as a habit of slipping between them at all the worst times, and the clutch had a movement of about one millimetre from 'engaged' to 'free.' Not only that, but the chair had a top speed of almost thirty miles an hour – and it had a mind of it's own, always trying to attain at full throttle. Most of the wheelchair scenes involved a speed of around four miles an hour, so invariably the chair and I were always in conflict. It was like having an uncontrollable crack-snorting Great Dane on a tight leash.

During the first week we shot the pre-war scene where Sir Clifford, Master of the Hunt, challenges his German friend Anton to a race home across the estate. Thanks to Billy Dillon, Jane's father, I felt reasonably secure. He'd taught me how to ride while I was at University. I knew from bitter experience what it was like when a horse falls on your leg.

On the day, we mounted up. It was autumn and the rain had been unrelenting for days. This was our first fine day, but the ground was very boggy. I was introduced to the real Master of the Enfield Hunt and his son. The latter told me, en passant, that they were no longer hunting because the conditions were proving too dangerous. This filled me with confidence, as you can imagine.

With the Royal Enfield Hunt.

Another problem was that the Master of the Hunt should look like the most accomplished rider, and I certainly wasn't that. However, I'd told Just and both producers, Frenchman Andre Djaoui and Chris Pearce, that I could 'ride very well' so I had to get on with it and show no fear!

Within ten minutes one of the horses belonging to a real huntsman decided to bolt and threw his rider. Though the rider was not injured, I knew these things could happen to anyone – even to a regular member of the hunt.

The day went well and by mid afternoon I was quite confident. There was just the last shot of the day to come; one that Just had been looking forward to. They had the camera down low, locked onto the back of a camera car. The idea was to drive the car down the two-mile elm tree-lined drive that lead from the road up to Wrotham Park. The main building is a beautiful Palladian house that had featured in over thirty-seven film and television productions, including *'Sense and Sensibility,'* *'Vanity Fair,'* and *'Gosford Park.'* In this scene we see Sir Clifford racing his German friend home. Anthony Head played the German. The angle Just wanted was one looking directly upwards at the underside of the horses' heads, with Anthony and me leaning over the camera, low and intense. The speed Just wanted was *"break neck speed please Schmucky."*

I have to say I thought the idea to be rather dangerous as the horses would be arching forward with each stride right over the Panavision camera lens, and if they stumbled they'd come crashing down on the metal. With me on top. I shared my reservations with Just. He simply laughed.

"Hey, Schmucky," he replied; that was his affectionate nickname for me during the shoot. *"Is not danger. It's a pièce de gateaux!"* he replied – he liked his bilingual jokes.

I then had my usual stroke of non-genius and offered him a challenge.

"Okay Just. You get on that horse and show me. You do it? I do it."

Just stared at me for a second or two, then jumped up on my horse.

As he cantered easily back to the starting mark, and the camera car backed up, the second assistant director confided in me. *"Not the smartest of moves, Shane. You know Just was a jump jockey in France for ten years before he became a director?"* My heart sank. No I didn't know. But a deal was a deal.

Just galloped like the wind, urging the horse's head right over the camera. He was perfect.

"Now you, Schmucky!" Just said, jumping down lightly.

Well, we did it eventually. Quite a few takes. I was terrified. I'm not sure how Anthony felt, but I managed to keep a smile on my face – albeit a terrified rictus – as we pounded along.

The ball scene in 'Lady Chatterley's Lover.'

We had a great supporting cast, featuring Elizabeth Spriggs as Lady Eva – a character she turned into a female Oscar Wilde, and Ann Mitchell – a very talented actress whose career was to surge forward very soon.

Robert Fraisse was director of photography, and what brilliant work he achieved; the picture should have won him an Oscar for photography. Fraisse's work has always been outstanding; *'Seven Years in Tibet'* with Brad Pitt, and *'Enemy at the Gates'* with Jude Law and Ed Harris. He made the already beautiful Sylvia look extraordinarily lovely. In an early scene the declaration of war is announced during a ball given by Sir Clifford. It was a lavish scene – one I loved. Sylvia and I (and all the extras) danced all day. Just as well it was a waltz because, as Bob Fosse knows, I don't dance!

Convincing an audience that you are crippled isn't as easy as it sounds. Audiences watch you closely so they can point to any movement in limbs that should have none.

I was determined not to make that mistake, so I came up with an idea – I would try to convince myself that I had no feeling in my legs all day, regardless of whether I was in my chair, in bed, or transferring from one to the other. The hardest scene physically for me was where I wake up one night and Connie is nowhere to be found. She's out with Mellors of course! Hoping against hope that she's asleep in her own bed, I struggle into my chair, trundle it to the bottom of the stairs, flop out of the chair and pull myself up the stairs to the first floor.

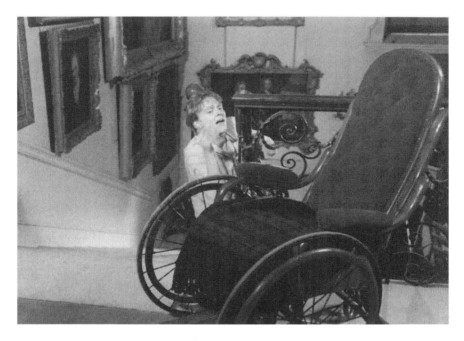

Climbing the stairs without using legs. 'Lady Chatterley's Lover.'

Now here's the thing, I could have cheated and asked Just where he was thinking of cutting to the close-up. In this way, I'd know when I could brace myself with my legs. But I didn't want to ruin anything by cheating. I knew if the work was hard it would show on my face, so I did it all by pulling myself up using the banisters. It was tough but I think it pays off in the film. I was *really* sweating, and *really* gasping – no acting necessary!

They referred to Wendy as 'The jolly brown Australian!'

In some ways it was odd working with Sylvia because the dialogue came back at me with a Belgian accent, which was perplexing and threw me a bit. But it had been decided that Sylvia would be dubbed, and this was fine with her, so that was a done deal. Other than that problem, there weren't any. She was always a pleasure to be around and she made me laugh every day – hugely. Sometimes, she became tired. I could understand why, as she was in almost every scene. So I'd tell her it was fine if she took it easy when it came to my close-ups; she could lie down and recover. At such times, I'd speak to a wooden pole with a gaffer-taped black cross to denote where Sylvia's eyes would have been. The reason I did this is simple. I've always thought it best not to expect your fellow actor to be there for your close-ups. Most directors insist on it. However, if the actor is too tired or lacks enthusiasm, their presence is self-defeating. I personally believe one's off-camera performance should be every bit as sharp as one's own close-up. It's only fair.

Just Jaeckin was always the joker.

One afternoon it began to pour with rain. Because we were really pushed for time we couldn't stop filming. We had a massive exterior scene to complete and it was coming down like cats and bulldogs.

This proved no problem to Jaeckin and Fraisse – they simply hoisted a fifty-foot tent, took out all the sides, lit the scene from underneath the tarp, and continuity made a note to loop all the dialogue later. It was the most bizarre afternoon – the actors could hardly hear each other for the pounding rain. We could smell it. But we were supposed to think 'sunny.' I challenge anyone to see flaws when you watch the film – Fraisse is a genius!

The gorgeous Sylvia Krystel in 'Lady Chatterley's Lover.

We had a very good-looking assistant director on the set who caught Sylvia's eye in a big way. She was single at the time and asked me to ask the young man if he'd like to join her at her hotel one evening for a few drinks. I asked her why she couldn't ask him herself and she replied that she'd rather I asked him.

So I did. I said, *"Sylvia thinks you're cute, John. She's asked me to ask you if you'd like to drop around to her hotel sometime this week and... have a few drinks with her."*

He just laughed at me. *"Sure. Sylvia Kristel wants me to bonk her? That'll be the day."*

"Hey, John," I replied. *'I'm really not kidding. Don't pass on this. Go for it!"*

But he wouldn't believe me. No way. At the wrap party I told him what a mistake he'd made, and even then he didn't believe me.

As least once a week Wendy and I would ask Sylvia or Just to dinner at our place – the flat above the Sunlight laundry in Pimlico that Adza had found me all those years before. Sylvia's driver would drop her off, and pick her up later. She was the best dinner party companion because she knew how to enjoy herself. She loved her namesake Champagne – Louis Roederer, Cristal. So did Wendy and I. Sylvia would always arrive with an ample supply. The ideal dinner guest.

On one occasion she called her driver at one o'clock in the morning to take her home. When she reached her hotel suite she called us and asked if we'd like to come over and watch a movie. *"I have plenty of champagne!"* she said. It's a pity she didn't have Eddie Knight and his box of tricks in make-up the following morning. She didn't miss a beat, though I'm here to tell you I felt a bit jaded.

As the production was half French funded, the major première was at the Normandie Film Theatre in the Champs-Elysées. It was a very old-style opening, long stretch limos arriving at the foot of a long red carpet, four giant searchlights shining beams into the night sky, and a mass of young fans pressed against cordons waiting to glimpse Sylvia and Just.

Playing Wendy's sugar-daddy – as an extra on my day off. 'Lady C.'

I had bought a white silk suit so that I could make the most of the publicity, but few people took their eyes off Sylvia. Her beautiful eyes twinkled as she waved her slim arms at the crowds, blowing kisses, taking her time to reach the end of the red carpet – wow, she knew how to work those fans!

Inside the theatre she remained standing while the whole audience gave her a standing ovation. She didn't cut them short, she simply kept blowing kisses. She was adored in France. I sat on one side of her, with Just on the other. I had no idea whether I should stand, wave or blow kisses too, so I simply sat there as she waved and blew kisses, occasionally waving idly. When the film concluded, she stood again and the whole scene was reinvented. Then we set off for the nightclub *'Regine.'*

'Regine' was then one of the world's most famous nightclubs, as was *'Jackie O'* in Rome and *'Annabel's'* in London. Andre Djaoui had taken the entire place over for the night and most of the Paris 'In' crowd came. Wendy and I had a ball. Sylvia mingled with everyone after joking to us that her tax bill was so gigantic that she'd have to marry someone rich within six months, so she was on the lookout. We both thought that was hilarious.

She remarried six months later. He *was* very rich.

One moment that night I shall never forget. I was at a table with Wendy, Just and André, when an extremely glamorous woman, with close-cropped blonde hair, dressed in the most beautiful men's dinner jacket, touched my shoulder.

"Would you like to dance, Sir Clifford," she asked. I remember her as being very lovely, around forty-something, with very shiny wet red lipstick and pale green eyes. She didn't appear to blink at all. Simply stare.

"I'd love to," I replied.

She led me to the dance floor where disco music was pounding, then took me to an alcove where she could speak to me confidentially. She told me that she'd organized a party for later that night and asked if I'd care to be her guest of honour. She informed me she was the head of a very famous Paris fashion house that has to remain nameless – hence her wonderful style – and made it clear I was to come alone.

"You see, my party is for women only. They have asked if you would like to come and share in the fun."

I felt struck by lightning. What an incredible event that might be. But I could hardly say yes. So I told her I had a steady girlfriend and she wouldn't like the idea of me swanning off to a private party with twenty girls of a certain persuasion. She just smiled and whispered some more. *"I'm sure I can find someone quite enchanting to pass some time with your girlfriend. Then you will be available."*

A very tempting invitation, had I been single. Wait till you are confronted with such a choice and know there's no way in hell you can take advantage of a trip on the wild side like this! It's a very cruel world sometimes.

Back at the table there was no sign of Wendy. My heart sank. Wendy could have chosen anyone she wanted without any help. I eventually found her chatting to Philippe Junot, playboy ex-husband of Princess Caroline of Monaco.

I told this story to a friend years later and he said, *"The thought of an intimate party with just you and twenty gay women of a certain age is probably best remembered as a 'what if.'"*

As an amusing footnote, when I told Wendy of my invitation, she told me of hers. *"Philippe asked if I'd like to have breakfast with him – a charming and very sophisticated man. Not a roué at all. Tempting, nevertheless. If it weren't for you…"* I didn't reply. Breakfast? Not a roué? Sure.

Not surprised that P. Junot was tempted.

Looking back, my favourite scene in *'Chatterley'* was one with Nick Clay, a scene in which Sir Clifford is absolutely vile to Mellors.

He's out with Connie, and deliberately drives his motorized wheelchair into a patch of deep mud, then feeling sure that Mellors is close by he calls out for him to help him clear the obstruction. When the gamekeeper arrives to push him free, Sir Clifford deliberately applies the brakes so that it's virtually impossible for Mellors to move him an inch. *"Have you got the brake on, sir?"* Mellors asks pleasantly, as he struggles. *"Of course not,"* Clifford replies, looking Connie in the eye as he clutches the brake hard.

"Is the brake on, sir?" Nicholas Clay as Mellors, asks.

Several minutes later, when they arrive at the hall, a footman comes to carry him in. Clifford again looks daggers at Connie and says, *"No! Let Mellors do it!"* He follows this cruel remark with the delightful easy aside to Mellors. *"Not too heavy, am I?"*

Poor Nick had to carry me up those stairs about twenty times, yet he never complained. He was a wonderful man. I was deeply saddened when he died so early in his life. He was just 54, leaving his lovely wife, Lorna Heilbron, and two daughters, Ella and Madge way too soon.

I shall never forget meeting Mel Brooks at the St. James Hotel in Park Place, just off St James Street. I'd only been home from the studio for about half an hour, when Sylvia telephoned. She sounded very excited. *"You have to stop whatever you're doing and come round to my hotel. Mel Brooks is here and he is making us all laugh so much I may split my side,"* she told me. I immediately called out to Wendy and told her what had happened – that she'd better get out of the bath and get into some clothes quickly. Ten minutes later we were driving far too fast towards Piccadilly. I'd just had sufficient time to snatch up an original movie poster of *'The Producers,'* that by sheer chance I'd recently bought. I hoped Mel would be kind enough to sign it for me. As we reached Sylvia's floor, the door to her suite flew open, and Mel and I almost collided. We stared at each other for a few moments. He had no idea who I was – we'd never met. But because he's such an original human being he stopped and said. *"Hello! And how are you?"* His delivery was so comedic that I replied in a similar comedic vein.

"Wowser! This is an amazing coincidence," I said. *"You will NEVER guess what I have under my arm?"*

"Well, you'd better tell me, kind sir. What have you got under your arm?" he replied in the music hall theme he seemed to have slipped into so effortlessly. His eyes were wide with feigned surprise.

I unrolled the poster across my chest and beamed a smile. He stared at the poster. Now he was genuinely surprised.

"Wow!" he said. *"That IS a coincidence!"*

Then he took the poster from me, got down on his hands and knees and rolled it out flat on the carpeted corridor floor.

"Give me a pen!" he barked.

I did so.

"What's your name?"

"Shane," I replied.

"Okay."

He then started to write on the poster.

"There!" he said at last. I looked at what he'd written. *'To Shane. You're tops in taps!'*

I had no idea what he meant, but then that's his humour – very left field. He could have said *'Shane is a small turkey'* and I would have been delighted.

"I got to go fetch something from my room," he said. *"You visiting Sylvia?"*

I told him I was, and he rushed off.

During the two hours that followed, Wendy, Sylvia, her friends Elaine and Alan Rich, and I listened spellbound as Mel told us a hundred stories of what it was like growing up in the Bronx as a kid. It was all off the cuff, and his delivery was brilliant – it was a tour de force; one Wendy and I will remember forever.

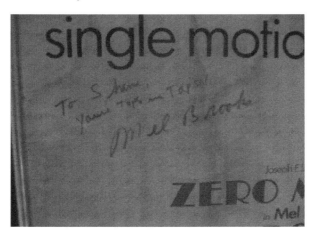

Funnily enough, the following morning – a Saturday, so no filming – the telephone rang and I picked it up. It was Mel – I must have given him my telephone number the night before.

"May I speak to Wendy, please," he asked.

"Sure, Mel," I replied. *"Of course. Hold on a second."*

Silence.

Wendy then took the phone, and the only thing I heard her say was, *"Well, yes, I'd love to. Brasserie St. Quentin, Brompton Road. One o'clock. I'll look forward to it."*

I wasn't invited. Why should I be? I understood. Mel wanted a quiet lunch with a beautiful girl with no strings attached – just a lunch companion. Wendy told me later he was, as ever, hugely funny, and that all the staff at the restaurant adored him. As one might expect, he was also the perfect gentleman.

When it came to the pudding, Wendy ordered the passion fruit sorbet. She told me that Mel had thrown up his hands in surprise. *"The only other woman I know who has ever asked for passion fruit sorbet is Ann."* Ann Bancroft, of course. His wife.

As it turned out they served Wendy a spectacular sunburst of seven flavours, created especially for Mel, and delivered personally by the executive chef.

Mel's humour is one of a kind, as most people know – there's no one quite like him. If you ever get the chance to listen to a record he made a long time ago called *'The 2,000 year Old Man,'* do yourself a favour – it's brilliant. I still have the framed poster of *'The Producers.'* I love it. It reminds me of the time I met a brilliant comedian. A man without any airs and graces.

During the *'Chatterley'* shoot I was given a director's chair with *'Alec Guinness'* stitched on the back that happened to be in the back of a grips truck. I felt wonderful every time I relaxed in it, as if his aura was around me. I have it today. Every now and then when I've been out of work for too long, I sit in it and more often than not I get a good job!

Working with Just was a happy time. He was always happy and knew exactly what he wanted and how to get it on screen.

Towards the end of the shoot we had a scene in an orangerie. Just told me his new girlfriend, who just happened to have been Miss Argentina the year before, had asked to be in the film. I suggested that Wendy should also take part, as I knew she'd be far more arresting on screen. How right I was. Just girl looked pretty good, but Wendy, complete with two huge Borzoi dogs on a leash looked breathtaking.

Wendy eclipsing Miss Argentina in 'Lady Chatterley's Lover.

There are some moments in any actor's life that are indelibly recorded in the memory. Meeting one's heroes, such as Newman, de Havilland, Mason, Palance the first time, with the prospect of actually playing scenes with them is magic. Looking at that giant photo of Sheelagh Cullen and myself on the walls of the Apollo Theatre in Shaftesbury Avenue was an early thrill. Another was walking down to Leicester Square and seeing my name in three-foot-high letters above the title of *'Lady Chatterley's Lover'* at the Leicester Square Theatre. Remember, I was a young man then, and this was the stuff of dreams.

My kind of billing – at last!

The first time any actor sees a close-up of himself/herself on a big screen it's something people react to in different ways. Initially, I was appalled by the size and detail. I got used to it over time; but now I am appalled again as the close-up lens does no one over the age of forty any favours.

So why was *'Chatterley'* the third major catalyst in my life? Because it was the Fox-Columbia promotional tour of the film that took me to Australia the following year.

My mother was born outside Sydney in the Blue Mountains in a town called Leura. When her father, Morven Nolan, was tragically killed in action in France her mother remarried an English Navy Captain by the name of Conway Colles and moved to England to start a new life. My mother didn't got the chance to return to her home country until she was in her sixties, when Wendy and I were living on the northern beaches of Sydney in a suburb rightly called Avalon.

When I was little, my mother had always talked about her childhood in Leura; walking to school in nearby Katoomba, seeing the galahs, cockatoos, rainbow lorikeets and budgies flying on the wing by the dozen. Over the years her words had stuck a chord in my imagination. Wendy had been born and raised in Adelaide. This proved to be a big draw card to go and check out Oz. So when I finally arrived in Sydney for the Fox-Columbia *'Chatterley'* promotional tour and felt the hot sun, took in the glorious beaches, drank the cheap yet superb wines, and discovered that the film industry there was undergoing a purple patch, I was hooked.

ENGLISH THEATRE WORK

THE THORNDIKE THEATRE & THE HAYMARKET, BASINGSTOKE.

It's odd that having begun my career in the theatre, and formed such a loving bond with the boards that the bulk of my work has been on a screen of some sort.

I loved acting with the Trinity Players. The immediate and thrilling experience of the countdown before curtain up, the light-hearted burble of the audience the other side of it, the knowledge that everything could be brilliant or pear-shaped depending on the night, the smell of the make-up; it was always an exhilarating experience. By contrast, filming is mostly 'un-thrilling,' in so far as you have no audience, yet thrilling nonetheless because you know you are playing to a vast audience all over the world – it's just they are not watching you at that particular moment, just the crew.

In 1974 I appeared in a play at the Thorndike Theatre; a two-hander called *'Old Contrary.'* I loved working at this theatre in Leatherhead – it's very intimate with great acoustics. I really can't remember too much about the play, other than the female lead was played by Maggie Jones and *The Stage* called the production *"A masterpiece of theatre in the round."* Always nice when you're in a production that someone says is a masterpiece of *some* kind. Quite why British actors pooh-pooh reviews by *The Stage*, I have no idea – maybe it's the done thing. As you can imagine, I now take them very seriously!

One of my favourite plays the following year was one by Egon Wolff called *'Paper Flowers,'* at the Horseshoe Theatre, Basingstoke. Helen Ryan played Eva, a lonely middle class woman who allows a young tramp in a South American capital city to take her groceries home for her in return for a tip, only to find that he intends to completely dominate her emotionally so that she will become his equal – a nobody. The play – again a two-hander – challenged me greatly. It was directed by Guy Slater, who had written two television plays I'd taken part in – I imagine that's why he thought of me for the role.

My character, named *'The Hake'* after a particularly aggressive and invasive type of fish, had many long monologues during which he demonstrates how well he can fashion paper flowers out of newspapers. Naturally, I had to learn how to do this, and it was an extremely complicated process. I had to be able to match exactly the progress of the demonstration of flower making to the speech, so that at the end of each monologue I had finished a stunning rose, lily, orchid etc.

In the end, when he has reduced Eva to an almost vegetative state, *'The Hake'* becomes completely unhinged, speaking at the speed of a machine gun, while tearing up newspapers and paper flowers. I loved it because it was so challenging. I'm not sure I'd be up to it now.

CARROLL BAKER, HELMUT BERGER IN ROME.

Over the years I've returned to the stage ever less frequently. I have no idea why – it's not as though I am a totally hopeless stage actor. Maybe I just think I'm a better film actor. It's my preferred medium because it's more intimate, and you generally have the evenings free.

In August of 1976 Peter Coe cast me in a play by American novelist and playwright Irwin Shaw called *'Lucy Crown.'* The stars were Carroll *'Baby Doll'* Baker and Roy Dotrice. Ralph Nossek and I were the support.

Carroll Baker in 'Lucy Crown.'

Ralph became a good friend – we both had Adza as an agent

and we both loved her dearly.

The novel was one of Shaw's first, but hardly his best work. A later novel 'Rich Man, Poor Man' was produced as a BBC television series and was a huge success, as was the book.

The story of 'Lucy Crown' was of a wife and mother who has a dalliance with a nineteen-year-old college student while on holiday in a resort in Vermont. Aged thirty, I was cast as the teenager because I never looked my age. Maybe now?

The critics found the play 'verbose and overlong.'

The plan was to tour England, and then slip into the West End somewhere. Carroll was the Hollywood draw card, and Roy was very well known to theatre audiences in London.

From the very start of rehearsals I felt extremely uncomfortable in the role. I was far too old to be playing a callow American teenager, and had no personal experience of the American college way of life to draw on. However, that was just too bad, I had to do my best until Peter Coe chose to fire me – which he once came close to doing! Only Carroll standing up for me saved my bacon.

Peter and I didn't get along at all well. Possibly because he realized I had been grossly miscast. He had a habit, during plotting, of placing my character in very unusual positions on stage. For instance, during one scene I was asked to lie on my back holding a chair above me. During these rehearsals, Peter would sit in the gods and shout down to me. "Can't hear! Can't hear!"

I know my voice then wasn't the strongest, but I had no problem with projection at the Apollo during 'Children of the Wolf,' so this chant soon began to irritate me, and I am afraid I let that show.

As I recall, we opened at the Billingham forum close to Stockton-on-Tees. It's a chemical town, once the home of ICI, and I found it rather grim. Carroll, Peter and Roy were housed in a nice pub, while the rest of us were farmed out to a ghastly building run by the council that had rooms to let. As a consequence I made enemies with bed bugs the first night, and had to grin and bear the appalling itching on stage every night for a week until we returned to London and I saw my doctor.

My mother had an answer for these establishments. When she was an actress on the road with a play, if her lodgings were 'horrid' and the people 'not nice,' she'd buy a fresh herring and nail it to the underside of the bed when she left.

Carole and I became close friends. Ralph Nossek was also a great pal. We played The Theatre Royal Bath, a very lovely theatre, then played the Richmond Theatre in Surrey, which just happened to be where I grew up, so that was a thrill. Even better was the thought that my mother had played this very theatre with her name above the title in a thriller by the name of *'Death on the Table.'*

Incidentally, my mother played the Lyric and Criterion Theatres too, as well at the Apollo. So in the 'West End Stakes' she's two up on me. Of course, hopefully I 'm not finished yet!

Finally we arrived at the Theatre Royal Brighton, which was to be our final halt before producers found a suitable West End theatre to move into.

During the run, Roy Dotrice would often play jokes on me on stage. If I were upstage of him, he would turn to me and make a face, trying to make me corpse. It was often difficult not to, as his 'faces' *were* very funny. There was no harm to it, but I have to say I didn't think that these gags added much to the performance. Otherwise, he was a consummate pro and a very gifted actor. On other occasions he would enjoy teasing me. For instance, before our third performance in Brighton, he popped his head around the door of my dressing room and said, *"You want to know who's front of house this evening?"* As I hate knowing who's out there, I begged him not to tell me. He nodded. *"Okay. Fair enough."* He then left, then reopened the door. *"Olivier! Want to know where he's sitting?"* *"NO!"* I almost screamed. *"Okay, fair enough,"* he replied, pretended to leave then said: *"Second row stage right!"* When I walked on stage, to speak my first cheery nineteen-year-old line (a real dog; *'Hi there!*

I'm Jeff Bunner!') I was acutely aware that Lord Olivier was just a few feet away, most likely heaving a sigh.

His chair was vacant after the interval.

Along the way, most actors do work they are not proud of, and this was definitely one of them. The lukewarm reviews persuaded the producers to forget about a London run, so that was that.

Carroll had been anticipating at least six months in London, so she had to change her plans radically, deciding to return to Rome where she had an apartment and had been living for some years.

One evening over a drink she suggested I should give Rome a try – it'd be a whole new experience, and she told me she knew everyone there and would be happy to introduce me.

This sounded like an amazingly generous offer – one I would be foolish to turn down, so I accepted her offer and within a few weeks I was in Rome meeting agents, casting people, and producers.

Almost immediately, I had secured an Italian agent, a short, swarthy, impeccably dressed man by the name of Vittorio Squillante. Let me say this; I'm sure there are several Vittorio Squillantes in Italy – probably all in the film business. I know that my agent then had that name, but on close research I see that a Vittorio Squillante was later the executive producer of one of my favourite films, *'King of New York,'* with Christopher Walken. Don't want to upset a man of such calibre, eh?

Within a few weeks I had a meeting with a director, whose name eludes me now, the upshot of which was that I was cast in a leading role in this film that had not yet achieved all its funding. During the following seven months that I spent in Rome I met with this director about once every ten days and on each occasion he assured me *"Two more weeks! Justa two more weeks. Then we begin! For sure!"* It never happened, and I never made it in Cinecita. A shame. But I had a great holiday. Carroll offered me a room in her huge apartment and it was like being on a very long holiday.

Living in Rome wasn't as expensive as I'd imagined. If you knew the right restaurants it was as cheap as chips.

One of Carroll's favourites was predictably called Mario's – a very small place that served the most perfect hot creamy chilli penne. The owner was always trying to get me to order *'un buon filleto'* because it cost more, but I always stuck to the pasta – it was divine.

In the evening, quite often Carroll would be asked to join friends in bars, restaurants and nightclubs as she was very much a part of the Roman party scene. The most popular spot was of course the famous *'Jackie O.'* It was always packed with showbiz people, a lot of whom wondered how close Carroll and I were. Well, these were showbiz people – they adore a gossip! And many had crushes on Carroll, such as famous pop star, *'Little Tony.'* There was no future in telling them we were just good friends, we had to bear a lot of teasing asides.

On one night, I was dancing with a girl and I was spun around by a young man who then kissed me full on the lips and wouldn't let me go for several seconds. Whoa! He then introduced himself as Helmut Berger. He'd also done a version of 'The Picture of Dorian Gray' in 1970, so we were kindred spirits. He was a real party animal.

Carroll sitting next to 'Little Tony' at Mario's in Rome.

On another occasion Carroll and I were in 'Jackie O' and 'Little Tony' was thinking of finally making a move on Carroll. But he still was convinced we were an item. So he made a phone call and twenty minutes later a lovely girl was seating herself at my elbow asking me to come to her place. Clearly, the singer had given this young lady an incentive to get me out of there.

One of Carroll's closest pals was a costume designer. He was short, rotund and very jolly. He was also very gay.

He told me this wonderful story – I'll give you the gist of it, exactly as I remember it. At the time a producer friend of his called Tinto Brassi was about to shoot a film called *'Caligula.'*

"So...I get zis call from Tinto. He say...'you wanna be in miya film?' I say 'Tinto! Of course. I would keel to design youra film.' Then he say, 'No, not design my movie. Act! I want you to act!' I say, "But Tinto. I am not actor. What you want me to do?' He then say, 'In the film John Gielgud look through a hole in the wall. I want to film a scene – eet is what he is supposed to see. An orgy!' So I say to Tinto, 'Okay...so whata I do? Be

naked?' And he reply. 'I want you to be ---- by a mule.'"

The costume designer was shocked to the core. Was Tinto serious? Or was it another of his bad jokes? I like to believe this was Tinto's idea of a joke.

I never saw the film but I believe there was an orgy scene in one of the director's cuts, one that Sir John was supposed to see through a hole in the wall.

During those months in Rome, Wendy came to visit me. She brought with her our great friend Rupert Byng. Each time we traveled on Rome's buses, we played 'The Bus Game.'

Bus driver's in Rome think they are Fangio reincarnated and have a habit of not only driving far too fast with no regard to their passengers, but like to swing the buses into each turn and jack-knife them out. So, the game is as follows. The players have to stand, not sit. They can't hold onto anything – that's immediate disqualification! It's a kind of 'Interior Bus Surfing,' and a lot of fun. Try it on any bus – it's not as easy as you think! Another thing Rupert enjoyed doing was attaching an ice-cream to a helium balloon, biting off the bottom of the cone and allowing it to drift over St. Peters Square and study the drips.

TV MOVIES

'THE FLAME IS LOVE,' LIMOS, & BEDS IN IRELAND.

In the winter of 1977 I was fortunate enough to be cast in a wonderful BBC *'Play of the Month.'* It was an adaptation of Georg Büchner's *'Danton's Death.'*

Yet again I was surrounded by the cream of Britain's finest thespians. Norman Rodway played Danton, and Ian Richardson was Robespierre. Ian had that signature clipped way of speaking, similar to Peter Cushing. Don Henderson was Mercier. All have now passed away.

I was fascinated by Rodway and Richardson's voices, as well as Richardson's way of staring at people to make them feel uncomfortable. Always in character of course. But he was the master of what I call the 1-2-3; the pause, the look, then the dialogue. Each one had a long beat in between.

A young Michael Pennington played Saint-Just. Even then he was a theatre star, and his work impressed me enormously.

Soon after, I was cast in a play for Yorkshire television called 'The File on Harry Jordan.' Directed by Gerry Mill it also starred Bernard Gallagher and Georgina Cookson.

I thought it a very original 'Play of the Week', about a young man with endless ambition who is determined to get to the top – whatever the cost. Once his promotion is announced, he enters the lift and ascends to the top floor. In a huge office that occupies the entire floor, he speaks to the outgoing CEO, a man who looks incredibly tired and depressed, yet welcomes Jordan to the top job. He then shares one secret with him. The CEO is never allowed to leave the 13th floor. He lives there all his life until replaced. Horrified, Jordan tries to leave but he's locked in. At that moment the retiring CEO leaps out of the window – the only option to leave.

In the spring of 1978 I was cast in what was to be the pilot for a series of all Barbara Cartland's romantic novels; 'The Flame is Love.'

My character, an English aristocrat, goes to live in late nineteenth century Paris, joining the 'Symboliste' movement. He falls in love with an American heiress who is there on holiday, and ultimately has to battle a satanic movement bent on sacrificing the girl he's fallen in love with.

The script was written by Hindi Brooks, based on Barbara Cartland's novella. Michael O'Herlighy directed, and the iconic Ed

Friendly produced. Ed was a man who seemed to have met everyone from Gloria Swanson to Douglas Fairbanks Snr. This time, incredibly, I was the good guy! That role was handed to Timothy Dalton. The heroine was Linda Purl. The legendary Joan Greenwood *('Kind Hearts and Coronets')* was to play *'The Duchess of Grantham.'*

It was the first time I had been cast as a squeaky clean, delightfully normal Englishman, and I knew I'd have to struggle mightily with this paradigm – bad guys are not only more fun, but easier to play. Good guys are normally rather dull because they don't have the inventiveness to be devilish.

The film was shot in and around Dublin, Ireland. This was a delight for me, as I couldn't wait to get back to the country that had been so good to me.

With producer Ed Friendly on the set of "The Flame is Love."

I flew back to Dublin, hoping everyone would be pleased that I'd made a modest name for myself and was about to star in another American television movie. I was to be a little disappointed with the reaction of the locals.

Even my old friend Bob Collins was less than thrilled when we met at our hotel. I found this sad, since for four years at Trinity we'd been as close as brothers. Maybe I am misremembering.

When an American show comes to Ireland, word gets around like wildfire, and every Irish actor wants a part of it. It was no different with 'The Flame.' All the usual suspects were cast, and then some more. My fiends on the Dublin theatre scene snaffled some great cameos – Godfrey Quigley, Jim Fizgerald, Maureen Toal, Meryl Gourley, Paeder Lamb, John Malloy, Ann O'Dwyer, and Eddie Golden amongst many others.

With the very kissable Linda Purl in Barbara Cartland's 'The Flame is Love.' CBS.

Our hotel was in Killiney, a small village a few miles south of Dublin. A very picturesque village right on the water. I'd had a wonderful working holiday, struggling a bit with my role because 'Pierre Valmont' being so desperately decent and ordinary. Michael O'Herlihy is a joyous man to work with – a consummate professional, and very much at home in Ireland. Linda Purl was a sweetheart and perfect for her role as the innocent American heiress *'Emmaline Nevada Holz.'* Each day I'd be picked up from my hotel in a beautiful white shiny Mercedes and driven to the set by an elegant chauffeur. A great day's shoot and a beautifully catered lunch later, I was driven back to my hotel to dine.

This was to change with the arrival of Tim who didn't arrive until late one evening after we'd completed a week of filming and joined Linda and I for dinner. I found him very affable, amusing and friendly. He had some great stories and enjoyed telling them. Tim was an extremely likeable man.

That evening, after dinner, as we made our way to our rooms, Tim asked if he could take a look at mine. I replied, *"Of course, but as far as I know, all the suites are the same."*

I don't think Tim was convinced.

He looked into my room. *"Hmmm. Interesting. Your bed is much bigger than mine,"* he observed sagely. *"Really?"* I replied. I couldn't see any difference. *"Really. Take a look at my bed,"* he said, crossing the corridor and opening his door. The room was exactly the same as mine, but his bedspread was blue while mine was cream coloured. *"Looks the same as mine,"* I said. He didn't reply – he simply muttered something indiscernible.

The following morning I was called late to set, so I had a leisurely breakfast, eventually walking outside at the appointed hour to climb into my dazzling white Mercedes. But instead of my lovely chauffeur driven limo, I was greeted with a ten-year-old weather-beaten Ford Torana. The driver was engrossed in a novel, chain-smoking. The ashtray was brimming with butts. I knocked on the window, unsure whether this was my lift to the set. The elderly man, who looked as though he'd just milked a dozen cows, climbed out and said hello.

"I'm Shane. Are you taking me to set," I asked.

"Royt!" was the reply. *"Hop in."*

I enquired where Alex and his Mercedes were that morning.

"Royt! Thaz Mister Dalton's car, sir. You only had it 'cos he was away."

Lovely.

I asked Tim about 'contracts, cars and stuff' over lunch, and he filled me in about a few things he'd learnt over the years.

"If you want the good things of life it's all got to be in the contract. Like the car – has to be a 'luxury' Merc. If you don't mention the luxury bit, they'll fob you off with some small cheap Mercedes. Not so good. Same goes for trailers, hotels and class of air travel."

So, that was it. Bye-bye Mercedes. Never mind, it was an unforeseen luxury – didn't bother me in the least.

When I arrived back at the hotel that evening, and strolled down the corridor I saw that my room door was open, and two men were struggling with my bed. Curious, I asked them what they were up to. *"Swapping your bed with Mister Dalton's."*

Amazing.

I have a suspicion that this was a way Tim made damn sure everyone took him seriously. Me? I'm sure production people think I'm just too easy. When it comes to Tim, they take notice and make sure he's comfy.

I watched the film again a week ago to refresh old memories, and was stunned by my Froggy accent. Maybe it's a fact that practically all English actors sound like Inspector Clouseau when they affect a French accent. Maybe not Daniel Day-Lewis. But I know I did. However, I was lucky enough to have an excuse because Pierre the symbolist painter was in fact an English aristocrat masquerading as a Frog. Well, that's my excuse when people cringe. My only tip with accents is to get the shape of the mouth right first – if the shape's right, you'll find it really hard not to speak their way.

Dublin has changed quite a bit since I studied law there. Then, the economy was struggling, the Irish punt was down against the pound, the pubs were so smokey you could hang a ham or a haddock in any of them, and as I mentioned before the Republican pubs such as the famous *'Brazen Head'* were a no-go zone for we English students.

Then for a while, Ireland became a financial haven for European money, and the cost of living skyrocketed. When I was last there the Aussie dollar didn't go very far. Now the wheel has come full circle and Ireland's economy is on the skids again, thanks to the world recession. Such a shame, the Irish people are again struggling. I hope things improve. In the meantime, as I write, the Aussie dollar is in great shape and I can afford to visit my favourite Irish pubs again –*Toner's'* in Baggot Street, *'Johnny Fox's'* in the Wicklow Hills, and *'The Old Stand,'* just off Dame Street. No better pubs in the world.

'The Flame is Love' was supposed to be the first of a series of Barbara Cartland's filmed books, but somehow or other it proved to be the first and last. I can't really understand why, after all her books sold untold millions of copies. It wasn't as if we didn't stick rigidly to the formula of somewhat unbelievable heroes, heroines and wicked dastardly bad guys in an historical context – possibly we were too squeaky clean and proper. It also didn't help that the night it aired across America everyone was watching the seventh game of the world series. This was never factored in as an excuse. Ratings, that's all that counts.

I returned to Los Angeles for the television premiere of *'The Flame is Love,'* to promote myself a bit, and to revisit all the friends I had made in the past. Barbara Cartland was kind enough to send me a telegram saying Pierre was just as she had imagined him; *"You were marvelous,"* she very sweetly said. This concerned me at the time because maybe I'd come across in too saccharine a way.

Of course nowadays she might have sent me an email of congratulations, or even texted me? Now, even the Queen's telegram doesn't exist as such, you have to *ask* the Palace for a note of congratulation. Progress without much charm.

While I was in L.A., Ed Friendly was kind enough to take me to the famous Musso and Franks restaurant.

As Hollywood's oldest and most famous grillroom, it's steeped in history. F. Scott Fitzgerald, William Faulkner, Raymond Chandler and Ernest Hemingway were habitués, and often Orson Welles held court there. The story goes that Charlie Chaplin, Douglas Fairbanks and Rudolph Valentino raced along Hollywood Boulevard on horses, the loser having to foot the bill. It's a good story, regardless of its veracity.

While I was eating there and chatting to Ed, the loo door opened and Steve McQueen walked towards us. I was certain he'd pass us by, but he spotted Ed and stopped. Ed introduced us and I shook another of my idols by the hand. He was very friendly indeed, asking me what I was doing in L.A. and wishing me the best of luck in my career. Like Newman he treated everyone the same; rich, poor, famous, not so famous. As I write, I am constantly discovering that people I loved working with have since died. The fact is, it's easy to miss a news report, and the Oscar's *Vale* doesn't include nearly enough people. Consequently I just found out that the wonderful Michael O'Herlihy died thirteen years ago. Only 68. At least he died in Dublin.

'MURDER IS EASY,' AND OLIVIA DE HAVILLAND.

In 1981 came the CBS telemovie *'Murder is Easy,'* which was shot in the English countryside just outside London. When the cast sheet was sent to me in Pimlico by the production company prior to the shoot, I was stunned to see I'd be working with legendary Olivia de

Havilland.

Sadly, a very shabby snap of a legendary Olivia de Havilland. 'Murder is Easy.'

"I'm going to be working with Melanie!" I told Wendy. She was puzzled. *"Melanie Griffiths?"* she asked. *"No! Melanie Hamilton – Gone with the Wind','* I replied.

If that wasn't enough, the cast included Helen Hayes, my former semi-nude screen girlfriend from *'The Sweeney'* Lesley-Anne Down, (now *much* more of a star) Jonathon Pryce, one of my favourite English theatre actors, Freddie Jones whom I'd worked with on *'Shades of Greene,'* and *'The Incredible Hulk,'* Bill Bixby.

It's always good to shoot a film on location in England when the weather is good; and this was summertime. Claude Watham directed. The production turned out to be good Agatha Christie material.

I was chatting with Lesley-Anne on set one day when her then husband, Enrique Gabriel, arrived. Two giant Borzoi dogs were dragging him along. Leslie-Anne saw her husband and the dogs and her face lit up.

"My darlings!" she cried out loudly and jumped up to kiss both

dogs. My kind of woman. Didn't kiss her husband – just the dogs. They *were* very kissable hounds.

In *'Murder is Easy'* I played a rather dull drug-running doctor. And while you always try to make what you can of a dull role, in this case no 'silk purse' came to mind. So my only option was to colour the 'sow's ear.' Confronted with dull material, it's a good idea to try to find a facet of your character that'll make him more striking without detracting from the other characters – that would unbalance the piece. Sometimes I make things up, such as giving a merciless killer one speck of humanity, such as a love mice. No actor should feel he's trapped by the script. Make the character your own. The writer has done his work – now bring the character to life by giving him a history. Roland Joffe is the master of this technique.

Working with Olivia de Havilland was a dream come true – the high point of the shoot for me.

I well recall one scene we shot.

When we were sent to relax, she asked me, *"Was I all right?"*

I couldn't believe my ears – Olivia de Havilland was asking me if she'd done a good job!

I replied, *"Miss de Havilland, you're asking* me *if you were all right?"*

She looked puzzled. *"We're all actors together, aren't we? Surely you have an opinion too?"*

She was quite right. *"You were perfect, Miss de Havilland,"* I replied.

She smiled and patted my arm with her hand.

'THE NAKED CIVIL SERVANT,' QUENTIN CRISP & JOHN

HURT.

In the spring of 1975, immediately following the theatre production of *'Paper Flowers,'* I was lucky enough to be cast in a television play that will live forever; in part because of the writing of Quentin Crisp and Philip Mackie, in part because of Jack Gold's direction – one of England's finest—and in part because of the award-winning performance of John Hurt.

Award-winning John Hurt as Quentin Crisp

The telemovie was called *'The Naked Civil Servant,'* and was the life story of Quentin Crisp, the English writer and raconteur who became an icon of homosexuals in the 1970s after publication of his memoir, *'The Naked Civil Servant.'*

The cast wasn't brimming with famous actors, barring John. However, it was the most marvelous ensemble piece, and Jack Gold pulled us all together and squeezed out whatever talent we had.

"Can I trouble you for a light?" Norma.

The rumour at the time was that many people had advised John Hurt not to take the role, as he'd forever be branded a gay actor. Of course this was nonsense and John had no time for this train of thought and neither did his agent. He won the BAFTA Award for best actor that year for his perfect portrayal. Jack Gold was nominated for Best Director, and the production also won the *Prix Italia* for Best Drama.

I didn't have a major role – not many people did; as I said, it was an ensemble piece with a huge cast. When I read the script I knew I had to play Norma, the first gay streetwalker that Quentin ever met – the 'girl' that introduced him to the dark and dangerous, raunchy side of London.

I met Jack and I scored the role. I was in heaven.

During rehearsals, Jack was at pains to tell us 'girls' that we were to shed any reservations we might have about playing up the roles—he wanted 'huge performances.'

"*Go for it,*" he told us. "*And when you think you're going too far, go some more!*" Well, I did just that, and loved very moment of those night shoots in London. We didn't dress in drag because in those days there weren't any cross dressers as such. The '*girls*' would dress in an extremely feminine way but still wear men's clothes. It was the hair and make-up that singled them out as street girls.

I had the most magnificent blonde wig swept up around the side, sitting atop of which was a gorgeous broad-brimmed Trilby. A long, elegant, blue-grey coat with the lapel turned up and a duck blue long tasseled scarf completed my costume. Roger Lloyd Pack and Adrian Shergold played two of the other 'girls.' Roger is the son of Charles Lloyd Pack, who'd played '*The Professor*' in '*Frankenstein and the Monster from Hell.*' It was a riot to be out in London looking so incredibly sultry. During a dinner break one night an elderly man sidled up to me and said, "*I say, can I interest you in a drink and a chat?*" I was so amused; I couldn't help replying in the falsetto voice I was using as Norma. "*Thanks, duckie. But I'm utterly washed out.*" I winked at him and walked back to my caravan.

The Black Cat Café

The male hookers' scenes were shot in two nights. It was hilarious. John Hurt set up a base camp at a delightful nearby hotel bar, where we would relax during takes and sample the wares. When I finally saw the film on television I was swept away by the brilliance of John's performance – it was deeply saddening, full of wit and humour and for once depicted gay men as people worth speaking to.

IDLE THOUGHTS ON SUCCESS

MY OLD FRIEND JEREMY IRONS.

If you are lucky enough to land the television role of the decade in *'Brideshead Revisited,'* you will most likely go from success to success.

Of course you have to make the right decisions. If Jeremy had decided to join the cast of *'Boxing Helena,'* after having finished shooting *'Brideshead,'* his career would have taken a sharp turn downwards. But he didn't. His next film was starring opposite Meryl Streep in *'The French Lieutenant's Woman.'* To follow there was *'Betrayal,'* written by Harold Pinter. How can one go wrong here? Roland Joffe's *'The Mission,'* David Cronenberg's *'Dead Ringers,'* and Barbet Schroeder's *'Reversal of Fortune'* followed, a film that earned him an Oscar. So, make the most of your first lucky break and make sure to turn it into another break. It's a little like letting the winnings of a single number ride in roulette. If you are outstanding in one production, and come to the attention of everyone in the business, don't snatch at your next role. Be patient. Sadly, I have never had Louis Malle, Mendes or Tarantino in a power struggle to hire me. But I know what I'd have to do if they all wanted me.

For most actors, when one film finishes, they are back to 'resting' and that's boring, as well as a struggle to make ends meet. My advice is always to accept the best work that pays little, rather than the worst film that pays big bucks and ends up ruining your career. I have made more then my fair share of 'money-spinners' simply because I needed the money, so now I am hoisted by my own petard here. Yet had I been cast as *'Charles'* in *'Brideshead Revisited,'* who knows what might have happened? Which segues nicely into my next point.

Sometime in 1981, Adza called me and told me they were casting the principal roles in *'Brideshead Revisited.'* Doreen Jones was in charge. I was really excited – this was a dream job. I went to a casting and met with Doreen and put down a test. At the time I thought I was up for Sebastian Flyte, the role played ultimately by Anthony Andrews, but curiously they saw me as a possible for Charles.

As the weeks passed I heard continuing fresh news from Adza. The casting was continuing and the list of actors was being narrowed down. Finally, Adza called me to let me know that there were now only three actors in the mix for Charles, and they'd let me know that day. I was thrilled, as well as mightily anxious that I might not land the role – I had no idea who the other two actors were at the time.

At six in the evening that day, Adza rang me to break the news – the role of Charles had gone to someone else. I was desperately disappointed. It was a crushing blow. Wendy did what she could to console me, finally reminding me that we were going out to dinner that night – to the house of Jeremy Irons, an old friend, and his gorgeous wife, Sinead Cusack. I'd met them both through Sinead's sister Sorcha, who I'd known well at Trinity – we'd been in a few plays together. So, with a heavy heart, I jumped into the car with Wendy, hugging a bottle of red, and we drove to Hampstead where Sinead and Jeremy had their house. When we arrived, I knocked on the door and it flew open. Jeremy was there, clutching a bottle of champagne. *"The most wonderful news, you two. I just landed the part of Charles in 'Brideshead.'"* He told me delightedly. Wendy didn't even look at me. *"Wonderful! Well done,"* she said. I caught my breath and said more or less the same thing.

I never told him that I was in the final mix. What was the point? It was a difficult evening for me emotionally – hopefully I didn't allow it to show.

I've often thought back to that moment when I saw Jeremy going from strength to strength, culminating in his Oscar win. Good for him – he beat me to 'Charles' fair and square, and went on to play exquisite parts, exquisitely well. He's a great talent. So if you don't land that role you've set your heart on, get over it and see what you can do instead. I did, and ended up in Australia having the time of my life. Sure, I never won an Oscar, but I've had a fantastic life and am still doing so.

Here's another thing. Jacki Weaver has been an Aussie film icon for decades. Films such as *'Picnic at Hanging Rock,' 'The Removalists,'* and *'Caddie.'* She started work in the late sixties, so she can't be much younger than sixty-something. And her role in *'Animal Kingdom'* landed her an Oscar nomination! She waited patiently all her life for the second shoe to drop and completed some terrific work along the line – so never give up!

MY MOVE 'DOWNUNDER.'

SUN, BEACHES, AND 'THE DON LANE SHOW.'

1981 had been a lean year, getting leaner by the second. So when I heard that Fox Columbia, the distributors of *'Chatterley'* were taking Sylvia to Australia on a promotional tour, I asked if I could go too. They agreed, and I packed my bags. Wendy was delighted; she'd always hoped we'd end up in Oz. Fox Columbia very cleverly sent Sylvia and me on separate flights. The reason was that they had to send Sylvia first class. I just wanted to get there and do the network television talk shows, introduce myself to Australia and see if they wanted to employ me, so I flew economy.

At Kingsford Smith Airport in Sydney, I was met by the friendliest young man imaginable, Fox Columbia's public relations guy Bob Nicol. A limo was waiting and I was whisked off. The sun was shining, the sky was blue, the pacific was shimmering with diamond sparkles, and Bob's gay humour made me laugh all the way to the hotel – I was being treated like a king and when you are, it's time to enjoy it.

That week I was taken to any number of publicity functions; there were radio spots, media interviews, magazine chats etc. When I had some time to myself, I took myself off to Bondi, swam and had a few schooners of Fosters.

The highlight of the promo tour was appearing on *'The Don Lane Show.'* Don Lane had been the Australian talk-show king for many years; it went to air each Saturday night in prime time and had a huge following, such as Parky and Letterman. Bob picked me up – I was staying with Wendy's sister, Robby, in Elizabeth Bay. We then collected Sylvia from her five star hotel and arrived at the

Channel 9 studios where we were welcomed by a gushing young guy who immediately confided to Sylvia that meeting *'Emmanuelle'* was a dream come true. Sylvia was always very magnanimous when people groveled like Uriah Heep – it was water off a duck's back. She'd lay a gentle hand on their arm and smile lovingly, then move on towards the dressing room where she knew the champers would be set up. On this occasion, she walked into the huge dressing room, took one look at the ice bucket containing the Moët & Chandon and said, *"I only drink champagne that has my name on it!"* By this she meant Cristal – it was a semi-serious joke of hers.

The young man backed out the door smiling. *"I'll see what I can do,"* he said.

Ten minutes later he returned with a bottle of Cristal in an ice bucket and Sylvia poured us all a glass.

By the time we were summoned – twenty-five minutes later – Sylvia was in such a delightfully relaxed mood she wasn't in the least inclined to chat to *any* talk show host. However, I impressed on her that Fox Columbia would be sorely disappointed if she didn't go to meet Don and show all of Australia how beautiful she was. That seemed to do the trick. She stood and we were led to the rear of the set.

Most people who watch *'Parkinson'* won't know that the back of the set is simply boards and gantries. Sylvia looked at the ladder she had to climb to appear at the rear of the set, ten feet above where Don was sitting.

"Hell, no. Count me out!" she said.

I could hear Don say, *"So please give a big Australian welcome to the stars of 'Lady Chatterley's Lover' Sylvia Kristel and Shane Briant!"*

"Come on, Sylvia. Up!" I replied, pushing her to the steps.

"Well, help me for Christ's sake."

Ten seconds later she was standing at the top of the set, waving her arms and blowing kisses to the audience as if nothing had happened. I stood behind her, waiting for her to walk down the steps towards Don, who had his arms out to her in welcome. Sylvia didn't seem to see Don, she simply continued blowing kisses for a good thirty seconds until I took her arm and guided her down to the seats. She was so happy to be there she was much more interested in the studio audience. I think that was why she showed little interest in the questions Don was asking her. Because the interview was rapidly grinding to a halt, I decided to answer most of Don's questions while Sylvia nodded her assent.

I have to say, she looked stunning that night, her eyes sparkling like emeralds.

Relaxing in Sydney after the Don Lane Show.

The show ended up a success. It was a great introduction to Australia for me because Sylvia allowed me to do most of the talking.

In Sylvia's suite in Sydney. Boy, she could party!

Back in London the film premiered at the Leicester Square Theatre. It was the first time I'd seen my name above the title. I stared at the size of the letters – who, me?

As I flew back to London I knew what I had to do. I'd been born in London and spent most of my life there, yet my genes were those of my mother rather than my Scottish father. I was an Aussie at heart. I had to return to Australia, my mother's and Wendy's country.

On the flight home from the promo tour of *'Chatterley'* one of the spectacularly beautiful Garuda attendants asked me very politely why I had chosen to fly economy class. I had no idea what she was talking about. Seeing my confusion, she continued. *"All the crew go see 'Lady Chatterley' in Seednay. Very nice film. But why you not fly… 'firstaclass'?"*

Now I understood. Like most moviegoers, the Indonesian cabin crew thought all film actors were insanely rich. I wasn't about to disappoint her, but I had to think quickly. *"Er…I am about to make a film in London about someone who has no money but flies around the world constantly. I wanted to see what it was like to fly economy; I've never done it before."*

The flight attendant smiled broadly. *"Ah! Of course. I see! Yes!"*

Ten minutes later she reappeared with a bottle of champagne from first class – in a plastic bag so my fellow passengers wouldn't be jealous.True story! I love Garuda. But I love Qantas a lot more!

THE POWER OF AN AUSSIE DE FACTO!

Back in London, I spent every day plotting how to get back to Oz. My dear friend and agent, Adza, had passed away several years back and I was now represented by a new agency – Richard Stone. Things were not 'happening' in the U.K. back then, while I knew they were in Australia. The Aussie film industry was on a hot streak, making dozens of movies every year. Many people in Oz had suggested I emigrate to Australia because English actors were highly thought of – it was an odd kind of 'cultural cringe,' one that's not so prevalent today.

But how was I to work in Australia without a visa? I had to find out what my options were. I visited the Australian Consulate in London and told them my mother was born in Australia. That didn't cut the mustard. I was surprised.

"What nationality is your father?" I was asked – clearly paternity was more important than maternity.

"Scottish," I replied.

The immigration assistant made a sad face.

"How much money will you be bringing to Australia?"

I thought long and hard about how to answer. Lie? No point, I'd be found out in minutes.

"Er...five thousand pounds," I replied.

An even glummer face.

"What do you do for a living?" she asked.

I knew that was the killer question. *"I am ...er...an actor,"* I replied, my voice the barest reed.

The official snapped the file closed. That was it. What else could I tell them? That my girlfriend was an Aussie? How would that help if the fact my mother was born in Sydney didn't count? It was worth a shot.

"My girlfriend is Australian. Does that help?"

An immediate smiley face. *"How long have you been together?"*

"Six years," I replied. *"We hope to get married really soon."*

Now, the woman beamed at me. *"With a de facto spouse, I don't see any problem in granting you a resident's visa."*

That was that. Mother? Nah. Girlfriend. Yes!

Odd.

Wendy and I thought it might be a good idea for me to test the waters before we uprooted ourselves completely from London, so we decided I would go out to Sydney first while Wendy held the fort in Pimlico. I had to tell my mum what I was planning, and I knew she'd be desperately lonely without me. So, to placate her, I promised I'd fly her out to visit me so she could again visit the country she'd left as an eight-year-old. That helped a lot.

I flew back to Oz six months later, leaving Wendy to organize what we'd bring with us, and what we'd sell.

I'd told the woman at Australia House that I planned to bring five thousand pounds, but I actually arrived in Sydney with two. My plan was to stay a year and see how I got on. It was going to be an interesting test. You may think two grand isn't enough to live on for so long. I'm here to tell you that in 1982 it was plenty if you were prepared to live frugally. The friends I'd made in Sydney during the promo tour became friends for life, and within a few weeks I was sharing a house in Paddington – the equivalent of Knightsbridge in London – with two lovely sisters from Coonamble. Fifty dollars a week. Shared bath and kitchen. Having little cash, I had to cut my cloth appropriately. I'd engaged the wonderful agent Shirley Pearce (Russell Crowe's agent – but he wasn't famous then.) I relied on her to 'make things happen.' I'd usually sit on my sun-drenched bedroom balcony, waiting it out with a cask of wine that cost about six dollars. Or nip down to Bondi and lie there, in the sun.

It was a very tough life!

In the evenings, I'd watch television, eat a jar of chili con carne bought at the corner shop, and revisit my cask of white wine.

The waiting game is a hard one for actors. But a necessary one. What makes it easier is knowing that you have an agent who cares about your career, has faith in your talent, and is busting a gut to get you work. Simply *having* an agent is not enough. Too many actors these days have agents who probably don't give them a thought for weeks, if not months, on end. The answer to that problem is to work like hell *yourself*, making connections, meeting people in the business, and putting yourself 'out there.' I was lucky enough to have a good profile because of all the '*Chatterley*' promotion. Casting people knew who I was, and I was the new 'English Import' in town. So I could afford to wait it out and allow my Australian agent Shirley Pearce to do her work while I lazed on the beach. Back home in England Wendy was doing her best to combine managing international sporting events with handling our move to Oz.

AUSTRALIAN FILMS & TELEVISION

'RUN CHRISSIE, RUN!'

In 1985 I made a film that had originally been titled *'Reunion,'* but underwent a sad name change later to *'Run Chrissie, Run.'* I believe it was also released somewhere, possibly America, as *'Moving Targets.'* I hated the new title because back in Dublin, the word *'Chrissie'* is a pejorative, otherwise known as a scrubber. It was produced by the South Australia Film Commission, directed by Chris Langman, and shot in Adelaide and the Barossa Valley. But at last I was seeing Australia.

Carmen Duncan and a young Annie Jones were a mother and daughter on the run from the IRA. Michael Aitken was the IRA renegade, and I was the man sent to kill him. On my team were Nicholas Eadie, a talented young actor, and Red Symons, the rock star front man of one of Australia's best known groups – *'Skyhooks.'* Red never stopped kidding around. I'm sure we bad guys had much more fun than the heroes, Carmen, Annie and Michael, as we did our best to be a very oddball threesome. Nick Eadie had his head shaved. He looked like the *'hoon from hell,'* in his black leather jacket and chains. Red imbued his character with constant sarcasm and razor sharp wit, and I did my best to be the cool 'silent one.' I ended up half *'James Bond,'* half *'The Saint.'*

Midway though the shoot the armorer showed me how to fire

my Uzi submachine gun.

To fire a single round was practically impossible for a novice like me, since the gun has a hair trigger. The best I could do was two rounds. The armorer suggested I fire the whole magazine, just so I could see how long it'd take. I was amazed. About two and a half seconds! When it came to the scene where I fired the gun, I made the stupid mistake of deciding not to wear earplugs.

I'd worn them at the demonstration and hadn't found the Uzi too noisy. What I failed to factor in was that the demonstration took place in an open field, whereas I would be firing through the windscreen of a car from the inside. Enclosed!

The safety officer gave me earplugs, but I took them out while he wasn't looking because I wanted to be able to hear all the dialogue crisply. Big mistake!

With rock star Red Symons on 'Run, Chrissie, Run.'

Come the moment, the windscreen exploded on cue and I began firing the Uzi through it. The noise within the enclosed car was like being at the epicentre of a category five cyclone. Never again – my ears buzzed for two days.

The Barossa Valley, the home of the Australian German community in South Australia, is absolutely beautiful, as is the wine of that region. One of the biggest scenes involved a festival well known in Europe amongst German speakers as the '*Schützenfest.*' In Adelaide and its surrounds, the South German Association has held the festival every year since 1964, although the first one dates back to 1865! Originally a shooting festival, it's now more of an excuse to eat, drink, dress up in dirndls and lederhosen, and play 'Oompah' music as loudly as possible. The spectacle was a great asset to the film, and I felt as though I was back in Germany – I'd my own baby Lederhosen when I was three years old and I loved wearing it when I was young enough to get away with it!

Every week one of the main cast members would be made 'Entertainment Officer,' and he or she would have to come up with something unusual and amusing to do on weekends.

A cross-dressing Barbie in Oz.

When my turn came I decided we would have a barbeque in drag, with a prize for the worst dressed. Not very original, but at least 'do-able.' Carmen came as Charlie Chaplin, Michael in a lovely organza dress and far too heavy rouge and lippy, and Nick Eadie wore stilettos, fishnet stocking and suspenders. Nick won.

At one point during our barbecue, the manager very politely enquired if we'd move our 'barbie' to a spot around the back of the hotel. Some elderly guests, arriving for lunch had been somewhat shaken by our appearance.

With Red Symons, director Chris Langman and DoP, Ernie Clark.

ALMOST A WILD DUCK.

Sometime in 1983 I heard word of a forthcoming film production of Ibsen's *'The Wild Duck,'* to be shot in Australia. I was doubly intrigued to read that Liv Ulmann was to play Gina, and Jeremy Irons, Harold. Though surprised that Jeremy wasn't playing Gregors, as far as I knew, no other actors had been cast. So the part of Gregors was still up for grabs. As a huge admirer of Liv Ulmann from my university days, I was determined somehow to contact Jeremy and have a chat. I hadn't seen Jeremy for many a moon, but I thought he could possibly swing things my way?

The reason I'm recounting what happened is to impress upon all up-and-coming actors that one should never even consider imposing on friends to do you a favour and put in a good word for you. It's a real 'no-no,' and actors hate being put in this invidious position. Not only that, but regardless of their fame, they're rarely in a position to be able to help you out. Of course, way back then it seemed like a good idea to chat to Jeremy.

It took me some time to find out from various sources that he was skiing in Verbier with his children. Determined not to be put off, I made further enquires and eventually tracked Jeremy to a hotel and called him at a civilized Swiss hour, and a very uncivilized Sydney hour. Jeremy sounded suitably surprised to hear my voice. Why wouldn't he? What on earth was I doing calling him from Sydney after all these years? The man was trying to holiday with his family – the last thing he needed was a ridiculous call from me.

"I hear you're coming to Australia to film the Wild Duck," I opened.

A pause, then he replied. *"Yes, that's right."*

Silence.

I continued. *"Would you believe it, I am meeting Henri Saffron in two days. Wouldn't it be fun if we could act again together – me as Gregors, and you as Harold?"*

Another awkward beat of silence.

"Yes, that would be interesting," Jeremy replied.

I then asked after Sinead and the children and enquired about the holiday snow conditions. I said no more about the production, hoping in a way that the next time he was in touch with Henri Saffron, the director of 'The Wild Duck,' he might mention my name, as he was about to begin the casting process and any help would be useful.

Anyway, this intensely awkward conversation ended after a few short minutes. I wished him well and he returned the sentiment. That was that. I met with Saffron a week later, but he cast Arthur Dignam as Gregors. I should never have suggested to Jeremy that he put in a good word for me. It isn't done and I cringe at the memory of it.

Many months later when Jeremy was finishing the filming I

called him at his hotel – the Sebel Town House; in those days all the celebrities stayed there. I was ushered into his suite by a butler – it may have been the very same one that I had met when I visited Paloma Picasso. He asked me to wait in the drawing room.

Jeremy didn't keep me waiting long. He appeared from the bathroom wearing a deep claret silk dressing gown, smoking a cigar. I thought, *'Zut! Noël Coward est mort, vive Noël Coward!'*

We chatted, exchanging our separate news. It was great to see him again after all those years. I asked him what he'd been up to and he told me how much he'd enjoyed working recently with Volker Schöndorff in *'Swann in Love.'* He'd starred with Alain Delon and Ornella Muti. I was envious to say the least. He was now definitely in the major league, could virtually name his fee and was set for an Oscar – I could feel that then. It came with *'Reversal of Fortune.'*

'ANZACS,' PAUL HOGAN & 'BUTCH LESSONS.'

My first major project in Australia was a mini series titled *'Anzacs.'*

At the time it was made, this production was the most expensive mini series ever mounted in Australia, costing thirteen million dollars. Ten hours of film, it took the best part of six months to shoot, and told the tale of a platoon of soldiers in the First World War from Gallipoli to the Armistice; a huge project, the brainchild of Geoff Burrowes and John Dixon. Pino Amenta, who was to cast me many more times over the years and become a good friend, directed along with George Miller, and John Dixon. I was cast as one of the key players – a member of the platoon of 'diggers.' It was all shot on a barren plain called Werribee, an hour outside of Melbourne. Unfortunately the schedule dictated that the winter in Europe would be shot during the Australian summer, and the European summer shots in the winter; this meant we wore great coats and scarves in the boiling heat, and froze in the winter with our sleeves rolled up.

The Sommes, or was it Ypres?

There were no major stars in the cast except Paul Hogan, who had been the comedic face of Tourism Australia for many years, but was still to become a big 'movie star' – *Crocodile Dundee'* was in the works but not filmed for a year.

A nice guy for a change! Kaiser.

Funnily enough, 'Hoges,' as everyone knew him, often mentioned how well the pre-production of *'Crocodile Dundee'* was coming on, telling us there were still parcels of investment we could buy. Each time he cracked on about his damned movie, we'd all chuckle – after all, how often is investment in a film a great idea? Once in a lifetime?

Of course we weren't to know that this *was* a lifetime opportunity. The screenplay was nominated for an Oscar. Every five grand invested made about a million. Were we ignorant jerks or what? Would we have leapt at the opportunity to invest in the sequel? Of course! And we wouldn't have made a penny. The old adage is never to invest your own money – use someone else's unless it's a short film project and you only stand to lose a few grand.

The casting of 'Anzacs' was interesting. As I mentioned before, when I was living in London I didn't normally have to audition if a reputable casting director recommended me. But things were very different in Australia where everyone tested for every role. They still do, unless you're Nicole Kidman, Naomi Watts, Hugh Jackman, Colin Friels, Judy Davis and a few others.

I had a meeting with John Dixon – who presumably had been informed by Shirley Pearce, my agent, that I had grown up in Germany after the war and I spoke passable German. The first thing he asked me to do was read a passage of the dialogue with a German accent. I did so. *"Too much,"* John said. I reduced the accent by fifty per cent. *"Still too much."* I reduced it to five per cent. *"Nah, still too much,"* he said, rubbing his chin. Frustrated, I spoke the dialogue in my normal English and forgot the accent altogether. John's face brightened. *"Beauty! That's perfect. I can just hear a hint of German coming though."*

So I became 'Kaiser,' and, apart from Hoges, the father figure of the platoon, the cast dominated by actors in their early twenties. All of us in the platoon bonded really well. We developed a camaraderie that mimicked what we would have felt for each other during the war. If Hoges was the father figure, then I was the uncle. Everyone knows Hoges, so I don't need to tell ·you he's a quintessential Aussie 'bloke.' As such, he saw me as a stitched-up, BBC Englishman. So he set about setting things straight by giving me what he referred to as 'Butch lessons' every day.

An example of such a lesson was how to hold a cigarette properly.

"You're holding it between you forefinger and middle finger like some sort of a faggot," he'd start. *"Chuck that ready made smoke away and roll yer own. Right! Now pick it up by squeezin' it between your forefinger and thumb. Point them at the sky—that's important. Then suck on it like that's the only thing that givin' yer lungs air."*

The way he did it looked bloody good. Unlike most comedians, who are depressive by nature, he was very funny and good-natured, twenty-four seven. He kept us all in stitches, regardless of how cold or hot it was. He introduced me to 'Aussie-speak,' such as the way one referenced male body parts – *'the beef bayonet, the pork sword and the mutton dagger.'* He also told me a wonderful tale he'd heard as a young man: -

"This bloke in the middle of Woop-Woop says to me, 'Yer know the definition of pain?'

"Nah, tell me.'

"He says 'Pain is when you're chocker-block up an emu's arse running across a salt flat and the bastard breaks his stride!'"

Even remembering this crude story now makes me laugh and brings back great memories of our 'phoney war' in Werribee.

With Paul 'Hoges' Hogan. 'Butch lessons.'

Hoges also taught me how to add the word 'mate,' to any sentence imaginable, so I could become a real Oz.

Example: *"nother beer, mate?'*

Despite the help of a master, I never mastered this. *"I'd like the sirloin, please. Rare, mate,"* It never sounded quite right. Sounds better with the word 'mate' coming after the word 'sirloin.'

Tim Dalton would never have stood for it, but I was given a small apartment in Melbourne that I didn't much care for. We all had similar apartments. Hoges was different – and justly so.

The solution was simple. I had a word with the production manager and asked her how much the production was paying for my dreary apartment. Then I made a deal that if I went somewhere else they'd give me the same amount. This meant I could go anywhere providing I paid any difference – another tip for the aspiring actor. It's worth a few dollars extra to be snug.

Of course once I was ensconced in *Gordon Place*, a lovely hotel in Chinatown, all my fellow actors wanted in, but it was the last one on offer. I stayed there for almost six months. *'Loverly,'* as *Eliza Doolittle* might have said!

Andrew Clarke played our Lieutenant. The perfect Aussie gentleman officer – but a very different kettle of fish from the English version.

Andrew loved a punt, and when it came to the Caulfield Cup that year he advised me on which horse to bet on. And how much!

"Everything you have, Shane. If you own a house, liquidate the asset and put that on too. I'm serious."

I bet ten dollars and won around thirty bucks. Andrew was in heaven the day that horse passed the winning post.

Then, come the Melbourne Cup a few weeks later he reminded me of his former advice. *"Same horse. Same advice. It's going to win the double. The house and everything. Right!"*

"Right," I replied.

I put twenty on this time and made another hundred odd dollars.

But Andrew was Andrew; he had to put all he had on anything he thought would win. How was I to know he was on a winning streak then? At the end of the six-month shoot, I had squirreled away quite a sum from my per diems; I believe he'd gambled quite a lot of his away. He'd had his fun–mine was still to come.

As we were a platoon of twelve, the core cast were in nearly all the scenes together, and this caused a few problems, primarily because the three directors would start every rehearsal by studying the script and saying something like *"Okay, guys, you're all in this barn, so come on in and sit wherever you like. Then we'll run the lines."*

That was the cue for a stampede, as all the young actors had been eyeing up the spots they wanted. These positions, in their opinion, were key. After narrowly avoiding being trampled three days in a row, I no longer joined in, and took whatever spot was left. Since Hoges wasn't about to indulge in this kind of race, I usually ended up close to him – which wasn't so bad.

Another thing the younger platoon members would do would be to busy themselves doing all the 'stuff' soldiers do, such as cleaning rifles, loading magazines, taking machine guns to pieces, shaving, polishing webbing, whittling a stick – anything that might attract the interest of the audience. The actors with dialogue had to do their best to concentrate – as well as being heard.

Every now and then I'd plead with director Pino Amenta to ask the up-stagers to cut the noise. He'd invariably help me out, though the result was always a few discontented actors staring at me.

The platoon – without Blakey.

I greatly miss that part of my life. It really was like being part of a very close-knit group of blokes who trusted each other with everything and anything. I'd never been 'one of the guys' before, but with these twelve people for the first and last time, I was.

It wasn't easy to replicate the extreme conditions of Ypres on a desolate landscape outside of Melbourne, but the art department managed it really well. The trenches were dug and looked outstanding, huge piles of car tyres were set ablaze in various areas, so the entire forty acre set was plunged into semidarkness (they stopped doing this when someone, three months into the shoot, pointed out that car tyre smoke was carcinogenic) While the tyres were operative we would always hear a shriek just before a take. *"Beef it up, Stewey!"* Stewey was our second AD. Our lungs would be black at the end of the day. The trenches were flooded with water as and when necessary, and when a particular scene called for heavy rain the local fire brigade would be paid to drench us. This was undoubtedly the toughest acting I've ever done. Thank heavens for Hoges' 'Butch Lessons.'

During the last two weeks of the shoot, Wendy finally arrived in Australia. All our belongings had been sold, given away, or shipped to Oz. To keep her dry during the autumn on set, I bought her an Australian icon, the *Drizabone* raincoat. She wore it to set everyday and most times she was up to her knees in mud. The platoon loved her – she'd chat with Hoges for hours. She didn't think an investment in 'Croc Dundee' was such a great idea either.!

When the film was aired on television it was a huge hit and beat all previous Australian ratings records for drama. It was nominated for 'Best Drama' at the Logies – Australia's answer to the Emmys.

'THE LIGHTHORSEMEN,' & 'NANCY WAKE.'

The second film I made that year was a thriller called *'Cassandra,'* written and directed by Colin Egglestone, a charming yet eccentric man who had already made quite a few smaller budget films in the eighties. I played a fashion photographer with a very strange and terrifying family.

I think it went into production way before the script was ready, and so veered towards the ludicrous too often to be taken seriously, either by the critics or the public. It was one of the films I mentioned before, those that actors accept because they hope it might turn out better than it looked on the page. I don't think this made it – and I feel to blame as much as anyone else.

Soon to be beheaded in 'Cassandra.'

My foremost memory of *'Cassandra'* was having my head sheered off by a madman with a shovel. That and the fact it was our beloved pidog, Coco's first film role. Though *'Cassandra'* turned out to be less than first rate, 1986 was a great year for me financially. The film, *'The Lighthorsemen,'* made up for having my head sheered from my torso. And the mini series, *'Nancy Wake,'* was wonderful too.

Of course most actors don't have the luxury to pick and choose – so I recommend that unless a film is patently ridiculous in concept, accept any leading role you're offered, make sure the price is right, then do your utmost to make your part, and the film as a whole, work.

'The Lighthorsemen,' was produced and written by avid war historian Ian Jones, and directed by Simon Wincer, the director of *'Phar Lap,'* and Emmy Award winning director of the American television series *'Lonesome Dove.'* Together the producers assembled a great team, including Dean Semmler as DoP, a man who was to go on and win the Oscar for cinematography in 1991 for *'Dances with*

Wolves.' Heading up the young cast were Jon Blake, with whom I had worked in *'Anzacs,'* Peter Phelps, Tony Bonner, Sigrid Thornton and, to hopefully boost the box office appeal *'Brideshead's'* Anthony Andrews. Even then, producers still considered it prudent to have a *'real'* English actor in the cast to lend the production a certain cerebral credibility. Ahem! I no longer qualified because most people in Oz now thought of me as a 'local' – so I could no longer be considered an 'import.' Instead, I was offered the German role, *'Captain Riechert.'* The wonderfully robust and oddball actor Ralph Cotterill played the German General, who before the battle headed for the hills. I was very happy to play Reichert, as the film opens with an overly long but very showy title sequence of Reichert's arrival in Palestine. So effectively I opened the film. Not only was I the central figure at the start of the film, I was also one of the pivotal characters at the end as 'Reichert' attempts to blow up the wells in Beersheba and the Aussie hero, played by Jon Blake gallops in to stop him.

The film centred on the Battle of Beersheba, also known as the Third Battle of Gaza. The British were intent on breaking the Ottoman lines that stretched from the Mediterranean to Gaza. The story centred on the historical fact that there was an almost complete lack of water available to the divisions of the Light Horse Brigade.

The finale of the film was the legendary charge of the 4th Light Horse Brigade – the last of its kind ever! I'm not sure of the exact number of horses assembled in this production, but word had been sent out far and wide across Australia that the last great cavalry charge was to be filmed and the producers welcomed horses and riders, wherever they might come from. It proved to be a magnificent turnout – farmers and *bushies* arrived many days before the projected shoot with their swags, and a tent camp grew. On the day of the charge, there must have been two hundred horsemen lined up on the ridge. It was a magnificent sight.

As the commander of Beersheba, I stood on the parapet of the fort and waited to see the horsemen show themselves. Imagine looking at a ridge a mile and a half away, and seeing just the ridge and the sky. Then seeing two hundred horsemen appear and halt on the skyline. It was breath-taking!

History tells us that the horsemen were quite widely spaced, so when the Ottoman artillery opened fire with shrapnel it proved mostly ineffective. The horse artillery also quickly took out the Ottoman machine guns.

With Ralph Cotterill in 'The Lighthorsemen.'

The charge started out as a walk, developing into a trot, then a canter, and finally into a full speed gallop. It was magnificent to watch – and looks absolutely fantastic in the movie.

One of the major flaws of the Ottoman defense was to underestimate the speed at which the horses kept on coming. The charge was so swift that before the Turks knew it, the Australians were under their guns. The horsemen leapt the trenches, dismounted in the rear and then engaged the Turks with bayonets. The Ottomans soon surrendered.

Keeping up with the trades in the Flinders ranges.

There were several cameras rolling for that charge, one of which was behind me – I was a kind of 'book end' on camera left with the ridge was between us. Simon Wincer stood beside our camera when he called the shot.

I'd been standing in awe for a good minute, when I felt a hand tugging at my left sleeve. Fortunately I knew better than to look around. I had the sneaking suspicion that Simon needed more space, so he simply pulled me to one side. I tried to make it look as though I had *chosen* to move but I'm not sure it worked. If you ever see the film watch me shift several inches to one side.

'The Lighthorsemen,' is to my mind a classic Australian film, and I recommend it.

As Captain Reichert in the final scene in Simon Wincer's 'The Lighthorsemen.'

I wasn't so much a part of the general camaraderie because I was playing a German and came and went many times during the shoot, but I had a wonderful time in the Flinders Ranges, where the film was shot.

The actors who weren't scheduled to film for a number of days were usually sent home in the small plane that serviced all the hospital supplies in the area.

I remember one occasion where I only just managed to squeeze into the small twin-engine plane because it was bursting with blood supplies and plasma. It would have made a grizzly find as a crash site. Blood for half a mile!

The last night of the shoot the producers threw a wonderful party out in the open; barbecues everywhere, and a copious supply of beer and wine.

The following morning tragedy struck. Not because anyone was inebriated – it was simply the most horrendous accident.

Jon Blake, one of the leads, had just become engaged to his girlfriend and rose early that morning so he could drive to Adelaide and see her. He'd just bought a beautiful property where they both intended to settle down. That fateful morning, as dawn broke, Jon headed home. But someone had parked their vehicle with the headlights on the wrong side of the road just outside of town, so that it was facing the oncoming traffic. Thinking he was on the wrong side of the road, John swerved to avoid it and he hit a tree. He was well below the alcohol limit.

He was airlifted to hospital within hours, but sustained severe brain damage. All of us visited him in his nursing home from time to time from then on hoping to see some reaction from him. But there was none.

A great many people had picked Jon as the new Mel Gibson. And then some more. I believe he would have been just that – a star.

On a lighter note, everyone knew that 'Blakey' could charm any girl – even nuns weren't safe when he smiled and started in on his 'chat.'

One evening during the 'Anzacs' shoot, he and I were out on the town in Melbourne and he saw two gorgeous young girls on their own at the bar.

"*Follow me, Kaiser,*" he said with a wink.

Jon Blake. Everyone loved him.

He then introduced himself, and offered the girls a drink, then started chatting. I watched in awe – it was the best 'up-chat' I'd ever witnessed, and I was making mental notes.

Within a few short minutes the prettier of the two girls confided to John that she was on her hen's night with her friend – she was getting married in the morning! Oops! Too bad, I thought, expecting Blakey to move on. Not at all, he simply upped the charm level to 'extreme.' As we ordered some more drinks at the bar, he winked at me and said; *"Now that IS a challenge, Kaiser. Let's see what I can do."*

Three hours later the four of us left in a taxi to take the girls home. When we reached the pretty girl's flat she got out. So did Blakey. They stood on the steps by her doorway for about ten minutes. Then Blakey took her in his arms and kissed her very passionately for another good ten minutes. Her girlfriend and I just watched goggle-eyed. I couldn't believe my eyes – the girl was hugging Blakey as if he was her soldier husband leaving for the front. It was the most intense 'pashing' I had ever witnessed. When we had dropped of the other girl John smiled at me and winked. *"I was sooooooo freaking close, Kaiser," he said, gesturing just how close with his thumb and forefinger.*

My next major project was a mini series in 1986 titled *'Nancy Wake'* in Australia and the United Kingdom, and *'True Colors'* in America.

It was the heroic story of an Australian woman by the name of Nancy Wake who traveled to France to join the resistance during World War Two. Nicknamed *'The White Mouse,'* she caused an incredible amount of disruption to the German forces, and was pursued as a matter of some importance by the Gestapo. She was never captured. The tag line to the telemovie was *'One Woman's Battle—An Entire World's War.'*

Nancy was a hero if ever there was one, and she was tough as Teflon when she had to be.

HE'S A REAL NAZI PIECE OF WORK!

THIS man with the sneering expression, soon to be hated by Sydney viewers, was among the few to escape a barrage of critical bombshells hurled by wartime heroine Nancy Wake.

The woman whose courageous life inspired the mini-series Nancy Wake, screening on Channel 7 on November 4 and 5, has blasted some aspects of the way her life as a French Resistance fighter in World War II have been portrayed.

Speaking at the series launch, to the embarrassment of Channel 7 management, the celebrated subject of the series turned out to be its staunchest critic.

She surprised guests with honest tales of script and detail arguments, saying "It's not Channel 7's fault. It's the script-writers."

And in another shot, even the star of the series Noni Hazelhurst, didn't escape her firing line.

"I liked her much better in the second half," she announced without a flinch.

Fearless

But Shane Briant was among the cast members (including leading man John Waters) to escape the lady's fearless tongue. Shane's efforts as the cruel-hearted Major Hermann earned him a glowing report. "He was fabulous."

But Shane had no

said the 75-year-old heroine.

"He was so good looking, if I would have kept him for a week, then shot him," she said.

Shane, who admits he's an expert villain, plays the archetypal evil Nazi who stalks Nancy in her five-year fight for a liberated France.

Shane said he was well aware of the horror memories his character could spark for the heroine, and spoke of his hesitations over meeting Nancy.

"I told her I could understand it if she didn't want to talk to me because I played Major Hermann," he said.

reservations about accepting what he sees as a traditionally despised role.

"It's a challenge to play a villain," he said.

And the lady in the spotlight had no intention of making apologies for her revelations either, saying: "I hope they don't mind my telling a bit of the truth."

By ANGIE KELLY

CHALLENGE: Shane

VILLAIN: Shane Briant as Major Hermann

ON THE SET: Nancy Wake and Noni Hazelhurst

The Daily Telegraph. Sydney.

One of Australia's best actresses played Nancy – Noni Hazelhurst. Englishman Patrick Ryecart, the 'English import', flew out to take part (you may have seen him recently in 'The King's Speech' as Lord Wigram) John Walton played Nancy's husband and, guess what, I played the bad guy – a Gestapo officer who Nancy did not wish to name. There were any number of harrowing scenes in the telemovie. Nancy was usually on site so that she could let us know exactly how it happened.

Anton Differing made a career playing Nazis, and I've followed in his footsteps playing cruel Germans. But just because you're playing a 'Nazi swine' doesn't mean you have to give the character narrow eyes, a nasty attitude, and clipped accentuated speech.

Experience has surely taught us that more often than not murderers look and behave as ordinary people do. If they didn't we'd all be able to spot them in a crowd, wouldn't we? So, each time I approach a character, I think long and hard about what might have made this person behave the way he does. Could he have been born bad? Science suggests this is unlikely. Did social conditioning make him a bad person? More likely. Is the character all bad? Nah. Very unlikely. He probably loves his mother and sister, respects his father, and, in the case of my character in Nancy Wake, believes he must do everything in his power to win the war. And if that means resorting to butchery of the worst kind – so be it.

Often the scariest moments in my life have been the quietest. For instance, I've always felt I'll die at night, so am relieved when the dawn breaks. Walking the three miles from Stuben to Lech in Austria through a forest with just a dash of moonlight to keep me on the road was scary – simply because it was dark and there were no cars or humans around. It was absolutely silent, with just a light breeze whistling around me. After growing up in Richmond on a busy main road, I found living in the country at Quendon almost spookily quiet. When I went to Haileybury, the boy who scared me most was the five foot two inch boy who was the quietest, yet always had that 'look' in his eye – *mess with me and I'll poke out both eyeballs.'* And it wasn't just me; even the toughest boys gave him a wide berth. So when it came to *'The German Officer,'* I played him as quietly efficient as I possibly could. He was always immaculately dressed, never a hair out of place. He moved slowly, almost languidly, and when he threatened his captives he would almost whisper, while performing some very mundane task, such as sipping tea.

My friend Pino Amenta again directed, and as ever we had fun.

At the end of the mini series, my character is finally captured trying to make it home. He notices Nancy Wake celebrating with her comrades just as he is led to the firing squad. I was so deep into my character that day that I felt genuine fear as I was led to the wall, to be shot. Strange but interesting how easy it is to invoke fear in oneself. When the guns fired, all the other characters against the wall instantly fell. To set my character apart, I let him hang there in limbo for a split second, with eyes staring in disbelief. Then I slipped very gently down the wall. It was just an idea at the time, but it must have worked since several people have commented on that microsecond when he is shot, and he looks totally bewildered in death. I always try to do the unusual.

The first time I met the real Nancy I was surprised by what a jolly woman she was. Why I expected her to be a dour and tough woman I don't know. Maybe because of what I had read in her autobiography – she was never shy to pull the trigger when she had to, as well as being very capable of ending lives with a knife or garrote.

"So you are the Nazi, eh?" she asked with a grin. *"I like what I see."* She chuckled, and then added, *"If I had captured you, I think I would have kept you for a few days,* then *killed you."* She was a real character.

"ONE MAY SMILE AND SMILE, AND BE A VILLAIN." 'OUTBACK!'

'Outback' a film that was released in America as *'The Fighting Creeds,'* and in Australia had its name changed to *'Minnimurra.'* It was directed by one of my favourite people, Ian Barry. I have worked with him many times now and he's always affable, supremely efficient, and an actor's director – if such a thing exists.

I was now represented by Barbara Leane, a very robust lady who reminded me somewhat of Adza – she didn't take 'nonsense' from anyone, and went in to bat for her clients with an outsize Gunn and Moore wearing no pads – she didn't need them.

I have no idea why the title was changed. *'Outback,'* has strength and says it's set in Australia. *'The Fighting Creeds,'* sounds like a B movie. *'Minimurra'*? Well, one day over lunch I happened to ask my friend, John Sexton, the man who produced the film, why he'd called the film *'Minnimurra* and he pointed to a street down the road called *'Minnimurra.'* I rest my case.

The American star of *'Silverado'*, Jeff Fahey, was cast as our hero; Aussie actress Tushka Bergin was the ingénue.

It was a well scripted, yet somewhat formulaic tale of a cattle station on the rocks about to be taken over by 'The Bad Guy.' To the rescue comes the best looking American that ever lived and somehow manages to get five hundred horses to the docks despite the evil shenanigans of 'The Bad Guy.' One might have called it a formula movie, but I was delighted to work with Ian again.

While I have it in mind, here's something actors must be careful about. When I was initially approached by the casting agent, via my agent Barbara, I was told that my role happened to be the last to be cast and the production had spent almost all of their budget.

"We really want Shane, but the thing is we have so little money."

Hummmm. Maybe. We've all heard that one in some shape or form, but this didn't really make much sense. Why cast the bad guy last – he was a pivotal character? Ultimately it was proving to be a standoff, so the production company asked what my weekly fee was. This circumvented the fact that I would be present as the bad guy throughout the final cut of the film.

"We can shoot all Shane's scenes in one week," the production supervisor maintained.

So my agent quoted a weekly fee. I made the film and, for all intents and purposes, I was featured through the film as a lead role. So they managed to hire me as a lead for the price of a week's salary. Don't let this happen to you.

As the cruel Allenby in 'Minnimurra' aka 'The Fighting Creeds.'

As ever, during the weeks before principal photography I read and re-read the script thinking of ways I could make this very bad dude original, while imbuing him with some features cinema audiences hadn't come across before – not easy!

I ended up thinking of *Allenby* – that was my character's name – as a man who always achieved everything he'd ever wanted with effortless ease, was extremely confident in himself, and supremely arrogant, as well as selfish and cruel to everyone around him, including the flora and fauna.

Ian is always enjoyable to work with because he allows you to introduce new ideas into both your character and dialogue.

On one occasion, when *Allenby* attempts to buy a horse that is very dear to our female lead, *Alice May Richards,* he is asked in the script to pay cash for the horse. In the earlier version one of his minions delivers the money in a huge bag. However, I thought it would be much more amusing – and might demonstrate the arrogant mindset of the man – for him to look casually at the auctioneer and say, *"Gentlemen don't carry cash."* Ian liked it and it was included. I was delighted.

It's always amusing to introduce quirky aspects of any character – if they are good enough, who knows, they may stand the test of time.

In one scene I am supposed to be shooting clay pigeons, while at the same time verbally threatening our beautiful young heroine. Clay pigeons, I thought? Nah! Why not a live white dove? A horrific idea, but that was the nature of my character. So I asked Ian if he liked the concept. Within an hour the art department had obtained a live snow-white dove. In the final cut we see *Allenby* about to shoot what we think are clays. After his final threat he nods to a henchman who reaches into a cage, pulls out the dove and casually throws it into the air. We watch the dove flapping it's way upwards, and then we cut on the shotgun blast. Adza would have hated it but many people recall that scene.

One last point of interest. Jeff Fahey introduced me to a novel sure-fire way of making your eyes shine in a close-up. It's worth giving it a try if you want your eyes to look remotely half as good as Paul Newman's. What you do is wait until the last second before a take, then strain every muscle in your entire body as if you wanted your eyeballs to burst from their sockets. That's when your pupils will dilate very suddenly and your eyes will look fabulous. I expect if you do this all the time, it will result in your eyeballs actually popping from their sockets, so my advice is to use this device sparingly. I never use it as I think it probably lead to a stroke!

No doves lost their lives in the making of this motion picture!

'*Barracuda*' was a telemovie directed again by Pino. I believe it was shot as the pilot for an ongoing series featuring the Sydney Water Police.

With pilots it's essential that your character doesn't die because that's the end of you. Sadly I was asked to play a powerful Sydney crime boss called Zoli Scone who ends up dead in the final scene.

In this pilot, Andrew McFarlane, an Aussie heartthrob for countless years, having become famous with a show called 'The Sullivans', headed the water police. Robert Taylor was another regular cop, and boxing legend Joe Bugner was cast as '*Crusher Harris.*' Zoli Scone's girlfriend (all crims have much younger girlfriends!) was played by Cassandra Delaney, an actress who'd made a name for herself in a film called '*Fair Game.*' Lots of gratuitous violence in *that* one.

It was around this time that she met John Denver, while singing at the famous Sebel Town House. It wasn't to be a happy marriage, but back then she looked happy as Larry.

Once again I was asked to dive elegantly into a swimming pool and again I looked very foolish – another tip, practice and get better at simple things like this so you can do them well on camera.

When '*Barracuda*' was aired, none of the major networks saw it as a continuing series, despite Andrew heading the cast. I was dead, of course. Drowned in Sydney Harbour. So I was never coming back anyway! Interestingly enough, many years later in 1991 Tony Morphett tested out the same idea, starring a host of Aussie regulars. This one translated into one of the most popular cop shows in Australian history, starring Colin Friels, Catherine McClements, Peter Bensley, Bill Young and Scott Burgess. Only goes to prove that one never can tell what's going to become a huge hit.

With John O'Brien, Cassandra Delaney in 'Barracuda.

There are television shows and there are soap operas. Then there are shows that overlap a bit. *'The Flying Doctors'* was one of those, a quintessential Australian drama series based on stories about the famous Australian Royal Flying Doctor Service. It ran from 1985 – 1991. Australia adored this series.

Just about every Australian Equity member had a role in this series over the years, and all the best directors had a go too – with Colin Budds directing twenty-seven episodes. Other directors were Pino, (he shot the first episode) Ian Barry, Dan Burstall, Peter Andikidis, and Steven Wallace.

The stories were always interesting and enjoyable to watch. The outback scenery was a huge plus.

Andrew McFarlane, Lenore Smith, Liz Burch, Maurie Fields, Rebecca Gibney and Robert Grubb were the regulars. I played a French rally driver in one episode, with my usual Clouseau accent, and a cruel wine baron in another. I was beginning to warm to this work in the outback – I *could* have been taking the Underground to work at the BBC in Acton. But here in the bush, I was spending my days under the blue, blue, Aussie sky in the perfect climate, making films that were not exactly Oscar material. However, I wouldn't have traded countries for quids.

The one thing that might have made things in Oz even more complete was if actors had been allowed to enjoy a 'tinnie' or two at lunchtime; but unlike most of Europe, including the U.K. this was frowned upon. In the good old days, every Friday evening when we finished shooting, there'd be a slab of beer on the back of a truck somewhere. Now, thanks to new laws concerning 'safety' this is no longer allowed. Presumably because, though the drink-driving limit in Australia is three standard beers (and all we wanted was one or two) we film people could not be trusted. Progress? Nah!

AUSTRALIAN THEATRE WORK

KENNETH BRANAGH AND DAVID WENHAM.

I'd been in Australia for five years before anyone thought of me for a stage role. I think people in Australia have a proclivity to compartmentalize actors. Because I was busy making films, and appearing in television series, I was not thought of as possible theatre material – even as a '*theatre* bad guy.' This is still the case, I feel.

I remember many years ago a good friend of mine bid for and won *'tea and a chat with Kenneth Branagh'* at a charity auction. It was organized through John Bell, the director of the Bell Shakespeare Company.

This friend of mine telephoned me, asking if I'd accompany her to the tea and chat, as she was shy and thought she'd be more comfortable with me there. She could sit beside me and talk as and when she felt like it. I said I' be delighted to meet Branagh. I admired his work. And I like free tea and cake.

By that time I'd appeared in leading roles in seven Australian feature films, and as many UK and American televisions series and films, but when I arrived at the Bell Shakespeare headquarters no one had the first idea who I was. Their entire focus was solely on the Bell Shakespeare Company and the Sydney Theatre Company. I don't think they ever visited a cinema or watched TV unless one of their theatre regulars was in a film or TV series. By contrast, I was familiar with both theatre actors and screen actors. I liked to go to the theatre as well as the movies.

When I arrived, I told the receptionist my friend and I had *'come for tea with Mr. Branagh'*. She asked us our names and we gave them. Then she asked us if we'd sit and wait. Then in came John Bell. He was very friendly. He shook my friend's hand, had a brief conversation, and then shook mine, asking what I did for a living. I told him I'd been an actor for fifteen years. He smiled. He'd no idea who I was, wasn't inclined to find out. This didn't bother me in the least. I appreciated that he probably didn't watch too much television, and was treading the boards most nights so seldom took in the movies. Then his wife came in and joined us, a lovely actress called Anna. She also asked me what I did for a living. *'Groundhog Day!'* I told her I'd been an actor for fifteen years. She smiled – no idea who I was, and not inclined to make enquiries. Of course I knew who they *both* were because I took an interest in *all* aspects of acting – the theatre included.

Anyway, we went backstage and were introduced to Kenneth, who was the epitome of charm.

During the two hours we were *'taking tea,'* we all asked questions of Kenneth; his insights into the UK theatre, as well as the state of the British Film Industry were fascinating. Finally, John wrapped things up and we all stood. It was at this moment, just before Kenneth left, that he turned to me and in front of John and Anna said; *"Nice to meet you Shane. I've always enjoyed your work.*

*"*I was taken by surprise – I'd no idea he was familiar with my work. Maybe he was being polite. Who knows? But his remark surprised the Bells, who both gave me a curious glance. The moments are golden, eh?

Director Peter Williams called my agent in July of 1987 enquiring if I'd be interested in playing Dysart in his production of *'Equus'* at the Glenmore Theatre, just outside of Sydney.

An newcomer by the name of David Wenham was to play Alan Strang, the part created by Peter Firth in John Dexter's famous production at the Old Vic.

Playing Dysart, with David Wenham as 'Strang' in 'Equus.'

I leapt at the opportunity, as I'd always found Dysart's lines sheer poetry, and though the psychiatrist is basically no more than *'First Voice'* in *'Under Milk Wood'* or *'Chorus'* in *'Henry V'*, it's a beautiful part to play. A kind of 'gilded voiceover.'

Peter was a showman of the old school – a charabanc-whiz. His matinées were invariably packed out because the plays he chose were directed at a less cerebral audience than the Sydney Theatre Company; people who wanted to see 'a darned good show.' How were they to know that, with *'Equus,'* they'd witness a naked lad slashing horses to death? As well as a stark naked girl. Peter knew how to sell – no question about that.

An example. A lovely actress named Linda Stoner was cast as Dysart's magistrate friend. Linda was then, and still is, famous for her very glamorous and voluptuous looks on television; she'd been a television celebrity for quite some time. So when it came to the production poster, Peter Williams had her name top left, with mine opposite. There was no mention of David. Why? Simple. The bus-tour ladies wouldn't have any idea who David was, and most wouldn't know me. But Linda? He knew what the golden girls would say as they read his advertisements in the local papers. *"Look here, Daisy. This one stars that lovely Linda Stoner – we have to see that."*

Rehearsals were intense. David was about nineteen at the time, but had a grasp of the theatre well beyond his years. He was a natural. It's fun when every so often one comes across a 'natural'; they stand out so much you simply can't miss them.

I remember midway through rehearsals I made the error of watching Richard Burton's film version. I was riveted from start to finish. Burton's portrayal of Dysart seemed perfect – it was everything I'd wanted to put into my own performance.

So what was I to do – change a lot of things just to be different so that the critics wouldn't say, *'Aha! He's seen Burton's version. A crude copy?'*

My good friend Robert Kenchington recently referred me back to Burton's version, and I immediately realized that though I had initially thought of my portrayal of Dysart as very similar to Richard Burton's, this couldn't have been further from the truth. While Burton's Dysart was a terse, angry man, filled with invective and bitterness, my Dysart was played at a much more sober pace. And while Burton seemed to be so convinced of Strang's motives and psychology, my Dysart was constantly attempting to conjure up the deep seated reasons for the young boy's behaviour, quite often at a loss to make any sense of his own personal darkest thoughts.

Just before the first night, as I went through the entire play at breakneck speed in the park – something I always find very useful – I thought to myself, *'I think we've a hit here. The play itself is outstanding, David is outstanding, and the support cast is terrific. I feel confident.'*

But the reviews were mixed. I hardly thought it possible, yet the critics took issue with Shaffer's play, suggesting it had been too highly praised in London when it premiered. Despite that, David received great reviews and we played to almost full auditoriums for a month.

Wendy and I got on famously with David, and every now and then we'd have him around to our home for dinner. He was so thin in those days!

I didn't see David again until 2007 when we were both cast in Roger Spottiswoode's film *'The Children of Hung Shi,'* otherwise known as *'The Children of the Silk Road.'* By then he was an Aussie film star, and had made a hat full of films, including *'Moulin Rouge,'* and a couple of *'Lord of the Rings.'* As I said, he stuck out as a star – he had nowhere else to go but upwards.

'WIT'

I hadn't acted on stage for about ten years when Sandra Bates, artistic director of the Sydney Ensemble Theatre, asked me if I'd care to play Harvey Kelekian M.D. in Margaret Edson's Pulitzer Prize-winning play *'Wit'* with Sandy Gore as Vivien Bearing. I accepted with pleasure. It's Vivien Bearing's play of course; Kelekian occasionally comes on stage when Bearing thinks of him. Nevertheless, it's a great play, and I was happy to be part of it.

Over the course of the play, as she confronts her terminal cancer, Bearing assesses her own life through the intricacies of the English language, especially the use of wit and the metaphysical poetry of John Donne. Sandy did a terrific job, as did Todd Warden as the doctor. Sandra directed impeccably.

However there were two very black moments.

I will never forget the dress rehearsal. Forty oncologists had been invited. Because our rehearsals had always run very smoothly, I anticipated a trouble-free run of the play. Wrong! The lights went up and Sandy started to speak. My cue was one minute later. I walk on stage, turn to Bearing and say *'You have cancer.'* I then sit down next to her and we both speak our separate dialogue over one another for a full minute at high speed.

However, for the first time ever, that night Sandy decided she'd ramp up her volume by about a hundred per cent, and since she was sitting just six inches from me, I got the surprise of my life.

I dried. Horribly.

I looked at Denise Roberts. She'd offered to be on the book that day, but she smiled a *'can't help you, Shane.'* No one had given her the book. Not her fault.

Sandy continued speaking for a good thirty seconds, then stopped. It was my line again. But which one? Extreme panic! My guides were looking after me that day. The line just popped into my head and all was well. Only those who knew the play well would have spotted my dry, as Sandy kept talking so loudly while I was silent.

However, the following morning I became increasingly panicked by what had happened the night before. My dialogue was a killer – medical jargon par excellence. Would I dry again? Horror of horrors. By mid afternoon I was in a cold sweat. When the half was called I was terrified, frantically thinking of any way I could avoid stepping onto that stage again. Could I feign a heart attack? Nah. Step in front of a speeding car? Possibly! There was nothing for it; I was a dead man walking. I had to go on stage. When my cue came, I stepped forward, feeling as a man condemned to the guillotine looking up at the blade. I turned to Sandy, told her she had terminal cancer and sat down beside her.

The gods were kind to me that night – the words came to me in a torrent and I never had that problem again. I just wish Sandy had told me she was going to shout the night before.

The year 2000 was a very dark year for Wendy and me because we could both see that our beloved Coco was so ill with her kidney problems that she would ultimately have to be helped to the other side. We finally agreed that we would only ask our vet, Alan Fridley, for help if and when Coco couldn't walk any more.

During the run of 'Wit' I took Coco to the theatre every day. Sometimes she'd relax on set. No one knew. I wasn't going to rat her out.

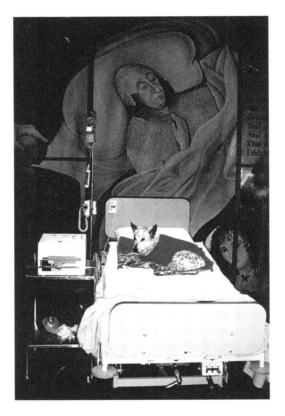

Coco on the set of 'WIT' at the Ensemble Theatre, Sydney.

We'd sit in the park before the show and I'd go through my lines. During the play she'd lie on the sofa in the Green Room. Then I'd take her home.

One morning a few days before the end of the run, Coco tried to get up but couldn't move her back legs. The time had come.

She now lies under a lovely tree on Geoffrey Simpson's property outside Berry. We planted it as a sapling and it's now a twelve-foot tree. We love visiting her, as well as staying with Naomi and Geoffrey.

COCO

PRINCES, PIGDOGS, AND PRESIDENTS.

Wouldn't it be fabulous if everyone loved animals and treated them with the respect they deserve? We've always had a dog or cat, and Wendy and I'd be lost without the friendship of animals. Coco the pig dog, a Blue Heeler cattle dog cross, lived with us for seventeen years. The breed is called *'Pig Dog'* because in the bush some Australians use them to hunt wild pigs. In their domesticated state they are very intelligent, athletic and loyal. Coco has a place in my heart forever, so she also has a place here. She came with me to almost every film I made. Sometimes she'd lounge in Winnebagos, sometimes she'd watch me act on set, and sometimes she even had a role.

In the horror flick I made called *'Out of the Body,'* the vampire looks into a window and sees two people making out in a seriously deviant way – a naked man is astride the naked woman while he feathers her naked body with a cut throat razor. Mary Regan and I were both buck-naked except for very skimpy flesh coloured underpants. I told Coco to sit and stay, and then we started to rehearse. But the moment Mary started her low moans Coco became jealous, marched forward and started to lick Mary's naked body. She was banned from the set. Coco – not Mary.

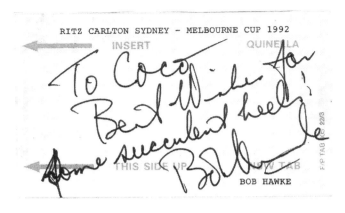

Aussie Prime Minister, Bob Hawke, signed a betting card to Coco.

I didn't think too much of *'Out of the Body,'* but I'd like to mention that the director, Brian Trenchard-Smith has done some fine work in his time, and it's said that he was one of Quentin Tarantino's favourites after he made *'Time Bandits'* and *'The Man from Hong Kong.'* This film was a bit of a turkey – I think, anyway.

Coco also played *'the dog on the station,'* in *'Cassandra,'* and was *'the lonely dog'* in an episode of *'Willisee's Australians — Jack Davey.'*

When she wasn't working with me, she'd be working with

Wendy who was Tournament Manager of the Australian Indoor Tennis Championships for ten years.

The *'Sydney Indoors'* was one of the top ten ATP Tour events on the world circuit, and the big names were always there – Lendl, Edberg, Becker, McEnroe, Connors, Agassi, Borg etc. It was a superb tournament with Graham Lovett the Tournament Director.

I was hired as the on-court announcer. Nepotism? Why not? I was the announcer during the day, and when the Channel 7 commentators arrived for the televised evening session I made my way to the players' box and helped myself to the catered food and wine. Delish!

Wendy with the charming Boris Becker. He won.

Wendy with a disappointed Stefan. He lost.

Coco's job was to mooch around in the car park while I was inside announcing, and be amused by the world's top tennis players as they arrived. She took her job very seriously. Ivan Lendl, a German Shepherd devotee, would play 'Catch 'n Spit' with her most days in the VIP car park, as would Andre Agassi, Boris Becker and a host of other guys – they were all charmed by her. Every year, after the Final there'd be an on-court 'bump-out' cocktail party. Wendy would very briefly allow Coco inside for a race around the court, and often the players would hit balls for her. She loved that.

Coco with Australian tennis legend, John Newcombe.

She had many famous friends. One Sunday morning in late 1988, Wendy received a call from HRH Prince Andrew. Wendy had been good friends with the Duchess of York when she was simply Sarah Ferguson, and had attended the royal wedding a couple of years earlier. When the Duchess visited Oz to see her sister Jane, she'd often call Wendy and occasionally take a trip up to Avalon for lunch with us. So when Prince Andrew's ship hit a technical problem that needed a day to fix, he took Sarah's advice and called Wendy to ask what might be a fun way to spend the day. She suggested Andrew drive up to Avalon, where we lived at the time, offering to take him up the Hawkesbury River to lunch at Cottage Point, a lovely restaurant sitting on a pontoon over the water. Great food and wonderful views.

Well, it seemed like a good idea at the time, but neither of us had factored in the entourage. There were Federal Police, State Police, and Steve, his personal protection officer. Plus there was Wendy, Coco and me.

It was soon clear we needed the use of a second boat, since my beat up fourteen-foot runabout with the outboard would fit just Prince Andrew, Wendy, me and Coco (had to have Coco in the number one boat) Plus Steve, of course.

I asked a friend, the larger than life Aussie John 'Just do it!' Miller, if he'd skipper a second bigger boat and follow us with the security guys.

"No worries, mate," he growled. *"Just don't expect me to put on shoes jest 'cos he's a prince, will yer?"*

Within the hour we were all on our way. No one except security knew where Prince Andrew had gone, so there were no paparazzi about. HRH had taken Wendy's advice to come disguised as Groucho Marx so that no one would pick him out as a Prince, and was suitably hidden behind sunglasses and a baseball cap.

As we docked at Cottage Point, Coco leapt from our small boat and ran down the jetty towards the restaurant, where a very irate manager immediately waved her away with a hand.

"Hey! No dogs, mate! Health regulations," he shouted.

However, the moment he recognized Prince Andrew striding towards him his attitude changed radically. So much for disguises!

I informed the manager privately that Coco was Prince Andrew's guard dog and had to be *'a leap away from HRH'* at all times. I've never told Prince Andrew I lied in this way, but he's probably far too busy to think of reading my autobiography. We'll see.

Coco sat at Andrew's feet throughout lunch and was even brought a plate of tender chicken morsels by the manager.

Another amusing incident occurred during the lunch.

Wendy, who was sitting next to Prince Andrew and opposite me, gave me one of her subtle *'look over there!'* glances. I did so and noticed Rutger Hauer of *'Blade Runner'* fame sitting at a nearby table.

Prince Andrew picked up on Wendy's glance, glanced at Rutger and told her Rutger was one of Sarah's favourites. *"She'll be disappointed that she missed him,"* he said.

Rutger Hauer and Coco up the Hawkesbury River for lunch.

However, I was thinking of Coco's biography, so my thoughts were of a photo opportunity for Coco.

Towards the end of the lunch, I rose and walked across to Rutger. Coco followed me, as she normally did.

I smiled at Rutger and held out a hand.

"Good afternoon, Mr. Hauer. My name's Shane Briant, and I wondered if..." I began. But before I could finish the sentence, Rutger rose and smiled broadly. *"Yes, of course. I would be most happy."*

It was at that instant I realized what he was thinking – that

Prince Andrew had asked me to invite Rutger to his table, which he had not.

This was embarrassing, but I had no choice but to continue my sentence. *"I just wondered if you might allow me to take a photo of you with my dog. I've so much enjoyed all your films."*

To give him his due, Rutger reacted like a gentleman.

"Of course! My pleasure."

He then picked Coco up and I took the picture. I thanked him and he sat down again and continued his lunch.

On the way home, no one wanted to drive our lead speedboat. Prince Andrew said he'd spent his life doing it and it was his day off. Steve observed with a twinkle in his eye. *"Got to have my hands free to protect the Prince."* I thought I'd had too much wine and I could hardly be DUI with the Prince aboard! So Wendy drew the short straw.

Not having had much boating experience she took off through the moorings way too fast, and within fifteen seconds we had a Maritime Services vessel behind us. They were signaling both boats to stop. Prince Andrew was unperturbed, he knew what would happen. Our second boat dropped back and the Federal boys held out the IDs and told the Maritime Services boys that they had to back off because there was a VIP on board the speedboat in front. They asked who it was and the Feds replied. *"You don't need to know, mate."*

They did as they were told. I revel in these kinds of *'nah-nah-ne-naaaah-nah'* moments, but then I'm a big kid.

Back home we had afternoon tea and Prince Andrew allowed me to photograph him with Coco.

It's a wonderful snap.

I think the years we spent in Avalon were amongst the happiest of our lives. We'd walk to the beach in ten minutes and watch the sun set as Coco swam and chased seagulls. Then home to a barbecue in the summer or an open wood fire in the winter. On the minus side, I was being bitten by grass tick and my allergy was increasing – on several occasions I was hospitalized. After eleven years it was time to leave.

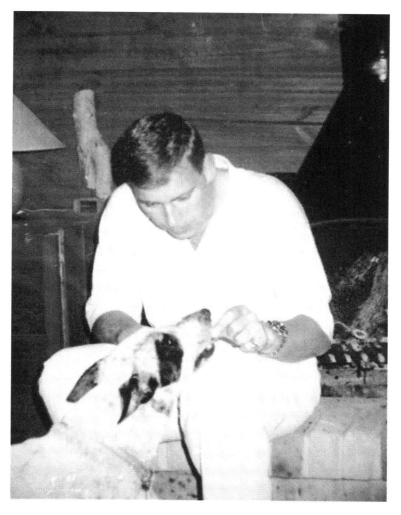

Coco and HRH Prince Andrew, in our Avalon home.

As a footnote to this story, the following week there was an irate *'Letter to the editor'* in the local paper, *The Pittwater Press,* complaining that there was clearly *'one rule for a Prince and another for the rest of us,'* when it came to the no dogs in restaurants rule.

Meal fit for prince

Prince Andrew, minus his popular wife Fergie, paid a surprise visit to Cottage Point restaurant at the weekend.

But he was not alone as he lunched. With him was an entourage of six and a pet dog who sat by his side throughout the two-hour meal.

Prince Andrew took staff and diners by surprise when he arrived by boat at the Cottage Point Inn at 1.30pm on Sunday. He was shown to the best table.

A mystery woman had earlier made the royal booking under a false name.

The prince and his group enjoyed the restaurant's specialty — a lavish smorgasbord with lots of seafood.

Restaurant manager Nick Heflink described the royal visit as a delightful surprise.

"According to the waitresses, the prince really enjoyed his meal as well as the surroundings," he said.

"Everyone was absolutely stunned when he walked in."

I don't believe Prince Andrew ever saw this letter. Nor was he aware he was causing anyone any inconvenience. All my fault – very bad form!

But that's the sort of hound Coco was, friendly to everyone. She wasn't impressed by princes, actors, directors, or sports celebrities; everyone got the same nip in the ankle if they walked past her too closely.

Oh! I completely forgot the letter President Bill Clinton sent Coco!

The first week of January 1999 I'd had enough of Mr. Starr harassing the President. Every day they were giving Bill a hard time, and to my mind it was proving damaging to his administration and America as a whole. Not that I thought he was blameless; far from it. But I eventually thought after he'd come clean about the events, that Starr might give the President a break. So, during a dull morning, I decided to write Bill a note of support. As I composed the letter, I noticed Coco at my side, pawing my shoe. She wanted to go for a walk, but I reinterpreted her behaviour as wanting to add her name. So I composed a very short note:-

'Mister President, all my friends in Australia think you and your administration have been doing a great job over the last few years, and we think the people who are giving you a hard time right now should back off. So, all the best from us girls in Sydney! Good luck.'

I signed it: *'Coco Briant,'* and sent it off, addressed to:

The President of the United States,

The White House,

Washington D.C.

U.S.A.

I never expected a reply.

A few weeks later I saw a letter in the mailbox that was certainly not Basildon Bond – it felt like wonderfully soft vellum. On the back was the understated embossed *'The Office of the President of the United States, Washington D.C.'*

I opened it carefully in the kitchen – Coco was too busy eating to listen to my reading it aloud.

'Dear Coco,

Thank you so much for your message. I've been touched by the many expressions of support and encouragement I've receive from people everywhere who cares deeply about my Administration and about the future of the United States and the world. I am doing everything I can to help us meet the crucial challenges that face all of us.

Sincerely,

Bill Clinton (signature)

A year later, I wrote another letter on my own behalf, thanking the President for his reply. I didn't mention Coco was my dog – I didn't want him to think I was having a joke at his expense. I did mention that Coco had a serious kidney problem and would be cheered greatly by a photo.

A week later a White House staffer sent me three signed photos – one of Bill and Hillary, one of their cat Sox, and one of their dog buddy. They remained in Coco's basket till she passed away.

President Clinton achieved some wonderful things while in office and continues to work tirelessly with his foundation, as well as in Haiti. He's still one of my heroes.

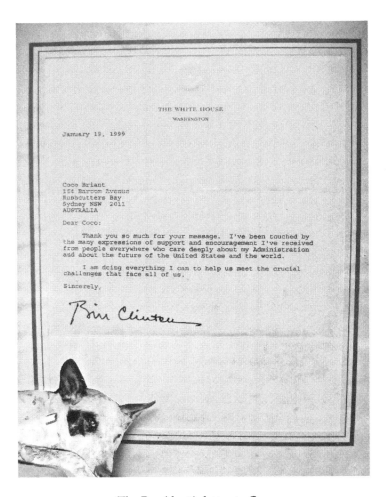

The President's letter to Coco

AUSSIE MOVIES.

ORGIES & SOUTH AFRICAN MERCENARIES.

The same year as *'Barracuda'* was aired, I started work on a film that had more of an edge to it. Written by Warwick Hind, *'Grievous Bodily Harm'* starred John Waters, with whom I had worked on *'Nancy Wake,'* and Colin Friels. Mark Joffe directed.

With John Waters on 'Grievous Bodily Harm.'

The story revolved around a schoolteacher who becomes obsessed with the idea that his wife Claudine did not, as everyone else thinks, die in a car accident. Joy Bell, played the girl everyone thought was dead. She was exceptionally beautiful so consequently was featured in close-up on all the film posters. She left Australia for America at the end of the shoot and appeared in the daytime drama *'Another World'* for many years. Joy Bell was terrific fun. She really enjoyed life and didn't take too much seriously. I'll give you an example.

One of the threads of the story took the form of a three-way sex tape that the twisted shrink, played by me of course, had made of John Waters wife Claudine played by Joy Bell, my wife played by Caz Lederman, and me. It had to look very sexy and cutting edge because everyone in the film is trying to hush up the tape's existence. So, naturally we had to spend some time shooting the sex scenes on videotape.

On the day we shot the tape, we had a stripped crew of just four people – make-up supervisor, wardrobe supervisor, one lighting guy, and Mark, our director.

"Okay," Mark began, *"why don't we take off our dressing gowns, hop into bed and see how this scene plays out."*

We all stripped buck-naked.

I've never been totally at ease in public in the nude. Who is? I suspected Caz felt the same, but with a long career in modeling, Joy Bell couldn't have cared less. We lounged on the bed for a few moments, and then noticing our shyness, Joy Bell took command. Thank heavens she did.

This is Joy Belle… No wonder she was on the poster!

"How about this?" he started. *"Shane's massaging K-Y jelly into my bum. Caz is stroking my breasts. Then she begins to go down on me. I'm just kind of…moaning with pleasure. Sound like a plan?"*

Sounded like a plan to me. Providing I kept a lid on my feelings. Not so easy when you're confronted with Joy and Caz's naked bodies – not too shabby.

"Right. Let's shoot the rehearsal," Mark said.

Within seconds I was massaging warm jelly into Joy Bell's butt and enjoying every second. Almost immediately Joy Bell started these incredibly convincing moans, with extempore lines such as *"Oh my God, that feels soooooo good."* I was taken by surprise at her intensity, especially when she pushed her backside into my groin. *"Do it to me…do it now…"* she continued, heatedly.

Somehow I didn't disgrace myself, but when I look at the finished product I am amazed at my restraint. Always the professional? Well, that's not easy sometimes.

We shot another two scenes in different sexy locations; one was in a spa pool and one, at Joy Bell's suggestion, was in an elevator.

Both were equally exhilarating. Take a look at the poster with Joy Bell featuring and tell me if it'd be hard to spend a day making a porn video.

In the summer of 1988 and the spring of 89 a dream came true for me – I worked twice with *'Jim Phelps'* in *'Mission Impossible.'*

I'd been watching the series from its inception in 1967, and had never missed an episode until the series ended in 1973. Now Peter Graves was to return as *Jim Phelps* in the new series, with a fresh cast, to be filmed in Australia at the Warner Brothers studios on the Gold Coast. I knew I had to score a bad guy role somehow. I let Barbara know I'd kill for a part.

She obliged. I played a man everyone hates – a Zurich gnome. A man who controls vast sums of Nazi money but won't say where. The joy of this role was that I would be the patsy who Phelps and his crew drug and manipulate. As I anticipated, Graves was a delight. I couldn't believe that even in close-up he looked as if he'd had just a two-week break from filming the previous series – and that was after a fifteen years hiatus! He never once stumbled over a line, lost his cool, did not miss a mark – even by half an inch – nor did he ever muss-up his perfect hair.

Producers very rarely bring back a guest star for a different role in the same series, as they're afraid the audience will spot the actor doubling up in another role. I was lucky enough to do exactly that with *'Mission Impossible.'* I came back months later as a KGB operative with an appalling accent.

It's no accident that people categories actors. If the first role you play is critically acclaimed, then producers will always want more of the same – or at least bear you in mind when a similar role is up for grabs.

Because I started out as a murderer in the grip of a psychosis in *'Children of the Wolf,'* those were the roles I played for a good while onwards; Emil in *'Demons of the Mind,'* Peter in *'Straight on till Morning,'* being just two examples.

When I came to Australia I was categorized firstly as: *'Englishman: Import,'* then as: *'Australian resident: Plays English bad guys: Can do accents.'*

That's most likely why I was chosen as the Russian Spy in *'Mission Impossible,'* the thinking being that if an actor can *'do German'* he can surely *'do Russian.'* I was lucky they hadn't seen or heard me *'do French'* in *'The Flame is Love.'*

It was good to work in American series television in Queensland at that time. At that time American producers had real money. The guest stars would be driven around in ridiculously long limos, stay at the wonderful Sanctuary Cove, and earn great money.

Incidentally, talking of accents, I remember on my first day working on the BBC series *'Huntingtower,'* in 1978. Bob Hird, the director, walked over to me and said, *"I know you are supposed to be a Russian, but since your character has spent so long in Australia, do you think you could play him as Russian but give his voice an Australian twang?"*

I was speechless. I was two minutes from shooting my first scene and he throws this spanner in the works. Should this ever happen to you, simply hide any expression of surprise, and reply without hesitation. That day I said something like, *"Russian with an Australian twang? Coming up."* I seem to remember I kept the accent the same as before, while constantly asking Bob if he could hear the twang. He usually nodded affirmatively.

One other incident comes to mind. The motorbike they gave me to ride – an original 1930 Triumph – was so heavy, when I mounted it for the first time the weight of it topped me over and I was trapped underneath it.

The crew simply looked at me in disbelief. *'Stupid boy,'* as Captain Mainwaring might have said in *'Dad's Army.'*

'DARLINGS OF THE GODS.'

In 1989 Thames Television got together with the Australian Broadcasting Corporation to make the mini-series *'Darlings of the Gods,'* a biographical representation of the period when Vivien Leigh and Lawrence Olivier toured Australia.

UK actress Mel Martin was picked to play Vivien Leigh, and Anthony Higgins was cast as Lawrence Olivier. There were a great many cameos to be had – Ralph Richardson, the young Peter Finch, Cecil Tennant etc so I put my hand up for Cecil Beaton, and the director, Catherine Millar, kindly cast me.

Beautifully written and observed by Garry O'Connor, as well as wonderfully realized by Catherine, it proved very popular in both the U.K. and Australia. Mel Martin was particularly touching as the emotionally unstable Vivien Leigh, and Jerome Ehlers was a very convincing Peter Finch.

It's a strange thing, yet very often the shows you believe will be successes, kicking your career forwards, don't amount to very much, while the work you accept because you've got nothing better to do end up changing the course of our life. You simply never know.

'Children of the Wolf' was the runaway hit of the 1971 Irish Theatre Festival but failed to impress the London critics.

I was certain I was part of a big hit film when I scored a role *in 'The Mackintosh Man,'* but how was I to know that the production had been put together in somewhat of a hurry as a money-spinner, and shot in the same vein because the major stars wanted to go skiing at Christmas.

So, despite three star names, and the legendary Huston at the helm, it remains one of Huston and Newman's weaker movies.

By contrast, I was once asked to take part in a pilot for an Australian children's series, one that was to be shot in one day, and it ended up as a European, Australian, English and Japanese classic series; one of the most enjoyable series I have ever been a part of. But more of that later.

'TILL THERE WAS YOU' & MARK HARMON.

In 1989 I was offered a really interesting role in a film that Southern Cross Films, in conjunction with Paramount Pictures, planned to shoot in Papua New Guinea. In some ways the script, written by Michael Thomas, author of *'The Hunger,' 'Scandal,'* and *'Ladyhawke,'* reminded me a bit of a Hemingway story. Jim McElroy was the producer and he'd offered the film to award-winning John Seale to direct. John had already been nominated twice for an Oscar as a cinematographer (*'Witness,'* and *'Rainman,'*) and was to go on to win one in 1996 for *'The English Patient.'* It was to be John's debut movie as director. Our Director of Photography was to be Geoffrey Simpson, winner of the Australian Film Institute Award for Best Cinematographer for *'The Navigator.'*

I became good friends with Geoffrey and his wife at that time, Sally. Wendy, Coco and I would later visit Sally and Geoffrey at their home in Berry. It's such an incredibly beautiful spot. Wendy in fact knew Geoffrey from the time they both grew up in Adelaide.

With these kinds of credentials it was hard to see how this film could be anything but a huge success; the script was great, Mark Harmon was to be the American lead, Jeröen Krabbé and I were to be the bad guys, and an Australian newcomer, Deborah Ungar, a girl who had already gained a reputation for herself in the television mini series titled *'Bangkok Hilton,'* was to play the female lead.

Before we even had time for a preliminary read through, it was decided it would be far too dangerous to even consider shooting in Papua New Guinea at that particular time – a shame, because I thought without this sense of danger Michael Thomas' script would lose it's edginess.

The new location chosen was The Republic of Vanuatu, an island nation in the South Pacific, around two hours in a plane from Sydney.

Filming in exotic locations was one of the prime reasons I decided to move to Australia, so this job was going to be a dream shoot – eight weeks living in a luxury thatched bure at the water's edge at the Le Lagon Hotel near Port Vila.

John Seale arranged for all the cast, other than Mark and Jeröen Krabbé, to meet before we all left. Deborah Ungar, Lech Mackiewicz – my fellow bad guy henchman – and a bunch of other actors attended. All went smoothly at the reading, and as I looked across the table at Deborah I thought, *'this is going to work really well, Deborah has a sultry, sexy look and is clearly a fine actress.'*

When I arrived on Vanuatu's Island of Effate, I met with and immediately bonded with Jeröen and Mark. Everything pointed to a great shoot.

It's at moments like this that things tend to go awry.

The first hiccup was to affect me directly. Before we'd even started filming, Jim McElroy asked if we could have a 'word privately.' This kind of remark never bodes well – avoid these private chinwags. He told me that the preponderance of opinion was that Jeröen, rather than me, should be *'the last bad guy standing.'* Apparently they felt he was a bigger star in Europe, and as such should be at the heart of it when the violent action took over. I couldn't believe what I was hearing. *"You want to change the ending simply because you think Jeröen is a bigger name in Europe? What about the integrity of the script,"* I argued.

In the script that I'd originally read, my character, Rex, was the cold-blooded South African mercenary who Krabbé's 'Vivaldi' character employs as 'security.' In the exciting conclusion to the film, the quiet man Rex finally takes over and excels.

"So what do you have in mind for 'Rex' now?" I asked Jim bluntly, over a somewhat incongruous glass of French champagne. Jim looked everywhere but at me, as if he hadn't considered this at all.

"He... There was a beat. *"He gets shot dead in the crossfire? Something like that?"*

"But the entire point of Rex being around as security for the entire film is because at the end he finally does something positive," I replied.

"Look, Shane. I'll be frank. It's been decided. It's a fait accompli. Sorry, mate. Oh, I'd like to let you know this has nothing to do with Jeröen – he didn't ask for the change."

I was stunned, as well as unbelievably disappointed; but what could I do? Get in a huff and jump a plane? Nah. Only in very complex American contracts is there any way you can wheedle out of a film merely because the script has been changed. It's just one of those things that happen – you have to accept them.

But I now had a dilemma. I had 'above the title' billing, same size and type as the other three stars, yet now my role had had its wings clipped in a big way. How could I avoid looking silly? Somehow I had to quickly think of a fallback position.

That night I lay awake in my thatched bure thinking of a way to salvage the situation. I knew I'd have to come up with something because I knew Jim wasn't going to lose any sleep wondering how to help me out – he was the producer. By dawn's early rays I had come up with a possible answer!

My idea was this. There was no way my character, the ultimate hard man from Jo'berg, was going be killed accidentally in any crossfire. It simply made no sense – the whole point of Rex was that he was capable of anything, so he could easily outwit the native

Vanuatans bent on killing him with bows, arrows and spears. It couldn't be a tragic accident either – Rex was worthy of more than a stray arrow.

Rex's death had to be the result of his one redeeming feature. A terrible irony!

I've always believed that no one is all bad. As I've mentioned before, serial killers sometimes have a real soft spot for dogs, cats or monkeys. Or keep birds in their cells. So how about this? Rex, the deeply racist South African mercenary – a man who has no hint of compassion or pity in his soul, just happens to be amused by the nerve of a young native Vanuatan boy. Every day Rex passes him by in his jeep, and every day the boy raises his thumb and forefinger and pretends to shoot him.

He's the only kid on the island that doesn't fear him. Rex, thinking the kid's got balls for an eight year old, smiles back every day and returns the gesture. Where is this heading, you may ask? Well, towards the end of the film when Mark Harmon assembles his native army to take down Krabbé, Rex decides it's more sensible for him to take his stash of gold and get out of Dodge. So he races back to his room, takes off his webbing, leaving it on his bed, and has a final shave. Next thing we see is the eight-year-old Vanuatan kid edging his way though the bedroom door, curious to peek inside. He looks at Rex's back, and then sees the gun on the bed. The Glock fascinates the kid; he's never seen a real gun before. So while Rex is shaving, oblivious to the small intruder, the boy picks up the Glock and points it at Rex's back, thinking he'll play their game again – just like every day. Rex suddenly becomes aware there's someone in the room. He looks in the shaving mirror, and sees the gun pointed at his back. But it's too late. Boom! Rex falls, a look of *how the hell did I let this happen,* on his face.

Horrified and frightened, the boy runs away.

With Mark Harmon and Jeroën Krabbé in 'Till There Was You,' in Vanuatu

I put this scenario to Jim and John, and thankfully they agreed to it. At last I had an end that actually meant something, one cinemagoers might remember when they left the theatre.

For a couple of months prior to principal photography, I trained every day for two hours in a gym in Bayview, Sydney. By the time I was dressed in the khaki fatigues, boots and T-shirt, the sleeves of my T actually hugged my biceps. For the first time ever, I thought I actually *looked* like a 'tough guy,' as opposed to simply acting the 'bad guy.' I'd had my fair hair bleach-blonded almost white, and cut to one inch in length. With some sunshine and make-up I thought I looked pretty much the way Rex might look – Cliff Robertson would have loved the tan!

On the very first day of filming I was reminded of Tim Dalton's sage advice on contracts, *'Got to have everything covered in the contract or you lose out.'*

Again I had practically none of the creature comforts covered, and again I lost out. Here's what happened.

The first day was very hot and humid, and in the minute it took me to walk to the unit base from where I'd been dropped off by my driver I was sweating like a pig, yet actually enjoying the tropical feel. After wardrobe and make-up I was taken up to the set, a huge wooden house built of wood on stilts in the jungle. It was there I saw the courtesy tents. Those provided for 'the stars.'

There were three for actors and one for the director. They were large brand new tents with the actor's name pinned to the front so that people knew it was for that actor and no one else. (There were also directors chairs for the cast but the locals always sat in them!)

Inside each tent was a camp bed with a pillow at the top, an 'Eskie' next to the bed with ice cold drinks inside, and a bedside table with mosquito repellent and a hurricane lamp. However, there were four of them. Not five. I did not see my name. I was surprised, since there were four actors' names above the title. An oversight? I immediately tracked down the Unit Manager and asked him in the nicest way where my tent might be. He pulled out some paperwork he had in his pocket and glanced through it. Then he looked up at me. *"Nothing in yer contract, mate. No tent, no bottled water. Nix."* He paused, maybe feeling a bit uncomfortable. *"See, Shane, I just go by what's in the contract. It's that simple."* I smiled and told him I understood—no problem. I did feel a bit stupid at lunchtime when Mark, Jeröen and Deborah repaired to their tents, lay down, turned on their fans and sipped their Perrier water. So…what to do? It was another test for my inventiveness – I would say nothing more about the tents. I'd shame them. That was the idea, anyway.

That evening I asked my driver to stop by a toy store in the capital, Port Vila. There I bought a kid's Indian tepee – small enough to accommodate a five-year-old.

The following morning I arrived early on set and erected the tepee right next to the four other adult tents. I stuck a note with my name on the front and placed a bottle of fizzy red soda inside. Then I left the area and watched the reaction.

No one other than me found my joke funny at all. They were mostly embarrassed. The result was that John Seale told someone to give his tent to me, since he said he never used it. John is a nice guy.

So, instead of giving us all a laugh, it all fell a bit flat. But I had my tent!

Take your contracts seriously. Tim Dalton is a wise man.

As the shoot progressed more problems with the script developed day-by-day and this didn't please Mark at all. One evening he told me that what bugged him was that he was seldom if ever consulted about the changes, and he felt that since he was the lead character, John and Jim should discuss any changes with him.

Over the next few weeks this caused more and more friction – Mark had accepted his role based on the script he'd been given. Now the script had developed in a quite different way.

I tried to distance myself from the friction, but it's practically impossible to do that. People will always ask you, *'What do you think, Shane?'* and that's not the time to be a wimp and prevaricate. You have to offer an opinion. Take one view and risk offending the producer and director, offer another and risk offending Mark. I thought it best to tell it the way I saw it, and that happened to be the way Mark saw it.

I think I ended up being as politically sensitive as possible, but I wasn't much help to anyone.

Despite these problems, I had the time of my life for those eight weeks. The weather was superb, the days I didn't work I spent swimming or sailing in the lagoon, eating fresh tropical fruit, and sipping cocktails.

'An actor's life for me!'

I spent a great deal of time talking with Jeröen as he painted his canvasses outside his bure – he is a famous painter back in Holland. I liked him a lot; he has a wonderful sense of humour and enjoys every second of his life, never allowing anything to upset him. He thought, as I did, that he was on the perfect junket – whereas Mark had more to lose since he was the principal star and would be blamed if the film ended up a turkey. During the shoot I met and became friends with Sandra Lee Patterson who acted as a voice coach. She now owns one of Australia's leading acting academies, 'On Camera Connections.'

When we returned to Sydney, Mark came to visit Wendy, Coco and me in our house in Avalon on the Northern Beaches, and we went water skiing on Pittwater.

Coco and Mark on our veranda in Avalon, Australia.

As you'd expect Mark was an expert mono-skier – but then he'd been a star college quarterback, and could probably have excelled at any sport he cared to indulge in.

The following year I visited him at his home in Hollywood – I don't think he'd enjoyed Vanuatu much and that was a shame. I know I did.

The film was distributed the following year. It set a new

Australian budget record (so I was told, anyway) of thirteen million dollars. But it didn't really cut the mustard with the critics, and as far as I know didn't do too well at the box office.

Jeröen went back to his European movies, Deborah Ungar went to Hollywood and starred in another forty-odd movies, and Mark went on to star and produce the longest running hugely successful cop series in American history – *NCIS*. I gladly stayed in Australia to make more movies there.

FAMILY SADNESS.

LIFESTYLES CATCH UP WITH MY FAMILY.

At 3 a.m. on the fourth of July, the telephone rang and the son of my mother's best friend, Peter Hambro, informed me that my mother had died of a heart attack. We talked for a long time, then I sat on the deck outside our Avalon home as the rainbow lorikeets arrived on the veranda thinking as birds do that it was breakfast time.

Mum always loved Australian native birds, and these beautiful rainbow Lorikeets made me feel my mother was with me in spirit that day. She'd had a tragic life. So beautiful as a young girl, she would have had a wonderful career had the war not come. When it did, she married the wrong man and her marriage was a disaster. She also suffered from asthma all her life and was never really happy. Towards the end of her life, she came to visit me twice with my Aunt Margaret. Finally she had some happy times. After sixty-four years she returned to the happy country of her childhood. On the final Saturday of the second visit, before mum and Marnie left, Wendy and I took them to a wonderful restaurant called *Jonah's*. It's on a hill overlooking Palm Beach, and has the most superb views over the Pacific.

"Can I have anything I like?" mum asked – she always worried

that maybe I couldn't afford something.

"*Of course, mum,*" I replied.

"*Then I'll have the lobster. With lashings of unsalted butter!*"

I'd never seen her happier. The lobster arrived accompanied by a sauceboat of melted butter, which she finished in ten minutes – the butter, that is.

"*Do you think I could ask for some more butter,*" she asked me. Rationing during the war had meant she'd had to go without butter for too many years and she'd never forgotten this butter famine.

I ordered more, and when she'd finished her lobster she looked positively radiant.

Wendy, my Aunt Margaret, and mum at Jonah's, Whale Beach.

Two days later she flew home. A week after that she suffered a massive coronary while in the kitchen of her best friend in Harlow Essex, Mary Hambro. Mary told Dermot that mum had simply muttered, "*that's really painful,*' and was dead before her head hit the floor. It had to have been all that butter. Her cholesterol count was as massive as her heart attack. Yet, as she told me many times, she always preferred to 'chance it.' It was a fact of life that all my family then liked to 'chance it.'

As I mentioned earlier, my brother Dermot was a chancer all his life. Because he'd screwed up his chances of a fine Oxbridge degree, he embarked on a career that saw him do so many varied things it makes my head spin just to think of them.

After dabbling in Egyptology and being blackballed by that particular community for not being exactly frank with them, he married Jane Attewill and had two divine daughters, Natasha and Rosalind.

He then interviewed for a job with the Ministry of Defense and was hired to research any 'secondary' questions the Minister might be asked in Parliament. I think this shows how bright Dermot was. I was proud to think the Minister was reading off a script my brother had prepared for him.

Naturally nothing ran smoothly for Dermot, and he soon had a falling out with the Minister's Office, was divorced, and remarried, this time his wife was called Trina. They had a boy named Toby. It was at this time that he chose to move to Hong Kong, but within a a few short months he'd talked *Radio & TV Hong Kong* into hiring him as a breakfast radio host. By this time his health was appalling. He'd never taken any care of himself – smoking and drinking far too much. He must have known it would take him down, but he was the kind of man who never thought about what might happen next, he'd simply say, *"My round!"*

The last time I saw him was at London Airport. We met for a drink in the bar – I had to fly off with the *'Mission Top Secret'* crew to Poland. I hadn't seen Dermot for a few years and we were delighted to see each other. By then he'd become a diabetic. Nevertheless he threw caution to the wind and decided to celebrate. An hour later, when I returned from the loo there was no sign of Dermot and his third wife Christina – Dermot was in a diabetic coma, about to be rushed to hospital. I had two hours to spare before my plane left, and I wanted to make sure that he'd be all right, so I drove with them both to the hospital, hoping that Dermot would regain consciousness; which he did an hour later. He looked at me, smiled and held my hand. Then said, *"Please don't leave me, I think I'm dying."*

What could I do or say? I had an entire film crew waiting for me. Without 'Neville Savage' they'd be up the creek.

I stayed with Dermot for an hour. He eventually fell asleep and I left for Warsaw – I had no alternative.

He didn't die that year; he died the following year. He was just fifty-two. Such a waste; he had a brilliant mind and was supremely witty. He could have done anything, but his problem was that he thought he was indestructible.

Despite his faults, his children Natasha, Rosalind and Toby turned out to be such wonderfully balanced, loving, funny people. I remember Dermot as the loving brother I grew up with. He'd have done anything for me, yet couldn't help being a rogue when it came to chancing his arm.

Theo, Jessica, Harriet, Jonah, Livvy, Beatrice.

Toby and Donna's son William - no fiction is too strong for him!

MEANWHILE BACK IN HOLLYWOOD...

'VERONICA CLARE.'

In 1990 my old friend Jeffrey Bloom (from the 'Dorian Gray' days) had been putting together an American cable series he was to call *'Veronica Clare,'* and unbeknown to me, was thinking of me as a regular.

Screen writer and director Jeffrey Bloom on the set of 'Blood Beach.'

Jeffrey had by then written eight Hollywood scripts, including *'11 Harrowhouse,'* which starred, Charles Grodin, Candice Bergen, James Mason, John Gielgud, as well as *'The Swashbuckler'* starring Robert Shaw, Geneviève Bujold, Beau Bridges and a heap of other heavyweights. He'd also had a stellar television career, the highlights of which were several episodes of *'Columbo,' 'The Right of the People,'* and *'Jealousy.'*

Jeffrey proposed to produce as well as write his new series.

By this time I knew Jeffrey well and appreciated his nature was to write the script, produce it, be cinematographer, operate the camera, and design and edit the film if at all possible. The cable channel, *Lifetime*, financed this essentially film noir series about a jazz club owner and gumshoe by the name of Veronica Clare; a gorgeous vamp who solves a variety of mysterious cases. It was all to be set in period Los Angeles.

Jeffrey told me he'd always had a vague thought to write something for me, and this had been the perfect opportunity. So he fashioned the role of Veronica Clare's business partner, 'Duke,' especially for an Englishman – me! I was touched. No one had ever written something for me before. Not only was I touched, I was also very excited. A lead in a continuing American series? This might be a break into American mainstream television – another way forward. Maybe I would make a name for myself in American TV after all. The decision to return to England after 'Dorian Gray' might not have killed that possibility. I few over to L.A. to celebrate the new series with Jeffrey and his wife Carole. But even the 'sure thing' has a habit of falling down.

Once Jeffrey had found his Veronica Clare, a very sophisticated actress, literally reeking of film noir, named Laura Robinson, and had contracted the other key regulars, Robert Sutton, Tony Plana and Robert Ruth, he organized a read through in front of the *Lifetime* execs so they could check out the main cast and listen to them perform.

By this time I had signed a lease on an apartment close to Studio City where Jeffrey had a lovely house, and I'd put down a deposit on a car – I'd always wanted a Mustang and had found a cheap one in a lot near Universal Studios.

The read through was short. I shook hands with the colourless *Lifetime* executives (I'm biased, of course) and then left Jeffrey to chat to them while I drove across town to the fashionable Beverly Hills restaurant Kate Mantolino's, where I'd booked a table for the three of us. It was my treat, to celebrate the final piece of the puzzle being clicked together.

I think I'd had way too many margaritas by the time Jeffery and Carole arrived. They were an hour late, and both looked decidedly glum. I wondered what on earth could possibly have happened in such a short space of time. I ordered yet more drinks and waited for their news.

Good news and bad news. The series was going ahead! *Wunderbar!* A sigh of relief.

Without me. Not so *wunderbar*.

How I felt mentally when I heard about Lifetime's decision!

Apparently the *Lifetime* execs had decided that the co-owner of the nightclub should be a Latino, rather than an Englishman.

"But I wrote it for an Englishman," Jeffrey had argued forcibly. *"I wrote it for Shane."*

However, the grey-faced *Lifetime* execs were in no mood to budge. Whose money was paying for the show? Theirs. Who made the final decisions? They did. It would be a Latino. End of story.

I'm not a producer, so I don't know all the ins and outs. People often tell me that those who supply the money like to flex their muscles every now and then. If they don't do this, then people will think they are weak. So they find something trivial such as firing an actor just to make a point. Robert Beltran took over the role and did a great job. They wanted their Latino and they got one. The apartment people were very obliging, as was the used car salesman.

"Hey, man. That's some kind of tough shit," he said and then shook my hand. *"Pity. It's a sharp car!"*

"Guess you get to keep the deposit?"

"Guess I do, Shane. Good luck."

I flew back home a few days later.

My advice here is simple – don't tell any of your friends at home you're starring in an American TV series until the director calls action and you've got a watertight contract. Even then there's probably something that can go awry.

A short while after I lost the role of *'Duke,'* Jeffrey cast me as a very odd psychiatrist in an episode titled *'Phoebe.'* I don't think *Lifetime* ever knew I was back on their show. Jeffrey has always been a very loyal friend.

Back in Oz, I was soon guest starring in an Aussie outback detective series called *'Bony'*, starring Cameron Daddo as the Detective, and the celebrated Aboriginal Australian by the name of Burnam Burnam as the tracker. I'd put all thoughts of an ongoing television career in America on the back burner, and I'm telling the truth when I say I wouldn't have been nearly as happy living in Los Angeles, making lots of money, as living in my adoptive home in Sydney, simply making ends meet. No contest!

I fell in love with Sydney the day I touched down there in 1981. It's the only city I've lived in where, at the end of a fabulous holiday overseas, I feel more excited just to be home. Sydney has everything; a vibrant culture of theatre and film, the Sydney Symphony Orchestra, The Sydney Theatre Company, numerous fringe theatre groups, a hundred galleries celebrating the work of gifted painters, the most beautiful harbour in the world, and wonderful Australian and New Zealand wine.

An apartment in Paris would be nice too.

WORKING IN EUROPE.

'MISSION TOP SECRET' - A JUNKET PAR EXCELLENCE!

'Till There Was You,' didn't exactly reinvent my career – as I'd hoped. I'd had visions of the American box office receipts being huge thanks to Mark Harmon's presence, but they were very modest. So when Shirley, my agent, called me asking if I'd care to do a day's work on a modest pilot for a children's series, I wasn't exactly thrilled. Especially when I heard that the day's work was paying Equity minimum. I think Shirley registered the lack of enthusiasm in my reply, because she added, *"Oh, come on. What are you doing next Thursday? You never know what these things may lead to."*

The result of this day's work was a job lasting several years – the best acting junket of my life!

Produced by the Australian doyen of children's programs for many years, Roger Mirams, and directed by the late Howard Rubie, the pilot was the story of a group of kids who use an obsolete satellite to communicate with each other across the world via a computer network they called *'Centauri.'*

When it was written in 1990, this futuristic concept was fantastically original. It was way before the explosion of Facebook, Twitter, Skype etc.

'Mission Top Secret' was one of four competing pilots made by Grundy, with ours winning out.

I don't remember too much of the story line of the pilot, which is a pity. But I do remember that a year or so later Shirley rang me with the news that Roger, as executive producer for the Grundy Organization, had been given the green light to mount a television series that would be filmed all over Europe!

There were initially six European partners. The idea was that each would have an episode filmed in their country. It was a masterly idea for raising a significant sum of money, and, as far as I know, each network had a separate contract with Grundy – some would furnish a portion of the budget, while others would take care of the filming costs in their particular country.

Yet again it goes to show that out of the least likely projects comes extreme joy. Two years after the small cheap-budget pilot I was to travel to Spain, Switzerland, Germany, England, France and Poland to film six two-hour episodes. Each would take about five weeks to film. And the following year, South Africa would be added to the list of locations.

As a point of interest, the role of 'Pamela' in the *Mission Top Secret'* pilot was played by Danielle Spencer, who was to marry Russell Crowe in 1993, and as well as being a talented actress is also a wonderful musician.

In 1992 Roger finally signed contracts with five European television partners, and his children's series, *'Mission Top Secret'* was ready to go into pre-production.

I looked at the schedule with amazed happiness. We'd start off filming for five weeks in Majorca – and that was just one segment of the trip!

The kids were the real stars, but there also had to be a 'good guy' and a 'bad guy.' Fred Parslow, an Australian actor of note who'd been around a long time by then, was the zany Professor. I was the criminal mastermind, Neville Savage.

It was the most perfect role. I could be amusing, wry, wicked, and dastardly at will. Because the children always foiled Savage's plans, I saw him as the cartoon character, *'Wile E. Coyote'* while the kids were *'Road Runners.'*

Savage in another disguise for Savage in Sydney!

Prior to leaving Australia, our line manager, Emmanuel Matsos, came to see me in order to give me my 'per diems.'

Generally per diems are just the barest amount to keep body and soul together. It might be ten dollars for a lunch and twenty for a dinner. I often wondered where Equity thought one could eat for this amount – McDonalds? On this occasion Emmanuel would hand me *all* my per diems for the next six *months!* All in the separate currencies.

Euros didn't start circulating until 2002, so I was handed various bundles of French francs, pesetas, deutsche marks, pounds, and Polish zlotys. Our meeting resembled criminals sharing out the loot after a bank heist – a surreal Monopoly moment! Six months of per diems felt very pleasant in a single wad. It didn't concern Emmanuel that Freddy Parslow and I would have to travel around Europe with a hat full of money – a walking target for muggers. Once I had signed for the cash – that was my problem.

It was hard saying good-bye to Coco and Wendy – oops, Wendy and Coco – because I knew I wouldn't see them for six months.

And while I was away, I determined to write a novel – one set in each country I'd be visiting.

My bizarre idea was to make up a story that depended entirely on where I was and what I saw. I'd simply see what came to mind; the ambiance of each city, the architecture, the nightclubs and restaurants etc. A recipe for a dreadful thriller, everyone told me – it'll have no central thread.' I hoped I could prove them wrong.

Before I left, I debated whether of not I should take a portable typewriter. Amazingly stupid. *"I suggest you buy what's called a computer,"* Wendy advised me with a wry smile.Embarrassed by my ineptitude, I bought an *Apple Mac*.

Apart from Executive Producer, Roger Mirams, producer Noel Price, and line co-producer Emmanuel Matsos, we took two directors, Howard Rubie and Marcus Cole, the production designer Nick McCallum, a continuity lady, a tutor for the kids, and a costumier – the now famous Margot Wilson. All other members of the crew would be hired in the various countries.

Our first stop was Palma, on the island of Majorca.

Before I talk about the work, something far more important – my memory of the best nightclub I've ever visited.

The *La lonja* district of Palma is home to the best nightclub in the world. *Abaco*, a club owned by two Spanish princes. This exquisite seventeenth century Mallorcan manor house is filled with fabulous antique Spanish furniture; chaise longues, graceful embroided armchairs, period Persian rugs and tapestries. The cocktails are served in cut glass crystal balloon glasses. Back then, a fifteen-dollar cocktail would last an hour, it was so generous.

At precisely midnight every Friday, the music would stop and a cascade of fresh rose petals would stream from a hole in the ceiling of the great room. Everyone would cheer and literally bathe in the petals as they fluttered down – basket after basket after basket! When the cascade was over, the music would re-start, and the dancing continued.

So impressed was I by Abaco that I set the first chapter of *'The Webber Agenda'* there.

HarperCollins*Publishers*

That was how I continued my story – I made the action to suit the most enchanting and interesting places I chanced upon. So when I visited the cathedral of *La Lonja,* across from the *Palace of Almudaina,* in central Palma, and saw the giant wooden cross there, I knew Sam Webber had to die beneath it, his last vision looking upwards at the crossbeam where it reads *'For those that died for King and country.'*

After five glorious weeks of good food, wine and breathtaking scenery–especially the northern area called Pollensa – we boarded a plane and flew to Switzerland to start filming in Lucerne.

I loved Lake Lugano. The highly polished antique wooden speedboats are glorious – they look brand new yet were probably built in the 1930's.

We had the final weekend in Switzerland free, so I asked Noel if I could take the Post Bus from in Lugano to St. Moritz for the weekend. He gave me the green light, making it very clear that I would be totally irresponsible if I were even to *think* of skiing. As the bus pulled out onto the road and headed for skiing heaven, I had no intention of skiing. But temptation was to prove far too much. I arrived in the Swiss ski resort just before lunch and checked into a pension. I immediately headed for the cable car that would take me to where I'd been told there was a great restaurant. But as I tucked into my wurstl, rosti, and sauerkraut on the café balcony at over three thousand feet, drenched in the hot sun, I watched the happy skiers swoosh past down the mountain. I was weak at the knees. I could not help myself.

An hour later I was skiing. As I had no ski clothes with me, I wore denim jeans, an open-necked shirt and a leather jacket. It was one of those perfect ski days, and although I knew Noel would be horrified by my lack of judgment if he ever found out, I placed my safety in the hands of Saint Christopher and Saint Jude, and my weight on the downhill ski.

In my opinion St Moritz is a rich man's resort – most of the lovely old restaurants in the town cost a fortune. But it is just possible to eat reasonably cheaply there. I did. Very well indeed.

One more divine day and I was back on the Swiss Post bus, driven at speeds that would have scared Fangio. Swiss bus drivers just hurtle into tunnels after sounding their horn very loudly for eight seconds. It's up to everyone else to get out of the way. Within a few hours I was back in Lugano, telling Noel how much I wished I could have skied. A white lie at this point hurt no one.

Next day, after a breakfast of Swiss pastries and hot chocolate, we drove to the airport and boarded a plane for Hamburg. How I managed to struggle through that arduous week I just don't know!

NOTE: Attention all producers! I can now be trusted not to ski if I am on a film shoot and near a ski field. (Exclusions apply: Zermatt, Lech, Val d'Isere, Kitzbuehel, Obergurgl, Davos, Gstaad etc etc…)

I happen to love Germany; I suppose it's because I lived there as a child for so many years. Hamburg is not the prettiest city in Germany but it's certainly one of the most fun. It has a vibrancy that I love – the *'Dom'* fun fair, jazz clubs, good German food and great beer.

We stayed in a hotel called the Hotel Bellmoor. It occupied the fifth floor of a vast nineteenth century building. The rooms were curiously varied in size. For one week I had a room that looked more like a ballroom, but because it was booked the second week, I was moved to what the manager insisted was a *'very similar room, Herr Briant.'* It turned out that in the very 'similar room' I could almost touch both sides of the room with outstretched arms.

The best thing about the Bellmoor was the elderly woman who served breakfast. She looked like the Witch of Endor. She never smiled. Every morning she'd wait for us to seat ourselves in the breakfast room before bringing each of us a boiled egg, and a dish of cold meats. She never spoke, even when I tried to engage her in conversation in my childish German – she simply looked me in the eye as if that was confirmation she had heard me speak.

Five weeks down the track, Fred and I arrived late for our breakfast. The Witch of Endor approached our table and smiled broadly. We knew something was very wrong.

"Vot vood zu like for breakfast?" she enquired.

Fred and I were dumbfounded.

"You mean there is a choice," Fred asked politely.

"Indeed! Zer is egg." Long pause. *"And no egg!"* she replied beaming at us.

In each episode of *'Mission Top Secret,'* there were guest players. Savage always had a dim-witted offsider. In Germany it was a criminal conjuror called *'Von Steinfurth,'* beautifully underplayed by German actor Ulli Lothmans.

Savage was a man of many disguises, as Clouseau was in the *'Pink Panther'* films. In the German episode he was disguised as a shepherd with a high hat, green Loden coat, long staff, and beard. He looked wonderfully ridiculous.

The German food on set? It was a very different quality to that of Spain, where we always lunched in a well-respected restaurant, and Switzerland, where we did the same. The German lunch consisted of a trestle table on which were placed two shiny aluminum cauldrons. A stout German would stand there holding a ladle. A typical example of such a lunch would be brown stew in one cauldron and mashed potato in the other. There was no choice. Soft drinks were available, but no wine or beer!

Every evening after work I'd walk the streets of Hamburg searching for unusual and interesting material for my book. In my mind I'd established that the money everyone was looking for was stashed in one of Hamburg's most respected banks by the evil Thomas Pirch, my very own 'Bad Guy,' a man who had survived his childhood by thieving; eventually joining a street gang that called themselves the *'Schwarzenkinder,'* the *'Black Children'*, so named because they felt the name mirrored their souls.

In that way I had neatly locked off the German material.

Next up was *La France!* This time our home base was the exquisitely beautiful Loire Valley. The town? Amboise. Our partner there was FR3, the French television channel.

If you've never been to Amboise, put it on your bucket list. It's the home of the eleventh century Royal Château of Amboise, overlooking the Loire River. Take it from me, the medieval architecture is breathtaking. What a set we had for our story!

The first day we shot inside the Château, I found it hard to concentrate on anything but the architecture, as well as the castle's history. I'd look at the Long Gallery where we filmed, and imagine Louis d'Amboise plotting against Louis XI; I'd see Charles VIII striding down the corridors in 1495. I'd close my eyes and imagine Henry II and his wife Catherine de' Medici playing with their children in the nursery. Magic!

As Leonardo da Vinci in Amboise, France.

Our first lunchtime we were in for a big surprise. We'd been shooting indoors in a Long Gallery, so we had no way of knowing that a huge van belonging to the local *traiteur* had arrived. The French, as we all know, take their food incredibly seriously, and it's no different on a movie set. Thirty or so tables had been set out in one of the halls of the Chateau. Each table had a crisp white linen tablecloth, and the correct combination of silverware one might expect when about to consume several courses. In the centre of each table were bottles of the local wine, both red and white.

It's difficult to remember exactly what I ate that first day, but I do remember we started with hors d'oeuvres, and then went on to a fish course, then a meat course, ending up with the cheese and finally something sweet and delicious.

In France, two hours is reserved for lunch, rather than the one allowed for in the rest of the world.

I expect many will think that drinking wine at lunch is a bad thing. All I can say in defense of a tipple at noon is that French crews drink responsibly; no one was slurring their speech during the afternoon. I am definitely in favour of a leisurely and civilized lunch.

Savage in yet another disguise in the Great Hall, Château d'Amboise.

In all the five weeks we shot in the Loire Valley, the quality of the food never flagged. On some occasions, when the *traiteur* was too busy, we'd eat in nearby restaurants – my favourite was the magnificent dining room at the Château de Chenonceaux. Simply spectacular.

Interestingly enough, on the morning of the second day, when I arrived on set I was told there was a chance that the day's shoot might be cancelled as the crew had threatened to go on strike unless the quality of the wine served at lunch did not improve.

True. Disbelieve me if you like.

You see, on the first day there were bottles of the local *vin du pays* on the tables, in this case '*Vin de Touraine.*' The sparks pointed out that we were in the region of *Bourgueil*, an *appellation d'origine contrôlée (AOC);* to serve *vin ordinaire* was an insult to the French.

The matter was soon resolved – bottles of *Bourgueil*, and *Chinon* were served from that day on.

On the French shoot we had a French director as well as Howard Rubie. His name was Benjamin Legrand.

Ben Legrand with Wendy in Paris 2009

He was an author, had translated many books of American best-selling authors such as Nelson de Mille, and had directed a lot of television in France. His brother is the equally famous film composer Michel Legrand.

Ben is a charming Frenchman, and we became best friends overnight. We still visit him in Paris each time we're there.

The aspect of the entire series that I found most intriguing was the way it was so educational for children all over the world, while not in the least appearing so. When kids watched the series, they not only enjoyed a great story, but by the time they took in the final twist of the French episode, for example, they were familiar with Leonardo da Vinci, they knew the names of his paintings, what he'd invented, that he'd lived and worked at the Clos Luce in Amboise, and that there was a tunnel connecting the Clos Luce with the Chateaux d'Amboise.

The French episode was titled *'The Mona Lisa Mix-Up.'* Neville Savage had found a way of reproducing the world's most famous paintings – not just copies but as good as the originals.

Savage's French offsiders were a useless pair of criminals named *'Little Bob'* and *'Big Bob'* played by Guy Machoro and Jérome Rebbot. They were an hilarious duo.

All in all, it was an enchanting five weeks in the Loire, reminding me of the novel 'The Lost Domain' by Alan-Fournier – an enchanting romantic tale. The sun shone warmly every day, the window boxes in every street in Amboise were a riot of red geraniums, and Jean Pierre was the perfect host at the Blason Hotel. And the special duck dinner he created for Nick and me was as good as the best I had ever eaten before – that of the *'Au Quai d'Orsay'* in Paris.

Ben and I also made great friends with a hugely charming girl called Géraldine Guiblin who was our very young clapper loader. She had very short boyish hair and a perpetual smile. Absolutely captivating. She always wore lovely French shoes that clicked on the cobbles. I loved the sound of it and put it in the novel. The Aussies referred to Géraldine as 'Madame La Clap.'

Each evening in the Loire, before and after a magnificent dinner at the Blason, I tapped away at my computer writing the French passages of *'The Webber Agenda,'* based on all the information I had garnered during the day. One fascinating location was the very famous 'Caves du Douillard,' caves that run underground from one side of Amboise to the other and were an escape route for fighting men from the fifteenth century onwards. This made these caves the location where one of the stashes of money would be unearthed – while a much larger stash would eventually be found in the old Jewish Quarter of Krakow!

That was France neatly accounted for in my story – decorated with all the history and romance I had discovered there.

Next I flew to England to film there. I knew I'd have to wrack my brains for the relevance of an English chapter for 'The Webber Agenda.' I needn't have worried, the ideas came thick and fast the moment I touched down. Sam Webber's mother had married a Polish resistance leader during the war! Of course she had! I came up with this idea because I knew the final chapters would take place in Krakow!

So while I relaxed in Leeds, I wrote some nicely lyrical passages about Mrs. Webber's reminiscences of Poland during the war. And I could finally reveal my heroine – the love interest – the gorgeous Marysia!

We stayed in Leeds, because Yorkshire Television was one of our partners in England. Our hotel, 42 The Calls, was a remodeled warehouse on the canals – a spot that used to be a no-go area, yet had recently become trendy. After midnight it returned to its dicey past. I remember one morning walking out of the hotel and seeing a bloodstain on the pavement the size of an open umbrella. A trail of blood lead down the street to the doors of a pub called the George and Dragon; a gay pub that was well known for its violence.

Warsaw is fascinating. Of course it's sad that there is so little left of the old Warsaw. My good friend and prominent Polish film star, Gosia Dobrawolska, owns a beautiful apartment a few hundred yards from the new Bristol Hotel in the old town. She married an Australian, Michael Ihlein, and they live in Sydney. She returns frequently for Polish film festivals and to make yet more films – she's a legend in Poland. In 'The Chasen Catalyst,' the sequel to 'The Webber Agenda,' I named my heroine Gosia Dobra after her. I was told 'dobra' meant 'super' and she was supposed to be very beautiful. Her brother Januj was kind enough to help me with all manner of research.

Award-winning Australian film designer Nick McCallum in Warsaw.

Warsaw has a huge outdoor market close to the Hilton Hotel. When I was there, I have to admit I hadn't yet taken a stand against caviar farming, so I couldn't wait to buy a jar at a price I could afford. It's against the law for tourists to take it out of the country, so if it's found in your luggage it's confiscated (and I firmly believe it's then sold back to the market store owners). I posted a jar to London – it arrived a week later. The one I posted to Ben Legrand in Paris never made it – those Frenchies have a certain *nose* for delicious things.

When we were filming in Warsaw, the Aussie crew and cast would be picked up after the Polish crew and then driven to the set. By the time I climbed aboard, the back of the bus was packed with very happy Poles. Why happy? Because it was their custom to breakfast on their homemade vodkas. It's one of those local things – everyone makes the best vodka at home, and it's insulting to refuse a taste.

So each morning at around 6 a.m. the grips and sparks would call me down to the back of the bus and offer me the most raw and pungent brews you can imagine. They would pour a couple of fingers into a plastic jar the size of an English teacup. Then it's customary to toss it all down in one gulp. The only problem is that if there are six men who want to honour you with their special tipple, this means you arrive on set having drunk around ten Aussie measures of straight alcohol.

I didn't tell my director Marcus what was happening, but I wasn't about to be a 'wuss' and say no to these guys, as they were such fun, laughing and singing all the way to set – a journey that often took two hours. They took great delight in translating all the 'interesting' phrases one might need into Polish, and then some more. Then they would sing. Somehow I never ended up pissed on set. I tell you, they breed 'em tough in Poland.

My favourite location in Warsaw was in and around the President of Poland's former private train. It had been parked in a siding close to the city somewhere and was absolutely beautiful inside. There were sleeper cars that must have been fabulous in their day, as well as dining cars with amazing inlaid wood decorations.

In the Polish story, the President's train is Neville Savage's personal mode of transport, and I immediately got right into the spirit of the first scene. Savage is eating caviar and drinking champagne while he ponders what to do with some 'Centuari brats' he's kidnapped.

"Why not use the real thing," I begged Marcus. *"Just for fun."*

"Just this once, then," he replied.

So in this scene it's Beluga caviar and French champagne. It's never happened since – to me, anyway. Damned shame!

The joy of traveling around Europe on a film or television series is that all the boring things are handled *for* you. All you have to think of, in between periods of filming, is learning your lines and enjoying life.

From Warsaw we went to Kraków, the capital of Poland from 1038 to 1596. It's Poland's second largest, and one of its oldest, cities, dating back to the seventh century. Kraków has traditionally been one of the leading centres of Polish academic, cultural, and artistic life, and one of its most important economic centres. The twin towers of Saint Mary's Cathedral dominate the central square, the Rynek.

There is so much history in Krakow that I couldn't help spicing 'The Webber Agenda' heavily with anecdotes, both historical and romantic.

My favourite true story concerns Saint Mary's. The legend concerns the time of the Tartar invasions.

When the Tartars were seen in the distance trumpets and bugles called to each other from high places all over Poland. In Kraków, atop the church tower, the trumpeter was unable to finish his call of alarm as an arrow pierced his throat. To this day, to commemorate this brave man, a trumpeter plays the same call as the first brave man, and it is cut short at the very moment the first trumpeter died. It is played four times, to the north, east, south, and west. It's very moving to hear each hour.

My second story is more of a fable, told to me by one of our Polish make-up ladies as we were walking across the Rynek. She turned to me and said, "You must buy me roses. It's traditional. Every day of the year there are roses in the Rynek. Legend has it that the day there are no roses the city of Krakow will die."

I did so, happily. It's a nice story – even better if you are a flower seller in the Rynek!

On our day off, a party of us drove down to the Vistula River and hired a raft. The experience was wonderful. You hire the boat and a traditionally dressed pole-man stands at the back directing you while you eat and drink lavishly. It was a stunning day and we were glad we'd thought to bring several picnic baskets of food and wine. Cheese, caviar, crusty bread and fresh butter, cherry tomatoes, fresh fruit – everything a traveling film troupe would need. I recommend this side trip.

The Polish film company was not as rich as the other

Europeans, like FR3 in France or Yorkshire Television, so they made up for the reduced budget by contributing more crew and locales.

We filmed before Poland joined the EEC, so the Zloty wasn't worth much. Today Kraków is a thriving European city; then everything cost so little. To give you an example. Nick McCallum – our resident *bon viveur* – scouted out one of the most famous restaurants in Europe, one that just happened to be situated in the Rynek. The *Wierzynek* restaurant has been visited by most crowned heads of Europe for over four hundred years, as well as every Russian President since the formation of the USSR; Gorbachev dined there the week before we arrived in the same room that Nick had reserved for us – the celebrated *Pompejanska Room* with its seventeenth century polychrome murals.

Nick threw the dinner to thank his Polish art crew who he knew were struggling to make ends meet. We ate everything on the menu, including lots of caviar, lots of wine, and some amazing desserts, yet the bill worked out at just under five dollars a head. It would be a very different story today. So you can see I simply *had* to put the *Wierzenek* in *'The Webber Agenda'* somewhere. I set a romantic dinner there between our hero and heroine. They ate the same food as we did.

It was a dark rumour that there was a Polish Mafia connection with the television company. I'm sure it was just because our Polish producer was young and very good looking, and had all the pretty girls on the end of a string. I once saw him down half a bottle of vodka without taking his lips from the bottle.

'MISSION TOP SECRET 2.'

On the second series of *'Mission Top Secret'* we flew Business Class. We took with us a wonderful man by the name of Stanley Walsh, one of Grundy's best producers. Also Tony Raes as designer because Nick McCallum was busy on a film.

I have a sneaking suspicion that the change-up in class was made because there was a fear that someone – a forerunner of *Wikileaks* – was about to blow the whistle that on the first series the producers and directors had flown on separate flights in, how shall I put it, more 'comfortable' surroundings. Not Emmanuel, he never believed in too much luxury.

"Everyone is equal in my opinion. I fly with you. Economy," he'd always said. Whatever the reason, it was a nice change – it meant we arrived in much better condition to act. Producers please note.

Germany, Ireland, England, Spain and South Africa were our destinations this time. Once again Emmanuel Matsos handed out the wads of per diems, and once more I allowed the production to feed me, provide me with wonderful accommodation, pick me up in limos, drop me home each evening, and arrange the entire itinerary for six months of my life, while I had the very best fun in the world playing the devious and devilish Neville Savage.

In the Madrid episode, Savage had perfected a machine that was capable of stealing the voices of humans – in this case a famous opera singer. One of the guest stars was a dog – a trained terrier that had a nice cameo role.

In one scene, by accident the dog exchanges its bark via the machine with that of the opera singer, and proceeds to run around Segovia singing Puccini, while being pursued by Savage and his gay off-sider.

In another scene the dog had to be trained to walk up to Savage, pee on his leg, then walk away.

Spanish trained hound peeing on my leg.

The trainer had assured Howard, our director, that the hound was trained to do this very thing. But on the day, it didn't feel like it, despite many treats. Eventually, after squirting another dog's pee on my trouser leg to see if our dog will sniff and pee as well, the dog was fitted with a very odd device. A syringe was strapped to it's off-camera side, alongside it's dick, and a length of tubing was cunningly concealed so that when the dog stopped by my trouser leg, they could pump yellow liquid out. In the final cut it looks very convincing.

In the final scene in the second Spanish episode Savage escapes by being plucked off the world famous aqueduct in Segovia by his offsider, Santiago Alvares, flying an ultralight. The aqueduct is hundreds of feet up and the small plane was surprisingly fast. It was a great escape act!

Plucked from the top of the famous aquaduct in Segovia!

I have to confess that it was all done with a crane and a harness – to have tried to catch me with a hook off the aquaduct would be akin to catching a split pea on the head of a pin.

I recommend Madrid to any serious tourist. The bars are a delight and the tapas scrumptious. The only problem was the social time frame of the Madrilleños. If you're at all 'cool,' you won't meet your friends in a bar before 10 p.m., eat in a restaurant before midnight, or enter a nightclub before 2.a.m. This proved a problem if the crew-call was 6 a.m. Of course on my days off I had a very good time.

I recommend a restaurant just off the Plaza Major called *'Botin.'*

I'm told it's the oldest restaurant in Europe and it serves the best *jambon* around.

The make-up lady in Spain was extremely eccentric. She was always singing, and as wide as she was tall. Each day when she finished making me up, she'd reach for a dark make-up pencil, pinch my chin together so as to give me a 'Kirk Douglas' cleft and pencil a false one in.

I told her we'd already filmed twelve hours without a cleft chin, and that possibly this would be a continuity problem, but she was adamant.

"Bu' eet look sooooo nice. Like Kirka-Douglas. You know heem?"

It was a nuisance wiping it off many times each day. Each time she noticed I'd done so, she'd always come hurrying over to me.

The Ireland shoot was, as ever, a joy. I showed Dublin and the Wicklow Hills to Ulli Lothmans. He fell in love with both.

However, on this six-month trip, the high point was without doubt our five weeks in South Africa.

South African actor Bill Flynn played the useless Professor Roux – brilliantly. He was funny, yet had the perfect poker pace. I was choking back guffaws almost all day, every day. Bill played his comedy straight and very dry.

I'd never been to Africa before, so this shoot was an amazing treat.

For convenience we stayed in Sandton, a reasonably safe suburb of Jo'berg. Each day we'd drive to locations in the Kruger National Park.

Filming in South Africa has to be one of the best ways to see the country as there are no other tourists milling around you, and you get to see everything in such a tranquil setting. We filmed amongst wildebeest and antelope, giraffe, impala, rhino, and elephants (my bareback ride was the best experience!)

On one occasion I visited animals that were being nursed back to health after accidents on the veldt. To lie on your back and stroke a cheetah was a thrill. As was stroking a pregnant warthog – not recommended since they can be very dangerous. *'Beauty'* the warthog was the ugliest animal I have ever seen, yet had an inner beauty. How can I adequately explain?

The only way to travel! Kruger National Park.

One morning I rose before dawn so I could walk from my thatched cottage down to the lake where I knew there were hippos. Because I'd not researched hippos as I should have I had no idea that they were the most dangerous animals in South Africa and had killed more tourists than all the 'cats' put together. But since I thought they were sluggish animals, I sat on the bank of the lake and watched a wonderful female that was bathing with her baby. Occasionally she'd look in my direction, but she manifested no aggression.

I was lucky. The rangers told me she could so easily have taken exception to me and trampled me – she was in the shallows and hippos are by no means 'sluggish,' as I'd thought.

Talking of narrow escapes, I had another during our last week in South Africa.

Our director, Colin Budds, producer Stanley Walsh, and I were having a drink after work in Sandton and I put it to them that we had never been down to Jo'Berg in the evening. Were we going to be too scared to see the city? No way.

So we drove down to Jo'Berg and looked for a fun place to visit, settling on a huge, very colorful building called *'The Lodge.'*

As we made our way inside and up the stairs I became aware that there were no other white patrons whatsoever. Initially I wasn't alarmed. The place was a maze of corridors, with various smaller rooms to either side. In each room people were lounging around, drinking –the corridors were full of lovely looking women from all over Africa – Namibians, Sudanese, Nigerians, Zambians – you name it. As we entered the poolroom it was already very clear we had unwittingly entered the largest and most popular brothel in Jo'berg.

Colin stands six foot four, and as such is usually a target for troublemakers with a few beers in them. You know, the *'Think you're big? Wanna piece of me? Come on!'* Well, Colin considered himself a useful pool player so he stepped up to one of the tables and was immediately challenged by two extremely lethal looking men. The bet was ten dollars. It was to be Colin and Stanley against the two thugs. I watched on and sipped a *Fransen Street* wheat beer.

Midway through the game, Stan and Col were ahead. Then one of the South Africans inadvertently sank the black ball. Stanley smiled.

"We won!" Colin said, smiling.

"No," replied the second South African, *"You lost."*

So saying, he stepped up to Colin nose to nose (well, nose to Col's chin) and took the bill that was on the side of the pool table. There were around twenty fit black South Africans in the room while we were three. Added to this I was never a fighter – nor was Stanley.

"Guess we lost, then," Colin sensibly observed.

"Wanna play some more, fellas?" we were asked. We declined and went downstairs to the bar where we had a few beers and I danced in the disco for a while with the most beautiful African woman I had ever seen. She told me she was from Namibia, stood over six feet tall, and had the blackest and most perfect complexion imaginable. And such incredible… cheek bones? Ahem.

In the South African episode I was given one of Neville Savage's best disguises. I was dressed as a Zulu warrior.

In disguise in Pretoria. 'Mission Top Secret.' Lucky not to be lynched.

I always look forward to disguises, mainly because there's usually the chance to wander outside the set when on location and see the reaction of the public at large. In Pretoria, where we filmed inside the National Museum, it was a very different kettle of fish because I didn't want any black South African thinking that *'whitey had blacked up to take the mickey out of the locals.'* The makeup was brilliant as were my very colorful Zulu traditional robes, topped off by a bright orange turban around my head. I was of course otherwise topless.

Despite this, during a break – this was a night shoot – I decided I'd wander just a short distance off down the road. Inevitably, I was soon approached by a local.

"You want to buy some gold, mister?" he asked me. Clearly he saw through my disguise at once, and concluded I was a sexually deviant tourist.

He held out a hand in which there were about fifteen heavy solid gold chains. They still had their price tags on them. Very expensive. I very politely declined. He didn't react badly; he simply shrugged and ambled into the night.

The South African crew was all young and highly efficient. The focus puller used to estimate distances entirely by eye. No tape measure. I asked him if this was the usual way in South Africa and he shrugged, telling me that he could judge the focal length as well as a tape measure – besides it saved time. Every shot turned out perfectly. Crisp and exact.

Before we left South Africa, Colin, Stanley and I drove to the magnificent hotel called Star City. It's an amazing mix of luxury hotel and amusement park. I recommend a night or two here – expensive, but what luxury. While lounging there by the pool one morning Whitney Houston took a chaise longue a few feet from where I was sitting. Bobby Brown wasn't with her, and I somehow refrained from introducing myself. She looked pretty gorgeous.

Savage being cruel to children in Sydney.

BACK IN OZ.

50. ALEX O'LOUGHLIN, ALZHEIMERS & PETER USTINOV!

Many years before I was to write *'A Message from Fallujah,'* I decided to attempt a short film for Sydney's Tropfest Short Film Festival. After all, all actors want to direct, don't they? Sure they do. Plus, I thought I had enough friends in the business to make the film quite cheaply.

Most Tropfest films are made for the love of it by young people who just want to give it a try. The great majority turn out really well, while a few are sensational.

So my first thought was to ask my celebrated film writer friend Jeffrey Bloom to write me a story – one that had to include a mosquito somewhere.

Within a week I had a funny eight-minute script about a man who invents a cloning system to rid the world of all mosquitoes, by cloning only females that cannot reproduce.

Using the same cloning system as he'd used on insects he decides to bring his adored wife back from the grave. As a young woman. The android he develops is a replica of his wife, aged twenty, perfect in every way except for having lost the ability to reproduce. But the side effects prove to be worrying. 'Jane' likes to bathe every few hours, and when she sings in the shower, she whines like a mosquito. Clearly his cloning system is not perfect.

I knew whom I wanted to cast as 'Jane,' a beautiful actress called Janneke Arent. I cast myself as the Professor, and then looked around for a young actor with great deadpan comedic talents.

On the second day of casting I found him.

At the time, Alex O'Loughlin, was yet to be accepted into NIDA, the Australian Institute of Dramatic Arts. It's a notoriously hard Academy to get into, but within two months he'd managed it. The rest is history. Two nominations at the AFI's for the film, *'The Oyster Farmer'* and *'Mary Bryant,'* and a move to America to become a star there with *'The Shield,' 'Moonlight,'* the film, *'The Back-up Plan,'* with Jennifer Lopez, and then *McGarrett* in the remake of *'Hawaii-Five-O.'*

Wendy and Alex O'Loughlin in West Hollywood. 2010.

I'm not blowing my own trumpet when I say I saw it coming – I think anyone could have. Alex was delightfully modest, had a killer smile, and a burning ambition. He had heartthrob looks as well as being a natural actor.

I asked my now firm friend Geoffrey Simpson, the Director of Photography of *'Shine'* if he'd light my film and he kindly agreed to do so.

Pfizer, the pharmaceutical company, agreed to let us shoot on a weekend in their laboratory, and three days later we had our short film in the can.

The post-production was far harder – something all would-be short film directors should know. However, Spectrum Sound came to our rescue, as did Vicki Ambrose-Barry, who did a fine job editing it.

Sadly, with all the talent I'd assembled, *'AVX86'* didn't make the finals.

A footnote. Alex has always pleaded with me not to distribute or post my film because he's embarrassed about his performance. Of course, since he asked I haven't. And won't. But he's wrong – he's very funny.

The cast and crew of 'AVX86.' Janneke Arent in the centre. Alex top right.

One of the shows I am most proud of came between two tours of *'Mission Top Secret.'* It was an episode of a drama series called *'G.P.'*

This series about a medical practitioner ran for a long time as Australia's version of *'Doctor Findlay's Casebook,'* and starred Englishman turned Australian, Michael Craig.

The strength of this series was in the writing, in the direction, in the casting of the actors, and finally in the production team.

'The Sorcerer's Apprentice' centred on Alzheimer's disease. Noel Hodda wrote a heart-wrenching story of a well-known composer who lives with a conductor. Mark Lee played the conductor.

Mark had starred with Mel Gibson in Peter Weir's *'Gallipoli,'* and always brings the softest touch to his performances. We were directed by Tony Tilse, to my mind one of Australia's best television directors. It was the first time for many years that I hadn't been a serial killer, psychopath, demon or vampire. It was such a refreshing change to be normal – albeit very ill. I loved it.

One week into the filming I was allowed to conduct one of my character's pieces in the Sydney Opera House. It was a very modern piece without any discernible rhythm. Today they call this music minimalist; Pierre Boulez is an exponent.

In the piece I conducted, there was neither a time nor a key signature, so I had to view footage of Boulez and Carl Maria Giulini conducting their own music to be sure I was even halfway convincing. The wonderful part of these few moments was the fact that the small chamber orchestra actually looked at me for direction! I felt I *was* conducting them. It was exhilarating.

Once an actor is cast, it's up to him to conduct adequate research. When this is complete he has to upload all the emotions that he's garnered and step inside the mindset of the person he's playing. Occasionally I get deeply moved by the state of mind of the character. In the case of Murray Booth, the composer suffering from Alzheimer's, I was emotionally shaken during every scene.

One day Booth goes for a walk after an argument with his partner, and finds himself on a pedestrian overpass with no idea where he lives. The cars and trucks are roaring past underneath and Booth is panicked. I remember being invaded emotionally by Booth's panic during those shots, identifying so intensely with Booth's situation. It's an odd profession, acting.

It's working with the *best and most committed* actors that's exhilarating. They may be *about* to become stars or have *been* stars – more importantly; they may be better actors than *both* of the prior categories and have never been fully appreciated.

An actor who for me falls into this last category is Mark Lee. He's had a great career but never made it to the summit. He should have.

There were two leads in Peter Weir's 'Gallipoli,' Mark and Mel Gibson. For reasons I have never quite understood it was Mel Gibson that rocketed to stardom, thanks to his next film *Mad Max.' The luck of the draw to be cast in an iconic film, I suppose.* I think Mark's performance in 'Galipoli' was much more sensitive and interesting than Mel's. That's showbiz, I suppose.

It was about the time I made 'G.P.' that another very curious thing happened. I was about to head to the beach with my dog Coco, a couple of chili salami sandwiches, pickles, a bottle of Chardonnay, when the phone rang. It was my literary agent, Tony Williams. He had a proposition – would I host a literary lunch at the Hilton Hotel.

"Did someone actually ask for me?" That was the first thing I asked.

It amazes me now that I didn't first ask who was the author I was to introduce, but there we are... vanity!

"Well, you sort of came up in the conversation, so it's an offer."

"Because I write great thrillers, or because I have a film profile?" I asked.

"Because we all thought you had Noel Coward's 'talent to amuse'," he replied, and then added wryly, *"On a smaller scale."*

"So who is the guest of honour?"

"Sir Peter Ustinov," came the reply.

I was stunned. It was like being asked to introduce Vladimir Ashkenazy at the Wigmore Hall by giving an impromptu performance of chopsticks.

"Come on, Shane," Tony continued, cutting into the silence. *"It'll be great fun, and you've got plenty of time to think up a short speech."*

I agreed, and my pulse doubled for ten hours.

Eventually the day came. There were approximately four hundred and eighty people seated, waiting for lunch to begin. Wendy and I were introduced to Sir Peter who was in a very jolly mood but looked a trifle frail. The lunch was delicious, and Wendy very kindly chatted to Peter throughout so I could concentrate on my short speech. Eventually I bit the bullet and stood. I looked around my table and saw all the faces; publishers, media people, publicists. Sir Peter was smiling in a very encouraging way – maybe he could smell my fear. Anyway, I introduced the author and told a few stories. I even made a few jokes and people actually laughed. When I sat, Peter stood and winked at me. As he mounted the rostrum he whispered, *"Not bad."* Peter then went on to make the funniest speech I've heard, rivaling Mel Brooks' reminiscences of the Bronx.

Before he left, he gave me a copy of the book he was promoting that day and signed it to me; *"To Shane. From one scribbler to another."* I treasure this book.

WARNER BROTHERS & MY FIRST NOVEL PUBLISHED.

The eighties saw the birth of the Warner Brothers studios on the Gold Coast in Australia. And with the studios came a man by the name of Jeffrey M. Hayes. Born in Los Angeles, he came to Australia during the boom years and set up shop at Warner Brothers. I'm personally delighted he did so because I appeared in many of the television series he produced on the Gold Coast to sell in America, as well as all over the world. He'd been an associate producer of *'Vegas,'* producer of *'T.J. Hooker'* starring William Shatner, and executive producer of the *'Mission Impossible'* series of 1988 and 1989.

Sometime in 1993 I was cast as the bad guy in an episode of a new series that didn't really stand the test of time but I thought was passably good, called *'Time Trax.'*

It starred American Dale Midkiff and Australia's Elizabeth Alexander. The log-line? *'A cop from the future is sent back to contemporary times to track down fugitives hiding in the past.'* I thought at the time, and still do, that it was a premise that should have gone places, but there were only four episodes produced.

All I remember of the episode titled *'Optic Nerve'* was that I had to wear some very painful hard contact lenses.

'Optic nerve.' Definitely a bad guy.

Nowadays there are more modern contact lenses – but these thick yellow lenses were very painful to wear for long periods, I can tell you. But since life as an actor is usually so comfortable, I tend not to complain on the odd occasions where I'm too hot, too cold or uncomfortable. I was to discover true discomfort a few years later when I played the brain-sucking beast, *'Karvock,'* in the series *'Farscape,'* but we'll come to that later.

It was about this time, way before I met Peter Ustinov, that Tony, my literary agent, rang with the news that he had sold my first novel to Harper Collins Australia. I was over the moon. My father had written plays, novels, and biographies – now I was to have my first novel published too. And to have sold it to Harper Collins was interesting because, before securing Tony Williams as my agent, I had foolishly sent the manuscript of *'The Webber Agenda'* to Harper Collins personally. Not a good idea – always secure an agent first. Never send out unsolicited manuscripts, they will always come back with a note from someone in the basement thanking you for thinking of them.

I felt that someone deep within the bowels of Harper Collins Australia had possibly read, or maybe speed-read, my manuscript a month prior to Tony suggesting to the publisher at Harper Collins that my thriller was highly commercial. I didn't tell either Tony or my publisher that it had been knocked back months before. That would not have been the smartest move.

I'd wanted the title of the book to be *'Savage Arena,'* but those who knew a thing or two at Harper Collins told me that the word *'Savage'* never sold well. I was tempted to argue the toss. What about Christopher Hampton's *'Savages,'* Robert B. Parker's *'A Savage Place,'* *'The Savage Garden,'* by Mark Mills? People in publishing think they know everything, yet everyone in Australia passed on J.K.Rowling apart from Bloomsbury so exactly how smart are they?

"Think of a title that tells us it's an espionage novel," I was told. *"Like all of Robert Ludlum's novels."* So I offered up *'The Webber Agenda'* and they liked it. Boring, but at that time my aim was to please.

After eight months of editing, I geared up for the book launch of *'The Webber Agenda.'* I asked Australia's foremost film critic, *'Mr. Movies'* Bill Collins if he would be the speaker on the day and he said he'd be delighted to take part.

The launch took the form of a lunch at the lovely old Tilbury Hotel in Sydney's Woolloomooloo. Harper Collins picked up the tab and everyone said a lot of nice things about the book. I invited all my close friends and it was a great day.

I followed this launch with another up on Pittwater where we lived. It took place at what was then *'Carmel's Boatshed'* café and was hosted by my friend and Chanenel Seven national news anchor Ann Sanders. She gave an inspired speech.

One of the most picturesque spots anywhere in Australia, the *'Boatshed'* is located on the Pittwater side of Palm Beach. The owner at that time was my very dear friend Carmel Walton. I organized a coupe de theatre involving a seaplane diving the boatshed, and an actor pretending to be a gangster racing towards a getaway speedboat – all with a soundtrack of sirens and machine gun fire to match. Carmel's son Russell and his former water police pals came up with some wonderful ideas. Everyone dressed in costume. Russell, and his pal 'Friendly' were policemen, of course. Ken Tarrant was a sleepy Mexican, Egle Tarrant was a dancer, and Egle's daughter Debbie Tarrant looked fantastic as a younger Mexican dancer. Even Roger Mirams and his wife Irene sailed across from

Mackerel Beach dressed as pirates. The food, care of Carmel, Gaynor Jones and Pat Dunphy was magnificent. I paid for the drinks. Lots of tequila.

NEW ZEALAND FILMS & TV.

ALMOST A WATERY GRAVE, 'CONSTANCE,' AND 'SHAKER RUN.'

When we returned from the second European *'Mission Top Secret'* tour, we had to shoot all the scenes that were supposed to look like Africa but were in fact going to be shot in New Zealand.

The two most memorable escapades in *'Kiwiland'* filming extra material for *Mission Top Secret'* both involved water, and both were very uncomfortable.

In the South African *'Treasure at Elephant Ridge'* episode, Neville Savage tries to escape with a huge gem attached to a spear, but as ever is foiled by the *'Centauri'* kids. In trying to evade the children he boards a small dinghy and sets off down a raging river in Africa. But because the rivers in South Africa had not been 'raging' when we were there, it was decided to film those scenes in the Shotover River near Queenstown.

It's on the Shotover that one can experience the *'Ultimate Jet Boat Experience.'*

The day we filmed on the river, it was really 'raging'! The week before a Japanese tourist had been drowned in a nasty accident on the river. However, I was assured, as actors inevitably always are, that 'all would be well.'

The scene called for Bill Flynn and me to negotiate the rapids of the Shotover River in an inflatable dinghy that supposedly had a broken outboard engine. Bill is the first to bail out as he sees the Niagara Falls approaching, while Savage, stubborn as ever, refuses to give up his jewel. As he screams invective at the kids, Savage accidentally falls backwards into the torrent and we see him carried down the boiling river until he disappears over the Niagara Falls.

As this certainly qualified as a stunt, a discussion was held, at which I was present, to determine the safety measures. I was to wear a wet suit under my shirt, a double-breasted business suit and Savage's signature heavy black brogues.

As the inflatable passes on the right hand of the camera, Savage stands, loses his balance and plunges backwards into the rapids. Then he's supposed to flail around, gasping in the torrent as he's taken down river, at what I was informed was then running at approximately twelve knots. There were to be two jet boats in the water ready to fish me out the moment I passed the camera stationed fifty feet down river on the opposite bank.

It's tempting to suggest you're a 'good bloke,' unafraid to do a stunt or two. What I had to do was pretend I wasn't scared.

When it came to the shot, my heart was pounding so hard I was in two minds if I should call it off. However, it was far too late to go back on my word, so when I heard a distant call of '*Action!*' and one of the assistants pushed my inflatable out into the centre of the raging river, I bit the bullet and hoped for the best.

I clearly remember sailing past the first camera and just managing to stand up in the boat to shout invective at the Centauri kids. Then I launched myself backwards and immediately plunged several feet below the ice-cold water's surface.

I came up for air and found no difficulty in 'gasping and flailing.' But the power and speed of the Shotover River took me by surprise, even though I'd been staring at it all morning. I'm here to tell you, it's a very different thing when you're in a mini tsunami.

It seemed like five minutes, but I am assured I was picked up within twenty-five seconds by a safety boat. I looked back at the second camera, where Colin was waving at me delightedly. Why had I not been picked up where I was told – fifty feet back? Colin explained later. *"It was such great footage. You seemed to be in control, so I let you run a bit,"* he said with no hint of an apology.

The footage looks great, but I choke every time I see it. I wasn't in danger, but I most certainly wasn't 'in control.'

It didn't matter – it was in the can.

The other incident involving water was at Milford Sound, a fjord in the south west of the South Island. Rudyard Kipling called it the eighth Wonder of the World, with sheer rock faces rising nearly four thousand feet on either side.

As you can imagine, this majestic lake is massively deep and also cruelly cold. And what was Neville Savage to do in this scene? He was to emerge from the icy waters of Milford Sound, dressed as ever in his black suit, shirt and brogues, pull a live fish from an inside pocket and toss it casually over his shoulder. The only problem was the extreme cold.

They gave me a wet suit; then I dressed as usual. When the camera was ready, I was handed a fish – sadly it was dead, so I couldn't 'accidentally' release it. I was asked to place it inside my jacket and walk as slowly as possible into the water to avoid making too many ripples – the water had to be absolutely flat before my head immerged.

When only my nose and eyes were above the water, I was given the thumbs up and crouched down, stayed there for several seconds then, very slowly, walked out, casually tossing the fish over my shoulder.

It turned out to be a great scene, as. Very funny, I think. But boy, was I frozen that day.

While we were in New Zealand we also shot the bulk of a new episode commissioned by a Japanese television company. My sidekick in this story was a Japanese born Australian actor called Kazuhiro Muroyama. His character was *'Tagahashi of the Seven Secrets.'* Think *'Kato'* in the *'Pink Panther'* movies. My favourite line was *"Tagahashi of the Seven Secrets, do you know what the eighth secret is?"* He looks at me blankly. *"You are an idiot,"* I answer. Very obvious, but it worked. It's all in the delivery, they say. This was dry as parchment.

I happen to love minimalist acting. Make one gesture that means something, rather than five that mean nothing. Shoot one glance that impresses, rather than stare at your fellow actor throughout a scene. If it's funny keep it dead pan and if you want to scare people never shout. Whisper when people think you're going to shout. Shout when the audience least expects it. Never be predictable.

I love performances where you have no idea quite what the actor is going to do next. Smile just before you do something quite violent. And if you are a pitiless killer, always find time for a quiet moment where you can smile – just the smallest one. It's the element of surprise that's exciting; the not knowing what's going to happen. That's what makes a performance dangerous.

In the New Zealand episode with me was my old friend Barry Quin whom I'd worked with on *'Darlings of the Gods.'* Unlike me, I think he's a better 'Good Guy,' because that's exactly what he is!

Oddly enough, with the exception of an episode of the television cop show *'Special Squad,'* the first film I was involved with in Australasia was one shot in New Zealand called *'Constance.'*

Directed by an up-and-coming wunderkind by the name of Bruce Morrison, and written by Bruce and a very funny man by the name of Jonathan Hardy, it was a wonderfully retro look at life in New Zealand just after the Second World War.

Donna Rees played a bored, movie-loving schoolteacher who begins to fantasize that she's a Hollywood star – with tragic consequences. I was the catalyst who shakes her to the core – a famous photographer that ultimately rapes her and changes her life.

I've made some silly films in my time – most actors *have* to, to survive. This wasn't one of them. It was well written and intelligent, and Donna was a formidable actress with just the right period look.

If you're going to write a frank autobiography you have to include the bad with the good, otherwise people will think you're simply blowing your own trumpet. Bearing that sentiment in mind, I'll now offer a cautionary tale.

During the third week of the shoot, we were filming a garden party scene. Lots of extras – maybe a hundred – were gathered on the lawns of the Governor General's residence in Auckland.

On the N.Z Governor General's lawn. 'Constance.'

This was clearly somewhere to behave oneself. Unfortunately for me, I had partied far too hard the night before, something one should never do during a shoot – though we all know the acting fraternity is riddled with 'piss-pots.' The result was that I had the mother and father of a hangover during the afternoon tea party, which started at eight in the morning. I think the only thing that might have saved me that day was a hair of the dog, but Eddie Knight was the other side of the world. So I had to grin and bear it. I was dressed in a white linen suit. Make-up had done their best to make me look young and attractive. At four in the afternoon, I knew I was going to be violently sick. It all happened so quickly that I couldn't even make it to a flowerbed. The Governor General of New Zealand and his wife had come out to see what filming was like and were seated about fifty feet from where I was standing.

I threw up like a cannon. Three times.

I managed to avoid soiling my white suit, but that wasn't the point – I had barfed in front of the Governor General, his wife, a hundred extras and the entire crew.

My advice is simple. Don't get pissed during a shoot – even after hours. It will come back to haunt you.

The film won the premier award at the Taormina Film Festival in Sicily the following year, and it was an official entry at Cannes. Donna was asked if she'd attend, but apparently was not a believer in film festivals and awards. Another piece of advice – take the opportunities when you can.

With director of 'Constance' and 'Shaker Run' Bruce Morrison.

'SHAKER RUN.' HELICOPTER ACTING!

I almost immediately moved on to another New Zealand film, produced by the same man who had produced *'Constance '* – Larry Parr.

This film was not so intelligent – not that there's anything wrong with that! It was a road movie starring Oscar winner Cliff Robertson as the hero, Leif Garrett as his offsider, Lisa Harrow as the glamour ingredient, and me as the bad guy.

Bad guy Shane meets tough guy Cliff Robertson.

Cliff had won the Oscar for his portrayal of the name role in the film *'Charly.'* I thought he was superb in the role I couldn't wait to meet him in person. *'Shaker Run,'* was directed again by Bruce Morrison. I spent almost fifty per cent of my role in a black CIA helicopter. It was an amazing experience to tour the entire South Island of New Zealand from the bad guy's chopper. Imagine what it might be like to swoop down low over the lake in Queenstown, flying less than three feet from the water's surface, and then peeling off to fly over the snow-capped *Remarkables*. It was magnificent!

I greatly enjoyed Lisa Harrow's company. However, I felt she wasn't exactly comfortable in such a crazy film – she's much more of a cerebral actress, whereas I'm happy to do most genres of film – after all, I started out in Hammer Films. Leif was a nicely crazy guy who had never seen fish served whole, but always in fillet-mode. And Cliff? I believe his heart wasn't in the project, and he wished he wasn't sixty-three – a tad too old to be playing gung-ho road heroes. He did a marvelous job driving the Trans-Am hero-car at high speed like a true pro.

One problem that Bruce, our director, had to resolve one way or another was Cliff's make-up. In true Academy Award fashion, Cliff had his own idea of how a superhero should look – deeply tanned and rugged. But, as Bruce pointed out, the character Cliff was playing had been living in New Zealand for over a year – so where had the tan come from? It didn't make sense. But Cliff wanted to look the way he thought he should look, so he insisted on a deep tan. *"The guy is an American hero! He's going to look great. Okay?"*

Bruce had a word with the make-up supervisor, but regardless of what make-up she applied, Cliff added his own product every day. He ended up looking very dashing – and lets face it, the film wasn't exactly 'Gosford Park,' was it?

I was looking forward to single long dialogue scene where the good guy, Cliff, meets the bad guy, me.

We rehearsed for thirty minutes or so. During that time Cliff never looked at me once. Perplexed, I eventually asked him the obvious question.

"Cliff, when we do the take, are you going to look at me at all?"

He looked at me, smiled and pointed to a light.

"That's my key light, Shane."

That was it. As far as he was concerned, that light was optimum, so he wasn't about to spoil things by looking at me.

Cliff was right – in a way. He looked great in that scene. Very well lit. The quintessential movie star. I didn't look nearly as good. But I have to say that I don't think it makes much sense never to check back at the actor you're playing a scene with – even if it's only once. Otherwise the moviegoer is going to wonder if there's actually someone else in the room.

BACK IN OZ

'TWISTED TALES' WITH GEOFFREY RUSH, & A SECOND NOVEL.

When I returned to Avalon I splashed out on a Mercedes. Not a new one, but a lovely silver 1982 model. I *loved* it. Coco the pig dog preferred the Beetle convertible I'd bought a couple of years before but was hammered to death in a hailstorm.

Christmas in Avalon. Coco dressed as Pigdog Santa.

I thought Coco looked much better lounging out the window of my first 'proper' car.

My next film production was not the best ever, but it was work, and I thank Phil Avalon for that. It was a thriller titled *'Tunnel Vision,'* starring English imports Robert Reynolds and Patsy Kensit. I played a police inspector, but was not overwhelmed by the power of the script. I was impressed by the performance of Rebecca Rigg, who went on to work on *'Jerry Maguire'* and *'Fair Game,'* with Naomi Watts and Sean Penn – her abilities were instantly recognizable, but sadly wasted in this one. Gary Day was as good as ever.

It's interesting to note that Phil chose to bring in his 'English imports' to impress, yet it was the Aussies who shone. And remember, all those years previously when I arrived to promote *'Chatterley,'* it was me that had been the import. Now I was chopped liver as far as Englishmen went. I didn't mind in the least.

That year I finished the editing on my second novel, *'The Chasen Catalyst.'* This was a thriller concerning the possibility of widespread drug trafficking via the diplomatic bag. Fortunately, Harper Collins liked it and it was all systems go. So I thought, anyway. No one told me that Harper Collins had allowed a zero budget for the promotion and marketing – not till a year later.

No point in publishing in a vacuum – you'd have thought they'd have known that.

When it was finally brought to my attention, I quizzed my publisher. Angelo told me this by way of an explanation: *"We spent forty thousand dollars promoting your first book—the second book had to sell on its own merits now people know you're out there."*

Of *course* no one knew *'The Chasen Catalyst'* was out there. Duh!

As I had done with *'The Webber Agenda,'* I worked day in day out, contacting radio shock jocks and reviewers and television talk show hosts. This was not organized by Harper, but by me. I gave twenty radio interviews all over Australia. I appeared on the television show *'Good Morning Australia,'* with the wonderfully generous and charming Bert Newton, as well as appearing on the morning show at NBN Newcastle. But when I went out into the centre of Newcastle to sign books I was told by the stores that they hadn't received delivery of the books. Yet, Harper knew of my television show. Amazing.

So the sales of *'Chasen'* were disappointing, mainly because of the lack of promotional cash and some distribution glitches. Simple.

I was also informed at that particular time that Harper had made the mistake of reprinting far too many copies of *'Webber'* when it began to sell well. Had they not done this, I would have sold ninety per cent of the print run. When they reprinted, they were left with thousands of books on their hands, so the sales figures showed only that I had only sold sixty percent of the run. Their fault, not mine, but guess who was blamed? Always the author – never the publisher.

In the same year I was cast opposite Geoffrey Rush in an episode of Bryan Brown's television series, *'Twisted Tales.'*

'Bonus Mileage' was a very amusing script, well written, and stylishly directed by Chris Collins. The story concerns a calling card that, when passed to a stranger, changes identities.

As one might expect, Geoffrey was extremely funny as *Harry Chisolm*. Bone-dry humour. He was a joy to work with, and at the time wasn't famous. I remember asking him during lunch one day what he was up to, and he told me that the film he'd just finished was getting some great reviews at the Berlin Film Festival. The film was *'Shine'* and would win him an Oscar. Which yet again demonstrates the truth in the saying *'you never know what's around the corner.'*

One last interesting tidbit from this show. An actress by the name of Kate Fischer played a flight attendant in the piece. To call it a cameo might overstate the case. But at the time she was engaged to Australian tycoon Jamie Packer, son of tycoon Kerry Packer, who was the son of tycoon Frank Packer. So when the television company started to promote the series, *'Bonus Mileage,'* it starred Geoffrey Rush and Kate Fischer.

That's showbiz.

With Geoffrey Rush in 'Twisted Tales.'

In the same way, when the video of *'Till There Was You'* was released, there were two snapshots on the cover, and two names featured – Mark Harmon and Kate Ceberano. Why? Because she was a big singing star in Australia at the time, and although she didn't actually *act* in the film, she did sing a Jazz song at the end of the movie.

The owner of the video rights has to hard sell. So he publicizes whoever arouses the most interest on the day. No use complaining – Jeröen Krabbé, Deborah Ungar and I were, again, chopped liver.

'LET GO' BY HARPER COLLINS. MAKE MORE MONEY!

Having had my second thriller published by Harper Collins

Australia, I must say I felt I had really found a home. I regarded the publisher who had said such worthy things about my first two books, and my editor at the time, as good friends.

However, I think it's important to point out to those as naïve as myself that it is thoroughly pointless to mix friendship with business practices.

I shall give an example.

When I came to Australia, I was looked after by a lovely man who was paid by Fox Columbia to show me a good time while I was in Oz. Many months later, when I tried to contact him he told me frankly that while I was promoting 'Chatterley,' it was his job to be my friend. Now that this period was over, sadly he had too many friends.

I was a bit shocked to hear this, but it was a salutary lesson. My editor at Harper was very kind and generous to me when I was favourably looked upon by the publisher. But this soon changed when the sales figures – due to the misjudged and premature reprint of 'Webber' – were analyzed negatively. I believe she was obliged to say positive things to me about my work while Harper viewed me as an asset. I believe she was a much more cerebral person and the kind of fast fiction I wrote was not exactly her cup of tea. As far as I was concerned, I saw her as a friend and colleague. I genuinely liked her, rather than viewing her as someone who could be useful to me.

I am not so naïve these days. I don't blame her in the least. Business is business, and you have to edit what you're given and seem polite about it.

I had written my third thriller, 'Hitkids,' in Santa Monica while waiting for Gary Fuchs at Contemporary Artists to find me a job. Scott Citron and Jen Perito kindly let me stay in their apartment, where I looked after their five cats while they were away, Scottie co-producing a television series in Berlin.

When I returned to Australia – Mr. Fuchs sadly never found me any interviews, let alone work – I submitted my third novel, *'Hitkids,'* to Harper Collins Australia.

A few weeks later, I was summoned to 'Harper Collins Australia Central.' In Ryde. To attend a meeting. I had no idea what to expect.

Eventually, I was directed to a boardroom where at least ten men and women were seated. My publisher briefly introduced them all. Marketing, sales, editing, etc, etc. He then made a short speech outlining how disappointing the returns had been for *'Webber,'* and pointing out that the sales of *'Chasen'* had been a tad disappointing too. At this time I didn't have a chance to mention this was their fault for rushing into a reprint on *'Webber'* and failing to promote *'Chasen.'*

Then came the clincher. The opinion of the board on *'Hitkids.'* The novel, about the gifted son of an Irish hit man living in Los Angeles who takes on the business after the tragic death of 'dad' in a freeway accident, had been 'read.' Interestingly he didn't say exactly by whom. The general opinion was that the whole premise was politically incorrect. He pointed out that because the anti-hero was only 9 years old – no women would want to read it.

"52% of all our readers are women!" he pointed out.

I thought to myself, *"Hey that's practically fifty-fifty isn't it?"*

When I was given a chance to speak, I made various points I thought made sense. It was *their* fault they printed too many copies of *'Webber'*; it was *their* fault *'Chasen'* didn't sell, as the reviews of both books were great. And, as for the age of *Harold*, my antihero in *'Hitkids'*, had no one in the room ever seen the classic film *'The Demon Seed'*? My story focused on whether humans were actually born bad, or whether an evil nature could be the product of a child's social environment. Yet all in the room seemed to think it *'wasn't nice'* to tell a story of a young lad that murders people.

Eventually I gave up. *"You don't want to publish my book?"* I asked.

"No, we don't think so, Shane," Angelo replied.

So that was that.

The following day I asked the head of distribution whether Harper Collins Australia would like to distribute the book if I paid for it to be printed in Hong Kong. The reply was that they wouldn't mind that at all.

So I had a cover made up by a very talented young friend of mine, Oliver Moreton-Evans.

Oliver Moreton-Evans' design.

Wendy edited it, and Harper Collins distributed it. As usual, I did all the presswork – radio and television. I made four times the amount of money with *'Hitkids'* than I'd made on my previous two books. It was another lesson. Yet no one at Harper Collins either thanked me for the money they made on the distribution deal, or admitted they had made an error of judgment in telling me I'd written a book that *'would never sell.'* Lets' face it, how many people have the courage to admit they made a mistake? That was a huge lesson.

However, I still had a lot to learn.

A FOURTH NOVEL. 'BITE OF THE LOTUS.'

When I first came to Australia in 1982, the film breaking box office records was George Miller's *'The Man from Snowy River.'* So when I heard all those years later that they were making a television series based on the same story, I asked my agent to see if she could find something for me.

Being cruel to my 'wife,' played by Fances o'Connor on 'Snowy.'

All my favourites, barring Ian Barry, were directing episodes. The cast was littered with good actors – inter alia, Andrew Clarke (who I'd worked with on Anzacs for six months) Guy Pierce, Hugh Jackman, and Wendy Hughes. There had to be a bad guy coming up soon, I thought. Indeed there was, a decidedly unpleasant man. One who arrives in town to take back his errant wife – beautifully played by Francis O'Connor – who has had the temerity to desert him. My old mate Pino Amenta directed this two-part tale, and this time I holidayed – sorry, worked bloody hard – in the hugely picturesque spa town of Daylesford.

Now that I had had two books published by Harper Collins, as well as one published by my own company and distributed by Harper, I was determined to keep writing.

The next novel I wrote was more of a saga than a straightforward thriller. By 'saga' I mean a much longer novel, over five hundred pages, set in Washington, Sydney, New York, Saigon, Moscow and Hanoi.

People have often asked me how I come to think up my stories. In the case of 'Bite of the Lotus,' the inspiration came as I read an article about a plane that was called 'The Money Plane.'

The more I read, the more astonished I was that such a plane existed. Apparently, every Friday a plane left JFK airport for Moscow carrying several hundred million dollars worth of freshly minted bills bound for the Russian banks. The US Treasury had printed this cash and the whole thing was, as we Aussies say, 'fair dinkum.' Eighty per cent of the Russian banks were then, and most probably still are now, controlled by the Russian *Mafya* and they needed the US currency in order to operate. Someone explained to me that providing the dollars printed in the USA remained outside of America, there was no problem to the US economy – the money merely supported the dollar economy outside of the United States. The more I read of this story, the more astonished I became. The money arrived in an armoured van and was guarded by just three armed men.

I wondered why no one had thought of a heist? The reason was made clear in the last paragraph of the article – who was going to steal a hundred million dollars from the Russian *Mafya*? Didn't they enjoy living?

'Bite of the Lotus' was my most ambitious project to date, and I loved every moment writing it. As ever, my characters only traveled to countries I'd been to myself, and they ate only in the very restaurants I'd enjoyed great lunches or dinners. I believe very much in sound research, and I love to be transported in a novel to places I've never been to, and feel I'm actually there. I feel this is only possible if the author has experienced everything he's writing about.

When Wendy had finished her edit I was again ready to approach Harper Collins for the distribution deal. I'd come to identify so greatly with my two central characters that when I wrote the final short chapter where they meet again and fall into each other's arms, I shed a few tears. To me it was like farewelling great friends.

You might have thought that the commissioning editors there would have been interested in reading my new novel, in view of the fact that they had published my first two books, and made quite a decent profit on the third, but it didn't enter their heads, and frankly I wanted to make as much money again as I had with 'Hitkids,' so I was merely surprised – not angry.

To this day I think their behaviour was odd. Over the years, I made a great friend of the late managing director of Harper Collins Australia, Barrie Hitchon. We'd meet in the Queen Victoria Building for coffee and chat about his experiences in the publishing biz. He'd told me he'd enjoyed my novels, but since he was basically running the business end rather than the creative end of Harper he had no say in commissioning books. It was Barrie who had told me of the disastrous reprint that did me such harm, and he'd thought it quite wrong when Harper decided not to publish my third book.

"You have to have a belief in the writer. If you give him a go, then stick with him for at least three books, and make sure everyone knows the books are out there in the market place."

Barrie was a great friend as well as a great managing director for Harper.

When I write my books, I find it helpful to visualize my

characters doing whatever it is they are engaged in. I like to see the actual streets, the food they're eating; often I can even feel their sadness or anguish. During *'Bite of the Lotus'* I always had a vision of Cate Blanchett as my heroine, with Russell Crowe as my *'tough guy.'* So it was a moment of serendipity when Wendy and I chanced on Cate at an art exhibition of a friend of hers – Tim McGuire. Rather than let this opportunity slip, I suggested to Wendy that we chat to Cate and her husband Andrew Upton. Not as a hard sell for my book, but because I had always thought her very intelligent as well as 'normal.'

They were both extremely friendly and charming. As I remember, we talked about the McGuire's canvasses, possible names for her soon to be born son, and our two cats. I didn't talk about by novel, but later I sent her a copy with a note enclosed. I tried to get a copy to Russell, but despite my vague connection, having once worked with Danielle Spencer in 'Mission Top Secret,' this proved impossible.

If the film were ever made they'd make a stunning team.

The connection with 9/11 is interesting. *'Bite'* had been in the stores for just three months or so when the planes hit the Twin Towers. In the exciting conclusion of the novel an elderly Australian decides he will take a terrible revenge on the Vietnamese tycoon who took advantage of his daughter and island hops his DC3 airplane from Sydney to Hanoi, and flies the plane into the home of the bad guy. As far as I knew, know no one had thought of this method of killing people before. But three months after the launch thousands died in New York and the sales of *'Bite'* slumped – no one wanted to read about planes flying into buildings.

Designed by Scott Citron in New York.

SEX IN LIMOS, & ROGER MIRAMS.

1999, and the two years that followed, were lean years in terms of my feature film work. The eighties were the Australian boom years with the birth of government incentive schemes such as one everyone knew then as 10BA.

Without going into too much detail, 10BA proved to be useful as a method of laundering money by investing in movies and obtaining tax breaks. I'm not sure when the government axed the scheme, one that had helped bring so many Australian films to the world, but I think it was around then. So, without a plethora of Aussie movies in the mix, coupled with the fact I was getting longer in the tooth and the Oz film industry, like America, was becoming obsessed by youth, it was back to television and more bad guys. One show was called *'Wildside.'* In my opinion this was one of the best cop series ever made in Australia. Great scripts and a solid cast, including Tony Martin and Rachel Blake. I wish I had been a regular on that series but it wasn't to be, so I played a crooked barrister. All I can remember of the episode I was in was that I had sex with the comedic actor Mary Coustas in the back of a limousine – not in real life, mind you.

That year saw the release of a film called *'Airtight.'* A film I'd made one year earlier, a futuristic piece written and directed by Ian Barry.

'Airtight' centres on futuristic air pollution. Imagine a time where crime families no longer deal in booze, prostitution or protection rackets. When air, water and energy are the new 'territories' fought over by underworld barons. I played on of these 'scurrilous chappies.'As the air quality becomes toxic, humans can no longer breathe it. All the major cities are enclosed in plastic bubbles and have recycled air pumped in. But corruption raises its ugly head and the *'Air Barons'* decide to take over all air supply and charge money for it. Ultimately only those who can afford it will have any air to breathe.

A great idea for a movie, I thought, though I have to admit I wanted to know what happened to all the animals and insects that lived outside the bubbles.

There's a great scene at the end of *'Airtight'* when our hero, *'Rat,'* guns down all of the bad guys with a machine gun. Lots of special effects, blood capsules and mayhem. The entire set was trashed, and every stick of furniture was left dripping with fake blood!

'Airtight' sold very well all over the world – America, Germany, Hungary, France, and Brazil.

That same year, I was asked up to the Gold Coast to play a wheelchair-bound, voice-boxed deviant criminal by the name of 'The Mongoose' in a futuristic television movie starring Bobbie Philips and Doug Penty. This time it was for American television. It was a full-on action pic, and incredibly violent to boot. I loved it. Because 'The Mongoose' had a voice box, my dialogue had to be changed in post production.

'The Mongoose' – one scary dude.

The chair they gave me was state of the art. Incredible. A far cry from Sir Clifford Chatterley's. I was supposedly a quadriplegic and had only the use of my forefinger and thumb. It definitely was a challenge to arrive on my marks with pinpoint accuracy because I wasn't allowed to look down; I just had to judge distances myself by what was around me.

'Chameleon 3' certainly had its moments. I especially liked the scene where everything starts to go wrong for 'The Mongoose' and he high-tails his wheelchair to a broom cupboard to hide, only to find himself locked in it. Many hours later the cops arrive, open the cupboard and begin questioning him. Of course, *'The Mongoose'* is such an arrogant sonofabitch, he refuses to talk. So they simply shut the door again in his face. From behind the door we hear a muffled voice-box croak, *"No...wait...!"* The silence that follows always makes me laugh – the Coyote-syndrome yet again. What does the crestfallen bad guy say when they re-open the door? *'I want... to speak... with my lawyer,'* he desperately crackles through his voice box.

It was too much to hope *'Mission Top Secret'* would go to a third series. Money is always hard to find, and although Roger Mirams worked like a beaver to get up series number three, he couldn't attract enough partners. Spain, as ever, was keen as well as Germany, but the others....?

It's interesting to note, as well as being a rather a damning indictment of American television executives, that when Roger tried to sell the first two series to Disney, the executives shook their heads, telling Roger apologetically; *"You see it's all set in Europe and Australia. Nothing in America! Kids here don't give a damn about places like Paris and Sydney. Most of them have never heard of Palma, and Madrid. As for Poland..."*

Probably this mindset has been around since the birth of television in America. There are channels such as PBS where the minority of Americans can watch film and television from all over the world, but correct me if I'm wrong, I don't believe any single foreign television series other than documentaries have ever been bought by the major networks in America. They have, of course, bought our concepts and crucified them. A case in point is the Australian series, *'Kath and Kim,'* which was originally gloriously irreverent, but when translated into *'Americanese'* became so politically correct, all sense of humour was gone! The same thing happened to the wonderful British sitcom, *'Absolutely Fabulous'* also known as, *'Ab Fab.'* In the series the two central characters, played by Joanna Lumley and Jennifer Saunders were binge drinkers, cocaine snorters and dope fiends, they swore like troopers and was a neglectful parent. In the American version the producers weren't allowed to air scenes that contained swearing, drug use, binge drinking and dysfunctional behaviour. You can imagine how funny that remake was.

And while this is the case in America, we in Australia are flooded with American material because the producers of this material have already made their money in the USA; so selling their series to Australia, Germany, and Japan etc is simply icing on the cake. How can Australia compete when it costs us twenty times the money to make an hour of drama here than to buy fourteen episodes of say, *'Bones,'* or *'The Mentalist?'*

There's no use complaining. One might just as well complain that the cost of making a garment in India or China is a fraction of that in America. That's simply the way it is.

So, instead of another *'Mission,'* Roger busied himself selling another pet project of his to a channel in Australia.

Ever since he was a child Roger had wanted to make Robert Louis Stevenson's *'Treasure Island.'* He believed now was the time to make his dreams come true, so he gathered the same writing team as on *'Mission,'* and soon had a pilot ready.

The story of *'The Search for Treasure Island'* was this. Seven people struggle through a tempestuous storm and come out the other side to be shipwrecked on an island that proves to be Robert. L. Stevenson's famous *'Treasure Island.'* But here's the twist, the island is inhabited by three separate and extremely odd primitive tribes.

With Tania Lawson in "The Search for Treasure Island."

I amused myself playing '*Dante*,' a Tolkien-esque oddball bad guy, but this series, for me at any rate, was hard work. My old mate from '*Mission*,' Freddy Parslow, was another lead, as was the beautiful Brittany Byrnes. I always thought she had an Audrey Hepburn air to her that was captivating.

Roger, '*The King of Australian Children's Television*,' Mirams, was the most wonderful, hilarious character. Here are some examples of this marvelously eccentric man.

On the second series of '*Mission*' I arrived in the breakfast room of the Madrid hotel where we were staying. Roger was tucking into a hearty breakfast with his lovely wife, Irene. He saw me enter and looked at me in blank surprise.

"What are you doing here?" he asked.

"It's me, Roger. Shane. I play Neville Savage," I replied.

"I know that!" he said. *"But you don't start working till Monday. Today's Thursday!"*

"I think the idea was, Roger, that the cast be given a couple of days to get over the thirty hour trip here," I replied. *"You know? Jet lag?"*

Not happy, he continued to eat his bacon and eggs.

"I don't know. These days actors are thoroughly spoiled," he mumbled.

But that was the producer of the old school speaking. Business class was a luxury for all other than producers, as were two days to rest and recuperate after flying around the world.

Over the years Wendy and I became good friends with Roger and Irene. They owned a house on Mackerel Beach about forty minutes from central Sydney. It was perched up on a hill above the beach and was only accessible by the old ferry that plied its way around Pittwater. Often Irene and Roger would invite us over for a wonderful lunch when he'd also invite his grandchildren. The garden and the inclinator that led up to his house were always packed with jokes, automated bloody hands, scary masks, and other intriguing toys. Children adored his wonderfully eccentric sense of humour. Even the inclinator itself was a wonder. When you stepped inside and hit the 'up' button, an audiotape would play *'The Chattanooga Choo Choo.'*

It really was a fun place to visit. When it came to personal generosity, Roger knew no limit, but when he put on his producer's hat he was a miser.

Another 'for instance.'

Many weeks after we had returned from France, Roger called me and after some initial banter, asked me what I was doing that day. I told him I had it virtually free.

"Then can you do me a favour and come to Grundy house – just for an hour or so," he asked.

I told him I'd be happy to help him out in any way, and then asked him what it was all about. Roger told me there was some problem about when I pulled off my *'Leonardo da Vinci'* facemask to reveal my *'Savage'* face.

"I'm sure we could fix it up in no time at all. Tell you what; I'll buy you some wine. How about that?"

All actors know what a re-shoot is. It's something you get paid for. But Roger was asking me 'as a mate' to settle for some wine. Because he was Roger, I agreed. Life's too short to see a friend disappointed. I arrived at Grundy house to find Roger in the basement clutching a Sony Handy cam in one hand and a hard plastic facemask of Ronald Reagan in the other.

"I don't think this is going to work, Roger," I said. *"It's clearly Reagan."*

"Just need a fraction of a second. No worries," he replied.

We shot bits and pieces for an hour or so, until he was satisfied.

"Well, I suppose I should buy you that wine," he said, as I went to leave. *"There's a drive-through around the corner."*

We drove into the bottle shop and stopped the car. *"I'll come in with you,"* he said, *"I know the specials here."*

'Specials?' I thought. I had my eye on one of my favourite wines – not overly expensive, but not a five-dollar a bottle 'special'.

"I say! Now that's *a lovely wine,"* Roger said, pointing to a red dot special. *"How about that one? Great value."*

I agreed it was good value, and that's what I received. Mind you, at his home he would have served a lovely wine. But that's Roger – the man, the producer.

My favourite story is one recounted to me by Howard Rubie.

Apparently, there was a screening of one of the *'Mission'* episodes at Grundy house and all the heads of departments were present. Roger was sitting between Howard Rubie and Emanuel Matsos. In the middle of the screening someone's mobile phone rang – one of Roger's *bête noirs*. Very annoyed he snatched up the television remote control and put it up to his ear.

"Hello?"

Silence.

"Yes? Can you hear me?" Roger shouted again into the television remote as Howard and Emanuel watched, fascinated.

"None of these damned newfangled things work," Roger muttered, and then slammed the remote down beside him.

The picture disappeared – he'd accidentally hit the 'stop' button.

"Now the television won't work, either!" he added.

Howard picked up the offending TV remote, clicked the television back on again, and replied soothingly, *"I'll get it fixed, Roger. No worries."*

Roger was always one for a party. So, aged in his early seventies, he determined to remarry Irene in a lavish ceremony.

After the beautiful lunch at his house in Mackerel, a small seaplane arrived and touched down on the water. Both Roger and Irene were dressed in white. Her dress was lovely and Roger's white suit and broad brimmed planters hat made him look like Ernest Hemingway. The whole wedding party walked them down the jetty, and they climbed into the seaplane which then took off.

As we gazed upward at the plane we saw something pushed out the window, to flutter lazily down to the sea. It was Roger's white trousers. He then appeared at a passenger window and started to play the trombone.

As a footnote, Roger always told me that he'd been fit as a flea all though his life until his doctor advised him it'd be sensible to have his heart checked. He took the advice of the old sawbones, felt rotten the day after the procedure, and never felt altogether well thereafter.

He died of a heart attack only a few years later.

With Roger Mirams on set (Madrid Central Railway station!)

PALM TREES, DICKENS & SCARY FACES.

There are shows that are well written and appeal in a serious way, and there are shows that pay good money. And don't forget, the 'pulp' films often take you to exotic places. *'Tales of the South Seas'* qualified as decent money as well as being exotic – lovely locations in Queensland right on the Great Barrier Reef.

Produced by Australia's Channel Ten, Gaumont Television, and Village Roadshow, *'Tales of the South Seas'* was a period series – the title really says it all. All the usual suspects were asked up to the palm-fringed set at one time or another, both actors and directors. The stars were young and attractive; William Snow and Rachel Blakely.

We all stayed in a very comfortable hotel in Airlie Beach in the Whitsundays, which is about half the way up the coast of Queensland. They say about Queensland, *'Beautiful one day, perfect the next.'* For those reading this book in colder climes, such as the UK, I'm here to tell you that with the exception of the devastating floods of 2011, this is true. I loved every minute of it, but can't remember a damned thing about the story.

I do remember that my old mate Mark Lee played a very stitched up clergyman and that we ate wonderful food and drank great wine every evening – a far cry from working at the BBC in West Acton.

When *'Tales of the South Seas'* wasn't picked up for another series, Jeffrey Hayes simply invented another production, called *'The Lost World,'* with the same two young stars, William Snow and Rachel Blakely. The same directors flew up and the same guest artists populated the cast. Almost a club!

It was always rumoured that Hayes had a little black book in which he made a note of actors he thought could act well, as well as being reliable. I'm sure it's true – too many directors have told me they saw it. Aussie actors have to thank Jeffrey because over the years he's provided us with a lot of good paying work.

This Queensland escape was followed by yet another Roger Mirams inspired children's series by the name of *'Escape of the Artful Dodger.'*

It was again made by the Grundy Organization and directed by a very talented Polish director by the name of Sophia Turkiewicz.

God bless Roger – what Jeffrey Hayes did for television series made specifically for the American market, Roger did for children's shows made for Australia. Incidentally, Roger was the first to employ a very young Nicole Kidman!

'Escape of the Artful Dodger.' Grundy Int. Films.

I made my choice to live in Australia in 1982 and during those boom times I made about two films a year as well as countless television shows. At that particular time, things were not so hot in England. So when the downturn came in the '90's I could hardly complain.

Australia has some wonderful directors such as Bruce Beresford, Roger Donaldson, Gillian Armstrong, Fred Schepisi and Peter Weir, but when they break through they usually go to Hollywood and are lost to we Aussie actors. So having spent the best ten years of my life in Sydney when the times were good, I wasn't about to complain when the lean years came.

'The Artful Dodger,' Roger's next television series had a great cast of kids, including my old friend, Brittany Byrnes.

The story was in essence 'What happened to Oliver Twist when he went to Australia?' When Oliver gets reunited with his grandfather he is sent to Australia. He is accompanied by Hannah, a girl from Hamburg, who is looking for her brother, Will Grady. When Hannah discovers that some bad guy wants to frame Dodger and Will for a crime he is planning to commit, she and Oliver make a plan to help Dodger and Will escape.

The 'Mission' and 'Treasure Island' team inventively wrote it, and the sets were a joy to behold, thanks again to Tony Raes. It looked so rich on screen, one had to believe Roger when he maintained that practically the entire budget was there to see. I played an incredibly stuffy English Colonel. Not so much a bad guy as a 'stitched-up' twit.

As good as the finished result was, the Americans didn't pick up the show, nor, as far as I know, did the U.K. channels. The reasons were the same. The American channels continued to believe that American kids like to watch only American based material, and have no interest in English literature. As far as the United Kingdom is concerned, the BBC and ITV thought they 'did' Dickens better than anyone, so why would they dream of buying an Australian show based on his material? A shame because I am a dual national, English/Australian. I was brought up at 'The Beeb,' and to my mind our show 'The Artful Dodger' was as good as any Dickensian television adaptation I had seen in England.

In 1998 a very odd thing happened. I went to see a writer/director called Esben Storm with a view to playing a role in his forthcoming film 'Subterrano.' The tag-line for the movie was 'Evil lurks on every level.'

It was pretty obvious I was too young for the role, which eventually went to one of Australia's stalwart actors, Chris Heywood. When Chris was cast, I forgot about the production until many months down the line I was telephoned by the producer, a nice man called Richard Becker of Becker Entertainment.

He told me that the film was now finished and edited, but in his opinion it still lacked… something. I was curious. What did his film lack, I asked? He told me that he was very pleased with the bulk of the movie, but in his opinion it started too slowly and lacked a sense of danger right at the outset.

Here is what Esban, the director, had in mind. *'Killers, revolutionaries, big business, God, romantic subterfuge, betrayal, bounty hunters, people trapped in a subterranean world, set upon by lethal, remote controlled toys. A game called Subterrano.'*

When I read that I thought, *'Whoooaaahhh. That's a big ask for a film. No way it's going to be 'The Day the Earth Stopped Still' nor even 'Blade Runner.'*

"So what do you have in mind, to make it…scarier?" I asked Richard.

I heard him chuckle. *"You can look dangerous and scary. I've seen it many times. You can just look at someone on screen, and the audience at once fears for him."*

I laughed. In a way bad guys who *look* dangerous were my forte.

"So I'd like to shoot a new credit sequence, with you sitting in a limo looking really scary. Then the film starts."

"Any dialogue? What do I say?" I asked.

"Just a couple of words. You're just looking at a video screen in the limo, and you see your new video game. You think it's absolute shit, and this makes you angry. Very angry! Somewhere, someone is becoming very afraid. That's the idea."

My 'scary' look. Me? Scary?

To cut to the chase, I went to work on a one-day re-shoot. It was a night shoot. I was dressed in black from head to toe, and had my hair slicked like a young 'Gordon Gekko.' I sat in a vast limo, staring at a huge video screen, which was of course blank - there was nothing to see. I squeezed a 'pup' – a small light – between my knees and held it tight, so the light would shine up into my face (like kids do at Halloween) and I did my best to look *'real scary.'*

A few hours later I went home. Richard Becker was pleased – he had his new opening. I was happy – I had a nice fee. Strange how things turn out, eh?

GIBLET, FREDDY AND SOME OF MY WORST NIGHTMARES.

That same year *'Giblet'* moved into our house.

A lovely tortoiseshell kitty, she lived a few doors down from us but visited most of the houses in the street scouting for nibbles. She's a very affectionate and somewhat greedy pussycat.

We could see she was pregnant, so we made sure she had extra snacks whenever she wanted them.

When she gave birth in our laundry basket, we felt obliged to take her home to where she lived, together with her five kittens. But within the hour she brought them all back to our garden, carrying them one by one in her mouth. How she managed to climb three garden walls I can't fathom. But she did. She's that kind of a cat – when she sets her mind on something she does it. She must have decided she was moving in with us. So, despite being taken home three times, she brought those kittens back each time. Eventually we no longer took her home. She stayed in the garden and we fed them all there.

I recall saying to Wendy, *"If you let that cat into the house, she'll never leave."* Wendy says it was she who said this to me. Either way, someone opened the back door and she moved in. She was originally called *'Simba,'* but as it was close to Christmas I renamed her *Giblet* because she was skinny. Believe me, she's a good weight now.

She had three litters of kittens before we adopted her and 'hung up her gloves.' All the kittens found good homes. Wendy called her last litter *'The Wobblies'* because they staggered around a good deal.

I was away on some shoot and she rang to ask how many kittens I'd like to adopt this time. We settled on one. The cutest – a marmalade kitten we named *'Freddy Kruger,'* because he was forever going outdoors and then, on his return announcing very loudly *'I'm baaack!'*

Coco was approaching seventeen at the time. She attended the birth of the final litter, like a wonderful doggy midwife, and Giblet was happy to have a protector.

As the kittens grew older, they'd jump onto Coco's back from a sofa and ride around the kitchen.

Giblet kisses her son Freddy.

ART AND BRAIN-SUCKING MONSTERS FROM OUTER SPACE.

I've always loved painting, though I admit I tend to be derivative in my amateurish efforts. But, as with writing, it's creative as opposed to being essentially interpretative. I love Arthur Boyd's work – incidentally Boyd lived in one of the Adeane's cottages in Suffolk when James and I were children. Those painting were known as *'The Bawdsey Paintings.'* I especially liked his dog pictures, so I painted a 'homage to Boyd' with a white Coco in a snowstorm.

One evening after I'd been to a gallery in Paddington, I marveled at a Rosalie Gascoigne in a gallery window down Macleay Street. As I could hardly afford to buy one at a hundred and sixty thousand dollars a pop, I decided I'd make my own.

Of course it's not the real thing, but it's the best I could do, and it makes me happy. It cost me two dollars in paint – the wood I found in a skip. People often ask me if I might part with my *'Gascoigne.'* I always mutter, *'no.'* My brother Dermot would, of course, have sold it on the spot.

During the run of 'Wit' Sandra Bates allowed me to have an exhibition at the Ensemble. That was fun. No one bought anything. In a way I was relieved, as I didn't want to part with any of my canvasses. Maybe it says something about my work?

My painting of Coco on Palm Beach.

When Wendy and I moved from the Northern Beaches to the Eastern Suburbs we began going to all the gallery openings. There would be on average two a week and the art was usually interesting, the wine tasty, and at the more important galleries such as the Saville Gallery, there were chicken sandwiches. They were very tasty ones indeed.

We made many good friends at the various galleries, and over the years a few gallery owners have asked me to launch their exhibitions. I always did my research so I wouldn't be talking rubbish to people who knew more about art than I did.

The first time I opened an art show I was tempted to use an excerpt from a Peter Sellers record called 'The Critics.' It was a spoof that went something like: "*Sensing the resurgence of the traditional stress is something that Bonstard had done, and is doing. He habitually used fragmentation of pigment to consummate his all prevailing sense of hermetic anarchy. It's as simple as that!*" Of course I didn't follow through with this gag, but I wonder how many of the art devotees might have taken me seriously.

Wendy and Charles Blackman, one of Australia's best known living painters.

I later opened a show for the talented landscape painter Robert Klein Boonschate, and he very kindly gave me a canvas, which I love.

On another occasion, our friend, gallery owner and painter Michael Commerford asked me to speak at the opening of an exhibition featuring the iconic pop artist Martin Sharp. An honour.

Over the years Wendy and I have made a lot of friends in the art community, Linda Dry-Parker, her husband sculptor Stephen Glassboro, Scott McDougall, actor cum painter cum funny man Max Cullen and his gorgeous talented wife Margarita Georgiadis, seascape master Neil Taylor, the beautiful Maggie Ferguson (also a hugely accomplished violinist who accompanied Nigel Kennedy so brilliantly at his jam session at the Basement Club in Sydney!) our lovely neighbour sculptor Caroline Rothwell, Sophie Gralton (love her canvasses) and our old friend, sculptor Sally Lee.

Margarita Georgiadis and Max Cullen at my 'Graphic' book launch. Max hosted it at the Commerford Gallery… and roasted me!

Phew. Remembered them all… I hope.

A couple of years ago our Austrian friend Florian Werner told us that he wanted to offer a painting prize to a worthy recipient in Australia. As well as being one of the leading hoteliers in Austria, he's a fine painter and sculptor himself. The prize would be a two weeks residency at his studio in Sankt Christoph, all expenses paid. He or she would work with Florian.

We told him we'd be delighted to help. The *'Florian Werner Prize'* is a dream prize for many reasons, not least of which is it includes food and accommodation at Florian's magnificent five star hotel, *'The Hospiz,'* one that dates back to the fourteenth century. Daniela and Florian gave Wendy and me, as a wedding present when we were married at the Hotel Alter Goldener Berg, a week at the Hospiz. We'll never forget the hotel; the award-winning cuisine and wines were stunning. The one glitch was the bar bill – we went to town that week! Oy! And when the prizewinner is not painting, he or she can ski in one of the world's best ski regions, the Tyrol.

Looking ridiculous the night I opened Martin Sharp's exhibition.

I at once contacted John Bloomfield at the National Art School in Sydney and the prize was set up. It's a joy every year now to be invited to view the work of the final students and award Florian's prize. This year's winner, Sophie Cape, also won the John Ohlsen drawing prize, and is widely touted as the next *'big thing.'* She's hugely talented, and was once on the Australian Olympic Ski team (we didn't know when we gave her the prize!) She's a good friend of another of our artist pals, one of Australia's finest young artists, the larger than life Luke Sciberras, who almost everyone finds 'curiously alluring.'

The hugely talented Luke Scibberas.

I loved being a part of the sci-fi series, 'Farscape.'

Though never previously a sci-fi fan, the characters conjured up in these series were fabulous. I would have loved to play Wayne Pygram's role of *Scorpius*, but I was never in the mix at the casting. He turned out to look über-scary, so maybe it was all for the best. And had I played *Scorpius* I would never have been cast as the brain-sucking *Karvock*!

Oddly enough, the role had been offered to another actor, Ivor Kants, but when he was told he'd need to have a complete head mask made, he bowed out. Well, it's a claustrophobic ordeal and I guess he couldn't face it. As for me, when I heard the news and was asked if a head mask would bother me, I replied, *"You can encase me in lead for the day if it's necessary. Count me in!"*

Brain-sucking Karvock in 'Farscape.' Academy-Award winner Dave Elsey's brilliant work.

Dave Elsey, Oscar winner in 2011, and the best creature designer in the history of the world, worked on my head for a day and came up with something much more spectacular than I had ever thought was possible. Forget the bleach-blonde locks of the old Hammer Films days; I now had the most terrifying head imaginable, some parts of it missing or oozing a mixture of puss and molten metal. And my hand was a miracle. It wasn't simply a hand, it had a spike that shot out before feeding time, and could be stabbed into the soft brain tissue of fair damsels such as '*Chaiana*,' played by the gorgeous Gigi Edgley, to suck out the delicious soft tissue directly up my arm and into my stomach.

Who wouldn't kill for a role such as this?

The basic story concerns an astronaut called John Crichton, who is on an experimental space mission, and is accidentally hurled across the universe into the midst of an intergalactic conflict, and trapped among alien creatures wielding deadly technology, hunted by a merciless military race. One such alien was my character. Each morning I would spend four hours in the makeup chair having my head created by Dave. Then I would struggle into my costume and head for the set. Because you get so incredibly hot when your head is completely enclosed – you lose the majority of heat through one's head – I was given a vest to wear under my alien costume.

This vest had tubes running through it that were connected to icy water. As I waited in my chair, the icy water would be pumped in. While I worked it would be disconnected and the water would become warmer – heated by my body. When we cut I'd be cooled down again.

Acting is often uncomfortable, yet actors often forget this as they read the script is that a film called *'Lost on an Ice Flow,'* is probably going to be filmed in Greenland for six months and it's going to be ****ing cold.

Another example is a mask such as mine. After a week it becomes a real chore.

I especially liked working with Gigi – she brought the most unusual physical quirks to her character, making it totally unique. Her silver hair fringing that perfect white face reminded me of Marcel Marceau's granddaughter.

I returned to *'Farscape'* eighteen months later to play a different role. It isn't customary to bring an actor back as another character, but since the only thing the viewer ever saw of *Karvock* were his devilish eyes, I was cast as a character that ultimately looked more like me – *Colonel Traso Talnell.*

He was a very amusing character. Not really a bad guy at all, but rather the perfect petit bourgeois bureaucrat. On the page,

Trayso is an annoying man in charge of a Scarran controlled space station. I like to think I elevated the character to someone we have all met in real life – that very annoying man we encounter in council chambers to discuss new dustbins, that irritating person who professes to know all about *'the Iraqi question,'* the recorded voice who gives you fifteen alternative numbers to punch into your phone to get the answer you want.

I love to take my characters to extremes. This doesn't apply to filmed adaptations of classic literature such as Chekov, Shakespeare, or Ibsen. But sci-fi? Why not work with the director and make your character truly memorable?

The ultimate galactic petit bourgeous bureaucrat Traso Talnell. 'Farscape.'

I enjoyed playing *Trayso* because he was so excruciatingly dull and boring. I made him vivid and interesting. I think, anyway.

Another brief footnote to this anecdote. My director friend Ian Barry happened to be directing a separate episode on a stage across from where Geoff Bennett was directing *'Fetal Attraction,'* when a fire broke out on our set. It was quite serious and out of control for some time.

Ian tells me that everyone rushed out of our stage very quickly.

Then several minutes later I ambled out (I promise I wasn't being brave – I simply didn't think I was in any danger) walked to Ian and said. *"Looks like an extra day, huh?"*

Hey, that's how actors feel about a well paying job – an extra day pays the electricity, *and* the water bills!

Wendy and director Ian Barry in Rushcutters Bay, Sydney.

During the early part of the new millennium I took various roles in Australia's best-known hospital drama, *'All Saints.'* It ran for many years on Australian television and was very popular. I played a surgeon whose hands were finally letting him down, and then came back as the love interest of the star of the show, Judith McGrath. There's not much you can bring to a hospital soap – all characters are normally pretty bland and actors are seldom allowed to go to town. This doesn't mean to say one can't have fun. On one occasion I was rehearsing a scene where the doctor I was playing was a patient. Halfway through rehearsals, a guy from the art department popped his head into the set and asked me the name of my character, because he had to make up a nameplate that would be placed above my bed. I told him my character was *'Dirk Diggler,'* – the porn star in *'Boogie Nights.'* My homage to Burt Reynolds. The art department guy left and soon was back with the name, which he stuck above my bed. No one noticed, and it went to air.

Judith McGrath is the ultimate Aussie professional television actress. I was looking forward to working with her, as her 'beau.' Less than a minute after we had started chatting at the read-through she told me, *"There will be no kissing."*

There wasn't.

Around this time I had an encounter with a well-known Australian director that at the time made me see red.

My agent called and told me that a casting agent had telephoned her saying that P.J. Hogan had specifically asked to see me regarding a role in his forthcoming film *'Peter Pan.'* Hogan had made two films that I thought were excellent, *'Muriel's Wedding'* and *'My Best Friend's Wedding,'* so I was definitely interested.

However, I was surprised because I'd been told that all the major and supporting roles had already been cast. However, since Hogan had personally asked to see me I drove over the Harbour Bridge to meet him.

When we met, he shook my hand warmly and we chatted for ten minutes or so about the production. Then he began to fill me in on the role he had in mind for me.

"It's a very important cameo. I pay great attention to the smaller roles because quite often they make or break a film." (These are my words, but based on my recollection.)

To my mind, he was dead right about the small roles. I listened some more.

"This character appears in just one scene," he said. *"But I think it's pivotal."*

One scene? Never mind – it's amazing what one can do in one scene. And 'pivotal' to boot!

"In fact, the character only has one line," P.J.Hogan continued.

One line?

Thoughts of Jack Palance's sage advice about his seven lines in *"Shane,"* sprang to mind. But this wasn't seven lines. Just one.

He picked up the script and carried on. *"It's a board meeting, you see, and Mr. Darling is chatting away about dogs."*

P.J was now getting quite animated; he clearly was going to enjoy his shoot.

"Then…suddenly…he can't think of a word. It's at this point that you lean across and whisper it into his ear. Kennel!"

I stared at Hogan. I resisted the temptation to stand and head butt the man. Had he really called me in to *audition* for a one-word role? I was flabbergasted.

"Let's do it a few times," he said.

I said the word 'kennel' twelve times. Don't ask me why, I think I was in shock. But on the sixth take I gave myself a limit. Twelve. Then I would poke him in the eye with a pencil.

He stopped on eleven, as though his guides were telling him enough was enough.

I left, smiling inanely.

I don't think he ever knew how insulted I was. He knew of my previous thirty-four feature films.

I was not offered the role. Since then I have discovered that many other seasoned Australian actors were asked to autition for the one-worder. I have no idea who landed the role. I hope he made the most of his split second in the sun.

'MURDER IN THE OUTBACK.'

'Murder in the Outback, the Story of Joanne Lees,' was the story of the terrible events that took place some years previously in Australia.

Joanne Lees and her boyfriend Peter Falconio were British tourists traveling around Australia when their car was stopped by a killer named Bradley Murdoch near Barrow Creek in the Northern Territory. Peter was ordered out of the vehicle and was never seen again – deemed murdered by Murdoch.

It was a fascinating case – the stuff of a great television film, so Granada Television and the New South Wales Film and Television office mounted a co-production.

Joanne Froggatt played Joanne and looked exactly like Lees. Richard Carter played Murdoch and was breathtakingly convincing. The barristers were Bryan Brown and John Wood. Spencer Campbell and Matt Carroll were the producers and the gifted Tony Tilse, with whom I'd worked several times before, was the director.

The story was researched within an inch of its life and I was asked to play the role of one of the two British journalists who were at the time closest to the action. My character, Richard Shears, was from the West Country of England. He wrote the novel, *'Bloodstain – the disappearance of Peter Falconio'*.

At the time of Falconio's disappearance he was working for the Daily Mail in London. I was sent a video by the producers, in which Shears talks about the case. The journalist had a very pronounced West Country accent – so pronounced that I knew I'd have to do some serious work on getting it right.

On my first day's filming I felt I had the accent nailed. It sounded a bit weird, but then broad West Country is a mouthful.

We rehearsed a few times. I noticed each time we cut that Campbell would stare at me and then whisper something to Tony. Eventually Campbell called out to me.

"What exactly are you doing, Shane?" he asked loudly.

I felt a bit stupid because Campbell was asking me this

question, as if I'd done something wrong. All the eighty of or cast and crew could hear him. Tony would never have done this, but for some reason he didn't say anything.

"Richard Shears spoke with a pronounced West Country accent. I was sent tapes. That's why I sound odd," I replied.

A long pause. Then Tony spoke, in a kind voice. *"I think we should lose the accent, Shane. It sounds ridiculous,"* he said.

"But…" I began again.

"Look, I appreciate it's accurate, but it comes out of left field like a cannon ball."

I lost the accent – but I tell you something, it's hard to do when you've had an accent in your head for a week.

During the shoot the director and producer conducted some very interesting experiments because they were curious about what so many people had found strange anomalies concerning Joanne Lees' version of events.

On the night of Falconio's disappearance, there was a full moon. A hell of a lot of people wondered how, on a night like that with a full moon and just short scrub around, Joanne could have hidden from the prowling Murdoch? Especially odd, since Murdoch had a dog with him. Surely the dog would have sniffed out Joanne Lees in a jiffy.

The scene was shot almost exactly where the incident took place.

First of all, the trained dog they hired refused to get out of the front seat, an identical white wagon to that of Murdoch, despite being ordered by its handler to do so. It was night and the hound was spooked. So maybe Murdoch couldn't get his dog out of the car either. That was our thinking.

To test whether Joanne Lees could have hidden from Murdoch, Spencer Campbell walked away from the set into the darkness and found that outside a perimeter of twenty feet he could see absolutely nothing but the moon above.

Doubly interesting.

I wonder what Richard Shears thought of my portrayal? Actually he wouldn't have known it was based on him as the production company altered my credit from *'Richard Shears'* to *'The Journalist.'*

It's disappointing when you can't be real and accurate just because people think an accent sounds stupid. I wonder if people in the West Country of England think they sound stupid too?

ALMOST AN OSCAR!

Most of the things I look back on I remember fondly, while others for some reason I choose not to remember. Perhaps it's because the film or television production doesn't turn out very well, so you forget it. Other moments you *prefer* to forget. Occasionally you remember a day such as when I was caught up in the power play between Peter Collinson and Michael Carreras and I instantly erase the memory.

In 2003 I was working on a screenplay idea I'd had for some time, titled *'Worst Nightmares.'* It was a concept very deliberately targeting the American *'Hannibal Lector'* market.

I'd loved Thomas Harris' *'The Silence of the Lambs,'* as well as both Anthony Hopkins' and Jodie Foster's performances, so I decided to write a thriller in the same genre, though it actually bore little resemblance to Harris' story – the 'darkness' was all.

The Vanguard Press hardback edition.

It concerned a man calling himself 'The Dreamhealer,' who has an Internet website where, supposedly, he finds cures for those who have terrible recurring nightmares.

In reality, he tracks his victims down and makes their worst nightmares happen somewhere far away from the madding crowd – amplified a hundred times.

I had been working on this project for over a year with a producer who had bought an option on it, when he asked me if I could come up with a script for a short film to showcase the talents of a well known and highly respected commercials director by the name of Richard Gibson who wanted to break into movies. I told my producer friend I'd give it a try, so I started thinking of suitable concepts. As I sat in my office thinking of ideas, my old friend Jeffrey Bloom emailed me. Since he'd written so many fine film scripts, I asked him if he had any brain-waves about my short film.

It took Jeffrey under a minute.

"Have you ever read 'An Occurrence at Owl Creek,' by Ambrose Bierce?" he asked me. *"It was made into a short film in 1962. The premise is all I suggest you work on. Put it into a modern context and you've got your script."*

I did some research and found the plot line. *'A Civil War civilian is to be executed by hanging, but when the plank is kicked away, instead of breaking his neck, he manages to miraculously escape unscathed. Or did he?'*

The idea had been used many times in films, most recently in Bruce Willis' *'The Sixth Sense,'* where both Bruce's character and the audience find out at the end that our hero has been dead all the time.

Having been given the idea, I immediately thought of Iraq. Instead of the Confederate Army executing a soldier, why not the execution of a businessman in Iraq? I'd been wanting to express my sorrow and horror at what was being done in Iraq in the name of religion. Here was the perfect opportunity to say something I believed in.

I wrote a second short story, but Richard liked what ended up titled *'A Message from Fallujah,'* best. So he got to work on the project, and like all directors, he began to make it 'his own.'

Without going too much into boring detail, Richard and I worked well initially, coming up with ideas that took the script forward.

Then he thought he'd make it better on his own, no longer discussing it with the writer. Oy!

We shot the film with Lance Henriksen in the lead role as the dead businessman. The first day we shot the Iraqi sequence on the sand dunes at the Kernel Oil refinery near Sydney airport the temperature soared to forty degrees Celsius. No need to light up the BBQ, just slide the meat on the bonnet of any car. The heat didn't stop Lance for a second. By contrast I almost passed out.

With Lance Henriksen and Wendy in that filthy heat!

The end result was a triumph – for Richard as director, Philip Rang as DP, and Lance as our lead. I couldn't have been happier.

With DoP Philip Rang on 'Fallujah.'

As it happened, the man who was to play a supporting role in the first scene couldn't make the shoot, so we had to find another actor. To my great surprise, both producer and director rubbed their chins. At such short notice, who could they find that might be up to scratch? Clearly they thought this a BIG problem. I humbly suggested that in view of my body of work playing leads in thirty-five feature films, I could help them out. They agreed, somewhat grudgingly I thought at the time. I didn't see them actually dance with pleasure.

A long time went by as the project went into editing and post-production. It lasted two months. I assumed all was going well because no one called me. Then out of the blue I got a call from the producer telling me in a very friendly chatty way that the director was asking me for half my writer's credit.

I was stunned. Why had he waited so long to even suggest such a thing? And why would he think he had changed the script to that extent?

I told the producer this was out of the question and his tone changed radically. And here was the thing – the film was about to be entered in various film festivals around the world, the deadline was just twenty-four away – if I didn't agree to their terms they would not enter the film in any festival at all.

Would you think this was a deliberate ploy? Many would.

If this kind of thing should ever happen to you, never cave in and think *'Oh my God, I've done all this work and unless I agree to their terms it will all have been for nothing.'* Don't do it. Be reasonable, sure. Don't roll over!

So, despite the threatening tone of my producer, I told him I was more than happy to have the Australian Writers Guild arbitrate on equal terms. If they thought Richard deserved half the credit – so be it. This seemed reasonable to me, but both director and producer would not have a bar of that – no arbitration. Instead they threatened to pull the film, saying they were saddened and offended at my unreasonable attitude. But by this time I was angry myself. The producer told me it would be my fault alone if the film wasn't in competition at the Montreal Film Festival, L.A Shorts, Palm Beach, and quite a few other festivals. And what did he suggest as a compromise? He suggested that I keep the 'Written by Shane Briant,' but there should be a separate credit later to the effect, 'Screenplay by Shane Briant and Richard Gibson.'

I told the producer that this was in no way the proper way to do things. It was a stupid credit that made no sense. But it seemed to placate Richard, so I let him have it. I had a very nasty taste in my mouth by this time.

In some ways I suppose I *did* give in. But I think arbitration is always the way. Let an independent body look at the facts and decide. Why would anyone not agree to that?

Wendy and I attended the Montreal Film Festival, and we had a ball. We didn't win, but we were very well looked after. And I got to meet the love of my teenage life, Anna Karina, the star of Jean Luc Godard's *'Pierrot le Fou.'*

At one of the daily cocktail parties I happened to see Anna sitting at a table with some younger people, one of whom was a very beautiful girl who was up for *'Best Actress.'* So I asked the festival director if he'd introduce me to Anna just for a couple of minutes. He said he'd be happy to do so, and led me over.

With French screen siren Anna Karina in Montreal.

At the table, during a pause in the general conversation, he said, *"Excuse me, this is Shane Briant from Australia who has written 'A Message from Fallujah.' He would love to meet..."* He paused and I saw the beautiful young girl wait for her name to be called.

"The woman Shane tells me he's been in love with all his life. Anna!"

The young girl stared at me, while Anna Karina laughed aloud. I actually preferred Anna to this young lovely – absolutely!

I sat next to Anna, had a drink, and we chatted – just for one minute. She looked radiantly beautiful, and a gorgeous sixty. It made the festival for me.

At the Montreal Film Festival with Wendy 1995.

As I left Anna, Wendy drew my attention to a group of four young people in one corner. They looked like they knew nobody.

"It's those Americans who were in that very, how shall I say, 'graphic' film we saw yesterday," she said.

I remembered the film well. It was yet another coming of age film set in America. The only thing I can remember now was that within five minutes of the opening of the film there's a three-minute sequence in a shower where the young lad masterbates very graphically. The scene seemed to drag on and on in lurid close-up until he achieved an orgasm. I couldn't fathom why we'd been treated to all of this. Nor could I understand the fact that every cast member masturbated during the rest of the film. It had a definitely documentary feel.

"No one's talking to them. They look so lost. Let's go over and say nice things about their film, eh?" Wendy suggested.

We walked over and introduced ourselves. A few moments later Wendy came up with this gem. *"We saw your film yesterday. You parents must be so proud of you."*

From Montreal I flew to Los Angeles. Wendy flew home to look after the cats – something she and I regret to this day because I wish she had been with me at L.A. Shorts.

Winner 'BEST IN FEST,' L.A. International Short Film Festival 1995.

'The Los Angeles International Short Film Festival' – such a mouthful that they call it *'L.A. Shorts'* – is an annual event with short films being invited from all over the world. In fact, it's the biggest short film festival in the world, as well as being the most prestigious.

Because the inspirational Jeffrey Bloom had steered me towards Ambrose Bierce's story, I insisted that he and his wife Carole attend the awards ceremony.

We sat with Richard Gibson near the front of the auditorium as the awards began.

Many people had said nice things about *'Fallujah,'* during the festival, so much so that our film was tipped as a front-runner.

To make the awards more interesting, the organizers stuck to the Oscar Format. Five names were read out, then the winner. When it came to *'Best Drama'* (we were one of the five) we didn't win.

I felt deflated. Richard looked as if he'd been snap-frozen in dry ice, and immediately walked out into the corridor to smoke a cigarette. The awards continued. As Jeffrey pointed out, there was still the *'Best of the Fest'* to go. A very long shot. Thank heavens Richard thought to return, because when it came to the last award we heard *'and the Best in the Fest is… 'A Message from Fallujah.'*

It was thrilling. Richard accepted all the prizes as director and made a speech about the current relevance in society of the film. I then stepped forward and thanked all the crew who had given their time free of charge and had worked tirelessly. Richard wandered off, while Jeffrey, Carole and I went out to a restaurant and celebrated. I called Wendy immediately and told her the great news – you can imagine how she felt to have missed out on this wonderful evening. It won't happen again.

All the winners at the various film festivals around the world are considered by the Academy Awards committee, and a lot of people in the know tipped us for an Oscar nomination, because L.A. Shorts is so highly regarded.

Wendy and I were skiing in Austria on the day the news of the nominations was revealed. We knew the time of the announcement, and we were expecting a telephone call should we be nominated. So we stopped skiing at 4 p.m. that day and sat with our gluhweins, waiting for the call. It never came.

One can't have everything, I say. Winning in La La Land was enough.

When I got home I continued work on a screenplay that Richard's company, Luscious International Films, had taken an option on. It wasn't the happiest time because of the fiasco regarding the credits on *'A Message from Fallujah.'* Everyone at Luscious made it clear that they thought I'd behaved badly by suggesting arbitration, so now it wasn't the same going to their offices. Before, I'd always got on well with everyone, had copious coffees and the occasional lunch. Now it was strictly business.

Of course I really should have seen it coming, but I didn't. I'd worked almost non-stop for two years with the Luscious producer on various versions of the screenplay. We'd look at the script together and he'd make suggestions. Lots of them. And so would I. That's the way it works – the producer looks at the writer's work and suggests how it could be bettered.

Around the twenty-second draft stage, out of the blue he said something to this effect – I can't remember the words, simply their import. *'I feel that I should get an equal writer's credit with you because I think I've come up with so much over two years.'*

It sounded like 'Groundhog Day to me. First *'Fallujah,'* now *'Worst Nightmares.'*

I remained calm, pointing out that the producer had in fact not written a single line – that had been done by me. He became defensive and instantly cold, telling me of all the ideas he felt he'd made that impacted on the script.

I had no alternative but to make it clear to him that business practice in America was this. The producer options a script. The writer either writes the script or starts writing it. At this stage the producer is still the producer and the writer is still the writer. During the time the producer and the writer work together, it is the function of the producer to say things like *'this is not right'*, *'this should come later,'* *'how about making the woman a man,'* *'how about having the man in a wheelchair rather than in a chair.'* This is commonly known as the producer guiding the script along. None of this logic helped. Again I was 'the bad guy,' and being incredibly difficult. I again suggested arbitration, since I had a fair idea about what the outcome would be bearing in mind that for two years I had typed every word into my computer. However, the more I suggested arbitration the angrier the producer became. Until we parted company and the option ran out. A shame. He had put a great deal of time and trouble into taking the script to Cannes and putting it about in L.A. but some people aren't content to be simply producers, they have to be writers too.

I haven't seen the producer or Richard Gibson since.

'GRAPHIC.' SYDNEY CRIMINALS.

In 2004 I published my fifth novel, *'Graphic,'* about a graphic novelist who undergoes a curious personal metamorphosis in which he feels himself changing into his fictional tough guy, *'Sainte Claire.'*

As soon as the manuscript had been expertly edited by Wendy, I contacted Harper Collins Australia, so that we could again work together and make money; me as publisher, they as distributors.

I was referred to the new distribution manager. He told me rather coldly that Harper Collins Australia had made a decision to no longer distribute books not written in-house authors.

I was surprised to say the least, and put some figures to him. I estimated they had made close to $50,000 distributing my last two books while I was an independent author.

It took the new distribution and marketing manager a few seconds to compose a plausibly logical explanation for not wishing to make another $50,000, while not stretching the sales team one iota.

"It's...er...a policy decision," he replied.

"Can you give me any logical reason this decision was made?" I asked.

"It wasn't me that made it, Mr. Briant. So, no, I can't."

"But you are in charge of distribution and marketing, aren't you?" I wasn't letting him off the hook so easily.

"Yes, I am but...er...it's policy. So I can't help you." He would have obeyed any order in Nazi Germany.

So I contacted another distribution company and had my books printed in Hong Kong – they do a good job there and, much as I would have preferred to use Aussie printers, as an individual I simply couldn't afford it. They were much more expensive.

'Graphic' is about criminal power struggles between the Aussie crims in Kings Cross, and the new Vietnamese crims in Paramatta. It had been a joy to write as there was a lot of humour in the book, and it goes without saying there was a great deal of me in the central character – a man who would love to be a tough guy.

Research?

I called the Paramatta Police station and asked to speak to a detective, explaining I was writing a thriller. I was immediately transferred to Chief Superintendent Deborah Wallace, who was cleaning up the Paramatta district. She invited Wendy and me to visit the station and promised to show me around her 'patch.'

She was nicely down to earth and not in the least stuffy. As she drove us around her area, she told me so many stories that my pen was practically white hot as it sped across my research notebook.

Chief Super Wallace is an inspirational cop respected by everyone including the local crims. All the petty criminals and dealers in Parramatta respectfully called her *'Ma'am,'* and in return she showed them respect. For instance, rather than publicly cuffing offenders and putting them in a paddy wagon, she'd tap the offender on the shoulder and tell him to present himself at the cop shop within the hour where he'd be charged. In this way the Asian criminal didn't lose face. They always arrived within the hour.

At 1 p.m. she took us to a local Vietnamese restaurant she was fond of. All the locals treated her like a friend because she'd brought the crime rate down by leaps and bounds.

"Try the 'Cop Soup'," was her suggestion as I read my menu. *"It's what all my officers choose to eat."*

I asked her what was in it, and she replied, *"Everything! The police in my station can never make up their minds what they want so Nuguen made up a soup dish especially for them. It has beef, prawns chicken, vegies...everything!"*

Detective Superintendent Deborah Wallace went on to become Commander of the Asian Crime Squad, and then Commander of the Middle Eastern Crime Squad. In 2011 she was awarded the Australian Police Medal in the New Year's Honours list. She'll be the Chief of Police soon. Bank on it!

When *'Graphic'* was published it received some great reviews, so much so that I entered it in the New South Wales Writer's Centre Awards.

What a surprise it was when I received a telephone call from the organizer of the award, Irina Dunn, to tell me I had won the Best Fiction award!

Well, let's be honest, what does a writer do when he or she wins a lovely fiction award? He or she tells the world at large! I started with Wendy, who was delighted, then told her family, then my friends, then everyone I passed in the street!

So here's one small piece of advice. Keep your powder dry for a few days, as with 'Veronica Clare.' There may be big problems ahead!

A week down the line, Irina called again. Her tone was subdued and a trifle conciliatory. "I am afraid we cannot allow you to win the award, Shane."

"But it's too late for that Irina, I've told everyone," I replied, hugely disappointed. I was going to look like a complete ass.

"The thing is, it's an Australian driven award and in the fine print you should have read that it's only open to books that are 100% Australian. 'Graphic' was printed in Hong Kong!"

Much as I argued the toss, pleading I'd be a laughing stock, she wouldn't budge – rules were rules,' But Irene has a good heart, so she came up with a face saving idea. The Best Fiction Award would go to someone else, while I would receive a new award.

You won't believe this, but this was the award; '2006 Best Self-Published Book Disqualified from Competition.'

Pretty wonderful, no? No.

No mention why I'd been disqualified – that was left to the imagination. Possibly the author had been caught with an underage girl, or had held up a bank, or the novel was considered too prurient and unsuitable for anyone other than deviant adults?

That award was my first literary award till now.

Wendy in Kings Cross, Sydney pretending to be a hooker for 'Graphic.'

COMMERCIALS!

JAMES BOND. AND 'M.'

Practically all actors make heaps of money making commercials because they've become famous – some can name their price. Even Olivier did the odd advertisement or two. And why not, some are short, witty and beautiful films.

Joan Collins and Leonard Rossiter in the famous 'Campari' commercials are examples of hilarious *coupes de film*. Those beautiful *Hovis* ads, directed by Ridley Scott were superb; brilliant, evocative, appetizing!

My personal favourites are the Al Pacino Vittorio coffee series, directed by the great Barry Levinson. Brilliant short films, performed with consummate ease that sell the product beautifully and are both amusing and tongue-in-cheek. And the *Dos Equis* commercials featuring Maximillian Schell. Wonderful!

Over the years I have been saved from penury many times by commercials – they always seemed to come along just when my back was to the wall and I worried about bills.

My first ad featured 'Hamlet Heaters' in Dublin after I'd played the role at the Eblana Theatre. Looking back at that ridiculous stitched-up photo of me in my black velvet coat I cringe. It saved my bacon then.

In America the actor gets a very small fee for showing up at the shoot, but is compensated by getting another small fee each time the commercial is aired. These are called residuals. So if it's for *Maxwell House* and shown for six months across America, that's amounts to a fortune.

Here in Australia, it's all up front; the fee and all the possibilities of how the fee might be augmented by street poster campaigns and the like.

I remember making two advertisements for *Colombian Coffee*

way back. Both were directed by one of Australia's best commercials directors, Pete Cherry, and produced by Paul Ibbetson. Both Pete and Paul became great friends over the years and without their commercials some years would have been very lean.

The first Colombian coffee commercial was shot in Australia for transmission in America. The deal was a buy-out–you get a certain amount of money and that's it. No more.

The ad, set on the Titanic as it went down, has been posted on YouTube because of its quality and popularity. As is the sequel, an advertisement shot on a wonderful replica of the Orient Express. Sitting in the train, you could easily imagine you were in the real thing.

One of Pete's little secrets, and something that makes his commercials so special, is his attention to detail. For instance, before we shot the Colombian ads he chatted to every single extra in the carriage and gave them a 'story' – why they were in the train that particular day. And because they felt the director considered their performances important, they worked more happily, injecting just the right amount of creativity to their performance.

"You are an old roué, married to an old bag, taking this delightfully young and beautiful girl to Venice to have your way with her," I heard Pete tell an elderly extra sitting at a table with a lovely young female extra. His performance in the background is a joy to watch.

The coffee ads ran for about six years across America, and Paul Ibbetson once calculated that had I been on an American contract (with residuals) I would have earned around a hundred and sixty thousand dollars, rather than the fifteen I earned as a flat fee.

Funnily enough, many years later I was in Los Angeles for the pilot season, and Pete cast me as the father of the bride in an *'I Can't Believe it isn't Butter'* commercial. It's hard to recall exactly what my fee for the day was, but I think it was a matter of a few hundred dollars. It was a major campaign and the product was an important one, so the residuals would surely have amounted to six figures.

But, damn it! The editor's scissors removed me from the final cut and so I had to make do with the few hundred dollars.

In this way I missed out on the Colombian Coffee ad because I was on an Australian contract, and on the margarine ad because I was on an American contract. As 'Norma' says in 'The Naked Civil Servant,' 'c'est la vie, I 'spose.'

It's the humourous advertisements I remember.

I was in an hilarious *Marlboro* commercial where I played a MI6 big-shot about to take off in my private black chopper from a barge in Darling Harbour in Sydney when James Bond races to the helicopter to ask some last second question, but the MI6 hotshot is not listening. He pushes a button and the window slides up, trapping James Bond's cigarette in the window. Rather than give up his *Marlboro*, Bond clenches his teeth and is swept upwards into the sky. How much do we love our *Marlboro*?

It's quite difficult to keep track of everyone that you've worked with. I usually remember a face but often forget names. I remember once a middle-aged woman came up to me at a gallery opening, all smiles.

"Hello. It's Shane, isn't it," she said.

"That's right," I replied, not knowing quite what was coming.

"You played James Bond in that Seiko watch commercial!" she continued.

I couldn't for the life of me put a name to the face, after all the Seiko ad was now almost twenty years old.

"I was Lady Godiva!" she exploded.

"Of course you were," I managed quickly, as a vision of the young naked girl I'd worked with all morning flashed through my mind. How could I have forgotten Lady Godiva!

Not all commercials work out the way you hope. On one

occasion I was up for a very lucrative commercial, and I knew the director very well indeed. In fact I'd given him a free option on my novel *'Graphic,'* and we'd been working on the script for over a year by then. I thought the job had to be in the bag.

Not so.

When I arrived for the final recall, I saw my old friend Barry Quin waiting to go in. I remember feeling a bit bad that Barry had no way of knowing the Kiwi director and I were best buddies and so he'd fix things for me. I was so certain about how things would turn out that I joked with Barry on the way out.

"How about his, Barry. There's just you and me left in the mix. Why don't we agree to share the fee now, so that the worst scenario is sixteen grand?"

Of course I wasn't serious, especially because I was certain the entire fee was mine anyway. I just thought the idea was an amusing one. If I'd landed the role, I'd have been a big pickle!

Next day, Barry landed the role. I continued working with the Kiwi director for another year, at which stage he lost interest in my screenplay project and just walked into the sunset. A free option is never a good thing, unless you know the director isn't going to get bored after you've put in a year's work with six drafts. It's the old 'free lunch' thing.

One last memorable commercial was one filmed for the Italian market starring Megan Gale – Australian supermodel – a girl who can no longer walk down any street in Italy without being swamped with fans. She has been Italy's reincarnated Sophia Loren for years now.

In the commercial, for an Italian telecom company, Megan is my CIA operative. She arrives in a very cool, classic, open-topped American car, and stops atop a dusty hill somewhere very barren. Almost immediately, a jet-black chopper appears out of nowhere with me inside. Megan hurries over to the still-hovering chopper and I give her a plastic card, telling her to *'look after herself,'* in

Italian.

Megan was very provocatively dressed in a low cut summer dress. She looked mouth-watering, while I looked like I'd been to hell and back with one glass eye and a scar that led from my forehead to my chin.

Beautifully shot in Broken Hill by Pete Cherry, I had the fun of spending hours in the chopper with Gary Ticehurst – the best chopper pilot in Australia bar none. In between takes he'd take me on jaunts around the plain, looking for kangaroos, and generally swooping across the landscape. Amazing!

Gary Ticehurst on a Sony ad in the Phillipines.

The final shot was looking out towards the approaching chopper as it weaves in between the huge electricity pylons. Had I not had Gary sitting beside me I might have been obliged to change my trousers later, but as it turned out it was safe as houses and looked terrific.

Big time CIA bad guy.

The Bigpond DVD rental campaign, *'Come Home to a Movie,'* was great to work on. The concept? An average family orders three DVD's and while they're out the three DVDs turn up in the house in person, and they have an armed standoff. One character is one of the *Blues Brothers*, another is one of the *Men in Black* and I was Harvey Keitel from *Reservoir Dogs*. We did a lot of pointing guns and shouting. Finally the family arrives home and one of us says, *"Hey, we're the DVD's you ordered."*

We even had *'Frank the Pug,'* a dog identical to the one in *'Men in Black.'* The dog had the punch-line. Check it out on YouTube.

At home, pretending to be Harvey Keitel in the Telstra commercial.

Very occasionally a friend tells me he's seen me on some billboard in Bangkok. That's the time to get your agent to check it out.

One last thing about commercials. One day you go to a casting where they're looking for a six foot, Caucasian, fair-haired actor with blue eyes, a BBC accent, experience in films and TV and you don't get the role – it goes to a woman, standing five feet nothing, with dark curly hair and a lisp. The next week, you think twice about turning up for an audition for the role of the ninety-year-old African American with a very strong Deep South accent, but you do just to please your agent. Guess which role you always seem to get and what you miss out on?

Many years ago I went to see Peter Bogdanovic at Fox Studios. He was about to make a film about Robert Wagner and Natalie Wood.

I'm not sure which role I was up for, but when I arrived in the outer office the producer, Richard Fischoff, took one look at me and called out loudly to Bogdanovich in the inner sanctum. *"Hey, Peter! We've got Christopher Walken here!"*

Bogdanovich came through to check out what all the shouting

was about. He smiled at me. *"No shit, Richard. It's Walken. But who the hell are you really?"*

I introduced myself, adding, *"I guess being Walken's good? In this film anyway."*

"'Fraid not, Shane. We want the twenty-five year old version. You look like," he looked me up and down, *"Forty plus?"*

The reason I mention this incident with Bogdanovic is because in 2010 my agent called me about a commercial. It was for a Sunday newspaper that was giving away CDs of Michael Bublé singing Christmas songs. They wanted someone to dance wearing a cool custom-made Santa suit as Bublé sings his new song. But here was the thing – they were thinking of Chris Walken's performance in the 'Fat Boy Slim' music video that everyone's seen on YouTube.

I was excited. This was good money, and people who knew me, such as Bogdanovic and Fischoff thought I was Walken's dead ringer. Not only that, but by pure chance I knew the video well and actually had a suit the same style *and* the same colour!

I worked all morning on the moves and even put one down on video and uploaded it on YouTube to see if anyone thought I was any good. The reaction was super. Surely this was in the bag.

I went to the casting and danced like a madman.

Two days later I was put on hold for the commercial. I wasn't too surprised – I felt no one could look like Walken quite the way I did, nor dance. Wrong. The role went to an older actor with white hair who happened to have been a principal dancer with the Australian ballet. Months later I watched the ad. The red suit looked great, the actor's white hair was perfect. The dancing was fantastic. Of course he didn't look at all like Walken, but the client didn't give a damn. My advice is this. Look for the Amazonian pigmy roles if you want to be in with a chance.

WEDDING IN THE SNOW.

THE LONGEST ENGAGEMENT IN HISTORY?

For many years prior to 2005 I'd considered various scenarios for the perfect marriage ceremony. I'd met Wendy in the summer of '76 on a tennic court in Battersea Park and for one reason or another we'd never tied the knot – neither of us thought the actual ceremony was something worth wasting large amounts of money on. As far as I was concerned I had a horror of church weddings with all the relatives, *'dressed up and looking in their prime'*, getting teary and drinking too much. So Wendy and I had put marriage on the back burner for twenty-nine years.

In 2004 I had an idea for a very unusual wedding. We'd go skiing in Austria, as we had each year for some time, and I'd arrange a surprise wedding half way up a mountain. Wendy wouldn't know anything about it until the time came to tie the knot. We'd wake up one morning in our hotel, have a champagne breakfast, step into our skis and take the lift to the top of the mountain. Halfway down the mountain I'd arrange to have a celebrant, two witnesses and a lavish lunch ready in my favourite restaurant.

Ultimately there were so many things I feared might not work on the day, that I knew I'd have to can the surprise element. It was only fair that Wendy be allowed to accept my formal proposal, rather than being offered a *fait accompli.* And what girl likes to be dressed in ski clothes on her wedding, clothes she hasn't bought especially for the occasion? And the make-up? And the hair? And the flowers? So many things to think about. So I ended up telling her my plans and she seemed to like the idea. It was the snow element, I think. I asked our great friend, hotelier Daniela Pfefferkorn, daughter of famous Austrian hoteliers, Franz and Gucky Pfefferkorn if we could be married on the deck of their fabulous hotel in Lech, the *Alter Goldener Berg.* We wanted a very simple affair; just the two of us, an Austrian celebrant and two witnesses. Franz and Daniela offered their serves in this regard – a big deal in Austria since witnesses at a marriage are in some sense responsible from that day on for the happiness of the bride and groom.

The morning of our wedding day in Lech, Austria. Haus Melitta.

We woke up in the Haus Melitta to a perfect day – blue skies and sun. It had recently snowed, so the piste conditions were perfect too. Frau Mathis served up a champagne breakfast I will remember forever, and we couldn't have been happier.

Later in the morning, we walked into town and I bought Wendy's corsage. Then we headed up the mountain.

Our good friend, Vietnamese/Australian-born clothes designer Alistair Trung had designed Wendy's wedding veil, many yards of beautiful fabric he wound around her white fur hat (no real animals involved!) in a fabulously original way in his showroom in Sydney. Wendy took the instructions so she'd know how to assemble it with hatpins in Austria later.

It's really hard to swoosh down the mountainside in a wedding dress, so Wendy wore a white jacket, white pants and white skis and boots.

At midday exactly Wendy and I were at the top of the mountain. I was to ski down to the hotel to let them know she'd be down in ten minutes. Wendy was to ski to another hotel where she'd stop to wrap her veil and make any final adjustments she wanted.

I then skied down to meet with our celebrant, Stefan Jochum.

Daniela had arranged a lovely table covered with traditional Austrian hearts made of twigs, dyed red, as well as other beautiful floral arrangements. There were four seats for the ceremony. I was introduced to Daniela's father Franz, who was freezing cold as I recall despite it being sunny. I think he was the only one of us who felt cold on the day. As I saw Wendy skiing down towards us, I was then amazed to see all the staff of the Alter Goldener Berg emerge, dressed in dirndls and lederhosen, forming up in a guard of honour leading from the ski slope to the wedding table. They were all carrying freshly cut long-stemmed red roses.

When she reached the guard of honour I could see that Wendy was stunned. She took off her skis and walked forward, looking absolutely beautiful. Ahead of her a young girl carried a basket of rose petals that she scattered on the ground as she walked forward – a carpet for Wendy to walk over. It was bliss.

I asked Stefan if he could read out my vows in German (just for old times sake, as I'd spent all those years as a child in Germany) and he agreed. Wendy glanced curiously at me when the German bit stated, as she didn't speak the language. Later I told her I had agreed to honour and obey till death parted us. Unless I changed my mind. (Not true).

Half an hour later, after Stephan's very amusing speech – not in the least stuffy and formal – he pronounced us man and wife and Franz popped the bubbly. It was an exquisite moment.

Lunch followed on the deck of the Alter Goldener Berg, the part of the modern hotel that dates back to 1430. It was magnificent. We ate a traditional Austrian cream soup of wild mushrooms, followed by crispy whole duck, and free-range game hens in wild mountain berry sauce, ending with a most beautiful wedding cake.

Wendy with Daniela Pfefferkorn and her father Franz.

Throughout, the sun shone down on us as though Mother Nature's Austrian representative was giving us his / her blessing.

Before we skied down to the village we were invited into the smallest and loveliest of rooms in the hotel, lined with wood that dates back five hundred years, and we drank some very old schnapps from glasses that had two-foot stems.

We skied down far too fast. But we made it. And guess what's the first thing we did when we took off our skis in the village of Lech? We headed for the nearest après ski bar and had a few more celebratory glasses of champagne. Everyone in the bar guessed we had just married because of our clothes – Wendy was all in white and I was wearing a silver ski jacket with a rose pinned to the lapel. We made many new Austrian friends that afternoon!

Celebrating our wedding in a Lech après ski bar.

I think this is the best way to get married. It doesn't have to be in the snow, it can be anywhere unusual. Of course, if you want a hundred people at your wedding and feel like spending many thousands of dollars, then be formal.

As I lay awake in the Haus Melitta that night, I remember thinking how lucky I was. Wendy was a female Dorian Gray, the perfect companion, she shared my sense of humour and was incredibly supportive. And now I had second family – a mother-in-law, Olive, and two sisters-in-law, Jilly and Robby.

La Familia Lycett. I call them the Lycett Mafia.

THE MAJOR LEAGUE AGAIN.

CHINA AND BOLLYWOOD! SPOTTISWOODE AND JOFFE.

It's always the same, just when you think to yourself, *'Hey, I haven't made a serious film for a while,'* one tends to pop up out of the blue.

So it was with what was originally titled *'The Children of Huang Shi,'* and became *'Children of the Silk Road.'*

It was directed by Roger Spottiswoode, the highly respected award-winning director of films such as *'Air America,' 'Turner and Hooch,' 'And the Band Played On,'* as well as *'Tomorrow Never Dies.'*

It was filmed entirely on location in China and starred Yun-Fat Chow, Radha Mitchell and Jonathan Rhys-Meyers, as well as the actor who played *Strang* to my *Dysart* in *'Equus'* all those years ago – David Wenham. My role was little more than a cameo, but as we all know by now it's not the length of the role that matters. A few weeks after being cast, I was flying to Shanghai. Out of interest I'd asked my wonderful agent, Monica Keightley, which hotel I'd be staying at in Shanghai and she'd informed me I was booked into the Hyatt. Naturally, as an actor, I immediately Googled the joint.

'Situated in the heart of Pudong, overlooking the world famous Bund, the Hyatt Shanghai is all about five-star luxury.' That's what I read. Very nice indeed.

There was a car at *Pudong* airport on my arrival. Forty minutes later we seemed to be heading into an industrial wasteland. We'd passed the *Bund* thirty-five minutes earlier, and since my driver couldn't speak English I had to wait and see where I'd end up. We halted outside a very nice hotel. I looked up at the name. It was 'The *Hyaart* Hotel.' It turned out to be the very comfy hotel where the bulk of the cast and crew were staying. Jonathan, Yun-Fat Chow,

Rhadha and David had insisted on being one star better – and on the *Bund*. But to give him his due, Roger was happy enough at the *Hyaart*, as was I.

I was only in Shanghai for one week. My scenes were set in a 1930's nightclub around the time of the fall of Nanking.

The shoot took place in an amazing ballroom with a spectacular '30's band and a Eurasian singer.

'I never met Radha nor Yun-Fat. My scenes were with Jonathan, David and a young Aussie by the name of Matt Walker.

When they came to cast the extras for the ballroom scene, there simply weren't sufficient white-skinned ladies to be had in Shanghai – the script called for a hundred or more young lovelies. There was only one recourse – several assistant directors were sent out to scour the best houses of ill repute in Shanghai to ask if any of the 'girls' would care to come and film with us. Most were delighted to have a more relaxing day at work, sitting down rather than prone. And most were stunning Russian beauties.

With David Wenham and Jonathon Rhys Meyers in 'Children of the Silm Road.'
Amongst all the Russian 'ladies.'(Shanghai)

Xiaoding Zhao was the director of photography. He spoke no English. In order to work with Roger, Zhao had an interpreter – a sweet bilingual Chinese girl aged eighteen.

From what Roger told me, the way the Chinese shoot is very different from that in America, Australia or Europe. To begin with the camera department doesn't keep camera sheets, so neither the director nor the DoP has any way of looking back and seeing what lens he used in a close-up the day before; he has to rely on his memory. Nor is there any continuity person, so if you are reading a newspaper in a wide shot, it's up to you to remember to have it open at the same page for your single.

It was fun working with David Wenham again. By then he'd become a star in Australia, and had played *'Faramir'* in the *'Lord of the Rings – The two Towers,'* and *'The Return of the King.'* Roger was a lovely man to work with – will must see how I can inveigle myself into one of his forthcoming productions.

Sometime in September 2010 my agent at Mollison Keightley, Tracy LeMin called with some very exciting news. As ever, the best news comes out of left field when you're least expecting it.

Roland Joffe was casting in Australia for his forthcoming film, *'Singularity,'* to be shot in Queensland and India. It would star Josh Hartnett and Bollywood superstar Bopasha Basu.

It's an epic story set across two time periods and continents. The plot involves a British officer in colonial India, Hartnett, the Indian woman he falls in love with, Bopasha Basu, an American marine biologist, Hartnett again, and his lover, a researcher played by Olga Kurylenko who is trapped in a wrecked British merchant ship.

I met with Roland, a man I'd admired since I'd seen the miraculous *'The Mission,'* and we chatted for ten minutes or so about all manner of things. He didn't ask me to read or put anything on tape. This took me back to my London days when directors took it for granted you were a good actor if the casting director said so.

Ann Fay, a wonderful casting director and even more wonderful friend, cast the film in Australia. She'd thought of me for the role of 'The Governor of Bombay.' It was a lovely cameo and just the kind of rich character I love to play. I couldn't have been happier when I heard that Roland had cast me.

I flew up to Queensland on the 11th of November and we shot the following week in a magnificent building that once was home to the Governor General of Queensland.

With directorial legend Roland Joffe on the set of 'Singularity.'

I'm not sure if Roland would like me to reveal his very individual rehearsal techniques, so I won't. Suffice it to say, they were a revelation to me and they worked wonderfully well. By the time we finished that day, we all had an intimate knowledge of our characters from their upbringing in England, to their moral and ethical beliefs. This paid huge dividends when we came to shoot the scenes.

My scenes involved a great deal of dining – there was a magnificent stilton right in front of me, so I worked it into the scene and ended up eating far too much.

As it was set in 1887, it was the custom to relieve oneself when necessary into chamber pots that were concealed behind screens. Roland thought it'd be a nice touch to begin one scene with the Governor pissing behind a screen while he chatted to his colleagues about the Maratha tribe. As ever, his direction was superb. *"We can only see your head, but I want you to demonstrate three things. Finishing peeing, putting it away, and then buttoning up. One, two three. Okay?"*

Say no more, I whispered to myself.

I've worked with great directors over the years, but that week with Roland was especially enjoyable. As was meeting Josh, who all the production runners referred to as *'Josh Heartthrob.'*

I also had the pleasure of working with some wonderful Aussie actors, including the very funny and bombastic Bille Brown.

OLD FARTS AND PEDOPHILES.

In 2009 I radically changed my eating habits. I'd seen the production called *'Rogue Nation'* on Australian television and felt I looked far too fat.

I'd played Lord Camden, Colonial Secretary, and was again directed by Peter Andikidis. But I was so shocked by my look I resolved that no calories would pass my lips until I had reached 82 kilos – I was 88 at the time.

It wasn't so hard.

I was cast that year in a U.K. / Australian television movie called *'False Witness'* in Oz and *'The Diplomat'* elsewhere. Dougray Scott, Rachel Blake and Richard Roxburgh lead the cast. As I was, shall we say, an older cast member, I was again cast as the head of MI6. Peter Androkidis directed impeccably and it ended up a very good show, I think. Richard Roxburgh was an inspiration to work with. It was all about terrorosts. Dougray played a British diplomat arrested and charged with working for the Russian Mafia. Don Hany was a newcomer then – not so now. He was the nasty Ruskie. Claire Forlani played the love interest. I've always warmed to movies about nuclear disasters – I've no idea why, they simply terrify me – so I liked this plot because bad things DO happen.

Richard Roxburgh in 'False Witness.'

I also appeared in an episode of the hugely popular television series, *'City Homicide,'* created by John Banas. The real lure of this job was firstly that I'd be directed again by Pino Amento, and secondly because my character, an aggressive gay pedophile, was so disgustingly interesting.

I wanted to give the audience a *real* insight into this kind of person, based on proper research – to give him colour and dimensions, a little light and shade. I'm more and more certain that sexual deviants are not, as most people might think, born bad, nor are they one hundred per cent evil. They acquire their sexually different tastes because of their childhood experiences. It would have been easy to simply play an evil person.

The episode was called *'Stolen Sweets,'* and there were two things that occurred that I remember well.

The first was rehearsing an interrogation scene.

One of the detectives, superbly played by Aaron Pedersen, was grilling me really hard throughout the scene, leaning in closer and closer to my face as he did so.

So I had an idea. What if my character, a Pastor by the name of Nieman, responds by teasing the detective sexually – indicating that he finds him sexually inviting. It was an easy device to introduce, since my only responses to his tirade were a succession of the word, *'Yes!'* So I gave it the element of *'When Harry Met Sally,'* and each time he asked me a hard question I would reply, *'Yes,'* raising the orgasmic intensity of the word each time as I stared into the young detective's eyes. When we finished the take, there was a curious silence in the room. I looked around and I saw a lot of faces, staring at me in disgust.

"It's not me – it's the character!" I found myself saying aloud. The editor chose to edit around my sexual innuendo. Probably right.

AMERICAN BOOK TOUR!

BREAKING INTO THE AMERICAN MARKET.

In 1995 I did my best to secure a literary agent in America. I knew that if I were to make any serious money from my books I'd need to be published there. Australia was all very fine, but the population is small.

And though I'd been published by Harper Collins Australia in Oz, that didn't necessarily mean Harper Collins U.K. would publish it in England. You'd think Harper Collins U.K. would want to take advantage of a Harper Collins Australia writer. But no. Quite the contrary. The attitude in England despite the common Harper Collins name, is 'We've got plenty of our own writers, thanks.'

An averagely successful trade format print run might be twenty thousand books in Australia, but half a million in the U.S.A. This was, of course, before the GFC – the Global Financial Crisis.

I couldn't have picked a worse year to debut in America!

Back then in 1995, I feared it'd be practically impossible to interest an American literary agent in my work, but I was going to give it a try – after all, I did have a film and television profile going for me which might make promoting me in America as an author a trifle easier.

So I looked up names of literary agents in the Writers Handbook, and compiled dossiers. Forty of them. They contained my film and television biography, a letter written by my then commissioning editor at Harper Collins, Louise Thurtell, in which she referred to me as 'a highly prized author,' various photos of me in movies, a sample chapter of 'The Webber Agenda,' and some great reviews.

A month passed. Then the replies began to trickle in. There were seven replies and thirty-three no-shows.

Seven was enough for me – I booked a ticket to New York and was off within the week.

When I arrived in the Big Apple, I called each agent and organized interviews. Some agents were lovely but said it'd be too hard to introduce 'an Australian' to the American market because publishers would think of me as a foreigner. Some agents had a single room on the sixth floor of a 'walk-up' on the lower east side. Others simply couldn't be bothered.

I'm sure it'll sound as though I'm making it up, but it eventually came down to the last literary agency, Curtis Brown Ltd, probably the most prestigious agency in the world. I had a heavy heart going in, as I knew I stood no chance.

Yet again it was a case of *'just when you think it's all over, your ship comes in.'*

A receptionist directed me to a room at the end of a narrow corridor. I knocked.

"Come in," I heard from within.

I opened the door.

Sitting behind a desk was a lovely young woman. Fair haired, probably no more than thirty, dressed in a smart suit, smiling at me.

"Please, sit down," she said.

Twenty minutes later I was Laura Blake Petersen's client! I couldn't believe it.

Of course having the best literary agent in the world is just the starter. One has to write a book she can sell – that's the thing.

I couldn't ask her to try to sell *'The Webber Agenda'* because it wasn't new. So I sent her the sequel, *'The Chasen Catalyst,'* and although she did her best to find a publisher, it somehow didn't have that 'wow' factor. Mainly, I believe, because it was set in England.

Eighteen months later I sent her *'Hitkids.'* Yet again she went in to bat for me. Two years later I sent *'Bite of the Lotus.'* This time she told me she'd come close to a deal but the publisher she'd had in mind (Heinemann, I believe) told her that though he liked the book a lot, they only had room for 'one financial thriller' that year, and they'd had to choose between me and Frederick Forsyth. Hmmm. Some choice.

Another two years and I sent her *'Graphic,'* knowing in my heart of hearts it would be an impossible sell since it was so essentially 'Sydney Underworld.'

Through all these years, Laura never lost faith in me or told me to get lost. Stunning. Never had she said, *'Hey, Shane, it's a lost cause. I'm afraid I can't do this any more.'*

In 2004 I sent her the manuscript of my sixth novel, *'Worst Nightmares.'* It was thirteen years after our first meeting, yet she still agreed to do her best.

I recall her sending me emails. One said that there were seven publishers on her list. Then there were six. Then five. Finally there was one publisher left. *'But the seventh has shown interest, Shane,'* she said. *"The Vanguard Press. It's a division of Perseus Books."*

I immediately Googled Vanguard. Their watchword was *'A Unique Collaboration Between Author and Publisher.'*

This sounded promising. At last a publisher who would work really closely with the author and they would have belief in each another. Vanguard didn't believe in advances. In return for no up-front money, the author received a bigger slice of the action. That suited me because I felt more confident about *'Worst Nightmares'* in the American market than any of my previous books.

'Worst Nightmares' was originally my screenplay. Usually screenplays come after the novel. Not this time.

'A serial killer professes to cure the nightmares of his cyber patients, but rather than offering a cure, he tracks down his favourites and visits their worst nightmares on them.' That was the gist of it.

Laura initially told me she had never read such a *'brutal'* novel, but had enjoyed the read enormously and felt it had a great chance of being published. She knew her stuff, and she was right.

Two weeks later she emailed to the effect that Vanguard Press would make an offer if I agreed to come to America at my own expense to promote the book at Book Expo America.

With Amanda Ferber at Book Expo America.

Wendy and I attended Book Expo America and stayed with our friends Scott and Jennifer Citron in their apartment on West 100th Street.

I was so happy. I remember constantly singing the song *'New York, New York.'* *'If I can make it there, I'll make it anywhere.'* Ever the big kid.

Wendy and I met with Roger Cooper, my new publisher, at a wonderful steak house. Also present were his two right hand people, Georgina Levitt and Amanda Ferber. They were wonderfully upbeat and optimistic, despite the oncoming GFC. Roger made me feel much more secure when he told me he'd personally loved the book. *'We're in this for the long haul. If the first books start slow, we move on to the second. We believe in you.'*

Two days later Wendy and I attended Book Expo America, and I signed copies of *'Worst Nightmares.'* I wasn't at all sure that anyone would show up because my signing was on a Sunday. I could see that Roger wasn't so sure either. We needn't have worried since

Book Expo America is primarily a trade event, all publishers make a habit of giving books away to people who might later help either promote or stock the book. It was heady stuff to be in New York with a queue of people asking for me to sign my book. My book signing lasted close to two hours. I was relieved, as were Roger, Georgina and Amanda.

Wendy and I stayed for another week, strolling around Greenwich Village, Soho, Tribecca – all the iconic places.

'Worst Nightmares' came out in hard back during the worst year in publishing history. I was very lucky to be published in America, now I was not so lucky with my timing. Because of the GFC, publishers had practically no money to promote their books. Vanguard was a small company. The budget for my novel was cut in half almost immediately. The result was that sales were initially 'iffy'.

Roger had promised he'd launch a mass-market edition and he was true to his word. However, in those desperately troubled times all the publishing houses cut their print run dramatically because they were afraid they wouldn't be able to sell enough books. So my paperback print run was very small. And without sufficient money to promote it through advertising and other modes of promotion, it stood as much chance of making it as a cardboard box in the sea off Cape Horn.

I realized I stood a good chance of an early departure from the ranks of Vanguard authors, so I organized a book tour at my own expense. I felt at the time that if I put my own money where my mouth was I'd be demonstrating to Roger that I was in earnest. Georgina emailed me to say she was delighted, and would help me in any way she could.

The first step was to ask favours from my old friends Sheelagh and Nicky Hippisley-Coxe in California, and Scott and Jen in New York. I asked if I could come back and stay with them. I felt rather like Freddy Kruger, so I had to apologize. Fortunately, they were all happy to see me back – unless they were simply very good at faking it!

I engaged the service of a publicist called Jackie O'Neal and told her to see what she could come up with in terms of TV interviews, radio spots, and book signings. Anywhere in America. I was in this for the long haul and would stick around for eight weeks.

I started off by flying to California, and then waited for Jackie to do her work. Very shortly the interview schedule started to take shape, but as luck would have it, they were all over the place – with none in California.

Jackie booked me in on the *Ken Hudnall Radio Show* in El Paso, and then followed this up with a community television interview in Dallas Fort Worth.

Within a week or so the interview offers started to come in thick and fast, but it was hard to juggle them so they made geographical sense – I didn't want to be constantly back tracking, because the air fares were quite daunting.

I left Australia on April 3rd, flying to L.A. On the 6th I was in Dallas chatting to Cheryl Nason on her show at CCTV Dallas Fort Worth. The producer was a lovely guy called James Carter. That's where I lost my camera – in a bar.

The following day I called in an interview via my cell phone on the *Frank Truatt Morning Show.* His show covered northern New York State and sections of Westchester County. Around half a million listeners every day.

On the 8th I flew to El Paso to meet and stay with Ken Hudnall,. He was very hospitable, treating me like a long lost son and driving me all over El Paso to book signings at Borders and Barnes and Noble. He also took me to Frank's Mexican Diner. Amazingly hot food! Across the Mexican border one could hear the sporadic gunfire as the cartels in Juarez terrorized the locals.

Because Jackie couldn't find somewhere to go to from El Paso, I had to fly back to L.A. Nicky was surprised to see me so soon, and I felt bad. The alternative was a hotel at $250 a day!

The first day I was back I lost my first cell phone.

While in Venice, CA, I was interviewed via my cell phone by Dr Beth Erickson on *'Relationships 101.'* I don't know how many people she reached, but as they say, any publicity is good. (Can this really be true?) She was a sweetheart.

The Mike Bissell Show was next, one that covered most of Nevada – via telephone again. There followed the well known *'Mike Dresser Show.'*

On April 23rd, while I was being interviewed via phone link with radio KZSB, the host, 'Baron' Ron Herron asked me if I was coming to Santa Barbara. Without thinking, and eager to please, I replied, *"Certainly!"*

He then asked me when I was coming, and I spluttered, *"Er... tomorrow!"*

That was it; I was now locked into driving the two and a half hours to Santa Monica – with no book signing set up.

Tant pis. My fault.

Typical reader reaction!

It turned out to be a sunny day and I enjoyed driving Sheelagh's car.

When I arrived, I sought out Barnes and Noble and introduced myself; informing the manager I'd been on the local very popular radio show the previous day.

"That's wonderful!" he replied. *"Perhaps you can sign the books?"*

I told him I'd be delighted to.

He found two copies. I bought both myself because they had a policy of re-ordering when they ran out of supplies. I went next to Borders, across the road, somewhat deflated. They had one copy. I asked if they had a policy of automatic re-orders and they told me they did – so I bought the single copy myself - at full price. Then I found a Mexican bar and ordered a very large margarita.

I found the Santa Monicans – if that's what they're called – extremely friendly, and while in that Mexican bar I started up a conversation with a young guy wearing a Dodgers shirt and his baseball hat back to front. He asked me what I did for a living and soon he'd dragged out of me what I'd been doing that morning. He laughed loudly then beckoned the young barman over.

"Hey Danny. You gotta hear this. My friend here, Shane, comes all the way from Australia to sell his new book. He drives all the way up here from L.A., spends about thirty bucks on gas, and guess how many books he sold. THREE! Okay? Now guess who bought 'em? That's RIGHT. The main man!"

Peals of laughter all around. I had three more stiff drinks, sat around on the sand looking at the ocean until the booze wore off, then drove the two and a half hours back to Nicky's place.

Back in L.A. I was interviewed on *'Celebrity Stars with Mike Kurban.'* The show covered Las Vegas. Handy.

Then there was the rather spooky *'The Midnight Bookworm, with*

Vin Smith.' He was a great guy – lots of jokes there.

I stayed with Nick and Sheelagh until heading off for Sacramento by air a few days later – Jackie had arranged a book signing in Roseville, North Carolina, a town I was told was very picturesque.

At the airport I picked up a car rental. I'd done some online research and had been surprised to note that a rental in North Carolina cost just $17! An amazing find, I thought! It was at the airport that an employee of *Dollar Rentacar* informed me the actual cost was $17 per day for the car, plus $240 a day for full insurance. So, much leaner in the hip pocket, I set off on the Freeway with my *'Nightmare-Mobile.'*

I'd sticky-taped my two foot by three foot colour posters of *'Worst Nightmares'* to both sides of the car as well as the boot. Any publicity? Never mind. It never occurred to me that other road users might be intimidated by a big black limo (upgraded for free!) with posters stuck to it that screamed *'Worst Nightmares.'* Each time I cruised up to a traffic light and glanced to my right, I'd enjoy giving them 'the look.' Usually, they'd look at my posters, and look away.

The scary 'Nightmare-mobile.'

While in Roseville I hooked up on Skype with Mike Johnson of the *'Indie Media Show.'* The same afternoon, I drove to Borders for my signing. This time there were fifty books ready to sign and a picture of me in the window. I stayed four hours, during which time I signed five books.

Barnes & Noble Ashville.

The next day I drove to Sacramento and met up with my actress friend Annalisa Bastiani, and we toured around town looking for bookstores. We found one store with no books in stock, so we settled on lunch in the old town. Great food. No book sales.

I flew to Asheville the following day, but due to the incoming plane arriving too late I arrived in the town at 1 a.m. There were two cabs waiting outside the airport. The first cab driver looked like first pick for *'Serial Killer of the Century.'* He was six foot four, lean as a beanpole, wearing a dirty bowling shirt, smiling, and chewing gum like it was the everlasting chew. I glanced at the second cabbie – he was African American and looked like a regular guy – but I could hardly ignore 'the killer,' as he was first in the queue.

I got in the back of the cab, told him my hotel address, and wondered if this would be my last ride. The cab set off.

Fifteen yards later he stopped

"Well, dang! Looks lark ah got myself a flat!" the murderer said as he opened his driver's door. *"Marne if I put on the spare? You gart tarm?"*

Ultimately this cabbie didn't end up slitting my throat, and I arrived at my hotel just in time to get down to the *'Texas Bar'* fifty feet down the road, where they were still serving beers at 3 a.m.

The Manager in Roseville read a chapter – then gave me a second look.

Next day I was up at dawn, trying to track down the 'good guy' cabbie. I was eventually successful and the African American drove me to the television station for my appearance on *'The Morning Show.'* The station was *WLOS TV (ABC)* and my interviewer was the very cute looking Victoria Dunkle. She was a smart journalist, asking all the right questions, and practically demanded that anyone watching should head down to Barnes and Noble at 5 p.m. to meet me and buy my books. I was, as you can imagine, elated.

Actress Jen Perito and designer Scott Citron at breakfast in New York.

However, at 5 p.m. I was again reminded that book signings, unless you are the Pope, President Obama, George Cluney or Adolf Hitler come back from the grave, are a thing of the past. I sold a dozen copies. But Asheville is a lovely old town and I could understand why President Obama had put it on his list of places to campaign.

Two days later I did something no one in their right minds would think of doing – unless they are kids who want to do something unusual. I paid for a trip on a Greyhound Bus from Asheville, North Carolina, to New York, Penn Station.

I phoned Nicky, telling him my plans, and he told me I was 'bonkers.' I told him I was going to save several hundred dollars. Besides, I'd be sitting on a bus for twenty-two hours and I could watch America go by. And sleep.

What I never factored in was that the bus stops every two to three hours and everyone has to disembark – no reason given – and then everyone gets back on again. This means you can't ever sleep for longer than a nap.

So I bussed to Winston Salem, Greenboro, Danville, etc, etc, etc, till we arrived in Washington and I had a brief look at the Pentagon before finally entering New York at five minutes to two in the morning.

That was twenty-three hours later!

I was mentally trashed, but felt I couldn't turn up at Scott and Jen's at three in the morning, so I dragged my bag into Times Square. I figured I'd have a few drinks in a bar, take a look around, and have a bite to eat someplace.

Nah. Not possible.

Why do people call New York *'the city that never sleeps'* when it's so hard to find a bar or a restaurant open at 3 a.m?

I did eventually find an Irish bar, but everyone inside was screaming at each other, and the three TVs were all showing very violent professional cage fighting. I had one drink and decided to move on – the patrons looked too scary.

I love New York – especially the Campbell Apartment cocktail bar at Central station, around the side where no one goes. May I recommend the *'Planter's Punch'* with the inch of Moët Chandon floating on the top? Best drink on the world. Drink the punch through the champagne or use a straw. Perfect! And less than twenty dollars! I love the atmosphere and buzz of the city, and I like the attitude of the New Yorkers. So I spent a week having a great time with Jen and Scott, then took the Amtrak train to see my old friend, theatre maestro Vincent Dowling, the director of my first West End stage show, who was now living near Huntingdon in Chester.

Vincent has his own radio show once a week on *Valley Free*

Radio called *'Shootin' from the Hip.'* It's in Northampton Massachusetts and covers the five college area of the towns and universities of Amherst, Northampton, and Holyoke MA. Vincent is assisted once a week by Walter 'Golden Voice' Mantani. Together they rival any twenty-something shock-jocks. In the afternoon Vincent had arranged with a friend who owned a lovely gallery to have a *'Meet the Author'* function. It turned out to be quite a success, with more than thirty people turning up. Afterwards, we ate a stupendous pizza in a local restaurant, drank a lot of wine, and finally drove back to Chester. Two more days of fly-fishing with Vincent, and I felt re-energized and very ready to fly home to see Wendy and the kids (cats – Giblet and Freddy)

I was acutely aware that my sixteen thousand dollar investment had earned me very little. As it turned out, very little *indeed*. Despite all my running around America, Vanguard couldn't be convinced to plough more cash into the promotion of the mass-market edition, and consequently it fell flat on its face. The sequel, *'The Dreamhealer'* was not taken up by Vanguard despite their promises of *'being in it for the long haul because - we believe in you.'*

There are no two ways about it, business is always business. Major publishing houses can weather any storm, even the GFC. But small ones such as Roger's Vanguard simply don't have very deep pockets, so despite their best intentions they find it impossible to take a loss.

But I'd been there before, with Harper Collins Australia, who had also promised me a long career. So, knowing that Laura Blake Petersen would never give up on me, I made plans to publish the sequel on the Internet while I wrote my next masterpiece.

'The Dreamhealer' is now available on *CreateSpace* and *Amazon*, and as a download on *Smashwords*. Week by week I'm adding all my previous books as downloads. They should all be up by the time this book is published.

It's no use looking back – always look forward and see the emerging trends. In publishing it has to be the Internet.

Another Scottcitrondesign cover.

MONSTERS AND VAMPIRES AGAIN!

It's not difficult for older actors to think *'Am I ever going to get that fabulous role?'* or *'Am I going to have to accept that very dull television role?'* There are exceptions, but more often than not that great role doesn't eventuate.

Why?

Because the international film audience prefers to see young lions doing fabulous things. People they can identify with.

What about roles such as the wizards and masters of the universe, you might argue? The chances are theatre actors who have earned a knighthood, or those who have won major film awards'll snap them up.

No need to despair. Just look at Jackie Weaver! She's in her mid sixties, has done a mountain of great theatre, film and television work all her life, then lands a great role in 'Animal Kingdom,' and she gets a Golden Globe and an Oscar nomination. Fantastic! A few years ago I wondered how my career was traveling. Things were looking bleak. Then along came Roger Spottiswoode and he made my Internet Movie Database profile look a lot better. Then another year passed and I wondered if Australia's best directors would ever come back to Oz and offer me something so I could show the world what I can do. They didn't return, but who should appear out of the blue? A hero of mine since 'The Mission.' Someone I thought I'd never have the pleasure of working with.

Which only goes to show – no one can tell what's around the corner.

In 2010 I was getting to know people on the Internet that I never knew existed, let alone had ever met. I knew that if my books were going to sell I needed as many people as possible to know they were out there in the market place. Who better to contact than the people who had enjoyed my early work – work that had become almost a cult. Hammer horror films.

I chatted to countless people on Facebook, I 'twittered' daily and worked on my website to make it worth a visit. Robert Kenchington and Melissa Brooks even went as far as to create websites in my honour!

Slowly but surely I made a great many friends – people from all over the world that'd seen my films. I got messages from a girl named Anna in Tver in Russia, Suki in Tokyo, Trevor in Manchester, Lavinia in Budapest – you name it. All one of them were very genuine people and wished me well.

I make a habit of replying to everyone who writes to me or contacts me on the Internet. One day it may not be possible because my profile may be too huge. That's the time to hire assistants. I'm dreaming, of course.

One person who contacted me is my good friend Robert Kenchington. Once a journalist, often a composer and sometime conductor, he had been running his Internet CD business for years, and had always loved Hammer films. I just happened to be one of his favourite Hammer actors. He told me he'd written some gothic horror short stories and I offered to read them and let him know my thoughts. I was delighted (and relieved) to discover that they were very well written, and I told him so. He's told me since, that without this kind of encouragement at the time he contacted me, he might not have continued writing.

Recently I was guest of honour at the Bram Stoker Film Festival, wonderfully organized by Mike McCarthy. Marcus Hearn and Nick Ransom represented Hammer Films—now once more a force in films with the release of 'Let Me In.'

In the auditorium there was an amazing exhibition of all things Hammer, from life-sized models of Sir Christopher Lee and reproduction heads of 'The Monster From Hell,' to production designs and scripts.

With Sharon Ankin and baby Leo Hearn in Whitby

I sat at a table next to Hammer film lovelies Caroline Munro, Martine Beswicke and Vera Day, and signed photographs for hours on end – I had no idea Hammer had this cult following.

With Martine Beswick at the Vampire's Ball. Where else?

The 'Vampire's Ball' took place on the last Saturday. Everyone came dressed in extraordinary costumes dripping with blood and gore. It was a great event – I recommend it to all Stoker/Vampire/Monster aficionados. McCarthy is onto a winner here.

Since meeting Robert Kenchington in person we've had a great time making short amusing videos for YouTube. Just for the fun of it. His original idea was to make a series of short *'whatever happened to him'* videos about the various Hammer characters I played, so we made *'Straight on Till Midnight,' 'After Frankenstein,'* then followed these with *'Beyond Dorian,'* and a short film about Bram Stoker for Mike McCarthy called *'Bram Stoker, Vampire Master.'* They can all be seen on YouTube.

Robert became my self-appointed biographer and published several picture books based on my films; *'Shane Briant, A Talent for Terror,'* and *'The Hammer Years.'* I recommend his book of short stories called *'The Chamber of Screams;'* it's very chilling.

At the end of my week in beautiful Whitby I returned to Australia and opened my mail to find my book royalty checks from Curtis Brown – a life saver! Then I began editing the sequel to *'Worst Nightmares,'* an even darker novel called *'The Dreamhealer.'*

To promote the new novel I made a series of dark and disturbing videos. A close friend, who wishes to remain nameless, very kindly offered to be the face of the *'Dreamhealer,'* and a scarier performance you will not find anywhere – Anthony Hopkins, maybe?

Then and now: Shane Briant has gone from blond film star to thriller writer

Horror hero is back in Whitby

Photos are 40 years apart. Reality bites.

JUST AFTER YOU'VE SUFFERED A DULL YEAR...

...you have a great one. You never know what's up ahead and that's the joyt being an actor.

In 2012 I was offered a lovely cameo in the A.B.C. drama/comedy series by the name of 'Rake' starring Richard Roxburgh. It's hilarious. I'd worked with Richard before and was delighted to find all my scenes were two-handers with him alone. The director, JeffreyWalker was a delight too. My character was masquerading as a mole within MI5. He wore a black suit and constantly smoked cigarettes - hence my name, 'The Smoking Man.'

Richard Roxburgh with 'The Smoking Man.'

Two months later I was offered a great ongoing role in the HBO ASIA / A.B.C. mini series 'Serangoon Road.' And guess what? I was to play the station head of MI5 in Singapore in 1965. It was as if *'The Smoking Man'* had gone legit! My outfit was a black suit and I was a chain smoker. Joan Chen, who had starred in Bernardo Bertolucci's winner of the Best Picture Oscar, 'The Last Emperor,' was the star as the owner of a detective agency in Singapore. A stellar Asian / Aussie supporting cast was headed by Don Hany, Chin Han, Ario Bayo, Pamelyn Chee, Rachel Blake, Tony Martin, Michael Dorman, Jeremy Lindsay Taylor and Ted Maynard. The two directors were my two favourites in Australia, Tony Tilse and Peter Andrikidis.

I had a ball for many months flying every two of three weeks to Singapore and then on to the island of Batam in Indonesia to stay in a resort hotel, sip a guava juice by a swimming pool and occasionally be driven to work with wonderfully talented people. And to be the wickedly *'bad guy'* into the bargain! Plus, I was being paid handsomely to do it! Sometimes an actor's life is fabulous. On one occasion Michael Dorman took me on the back of his motorbike around the island to lunch at his favourite fish restaurant over the water.

We ate spicy deviled crab and delicious local fish finishing the day with a round of golf at a spectacular nearby course - our Indonesian caddy was twenty-two, very beautiful, and could judge the distance to the pin to within a meter. I let her chose the clubs I used, since she was never wrong.

On the back lot at the Batam Studios

With Miss Myanmar 2006 at the wrap party.

WHAT NOW?

Why *would* any actor retire? Sometimes they are *retired* because people are sick and tired of the same performance. But if you're any good at all, and have kept learning throughout your career, then you'll feel, as I do, that the best is still to come, provided writers come up with those great roles for 'the mature actor.'

There are so many roles I'm dying to play. Some classic, some modern – maybe even a return to Hammer? Surely someone has to step into the breach now that my great friend Peter Cushing is dead, and Sir Christopher Lee is now quite old, possibly preferring a supporting role rather than the lead? Why not someone to fill the gap that Vincent Price left when he passed away?

As well as making contact with people who remember me as an actor, I hear from my thriller readers from all over the world.

Last year I had a huge thrill when *'Worst Nightmares'* was published as a translation in German across Europe – *Traum Mörder.'*

As I write these final lines, I think back to the day I started to write this book. Who's going to read it, I asked Robert? Sure, I'd made a number of films, yet I wasn't exactly a household name. Then I'd heard that until Oprah brought Sydney Poitier's autobiography, *'The Measure of a Man,'* to the attention of the American public, it wasn't selling as well as one might have expected bearing in mind Poitier's huge profile as a legendary actor. So I knew my book would have to stand on its own merits simply as a *'good read.'* Subsequent to it's promotion on Oprah, *'The Measure of a Man,'* has sold millions. (If you know Oprah please tell her I've been trying to reach her – at present unsuccessfully.)

I never thought I'd remember even half of my stories. Of course I shed many tears as I wrote about friends and colleagues that have passed away; Ralphie Bates, Nick Clay, Paul Newman, Jack Palance, Roger Mirams, Stanley Walsh, Megan Williams, and very recently

Jon Blake.

It's been a wonderful ride so far, and beside me always has been my lovely Wendy. Who could ask for anything more?

Well, I believe the best is still to come. It's just around the corner and will happen when I least expect it. I may not have won any major awards, but maybe I'm one of those actors who people see and say...

'Look, it's him. That guy. The bad guy. What's his name? Remember? He was that heartless cruel man in...you know...that film!'

'You mean the bad guy?'

'Yeah! Him. Always the bad guy!'

My wonderful agent Adza Vincent

Horst Jansen kills the vampire!

German translation.

The Dreamhealer of 'Worst Nightmares' and 'The Dreamhealer.'

Spanish 'Straight on Till Morning.'

My mother when she was at her happiest.

Our dear friend Geoffrey Simpson. A magnificent Director of Photography.